Praise for *Equity Happens*™

"I thoroughly enjoyed Equity Happens. Robert and Russell have created a masterfully comprehensive guide to the why and how of real estate investing. The Real Estate Guys really know real estate. They know an effective plan depends on the property, the market, and the location...not some "one-size-fits-all" system. Read this book. You'll learn from it just as I did."

Gary Eldred, PhD.
Trump University Faculty Member
Best-selling Real Estate Author

"I highly recommend this book to anyone committed to winning the game of real estate investing. Robert Helms and Russell Gray walk you through the do's and don'ts of real estate investing in the most engaging and creative manner. If you are a real estate professional, then this book is a must-read for you and your clients. It has the power to positively change their lives and your business forever."

Shayna Goldstein, Realtor
Coldwell Banker Premier Realty – Las Vegas, NV
Candidate for *Realtor Magazine's*
Top 30 Agents Under Age of 30 Award

"Equity Happens blasted open my long held beliefs... After reading the Tale of Two Investors, I knew it was time to shift my thinking... Robert and Russ are masterful at taking seemingly complicated real estate concepts and making them totally understandable for the average consumer. I now highly recommend Equity Happens to all my clients and readers."

Judy Lawrence, Budget Coach
Best-selling Author of *The Budget Kit Workbook*

"Conventional real estate wisdom is to buy, hold and hope. If you're looking to collapse time frames and create sustainable wealth, read Equity Happens...at least twice!"

Jim Rohn, Business Philosopher
Author of *The Five Major Pieces of the Life Puzzle*

"...fantastic and fun to read... easy to understand...Equity Happens will become a must have for all beginners to professional investors for years to come. I can't wait to...offer these books to my clients."

"Coach" Mark Soto, Mortgage Broker
The Home Loan Coach-Granite Bay, CA

"Equity Happens is a breath of fresh air. Robert and Russ have a wonderful way of making complex topics simple."

Kyle Wilson, President
YourSuccessStore.com

Real People Having Real World Success with the Concepts in *Equity Happens™*

"This is "Education for Effective Action"! My net worth is on track to increase by over $500,000 [after] just 18 months...thanks to the education and learning through real-life examples. I am able to recognize an opportunity, and act with confidence and competency!"
S.B.D. – San Jose, CA

"I'd gone to seminars and read many books. I never was able to know what to buy or actually go and buy a property. I am so grateful that after getting "Education for Effective Action"...last year I actually made more money from my properties than in my day job!"
Roland S. – Cupertino, CA

"I realized that if I didn't plan for the future, no one was going to do it for me. My knowledge of real estate investing continues to grow. Since the first of the year I have purchased three properties personally, and have formed a partnership to purchase a fourth property. I don't see any way that this could have happened left on my own."
Dan D. – Watsonville, CA

"My 'unenlightened' colleagues are still mired in over-analysis paralysis, still having taken NO action. There is no substitute for getting educated. We were able to take action quickly and with confidence. We took your advice and spent the time, effort and money to assemble a good team. The early success of our investments is a direct result... positive results way beyond our expectations. Thanks for a great program. It really glued it all together for us."
Rich R. – Mountain View, CA

"Since learning of you guys nearly two years ago, I have built on my previously limited knowledge of investing. More importantly, I have taken action with the knowledge I have gained and have seen my net worth more than double. Thank you!"
Tim H. – Santa Cruz, CA

"For the first time in our 27 years of marriage my wife and I, thanks to the Real Estate Investor Development Program, are taking action to secure our retirement based on mutually set goals. Thanks for helping to keep us on track."
Jim E. – Laguna Niguel, CA

"One year has changed my life. I was renting a one-bedroom apartment. In one year, I went from owning nothing to having two properties and I have almost doubled my net worth. I have built my team of advisors and I have created my personal investment philosophy. There is no other program like this one. Thank you so much!"

Alice T. –San Jose, CA

"The best program of its type. Our confidence began to soar and we realized we can do this and be successful. We have secured partners, a process that was fairly effortless to our great surprise. We've learned when you have a great deal, you don't have to hard-sell it. This program helped us begin the journey toward our unique goals."

Henry H. – Cerritos, CA

"Robert and Russ gave us the tools to think creatively and propel our real estate investment gains to new heights. A well-positioned equity growth strategy enabled us to purchase over 40 properties…appreciating from 15% to 50%. We have seen substantial cash-on-cash returns using this model and believe it is a tool to cut time frames in half."

Jeff S. & Jeremy G. – San Jose, CA

"…provided a solid education in the fundamentals of real estate investments, including finance, due diligence, establishing investment groups, landlord issues, etc. Purely due to this program I have gone from owning no investment real estate to controlling five properties in less than one year."

Jeff H. – San Jose, CA

"One of the financial strategies I learned allowed us to take idle equity out of our existing property and apply it to additional real estate investments. This, combined with proven real estate concepts I received such as team investing, phased equity and finding the "hot" markets enabled me to take action much more quickly than I thought possible. Thank you for providing this program!"

Greg S. – San Jose, CA

Robert & Russ have changed our lives! We were stuck in analysis paralysis. Robert & Russ' approach is straightforward, practical and can be applied in up or down markets. It's not a get-rich scheme, but rather a thoughtful analysis of fundamentals. Thanks for educating us so that we can take action!

Robert & Sandy T. – Cypress, CA

EQUITY HAPPENS™

Building Lifelong Wealth with Real Estate

Robert Helms & Russell Gray

LIGHTBULB
PUBLISHING

www.EquityHappens.com

II

The stories and case studies in *Equity Happens*™ are based on real-life people and circumstances. However, names and certain details have been changed to protect the privacy of the parties involved.

The investment strategies presented are based on the research, experience, education and opinions of the authors. In no circumstance should the ideas and strategies presented in this book be construed as professional advice for any particular reader's unique situation. The reader is strongly encouraged to seek qualified professional advice before entering into any specific investment. In all cases, the authors, the publisher, and their employees, affiliates, agents and vendors accept no liability or responsibility for the reader's investment decisions or investment results.

EQUITY HAPPENS™ and
are trademarks pending with U.S.
Patent and Trademark Office.

Cover Design: John Guzman

Book Design: Morris Jackson

Library of Congress Control Number: 2005910409

ISBN: 0-9774887-0-5

Lightbulb Publishing Limited
Carson City, Nevada

First Printing January 2006

10 9 8 7 6 5 4 3 2 1

Printed in United States of America

Foreword

Congratulations on your decision to read *Equity Happens*. I'm excited to see this book in print, and grateful to be writing its foreword! I've had the pleasure of working closely with Robert Helms and Russell Gray during the creation of their very successful Real Estate Investor Development Program. I've seen firsthand the remarkable influence they've had in educating, mentoring, and helping investors achieve the success most had only dreamed of.

Equity Happens not only discusses *why* investing in real estate is the best avenue to wealth for most people, but it also shows *how* you can use the information and concepts presented to maximize your likelihood of success.

When I participate in the various seminars and mentoring clubs with Robert and Russ, they refer to me as "The Godfather of Real Estate" - probably because I am the oldest living investor that any of the team knows personally! I bought my first investment property in 1957, and while I don't yet know everything about real estate investing, I have been investing for decades and decades and decades, so I have a clue about what works and what doesn't. Although I've been reasonably successful as an investor, I would have given anything to have had the benefit of the information in *Equity Happens* earlier in my own investing career. Getting the right ideas and then putting yourself in the right environment with the right mentors is a huge shortcut to success!

I think the ideas and methods discussed in this book will profoundly affect and impact your thinking, and thereby will directly impact the results you experience in your real estate investing endeavors. If you want to succeed in real estate investment, it's imperative to obtain and continue to improve your financial education.

Robert and Russ are both impassioned about teaching and helping others to achieve success through investing in real estate. Although they've devoted time teaching real estate to both college students and real estate professionals, neither of them are classic academics. Rather, both are active investors who make much of their living by investing, not just by teaching. The key to becoming a successful investor is to take action, but lack of adequate education is what holds most people back. Appropriately, the thrust of the guys' program is reflected in their motto, *Education for Effective Action*™. Robert often asks the audience at the live seminars, "How much money will you make on property you *don't* own?" What an important question to consider!

As you will discover, *Equity Happens* offers a different approach to real estate investing than is found in most writings about this topic. While the book embraces many of the classic methods used by professional investors, it also contains many ideas and techniques not widely used or understood, but which can dramatically affect the results attainable. We all realize that equity happens. The question we should *all* ask ourselves is, "How can I make sure it happens to *me*?"

In a few short years, Robert and Russ have been able to help hundreds of investors create many millions of dollars in new equity using the principles explained in this book. I think this is directly attributable to their beliefs, their attitudes, and to the core values they have adopted in both their businesses and personal lives.

One of the key concepts that the guys believe in is "abundance mentality". In short, there is plenty of real estate investing opportunity for everyone. So whether you're new to real estate, or have been investing for decades and decades like me, I highly encourage you to embrace the information you find here. Then go for it! There are plenty of good deals for all of us!

Happy Investing!

Bob F. Helms
Laguna Niguel, California
October 2005

Equity Happens is dedicated to our
Real Estate Investor Mentoring Club.
Thank you for your support, encouragement,
faith and perseverance. You have taught us
much more than we have taught you.
May you succeed beyond your wildest
expectations and become an inspiration
of success for the next generation of
real estate investors.

VIII

Preface

There is an old saying: "When the student is ready, the teacher appears." We trust you are reading *Equity Happens* because you are ready to make significant and lasting changes in the financial results you are producing in your life. We are passionate in our belief that real estate is the greatest wealth-building vehicle available to ordinary people. If you master and practice the fundamental concepts of real estate investing, we are extremely confident you will achieve phenomenal results.

As educators, we strive to find the most effective teaching methods. We categorize learning into three methods: *Listening, Watching* and *Doing*. Technical books feed you information. We have found many seminars, books and audio/video programs, especially those at the college level, feed the student information – lots of it! We believe information without real-world context is ineffective at best and irrelevant at worst. It's why Russ hated math as a child and never passed a high school math class after the ninth grade. He saw no value in learning the information.

However, by the time he got to college, he was already married and working in sales, had co-founded and sold a business, and had bought and sold a property for a profit. In college, he became a 4.0 GPA accounting student with much less effort than when he was struggling with math in high school because he finally understood the context of the information. In other words, he was interested in the information because it became relevant to his real-life experiences. He didn't have to fight against his desires and interests to learn the material. Instead, he was motivated by a strong desire to learn. This motivation made all the difference. In our educational events, Russ jokes with the audiences about having "arithmephobia" as a child, but then becoming suddenly cured when the text books starting placing dollar signs in front of the numbers!

The Magic Formulas

Taking life-changing action isn't complicated, but most people think the secrets to success are knowledge and information. They aren't! While very important, if knowledge and information were truly the keys to success, then college professors and librarians would be the most successful people on the planet. However, if you *are* seeking the magic formula, there are actually two of them which we will share with you right now.

First, you must understand that if a=b and b=c, then a=c. Do you remember this from high school geometry? It was true then and it's true now. That's the beauty of mathematics! Here's how it applies to you and your success: "a" = what you think and believe; "b" = what actions you take; and "c" = the results you produce. So, to restate the formula, it would read, "What you think and believe affects what you do, and what you do affects the results you produce, therefore what you think and believe affects the results you produce." This is why you *must* work on training yourself to *think* like a successful person. The Bible says, "As a man thinks, so he is." We agree.

The second magic formula is V+K+D = EA. It stands for Vision + Knowledge + Discipline = Effective Action. For the formula to work, you must have all three components working together. We see people spend so much time, money and effort seeking knowledge (which isn't a bad thing), but next-to-no effort on clarifying their vision (what they want and why they want it) and then developing the discipline (doing what needs to be done whether you feel like it or not) necessary to realize their vision. An ancient proverb says, "Where there is no vision, people cast off discipline." A more modern saying is, "If you don't know where you're going, any road will get you there." To be effective, you must have a compelling Vision, the accurate Knowledge of how to do what is necessary to achieve your vision, and the personal Discipline to do it, and do it, and do it, until your vision becomes reality.

If you don't put what you learn into action, then of what real use is the education? On the other hand, just taking action without learning won't lead to riches either. Business philosopher Jim Rohn says it best, "If you take an idiot and motivate him, you have a motivated idiot!" We've also heard it said, "Direction is more important than speed." In other words, the shortest path between two points is a straight line. Knowledge and vision provide direction, while action provides motion.

This book is designed to enlighten, entertain and inspire you to take *effective* action. We'll do our best to explain concepts and ideas we think will help you in your real-world quest to create wealth with real estate investment. We'll share true stories about ourselves and investors we know, and what we have learned from both the successes and the failures. We'll give you some tools you can use immediately to start or continue your personal real estate investment plan. Our sincere hope is we will help lead you to owning more property tomorrow than you do today and this property ownership will produce the financial means to give you the lifestyle you dream of. As you succeed, you'll grow beyond simply worrying about survival. After a short season of well-earned self-indulgence, you'll likely move on to the final destination for all truly successful people:

giving back. We desire for this book to help inspire and equip you to thrive to the point where you choose to give back to your community. It's in giving back that deep and lasting satisfaction is found.

Lastly, we realize this probably isn't the first book you've read on real estate investment. It certainly shouldn't be the last! No matter how much you may think you already know about investing in property, we're confident you'll find new ideas, hear inspiring stories, learn new strategies and techniques, and most importantly, gain further clarity about your personal vision for your future. When you have clarity of vision, strategy and tactics become self-evident. When you know what to do, effective action becomes easier. Ultimately, effective action is the real key to success in anything.

Successful Investing!

Robert Helms and Russell Gray

P.S. Throughout the book, whenever we need to refer to a generic person, we just say "he", "him", "his", etc. We know this probably isn't politically correct, and we aren't trying to be chauvinistic, but hey, after all, we are *The Real Estate Guys*™.

Table of Contents

XIV

XVIII

Eq-ui-ty (ek`-wi-tee)

1. The residual value of a property beyond any mortgage thereon.
2. The phenomenon which enriches persons intelligent enough to own real estate whose value increases as a result of persistent demand and inflation.

xx

EQUITY HAPPENS™

BOOK ONE

A Tale of Two Investors

XXII

Introduction

A *Tale of Two Investors* is the fictional story of two characters, Conrad Soomer and his friend, Juan Tunavest. These characters and their attitudes and actions are an amalgamation of the many hundreds of people and circumstances we have experienced in our years of teaching, investing, and professional practice. As you read the story, we want you to evaluate the financial decisions each of these characters make. Look past what they do and focus on *why* they do it. What attitudes, habits and beliefs are influencing them? What fundamental concepts of real estate investing are they implementing or violating? Which decisions do you agree with or disagree with, and why? This critical thinking will help you learn important lessons about your own investing psyche.

Real-world real estate investing is relatively slow-paced for most people. Even active investors may only be involved in a few transactions per year. Many will experience a transaction only once every two or three years. It's easy to lose focus, and thereby miss opportunities. The reason why most people never take effective action based on the knowledge gained from a how-to book or seminar, is there is just too much time between the education and the time they actually put the education into *action*. Therefore, it is imperative to put yourself in an environment which reinforces and utilizes your education quickly and regularly. Investment clubs have grown in number and popularity because a well-run club provides an environment to incubate beginning investors while they are learning the fundamentals, and helps take experienced investors to a whole new level of achievement, professionalism, and connections. If you have the opportunity to join or start an investor club in your area, take advantage of it! Success is much easier and much more fun when you are sharing the journey with other like-minded people. For now, we want to help you learn vicariously through the characters in our story.

We hope you enjoy *A Tale of Two Investors* as much as we enjoyed writing it. Best wishes for a successful investing career!

CHAPTER 1
The Thirties

Any plans for the weekend, Juan?" called Conrad Soomer from the water cooler in the employee lunchroom at Stone Cold United Manufacturing Company. His co-worker, Juan Tunavest, was seated at one of the tables, eating his lunch out of a plastic lunch box. Juan's thermos and cup were set off to the side to make room for a book he was reading while he ate. Juan looked up to see who was calling.

That Conrad Soomer sure is a sharp dresser, Juan thought, admiring Conrad's freshly pressed slacks, bright shiny shoes, and colorful tie.

"Hi, Conrad!" Juan responded warmly. "As a matter of fact, I have a great weekend planned. I'm going to a real estate investing seminar at the Moneytree Hotel, downtown."

"*Another* seminar?" Conrad asked incredulously. "Juan, you really should get out and live a little! The weather is supposed to be great this weekend. Connie and I are headed to the lake with the kids. Why don't you and your family join us? We're taking the boat, the jet-skis and the ATVs. Our cabin is big enough for everyone. It'll be great!" Conrad smiled encouragingly.

"That does sound really great," Juan began apologetically, "but I'm afraid I can't make it this time." Conrad looked confused. Juan smiled sheepishly.

"But thanks for the offer," Juan followed up. "I really appreciate it. You and Connie are very kind." Juan's face brightened, "I'm just really excited about this seminar. I want to hear what these guys have to say. I've wanted to get going in real estate investing for a long time and I don't want to put it off any longer. My last high school reunion made me realize how fast my life is passing by. I don't want to end up poor and living on social security like my dad. You know what they say: 'If nothing changes, nothing changes.' I'm ready to make a change!"

Conrad could see why Juan would want to make changes. The Tunavests didn't live in as nice a neighborhood as the Soomers did. They certainly didn't have many of the nicer things in life – at least Conrad never heard Juan talk about anything fun. And Juan's car certainly wasn't much to look at! By comparison, Conrad's sales career had always generated a very comfortable income. Now that Conrad's wife Connie was back to work, the Soomers were able to afford an even more enjoyable lifestyle. Conrad actually felt a little bit sorry for Juan, so even though they worked in different departments, Conrad always made an effort to encourage Juan. He seemed like such a smart and likable guy with lots of potential. *Maybe if Juan spent more time with an upwardly mobile person like me,* thought Conrad, *he would catch on and get out of that crummy storeroom. Maybe it's time for a little tough love?*

"You know, Juan," Conrad began, lowering his voice so no one else would hear, "if you would spend as much time on improving your job skills as you do going to those 'get rich quick' seminars, you'd be out of the storeroom with a high-paying office job. Have you ever thought about getting into sales?"

Conrad didn't wait for an answer. "I could probably pull some strings and get you into customer service. From there, it's a quick jump to sales – maybe even management! I'd be willing to mentor you along." At this point, Conrad was feeling quite charitable.

Juan's expression became serious as he considered Conrad's suggestions. "I don't know, Conrad," he said. "I'm not sure climbing the corporate ladder is what I want to do. That's okay for some people, but not for me. It seems so political. I just don't think I would fit in very well." Juan paused.

Conrad felt both sorry for Juan and a little offended. *Here I am trying to help you out and you make it sound like I'm some suck-up corporate politician. I'm just trying to get somewhere in life!*

Juan continued, "I'm just really ready to make some serious changes in my life. I'm hoping this next seminar will give me some ideas." Smiling, Juan added, "Thanks for the offer, Conrad. I really do appreciate it – and you! I hope you understand. I hope you, Connie and the kids have a great time at the lake!"

Conrad managed a small smile as Juan packaged up his lunch box and left the lunchroom to return to his duties as storeroom clerk in the SCUMCO supply room.

Conrad stood by the water cooler for a moment and watched Juan walk off. *You know, life is going fast,* he thought. *I don't think Connie and I will end up poor, but the kids will be heading off to college before too long. That won't be cheap. And then maybe some weddings to pay for after that!* His anxiety level began to climb. *I'm not sure we'll be ready. I've been letting Connie handle all the financial stuff up to now. My job has been to earn the money, but maybe I should start paying more attention to our finances. Maybe Connie and I should go check out Juan's investing seminar this weekend?*

Suddenly Conrad's thoughts were interrupted by the voice of his secretary as she poked her head into the lunchroom, "Conrad, Mr. Dover is on line two for you."

Conrad crumpled up his paper cup and tossed it in the waste can. Walking quickly towards his office to take his boss's call, a feeling of trepidation came over him. *I wonder what Ben wants?*

• • •

"Have a great practice, honey! Work hard and listen to your coach – and be careful! Mrs. Deeds and I are going to Sun Dollars for coffee. I'll be back to pick you up in about two hours. I love you!"

Connie Soomer rolled up the window of her late model sport utility vehicle and watched her son jog off to soccer practice. She turned and smiled at her friend in the passenger seat.

"He hates it when I say 'I love you' in front of his friends," Connie reported with a smile, "but I don't care! I'm not ready to let go just yet. They grow up so fast, don't they?"

Karen Deeds nodded in agreement, "Yes, they do. Sometimes I miss those days when the kids were little. Their games looked more like rugby scrums than soccer matches! All the kids would hover around the ball and swarm around in a bunch. We called them 'the killer bees'." Karen chuckled at the memory.

Connie smiled in agreement and added, "Now, it seems all they do is eat. Little Simon isn't so 'little' anymore. He eats like a horse! My grocery bill is probably bigger than my house payment." Both women laughed as Connie navigated her car out of the school parking lot.

"So, Connie, how's your new job?" Karen queried to keep the conversation going.

Connie's demeanor changed as she contemplated the question. "The job is okay," Connie replied with half-hearted enthusiasm. "After all those years at home with the kids, I wasn't sure I would fit in well at an office again. But my boss is pretty good, and the people in the office are easy to get along with." She was searching for a positive spin. "I suppose being the big boss's admin gives me special status, so no one gives me a hard time." She paused for a moment, and then continued, "It's not bad. I guess you do what you have to do to survive." Connie activated her turn signal and looked over her right shoulder as she changed lanes. Karen could see in Connie's expression there was more on her mind than her job.

Karen was contemplating Connie's comments as they pulled up to Sun Dollars. Connie parked the car, shut off the engine, and stuffed her keys into her purse. The two women got out and walked into the store, chatting about what types of coffee they preferred.

After being served, Connie and Karen sat down and their conversation continued. They explored a variety of topics from fashion to health. Then Connie sat quietly for a moment. She had something heavy on her heart.

"Karen?" Connie began contritely, "May I ask you something a little personal?"

Karen looked up from her coffee and into Connie's face. She could see the need in Connie's eyes.

"Sure," Karen said with a reassuring smile.

Connie leaned forward and locked eyes with Karen. "You and Grant seem to be doing so well. I mean, I never hear you complain about money. You have a gorgeous home. You drive very nice cars.

It's as though you have no worries. Is it really as rosy as it seems? I feel like Conrad and I work so hard, but we can't seem to get ahead."

Connie felt a little embarrassed at revealing her concerns about their family's financial picture. She looked down at her cup before continuing, "Conrad had a pretty good amount in his 401k, so a few years back we had our financial advisor set up some mutual fund accounts for the kids' college. The funds were doing pretty well until the last recession. Then one day I opened up the mail and all our funds were way down! I called our financial advisor and she told us to just hang in there. She says our portfolio is set up for the long term and eventually our accounts will go back up. Well, I don't know how long 'eventually' is, but it's been a while and they still aren't back up to where they were." Connie's voice became anxious, "College is coming fast!" She paused to calm herself down. "I think we should be doing more than just sitting around waiting." Connie sat up in her chair with her elbows on the table. She held her cup in front of her lips and watched Karen for her reaction.

Karen gazed at Connie and carefully considered how to respond. She wanted to encourage Connie, and didn't want to speak negatively about the Soomer's situation. *It's hard to be gracious,* she thought, *when you have such strong opinions about these things.*

Connie noticed Karen's hesitation and apologized, "I'm sorry. I didn't mean to get emotional…and I'm not trying to pry. I…I guess I'm just a little scared and I don't know where to turn for help." Connie turned and gazed out the window, watching all the people and cars shuffle around the shopping center.

"Connie," Karen reassured, "there's no need to apologize. I'm not offended, and I want you to know that even though Grant and I are doing well financially, everything isn't 'rosy'! I don't think anyone's life is truly rosy. We're happy, but Grant works hard and travels a lot, so we have our share of stress. It's just a different kind." Karen smiled at Connie.

Connie's curiosity grew. "What kind of traveling does Grant do?" she asked. "I've noticed you get to go away on a lot of fancy vacations."

Karen laughed. "Grant is a real estate investor. He travels to different parts of the country to research properties and meet with his management teams and advisors. He also teaches. Occasionally he'll write an article or book on investing. Some of those 'fancy vacations' are really trips to look at properties, teach a class, or get away to some quiet place so he can write. The trips are fun, but there is always work to do. Sometimes we don't get much notice. Something will come up that needs his immediate attention, and off he goes! I tag along every once in a while so we can spend more time together. We try to make it fun, so it doesn't seem like work." Karen was careful not to complain, but she also didn't want to come across as boastful. The Deeds' business and lifestyle were very different than those of most people working in corporate jobs.

"Grant works hard because he loves what he does," Karen continued. "Real estate is his business, but teaching is his passion. Perhaps you and Conrad should talk with him?"

Connie was puzzled. "How does Grant find time to travel just to look at real estate? Doesn't his boss get upset when he takes off work all the time? Conrad only gets two weeks of vacation a year, plus some sick days, but when sales are down, he can't even get away for a planned vacation. One time, Conrad's boss refused to let us take a Thanksgiving vacation we had been planning for months, and it was only going to be for three days! I can't imagine just taking off at the last minute because 'something' comes up."

"Actually," Karen responded, "Grant is a *full-time* real estate investor. He doesn't have a 'job' with a company, and he doesn't have what you'd call a boss – except for me!"

Astonished, Connie looked at Karen for a brief moment considering her comments, and then both women broke out in laughter.

• • •

"Honey, I'm home!" Conrad announced as he walked through the door of the Soomers' suburban home.

Connie emerged from the kitchen and the two exchanged a warm embrace. After a quick peck on the cheek from Connie, Conrad headed to their bedroom to get out of his work clothes. *Another long day at the office*, he thought as he crossed the threshold into his walk-in closet. His boss, Mr. Dover, was really pressing him to finalize some pending contracts. Dover wanted the sales numbers to look better for the current quarter. There was a big promotion on the line and Dover was determined to get it.

Connie had followed Conrad into the bedroom and plopped herself down on the bed.

"I've been thinking..." Connie started as she gathered her thoughts. "You know, I'm a little worried about our finances. Even though we're doing okay, I'm wondering if there's a better way? Mia tells me not to worry about the ups and downs in the stock market. She says we should just ride it out and suggested we 're-balance' our holdings. She says 'buy-and-hold' is the way to go and that the stock market has grown an average of nearly twelve percent a year over the last sixty years, even including the Depression! Twelve percent sounds pretty good to me. What do you think?"

Conrad did not respond.

Are you paying attention to me? Connie fumed in her mind. She wanted Conrad's undivided attention.

As he unbuttoned his shirt, Conrad's mind was still dwelling on the pressures of his life at SCUMCO. He only half-heard what Connie had said. *Why does Dover think the whole world revolves around him?* Conrad's thoughts pounded in his head. *Why should our guys bust their butts to earn him a promotion so he can use his new position to cut our commissions to impress the CFO with cost reductions?*

Suddenly, Conrad became aware of Connie's droning. *What did she say?*

"Who's Mia?" Conrad asked, trying to buy himself some time to focus his attention on his wife's comments.

Connie sat up on the bed and replied, "Mia Portu! She's our financial advisor from Dim Witty and Associates. You know, where we have our brokerage account. Remember? She put together our financial plan. How can you not remember? Don't you care about our finances?" Connie was becoming frustrated.

"I remember her," Conrad defended, "I just forgot her name, that's all."

Actually, he didn't remember Mia Portu at all. All Conrad recalled about their financial plan was that $2,500 seemed like a lot of money to pay for a spiral bound booklet with some charts and graphs in it. But Connie seemed to accept his explanation, so Conrad decided to continue down the track of discussing their finances, even though every time they had these discussions, they always ended up fighting. He concluded that if he were to have a chance of persuading her to go to Juan's investing seminar instead of to the lake, he would need to risk broaching this touchy topic with her. Sooner or later, they would have to deal with their finances because Juan was right – life was passing by very quickly.

"What do *you* think?" Conrad asked, putting the conversational ball back into play as he hung up his slacks. "You've read all those personal finance books. What do they say we should do?" He pulled the closet door closed.

"Well, that's just it," Connie replied, repositioning herself to face Conrad as he walked into their bathroom. "I *think* we're doing everything right. I was watching TV the other day and I saw that author I told you about – Ivana B. Padov. I read her book, *Debt Free, as Free as the Wind Blows*. She was talking about how important it is to get out of debt and set up an emergency fund."

Conrad was sure he remembered Connie talking about this once before, so he decided to prove he was interested in their finances, "You set us up with an emergency fund, didn't you?" he asked. *See?* he thought, *I pay attention.*

"Yes," Connie replied, "but it only has enough in it to last two months. My goal is to get it up to at least *six* months. Grandma reminds me all the time about the Great Depression and how important it is to have lots of savings. She even keeps a stash of cash under the mattress in case the banks go out of business!" Connie laughed at the idea.

"Do we have cash under the bed?" Conrad joked, pulling up the mattress and peering under the bed Connie was sitting on.

"Noooo," Connie responded with a smile as she righted herself on her perch on the bed, "but Ivana B. Padov recommends we have a full twelve months of living expenses in cash for our emergency fund, because sometimes it can take that long to find a job if you get laid off."

Conrad was surprised. "*Twelve* months?" he asked. "How long did it take you to save up *two* months? We've been at this a while, haven't we?"

Now Connie felt a little defensive. *Why can't we ever talk about money without fighting?* she thought to herself.

"Conrad, the reason it took so long to save is because the kids were little and we didn't have anything yet. I wasn't working and you were just getting your career started. We needed furniture, appliances, dishes, and all those things! We were paying off our student loans and saving up for a down payment on the house. Those were the things we had to do back then." Even as the words left her mouth, she started thinking about the boat, the jet-skis, the ATVs, the sound system, and all of the other things they had bought on credit. *But those were his decisions, not mine*, she thought, although she certainly enjoyed all of their toys as much as he did.

Conrad did not want this conversation to become negative. He could tell he had struck a nerve with her. He was still trying to direct the dialog toward the idea of going to the seminar with Juan. "I'm sorry, Con," he said in a reconciliatory tone. "I wasn't criticizing. I think you've done a great job! I guess I'm just having a 'pre-mid-life' crisis. It seems like life is passing by so quickly and even though we work hard, we aren't making any real progress. I'm not mad at you. I just want to feel like I know where we're headed." He smiled at her. "Do you understand?"

Connie was relieved Conrad wasn't angry. Maybe she was being overly sensitive. It bothered her that Conrad never seemed too interested in their financial affairs until he thought she'd made a mistake. Then he seemed *very* interested in pointing out all her inadequacies…at least that's the way it felt to her. Maybe Conrad's interest was truly sincere this time. Perhaps he would actually be willing to talk with Karen's husband about real estate. *Wouldn't it be great if this time he would listen to someone else instead of always having to be the one with the answers?*

"I'm sorry, too," Connie responded in a gentle voice. "It's funny. I've also been thinking about how life is passing too fast. Karen and I were just talking today about how quickly the kids are growing up. They'll be heading off to college before we know it!"

Connie's tone became more serious as she returned to the subject of their emergency fund. "Since we already have two months of cash in our emergency fund, I figured out if we could put one-sixth of our income aside each month, it would only take about five years for us to build up the other ten months of emergency money."

Conrad thought about that for a moment. *Save one-sixth of our income? How much is that?* He opened the calculator function on his cell phone as Connie watched.

"Sixteen and two-thirds," she said.

He looked at her curiously while she repeated, "Sixteen and two-thirds *percent.*"

Conrad was shocked. "Are you telling me we need to save nearly 17% of our income every month for *five years* to build up an emergency fund? Is *that* what you're saying?" Conrad couldn't disguise the frustration in his voice.

"It isn't as bad as it sounds," Connie reassured him. "Ivana says you can speed things up by investing in your debt."

Conrad's expression softened from angry frustration to confused frustration. "Invest in your debt? What does *that* mean?" he asked, still trying to comprehend living on 17% less money each month – or, conversely, what it would take to earn 17% more. *Would that work? But If I make more, then doesn't my emergency fund need to go up too? What about taxes? If I have to earn enough to net 17% more, how much do my bonuses have to be?* He felt himself winding back up into "office mode" as he started thinking of sales and marketing ideas to grow SCUMCO's sales and get those bonuses.

His thoughts were interrupted by Connie's response to his question.

Connie explained, "Ivana says people in debt use too much of their income making interest payments. She says if you pay your debt off, the income used to make the payments can be redirected to first establishing your emergency fund and then into funding long-term investments." Connie was surprised and pleased she understood the concepts so well.

"So it sounds like getting debt free is the first objective?" Conrad asked rhetorically. "Okay, so what's the next step?" *I hope this is simple*, he thought.

Connie perked up. "Well, I think we need to look for ways to cut spending so we can redirect the money we save to paying down our debt." She reflected on that idea for a moment. "Then," she continued, "we should try to reduce our interest expense. I suppose we could change our mortgage again, too. Don called and said rates are down. We can refinance and lower our payments another $120 a month, or we can get an even lower interest rate by getting a 15-year loan. Our monthly payments would go up by $420, but I'm already adding another $100, so it would only be like we were paying $320 a month more."

Conrad was trying to absorb all of this while he shuttled between the bedroom and bathroom. "Why are you paying $100 a month extra on the house?" he asked.

"I set up another one of those *Loan Acceleration Mortgage Eliminator* programs," Connie explained. "By using this LAME program, we save thousands of dollars of interest and pay the loan off several years early!" She paused for emphasis. "The house would be paid for in *fifteen* years, instead of twenty-five. Can you imagine how *great* it would be if we didn't have a house payment?"

"That would be nice," agreed Conrad, "but can we afford to pay an extra $320? I thought we were trying to build up our emergency fund and save for the kid's college." Conrad leaned over the sink to wash his face. *I wonder how Juan is going to handle college? I make a nice salary and we're worried. Juan doesn't make nearly as much as me. How do people expect to pay for these things, much less save for retirement?* He continued to ponder these questions while he dried his face and hung up the towel.

Conrad's thoughts were interrupted once again by Connie's voice. "It seems like everything we do is just a drop in the bucket, you know what I mean?" she said. "I guess we should pay the extra money toward the house payment. We can always get an equity line on the house when the kids are ready for college…or maybe we'll have moved up to a bigger house by then." She smiled at the thought of a bigger, newer home.

Conrad thought about that for a moment. He was getting confused. *How does buying a bigger house help us pay for college or establish an emergency fund?*

"Connie," Conrad asked "why would we want to go to all the trouble to pay the mortgage down if we're just going to borrow the money back out again later? That doesn't make sense to me."

Connie looked perplexed. *I hadn't thought about that*, she thought. "I'm not sure," she said. "I'll have to give Don a call and see what he says."

"I'm not so sure I trust that Don Nojak!" Conrad objected. "I don't see how he can keep re-doing our mortgage for free. Are you *sure* it doesn't cost us anything? It doesn't make sense to me that a mortgage company would spend money advertising free loans. Have you seen the car Don drives? That car doesn't go with 'free'. Isn't there someone else you can ask? What about that CPA guy? What's his name? Katz?"

Conrad pulled his sweatshirt over his head, and walked towards the bedroom door on his way to the kitchen. Connie hopped off the bed and followed him into the hallway and down the stairs.

"I think Don is a nice man!" Connie defended as she trailed Conrad out of the bedroom. "He seems to be very smart. Did you know he's a *Direct Underwriting Mortgage Banking Acceleration System Specialist*? He knows all about those equity building programs Ivana B. Padov talks about. I think the reason he does our loans for free is because the bank pays him for us."

She caught up to him in the kitchen. "*You* shouldn't be so cynical," she scolded.

"I'm not cynical," Conrad retorted. "I'm just a businessman. It doesn't make any sense to me that Don is working for free. Even if the bank is paying him, where does the bank get the money? Common sense says we're paying for it somehow."

"I suppose you're right," Connie conceded, "but, when I look at the loan papers, I go over every charge and I don't see where we're paying anything."

Conrad realized they'd derailed again. He decided to direct the conversation back to the CPA, "What about Katz, the CPA? Have you talked to him?"

"Freddy does taxes," Connie answered. "Besides, whenever I talk to him, he doesn't really give me advice, he just answers my questions. I don't think emergency funds, loans and college savings are tax questions, are they?" *Why can't this be easy?* she wondered.

Conrad turned to her with a look of puzzled frustration, "There must be some kind of class or somewhere we can go to learn about this stuff! This is crazy!" he lamented. "We both went to college, but neither one of us is sure how to run our finances. And it seems like our 'advisors'," he continued, holding his hands up and making mock quotation marks, "aren't really giving us useable answers!" Conrad sat down at the kitchen table perusing the mail, "I think we need a fresh approach."

Just as the words left his mouth, Connie's eyes lit up. *Now,* she thought, *is the perfect time to tell Conrad about my conversation with Karen.*

At the same time, Conrad thought, *Now is the perfect time to tell Connie about Juan's real estate seminar this weekend.*

"I have an idea," they both said in unison.

Laughing, Conrad deferred to Connie. "You go first. What's your idea?"

Connie began, "You know my friend from Simon's soccer, Karen Deeds? Well, her husband Grant is a real estate investor. Full-time! I was telling her a little about our situation and she suggested we talk to him. She said he would probably be willing to give us some ideas." She waited for a response, but Conrad was busy wrestling between being happy Connie was interested in real estate and being angry she told her friend about their personal financial issues.

"What do you think?" she asked eagerly.

Conrad looked at her for a moment. "That's interesting," he said trying to sound open-minded, "but I'm not sure I like the idea of you sharing our personal situation with some woman you met at soccer." He quickly redirected the conversation toward his own agenda, "I had an interesting conversation with Juan at my office today."

Connie was disappointed. She really hoped Conrad would be excited about meeting with Grant. "What did Juan have to say?" she inquired politely.

"Well," replied Conrad, "I invited him to come to the lake with us this weekend, but he said he was going to a seminar. I razzed him about it, but then he said something that kind of hit me."

Sometimes I'd like to hit you she mused in the privacy of her own thoughts. "What kind of seminar?" Connie asked, feigning interest.

"It's a real estate seminar," Conrad answered. "Not like a homebuyer seminar, but more of an investing seminar."

Connie perked up. "Really?" she said enthusiastically. "Real estate investing?" *Didn't you hear anything I said?* she thought to herself. *Why does it always have to be your idea?*

Conrad noticed her interest and was relieved. "Yeah," he said nonchalantly, "it didn't sound that interesting to me, but it was obvious he would rather do that than come boating at the lake with us." He was afraid to over-sell, yet he was trying to persuade her to want to go.

"Are you sure it isn't your breath?" Connie quipped.

"Funny," he deadpanned. "No, I don't think it was an excuse. I could tell Juan was really excited about going. He talked about wanting to improve his finances so he could provide better for his family and his future. I could really relate. He said 'If nothing changes, nothing changes'. He talked about his high school reunion and how fast life is going by."

"Doesn't *that* sound familiar," Connie agreed.

"Exactly my point," Conrad affirmed. He decided now was his best chance of asking Connie to cancel the lake trip and go to the seminar, "Soooo, I was thinking. Maybe we should go to the seminar? You know, the lake will always be there, and Juan has a point. Life is going pretty fast. Maybe we need to make some changes, too." He looked at her for a buying signal. Her eyes were bright and welcoming.

"Do you want to go?" he asked. *She's mine,* he thought.

A smile slowly grew upon Connie's face. *I thought you'd never ask, you big dork.* She looked him squarely in the eye and said, "Sure."

• • •

"We're looking for the real estate investing seminar?" Connie asked the sharply dressed young man at the hotel lobby. "Can you tell us where it is?"

"The real estate seminar is in the Cinderella Ballroom. Just go across the lobby and down the hall to your right," the young man replied, pointing out the way.

"Thank you," Connie called out as she and Conrad followed the young man's directions. They walked quickly across the hotel lobby. Approaching the hallway, they saw the marquee:

Rags to Riches with Real Estate – Cinderella Ballroom

"Here we go!" Connie exclaimed. She grabbed Conrad's hand and led him down the hallway. As she accelerated her pace, he jogged along behind her to catch up and then settled into a brisk walk.

As they neared the ballroom, they heard music playing and the clamor of people chatting. They rounded the corner and saw the seminar registration desk. There was a short line of people waiting to exchange their tickets for workbooks. Taking their place in line, they looked around at the variety of people milling about. Some were well dressed, but others looked a little ratty. Old and young, men and women, couples and singles, even a few teenagers.

I wonder if these people are all real estate investors? Some of them look pretty ragged, thought Conrad. *What kinds of people come to theses things?* Suddenly, it occurred to Conrad that others of his co-workers might be here, too. *I hope Juan didn't invite anyone else from SCUMCO!* He casually glanced around looking for anyone he knew.

"Conrad?" called out a familiar voice from behind. Conrad turned around and found himself face to face with Juan Tunavest.

"Hey, Juan!" Conrad greeted. "How ya' doin'?" The two men shook hands vigorously. Conrad turned to Connie to make introductions.

"Juan," Conrad said, motioning towards Connie, "this is my wife, Connie."

Juan reached out and grasped Connie's outstretched hand. "It's nice to finally meet you, Connie," Juan said with a big smile. Then Juan looked to the woman next to him, "This is my wife, Luv."

Luv Tunavest smiled warmly at Conrad and Connie and they exchanged greetings.

"I didn't expect to see you here!" Juan exclaimed excitedly. "I thought you two were going to the lake?"

"We were," Connie replied, "but Conrad said your little talk at the office convinced him we should come to this seminar instead."

Juan looked surprised. "Something *I* said?" he marveled. "I didn't think you were even interested in this stuff. But I'm really glad you're here! I understand today's speaker is pretty awesome."

By this time, the Soomers had advanced to the front of the line. "How many?" asked the young lady at the registration table.

"Two," Connie answered, holding up two fingers.

"That will be two hundred and ninety-eight dollars please," said the young lady. "Will that be cash, check or charge?" She smiled and waited patiently for a reply.

"Two hundred and ninety-eight dollars?" exclaimed Connie in disbelief. "Are you sure?" She looked at Conrad for guidance.

"Yes, ma'am!" the young lady replied confidently. "Tickets are one-forty-nine per person, which includes your workbook." She held up a spiral bound booklet, "There's lots of valuable information in here!"

Conrad stepped up beside Connie at the registration table. "How much without the workbook?" he asked the registration clerk. *I never keep those things anyway*, he thought. *Besides, I can photocopy Juan's at the office if there's anything good in there.*

"There's only one price, sir," the young lady replied, "and it includes the workbook." She smiled and waited for their decision.

Connie looked at Conrad. Then they stepped out of line. "Two hundred and ninety-eight dollars is a lot of money!" Connie stated, staring at Conrad. "Do you think it's worth it?" she said. "Did you know it was this much when you decided to come?"

"When *I* decided to come? I thought we decided on this together." Conrad was a little miffed at being blamed for an unauthorized expenditure. *It isn't like the earth will explode if we are over budget one month*, he thought. *Besides, we would have spent something on gas, food and parking if we went to the lake with the kids.*

The Soomers debated back and forth for several minutes. Meanwhile, Juan and Luv Tunavest had purchased their tickets and received their workbooks. Standing at the entrance to the ballroom, Juan looked back at the Soomers. "Are you two going to come in?" he called. "We can sit together if you like!" Juan stood waiting for an answer.

Conrad looked over and flashed a half-hearted smile at Juan.

Juan walked over to the Soomers, while Luv started into the ballroom. "What's the matter?" Juan asked. "Is everything okay?"

"We just didn't realize this was so expensive," Conrad commented. "Do you really think it's worth it? You said you've heard this guy speak before?"

Juan replied, "No, I haven't heard this particular speaker, but I've heard good things about him."

Conrad wasn't impressed.

"I read his book," Juan offered. "Besides, I figure 'nothing ventured, nothing gained'. Even if I get one great idea, it might it worth the price of admission."

No wonder Juan drives an old car, thought Conrad. *He throws his money away on chasing pie-in-the-sky. At least my boat is an asset and has some value left after I'm done using it.* Conrad felt a bit superior to his less affluent, and apparently less intelligent, co-worker.

Juan flipped through his workbook. "The speaker is Grant Deeds," he said, holding up the page with Deeds' picture and biography. "I've heard he has an amazing mind and really knows a lot about investing. He owns property all over the country."

"Did you say *Deeds*?" asked Connie incredulously, "*Grant* Deeds?"

"You've heard of him?" Juan responded with surprise.

"I'm friends with his wife, Karen," replied Connie. "At least if it's the same Grant Deeds I'm thinking of. She said he taught classes and wrote articles, but I thought it was just some little breakfast meeting and a newsletter or something." She looked around at the growing crowd and the sizeable book display, "I had no idea it was anything this big!"

Just then an amplified voice boomed out of the auditorium, "We are taking our seats! We are taking our seats! If the person next to you is talking, STOP LISTENING! We're about to begin today's program. Please make sure your cell phones and pagers are powered off or set on silent!"

Juan turned and hustled for the entrance to the seminar room. "We better go!" he called back to Conrad and Connie, "I don't want to miss any of this!"

The Soomers looked at each other in astonishment. *This is like a circus*, thought Conrad. He spoke first, "Connie, if this is the same Grant Deeds you think it is, maybe you can get Karen to ask him to give us some tips without having to pay all this money and sit here all day?"

Connie nodded in agreement, "I think so. After all, it was her idea for us to talk with him." She paused to think and then continued, "But since we're here, maybe you should just go in by yourself. That will save us $149 and you can sit with Juan. Afterwards, you can just come home and tell me all about it while we watch *American Idle*. I have some errands I need to run and there's a sale at the mall. I've been meaning to pick up some gifts for the kids. I'll use the money we just saved!"

Conrad agreed with the plan. "Sounds good," he affirmed.

Conrad kissed Connie good-bye and stepped back up to the registration table to pay for his ticket. *At least the line is gone now*, he thought. He purchased his ticket and entered the ballroom. It was packed! Looking around he saw an empty chair in the back corner against the wall next to a plant. When he sat down he couldn't see much of the main stage because a large pillar blocked his view. *No wonder no one was sitting here*, he thought as he settled in and tilted his chair back against the wall. *Oh well, at least it's comfortable.*

• • •

Conrad's head was still spinning that evening when he walked through the door into his home. He couldn't remember everything he'd heard at the seminar, but one thing he was sure of – Grant Deeds passionately believed in real estate as a wealth-building vehicle. He had such an energetic way of making the topic interesting, understandable, and even funny. Though Conrad didn't understand everything Grant taught, he was confident he could learn. For the first time in a long time, Conrad felt like there was legitimate hope for his financial future. It was like being a wide-eyed graduate again. He felt like he could conquer the world!

"How was it?" Connie asked enthusiastically. "Was it worth it?"

"You know," Conrad replied with cautious enthusiasm, "Grant Deeds is pretty good. I have to admit I actually enjoyed the entire seminar."

Connie waited, anticipating more information, but Conrad wasn't providing any.

"That's it?" Connie asked. "Well, what did you learn? Did you get any ideas? What do we do now?"

Conrad sat back and in his mind he began to sift through the eight hours of lecture, stories and visual aids he'd seen and heard. His head started spinning again. *Where do I start?* he wondered.

"Well," he began, picking the first topic that came to his mind, "Grant talked about things like 'leverage' and 'idle equity'. He said most people try to save their way to financial independence, but most people can't out-earn inflation. Real estate goes up faster than most people can save, which makes it hard to buy. But he said once you're in, real estate makes you money. He talked about 'good debt' and 'bad debt' and how you can make money with other people's money." Conrad's brow furled as he tried to organize all the thoughts floating around in his head.

Connie listened intently. This was the closest she and Conrad had ever come to actually both being interested in their finances at the same time. She really wanted to understand!

Conrad went on, "He talked about how to borrow money at one rate and earn more with that money than it cost to borrow it. He said real estate is a good investment because it tends to go up steadily over time and protects you from inflation. He said you can actually use real estate to benefit from inflation."

Connie prodded, "Did he give any examples or specifics?"

"Sure," Conrad said, as various images and sound bites flashed through his mind, "He had lots of stories about deals he or his students had done. Some of the investors he's worked with were actually there. In fact, I found out today Juan already owns a rental property!"

Connie was surprised. "Really? Juan? How can Juan own rental property? I thought he made less money than you do. And his wife doesn't even work. How can he afford to buy rental property?"

Conrad answered, "I don't know. I was surprised, too. The way Juan talked about wanting to get started, I assumed he hadn't done anything yet, but, I guess he goes to a lot of these seminars and reads a lot of books. He said he belongs to an investment club and they meet once a month to talk about real estate investing."

Connie was still confused, "I still don't see how that helps him afford a rental property."

"Well," Conrad continued, "Grant gave an interesting example that helped me understand everything a little better."

Conrad then proceeded to try to tell Connie how Grant explained the process of transferring equity from one property to use as a down payment on another property, then using the tax breaks and rental income to cover all the holding costs. But even though it all made sense when Conrad heard it at the seminar, he struggled with the details. Connie remained confused and was becoming frustrated with Conrad's inability to clarify. With each successive question Connie asked, Conrad found it more difficult to explain. Eventually, Conrad began losing the feeling of confidence he had when he left the seminar.

Even so, Conrad couldn't help but marvel that Juan Tunavest already owned rental property.

● ● ●

"Hey, Conrad! What did you think of the seminar?"

Looking up from the water cooler, Conrad saw Juan Tunavest walking towards him. "It was good," Conrad replied with subdued enthusiasm. Afraid to reveal he still really didn't understand much of what was taught by Grant Deeds, Conrad tossed the question back to Juan, "What did *you* think?"

"Awesome!" Juan said, beaming with enthusiasm, "I got several great ideas and confirmed some other things I already knew. I met Grant's real estate agent and his financing guy. I stayed after and had a chance to talk privately with them for nearly half an hour!" Juan paused, then asked, "What happened to you? I looked around for you. I thought we might talk afterwards. I figured with all your business savvy, you might have picked up some things I missed."

"Oh," Conrad replied sheepishly. "I needed to get home because Connie and I like to watch *American Idle*. It's our favorite TV show. It's our little thing we do together. Connie really likes it." Conrad felt like he needed to justify having left early, but remained embarrassed he had, especially in light of Juan's enthusiasm. Conrad continued, "But actually, we didn't end up watching TV after all. I spent most of the evening trying to explain that free rental property idea to her." *Great*, thought Conrad, *now I just exposed what a dunce I am.*

"What did Connie think about it?" Juan asked with genuine interest. Juan had always admired Conrad. As a supply room clerk, Juan didn't have much professional status at SCUMCO. Most of the "suits" treated him like a second-class citizen, but even though Conrad was a sales manager, he was always very friendly to Juan. Conrad treated Juan with respect and Juan appreciated it.

"To be honest," Conrad confided, "I had a hard time trying to explain it to her. It all seemed to make sense when Grant was saying it, but when I got home it was hard to repeat." *It would have helped if I hadn't left my workbook under my chair at the hotel,* he chided himself.

Juan agreed, "I know what you mean! That's why I always bring Luv to all the seminars. It makes it a lot easier to make decisions because we can spend time talking about what to do, instead of me trying to teach her in thirty minutes everything I learned over eight hours."

Conrad thought about it. "But don't you think it's expensive to pay for two tickets every time?" Conrad asked. "They should offer a family discount or something."

Juan laughed. "Expensive? Compared to what? Compared to spending twice as long to do a worse job of explaining it to Luv, or not being able to agree on what needs to be done and ending up doing nothing? I think it's cheap compared to the money we'll make!"

Conrad was amazed at Juan's attitude. *Man, has someone sold this guy a bill of goods,* thought Conrad. *What a racket. They must see guys like Juan coming a mile away! And besides the rental property, I don't see any evidence Juan and Luv are making any real money.* Conrad felt his insecurity being replaced by a feeling of superiority.

"You know what I mean, Conrad?" Juan continued, "Remember that rental property I told you about? I bought it less than a year ago and it's already gone up $35,000! Plus, I just had my taxes done and I'm actually getting an extra $2,400 refund just because of the tax deductions from the property. Isn't that great?"

Conrad was surprised. *How does a stockroom clerk get so smart about finances?* he thought. "Really?" Conrad asked. "I don't mean to be nosy, but how did you do that? Connie and I really want to get started in investing, but we aren't sure what to do next." Conrad was now feeling much less smug.

Wasn't this guy in the same seminar as I was? thought Juan. *I don't get it. Grant explained the whole thing in his lecture. Were you sleeping?*

"Did you buy Grant's book?" asked Juan with a very slight hint of sarcasm.

"No," Conrad replied, not picking up on Juan's irritation, "It seemed a little pricey to me. I mean, fifty-nine bucks for a book? Are you kidding me? It probably only cost four bucks to print! If he sold a hundred copies, he probably made five grand that day. I don't even know why he charged for the seminar. He should have paid us to come listen to him pitch his book!"

Juan was shocked. He stared in disbelief as Conrad continued, "I'm sure the book has the same stuff as he taught in the seminar. I've already heard all of that. Was there something *new* in the book that he left out of the seminar?" He looked at Juan, who remained flabbergasted.

"Maybe you can give me some of *your* 'secrets' for success?" Conrad said with a wink and a smile.

Trying to be polite, Juan returned an unenthusiastic smile. In an attempt to get the conversation back on a positive track, Juan suggested, "I hear Grant's got another seminar coming up. Why don't you and Connie go to it and brush up on the basics?"

"*Another* seminar?" Conrad asked incredulously. "Are you going to it or have you been to this one already? How did you find out about it?"

Juan replied, "Actually, it's a repeat of the seminar we just went to, but yes, I am going again. Maybe he added some new material or will have a different guest speaker or a new case study. Even if he doesn't, I might catch something this time that I missed last time."

Incredible! What an optimist, Conrad thought. Juan's enthusiasm for real estate investing was almost contagious.

"How did you say you heard about the new seminar?" Conrad asked again.

"From the e-mail announcement Grant sent out," Juan answered. "Didn't you get it? I thought everyone who went to the last seminar was on the list."

"Oh," Conrad said, "we never sign up for mailing lists. I get too much spam as it is. Maybe you could just forward a copy to me when something important comes up?"

Juan was getting annoyed. He glanced at his watch and then said to Conrad, "I need to go. I have an appointment to sign some documents for another property we're buying. Why don't you check out Grant's web site? I'm sure you can get more information there."

Conrad stood dumbfounded as Juan walked away. *I don't get it,* Conrad thought. *How can Juan be buying another property already?*

• • •

"Karen? Hi! This is Connie Soomer...you know, from soccer?"

"Oh, yes!" answered the woman on the other end of the phone. "How *are* you? It's so *nice* to hear from you!" Karen Deeds genuinely cared about other people and her interest showed in her voice. She and Connie hadn't spoken since soccer season ended.

"I'm doing well," Connie replied. "I'm calling to see if you and Grant would like to get together for dinner or perhaps a day at the lake? Conrad really enjoyed Grant's last seminar and we would love to learn more about real estate investing."

"I didn't know you went to the seminar, Connie," replied Karen. "That's great! What did you think? Did Grant answer your questions? He tries to stick around after each presentation to meet people. Did you tell him we're friends?"

"Actually," Connie answered, "I wasn't able to attend the seminar, but Conrad went and he really liked it. We were invited by some other friends. We were so surprised to find out Grant was the speaker. I didn't realize Grant was so popular! When I told Conrad you suggested we meet with Grant, he wanted me to call and set it up. Do you think we can get together?"

"I'm sure it would be fine," Karen responded. "But Grant is very busy, so please don't be offended if it takes a little time to get it scheduled."

"No problem," Connie answered. "Just give me a call when you're ready and we'll set it up. We're very flexible!"

• • •

"Connie? Don Nojak here! How are you doing on this fine evening?"

"I'm fine, Don," Connie Soomer replied politely, cradling the phone between her chin and shoulder, "I'm just putting out the dinner dishes. How are you?" She hoped he would pick up on the clue she was in the middle of dinner and not available to talk.

"It's a beautiful day at Hardy Sellers Mortgage!" Don responded with his trademark greeting and singsong voice. "Rates are still down and I was just thinking about our conversation. Guess what? Great news! We can still re-do your current loan and reduce your payment $120 a month using a 30-year, fixed-rate, no points and no out-of-pocket expense loan – or you can reduce your interest rate by nearly 1% with a 15-year fixed-rate loan. If you combine the 15-year loan with our *Loan Acceleration Mortgage Eliminator* program, you'll be paid off in no time! But don't wait! Rates look like they might be moving up…probably tomorrow…maybe as early as first thing in the morning. You can pay off your loan faster or reduce your monthly payment, which would you prefer?"

Don went silent and waited patiently for Connie's reply.

Gosh, Connie thought, *I'd hate to miss this opportunity. If rates are going up first thing in the morning, maybe I should handle this right now – but, then again, maybe we should wait and talk to Grant first?*

Connie hesitated. "You know, Don," she said, "we're going to be getting together with someone to talk about real estate. I don't think we want to do anything until after that meeting."

Don was surprised. "Not another mortgage man, I hope," he said with a twinge of concern. "We've been together for a long time, you know! I'd be insanely jealous if you had another mortgage man in your life!" Don joked to try to keep it light, but Connie could tell he was worried.

"Oh, no…nothing like that," Connie reassured Don. "He's a real estate investor. We're interested in getting into real estate investing and we're hoping he can give us some guidance. By the way, do you own any investment property?" Connie felt a little awkward asking such a personal question, but decided to ask anyway. After all, Don knew everything about the Soomers' personal finances. Besides, Connie reasoned, if she was going to get advice on real estate investing, it made sense to get it from someone who actually owned investment real estate themselves.

"Not yet!" responded Don confidently, "but I plan to some day!" He wanted to quickly redirect the conversation back to his pursuit of additional loan business. "You know, Hardy Sellers also does investment property loans, so if you decide to do anything with investment property, give me a call and I'll set you up with a great program. Have I told you I am a *Direct Underwriting Mortgage Banking Acceleration System Specialist*? And last month, I was the number one loan officer in my cubicle. You know, I take new clients by referral only now. Oh, by the way, if you know anyone looking for a great deal on a home loan, won't you please pass my name along?"

Do you take classes to learn this stuff? Connie thought to herself. Even though Don was a little corny, he was a nice guy, but it got a little tiring listening to him promote himself at every opportunity – especially with dinner getting cold.

Don's monologue continued, "Meanwhile, don't you want to take advantage of these great rates? It doesn't cost you anything. I'll do the loan for free and it'll save you $120 a month! You'd like to save $120 a month, wouldn't you?" Don once again went silent and waited patiently for her reply.

"Hmmm..." Connie murmured as she thought about how to get Don off the phone. The silence on the other end of the phone grew thick and eventually awkward. Don remained steadfastly silent waiting for her to answer. Eventually, Connie stammered, "Well, I ...um...I suppose...well..." and then her voice trailed off.

Don Nojak realized he wasn't going to get the "yes" he was so accustomed to from Connie, so he decided to try a different tact.

"Connie," said Don in a paternal tone, "you and Conrad have been my clients for a long time. I've always done you good, haven't I? I mean, you haven't paid any points for the last three loans I've done for you, and every single time I've lowered your payment. I know you've told me several times how happy and appreciative you are. Is there any reason you wouldn't want to lower your payment again? Remember, it doesn't cost you anything out of pocket. C'mon, whaddya say?" He stopped speaking and aggressively waited for her answer. She could almost feel his stare through the phone.

"Gosh, Don," started Connie, "it seems like a no-brainer, but we were thinking about getting some extra cash out this time. What do you think about that idea?"

Cash out means a bigger loan! thought Don immediately. He would love to do a bigger loan, but suddenly he was concerned. He was sure this wasn't an idea the Soomers had come up with on their own. *They must be talking to another mortgage guy,* he reasoned. He decided to take a contrary position to avoid inadvertently endorsing the competitor's advice.

"Why would you want to do *that*?" Don asked with exaggerated surprise. "Usually people who take cash out of their homes have credit problems and want to consolidate their debt. You didn't have much debt the last time we ran your credit report. Has anything changed or are you just planning some home improvements?" Don was fishing for some insight into Connie's motivation, but he also wanted to keep the door open for a bigger cash-out loan if it just turned out to be something Connie thought of herself.

"No," Connie said, "we only have the loans on the two cars, the boat and the RV. We just paid off the jet-skis and ATVs, and we don't have any credit card debt since we paid them off with the 401k loan."

Connie felt good about the progress she'd made getting out of debt. Ivana B. Padov would be so pleased!

"I think we're in pretty good shape debt-wise," Connie continued, "though I suppose it would be nice to remodel the kitchen, we don't have any current plans for home improvement. We just want to build up more equity and thought if we took some cash out we could use it to buy another property."

Don Nojak paused for a moment. *Where did THAT come from?*

"Connie," Don started, "I'm confused. How does taking cash out of your property help you build equity? It seems to me, you'll end up with a bigger payment on your home and another mortgage on the new property. That doesn't increase your equity. It increases your debt."

Connie was silent as she was processing what Don had said. *That makes sense,* she thought. *But Conrad was so sure after he came back from Grant's seminar. Did he misunderstand? I wish I would've gone to that seminar after all! I can't wait until we meet with Grant.*

Connie's silence was troubling to Don. *Maybe I offended her,* he worried. *What if this other advisor is a friend of hers? Think fast, Nojak!* Don was struggling to figure out what to say next. He was losing control of the conversation and needed to say something quickly. Then, he remembered an old sales truism, *'People don't care how much you know, until they know how much you care'.*

"Don't get me wrong," Don started again. "There's nothing I'd like more than to make you a big loan on your house and another loan on your new property, but I just don't think that would be in your best interest. I think it makes more sense to re-do your current loan and get a lower payment. If you can afford more than just the minimum required payment, why don't you make extra payments to accelerate your loan and pay it off sooner?

Then you really *are* building equity. In fact, if you think you can handle the bigger payments, why don't you get the 15-year loan? You'll get a lower interest rate and all of the bigger payment will go towards paying your loan off. We have a great program from Capital Resource Asset Partners. It's called the *Home Equity Accelerator Program* because you end up with a HEAP of equity! This is a very popular program. In fact, I've helped more people get into a CRAP HEAP loan than any other loan officer in my office."

Connie was impressed. "Wow!" she said. "Don, you are so smart! When you put it like that it just seems so obvious."

"No need to thank me ma'am," Don said with Joe-Friday-like matter-of-factness, "just doing my job." Connie laughed.

Don moved in for the close, "When can you come in to sign the loan application? I have an appointment available Tuesday in the afternoon or Wednesday in the morning, which would be better for you?"

• • •

CHAPTER 2
The Forties

"**D**o you, Bill Formor, take this woman, Hope Tunavest, to be your lawfully wedded wife?" the reverend asked the handsomely tuxedoed young man standing before him.

Bill Formor looked into the dark brown eyes of his lovely young bride-to-be and answered resolutely, "I do."

Hope Tunavest gazed back into Bill's eyes. The reverend turned to Juan and Luv Tunavest's oldest daughter and asked, "Do you, Hope Tunavest, take this man, Bill Formor, to be your lawfully wedded husband?"

"I do," she said softly.

"Then," the reverend responded, "by the power vested in me by the state and by God Almighty, I now pronounce you man and wife!" Turning to the groom he said, "You may kiss your bride."

The newly married Bill and Hope Formor exchanged a loving kiss before turning to face the witnesses and guests which filled The Good Shepherd Christian Chapel.

"Ladies and gentleman, I now present to you Mr. and Mrs. Bill Formor!" the reverend exclaimed as applause, laughter, cheers and tears erupted throughout the chapel.

Conrad and Connie Soomer stood together in the pew as the bride and groom walked down the aisle. The newlyweds were followed closely by the wedding party and honored guests.

When Juan and Luv Tunavest passed by, Connie looked over the handkerchief she was using to dab her moistened eyes. Her eyes met Luv's and the two women exchanged maternal smiles. Conrad smiled and nodded his approval to his long time co-worker. Decked out in his handsomely tailored tuxedo with his wife of twenty-seven years on his arm, Juan was the picture of pride and joy.

"Isn't this beautiful, Conrad?" asked Connie with admiration as she gazed around the spacious chapel. "I can't wait to see the reception! I'm trying to get ideas for Sara's wedding." Connie smiled at her oldest baby, now a beautiful young lady standing beside her father.

Conrad tried to be happy, but he was fighting back thoughts of worry and dread. *How in the world will we be able to pay for Sara's wedding?* he fretted. With Susie still in college and Simon just starting, Sara's engagement announcement nearly put Conrad over the top. Faced with mounting pressure from international competitors, SCUMCO's sales were soft. Even with Conrad's increased salary as Sales Area Director, so much of the income the Soomers depended upon came from bonuses. Conrad's boss, Ben Dover, was recently promoted to Wide Area Director and Conrad was sure this meant inevitable changes to the bonus model – again. Dover had a well-deserved reputation for reducing sales costs through cleverly disguised commission cuts. This made it increasingly difficult for Conrad to attract and retain top performing sales people. His best salespeople were always being recruited by the competition, who offered higher commissions. Conrad was constantly training new people to replace those who left. The problem was, as soon as a new rep was competent and productive, the competition noticed and recruited them away. Conrad felt like a training manager for his competition.

Doesn't SCUMCO get it? If they want profits, they need sales. To get sales, they need customers. To get customers, they need skilled and motivated salespeople. To get skilled and motivated salespeople, SCUMCO needs to offer attractive compensation. To provide attractive compensation, they need profits…which come from sales which come from customers which come from skilled salespeople. They are all interconnected. It seemed so simple to Conrad – offer attractive compensation to attract great salespeople, and profits will follow. Unfortunately, Dover didn't see it that way, so Conrad had to deal with constant turnover. It was a miracle that Conrad's sales team hit the sales record which catapulted Dover to Wide Area Director. Ironically, Conrad's work actually helped Ben Dover become SCUMCO's biggest WAD.

"Conrad!" Connie Soomer reprimanded. "Are you going to stand there daydreaming all afternoon? Let's get over to the reception!" Looking past her husband to her oldest daughter, who was standing on his other side, Connie called out, "Sara! Bring your father and let's get going!" Connie moved hurriedly into the aisle and headed for the chapel door.

As they hustled out of the chapel and into the parking lot, Connie updated Conrad, "Bill Formor is a very successful attorney. Hope met him at Harvard when she was just a freshman and he was a senior. He's been working in a private practice for two years since graduating and I understand he does very well!" Conrad nodded his acknowledgement, but didn't respond as he opened up the car door and climbed in.

During the drive to the reception, Sara and Connie talked incessantly about all their plans for Sara's wedding. Conrad's mind kept drifting back to the situation at work and the financial challenges facing him. He wanted so desperately not to disappoint his wife and children. *I don't get it,* he thought. *How can Juan afford to send his kids to Harvard? Just getting Sara through Okayfer University was hard for us. Susie had to start at Se Nada Community College and now that she's ready to move on, Simon will probably need to start there, too. I sure hope Susie doesn't get into a serious relationship with anyone soon. I can't afford another wedding. It'll take me years just to pay for Sara's!*

As Conrad continued wrestling with his thoughts, Connie announced that the hotel was in view. "There it is!" she said in awe. "Oh, my goodness! Look at this place! It's absolutely *gorgeous!*"

Conrad pulled the car up to the lobby of the Equity Palace Hotel. Indeed, the hotel was very beautiful. The valet greeted Conrad, and the doormen opened the car doors and helped the two women out. Conrad stepped out of the car and handed the keys to the valet. After pocketing the claim check, Conrad rejoined the women in the hotel lobby.

Connie glanced around the surroundings. "This is exquisite!" she exclaimed.

"Hey, Mom!" Sara called out from the hallway on the right side of the hotel lobby, "look at this!" She enthusiastically beckoned for Connie to come over to her.

Connie grabbed Conrad's arm and clacked along the tile floor in her high heel shoes until she reached her daughter. Stepping onto the plush carpeting, she peered into the banquet room which had been prepared for Bill and Hope's reception. Inside were dozens of elegantly decorated round tables with white tablecloths and tall, floral centerpieces. Crystal goblets and fine china were surrounded by silver cutlery and decoratively folded linen napkins. On one side of the room was a table with hors d'oeurvres and a tall fountain flowing with milk chocolate.

"Mom! Do you see that?" Sara squealed giddily, pointing to the chocolate fountain. "That is SO cool! Don't you just love it?"

Connie nodded and smiled. "It's wonderful!" she agreed. *What an exciting thing to be young and full of hope.*

"Daddy," Sara said, looking at Conrad with her big blue eyes. "Can I have one of those at *my* wedding?"

Conrad looked at the angelic face of his grown up baby girl and smiled. *How can I possibly tell her no?*

"Of course you can, sweetheart," he replied. "Of course, you can. I love you."

Sara smiled and gave Conrad a tight hug. "Oh, Daddy! Thank you!"

• • •

"What do you think of these?" Connie asked Conrad. She was holding up two different sets of crystal goblets. "Which one do you think would go better with these?" Connie set the goblets down and picked up two different fine china dinner plates.

Conrad stared at the goblets and china. He was trying to be interested, but he couldn't get his thoughts off the previous meeting with the catering company. *Eighty dollars per person? What are we serving? Caviar?* He wondered how a simple wedding could be so expensive. *It's only one day and then it's over! Then you have nothing to show for it except a twelve-inch stack of receipts, none of which are deductible. Why couldn't we have had three boys instead?*

"Honey, which ones do you like?" Connie asked again. She held up one of the crystal goblets, "I think I like these the best," she said with enthusiasm. Conrad seemed disinterested.

"Are you okay?" Connie asked with concern.

Conrad looked at her. She could see something was really bothering him. Maybe Sara was right. Maybe he didn't approve of her fiancé. Whatever is was, it had been going on for several months, but Conrad never wanted to talk about it. "Pressure at work" he would always say. Connie didn't know if she should be angry or sympathetic. She decided to take a gentle approach.

"Conrad," Connie began sympathetically, "what is it?" She looked at his face, but he stared at the table.

"Are you upset that Sara is getting married?" she asked. "Is it Beau? He seems like a nice young man. I think he really loves Sara and he'll work hard to take good care of her."

Conrad looked up at his worried wife. "No, that's not it," he said. "I have no problem with Sara getting married. I'm very happy for her and I think Beau is a fine young man. In fact, I think he's a whole lot sharper than I was at his age." *Thank God for that*, he thought, grimacing over the person he'd been in his younger days.

"What is it then?" Connie persisted. She was growing insecure. "Have I done something?"

"No," Conrad said with firm reassurance, "not at all. You're great. Sara is so lucky to have you for her mom. It's fun watching the two of you carry on over this wedding." He smiled bravely.

Connie refused to give up. She prodded, "Well? What is it then?"

Conrad became tense. He was hoping she would just back down and leave it be. "I don't want to fight," he said, trying to be patient. "I just have some pressure at work, that's all." Whenever he was backed into a conversational corner with Connie, he always threw out this catch-all smokescreen.

"I think it's more than that," Connie rebutted steadfastly. "You've always had pressure at work, but it's never stopped you from being a fun person. You've been moping around ever since Hope's wedding. Why don't you just tell me the truth?"

Conrad panicked. *She's on to me,* he thought. *Stick with the pressure at work thing,* he coached himself, *there's enough there that's real. She'll buy it until I can figure out what to do.* He didn't want her to know he was ashamed he couldn't provide the lavish wedding his daughter dreamed about and deserved and he so dearly wanted to give her.

"Work has been really tough lately," Conrad maintained. "Ever since Dover became the top WAD, he's been horrible to work with. It's like that Peter Principle thing. He's hit the top of his ability and he's always stealing my ideas. Then he undermines me to my team and the president. I think he's afraid I might get his job, so he tries to stay ahead by cutting me down and using my ideas to make himself look good. I feel like I'm painted into a corner. I can't implement anything without his permission, but as soon I tell him my plans, he steals my ideas and takes the credit for himself. Basically, he's a jerk and I don't have anywhere to go in the company." This humiliating admission was the lesser of two evils. He certainly didn't want to admit his feelings of being inadequate as a provider, but at least if it did come out, it would all be Dover's fault.

Connie nodded and decided to go along, "I was talking to Ben's wife, Eileen, at the last company party. She confided in me that Ben is worried about the direction of the company. She said if they can't get on track they might need to merge with a stronger competitor. If that happens, there will be fewer top jobs and most of them will go to the management team of the stronger company. Is that right?"

"Yeah," Conrad affirmed, "I see that too. Sometimes I envy Juan. His job in the storeroom seems so peaceful. The biggest crisis in his life is when we run out of copy paper." He chuckled.

"Oh, I don't know," said Connie, "I talked with Luv the other day to get some ideas about Sara's wedding. She said they had a big problem with one of their rental properties. Apparently one of the tenants stole some hubcaps from a neighbor. The neighbor came over and beat the guy up, then threw him out the front window! The police came and everything."

Conrad laughed. "I hadn't heard about that! No wonder Juan doesn't seem to like talking to me about his real estate investing. I guess it's not as easy as those TV infomercials make it sound." Conrad felt relieved he wasn't the only person in the world with problems. Then he became curious, *I wonder what else Connie learned from Luv?*

"What else did Luv have to say?" Conrad inquired. He was chumming for insight into how the Tunavests were doing financially.

"We mostly talked about Sara's wedding," Connie replied. "They did such a nice job on Hope's! It would be great if Sara's could be half as nice."

Half as nice? Conrad was offended. "What do you mean 'half as nice'?" he retorted. His competitive nature took over, "Why can't Sara's be even *better?*" He looked at Connie angrily.

Connie became defensive, "You've seen how expensive everything is! I'm doing my best to make it as nice as I can for what we can afford. As it is, we've had to cut corners on little things to try to stay in our price range."

Conrad was becoming more agitated, "I make three times more

money than Juan! Anything he can afford, we can afford. You must not be doing a very good job negotiating with the vendors. I probably should have handled all this myself. You're just not business-minded. In fact, maybe I should take over *all* the finances. It seems like we *never* have enough money. If Juan Tunavest can send his kids to great colleges and throw huge wedding parties, we can too! We just have to be smarter about managing our money." Conrad stared intently at Connie.

Large tears began to fill Connie's eyes. Her lip began to quiver and her chest began to heave. Soon, sniffles built into a crescendo of sobs. Conrad looked at his wife and hated himself for losing control. He had just vomited all his frustrations onto this beautiful woman who had stood by his side through all the ups and downs of raising a family and building a life. He cursed at himself, *Damn my stupid pride!*

"Con… honey… aw, c'mon… honey, I'm sorry," he said gently. "I didn't mean that." He reached for her, but she spun away from him and continued to sob.

"Look," he said, repositioning himself to get face to face with her. "It's not you," he reassured her, "It's me." He took her hands and held them, "Try to understand. I just want you and the kids to have the best of everything. I get upset when other people who make less than me can do more. I just don't understand it." He paused to gather his thoughts and choose his words carefully. He kissed her gently on the forehead and continued, "I know you're doing your best. So am I. We'll figure this all out. We just need to work together. I should never have said those things. I'm really sorry."

Connie looked up at him. Her eyes were swollen and moist.

"I love you," he said softly, hoping she would forgive him.

"I love you, too," she replied. In her heart, she forgave him, but she still felt wounded.

• • •

Conrad walked into the company lunchroom to see Juan sitting with a laptop computer open. Juan was gazing intently at the screen while he used his peripheral vision to reach for his sandwich.

"Hey Juan!" Conrad asked in a chummy voice, "Nice laptop! Is it new?"

Juan looked up, his concentration broken, "Oh, hey, Conrad. What's up?"

Conrad answered, "I just saw you sitting here with this fancy laptop and wondered what you're doing. I thought I'd stop by and say 'hi'. What are you working on?"

Juan returned his focus to his laptop and fingered the touchpad to scroll through the display on the screen, "I'm just looking to see if I have enough equity in my properties to refinance."

"Hey! We just refinanced again," Conrad said proudly. "Check it out – we got another 15-year fixed-rate loan for only…are you ready? Five and a quarter percent, no points and no fees! Isn't that great?"

Conrad watched for Juan's reaction. He was sure Juan would be impressed.

Juan looked up from his computer with a perplexed expression. "Why would you want to do *that?*" he asked with surprise.

Conrad was vexed. "What do you mean, 'Why would we do that?'" he said with some irritation. Juan had not reacted at all like he had expected. "We did it to build up equity. We're investors, too!" Conrad asserted.

Juan's expression changed to one of excitement. He was genuinely happy the Soomers had finally taken the plunge. Juan and Luv Tunavest had purchased several more properties since that first Grant Deeds seminar so many years ago. For all their apparent interest in real estate investing, Conrad and Connie hadn't really taken any visible steps towards actually investing. Conrad always seemed interested in *talking* about investing in property. Occasionally, Conrad would show up at a seminar. A few times, Conrad would bring in an information sheet on a property he found in the paper or on the internet and ask Juan to take a look, but as far as Juan knew, the Soomers had never actually closed a deal. In fact, Juan wasn't sure if they had even ever made an offer. *I guess I was wrong about Conrad,* Juan thought.

"Congratulations!" Juan exclaimed, "When did you get your investment property? Tell me all about it!"

Conrad clarified, "No, we don't have an investment property yet. We're investing in our home first by accelerating equity growth on our home loan. Once it's paid off, we'll start saving towards getting our first investment property. I mean, equity is equity, right? We just can't afford to increase our monthly payments more than we already have. Sara's wedding is coming up and Susie is still in college. You know, the payment on a 15-year loan is a lot bigger than the 30-year loan, but it really piles on the equity! We got one of those CRAP HEAP loans. Are you familiar with that program?"

Conrad was clearly enthused, but Juan was aghast. Was he really hearing this?

"How did you come up with this plan?" Juan asked, trying not to be condescending or rude.

"My wife has this great mortgage guy, Don Nojak," Conrad answered, eager to boast about his connections. "Have you heard of him?"

Juan shook his head, but didn't say anything. Conrad went on, "When Connie talked to Don, he had a chance to sell us a big cash-out loan and then another loan on an investment property, but he explained to us how doing that didn't really build our equity – it just spread it out, increased our debt, and put us on the line for huge payments. Don said the best way to get equity in our property was to get the interest rate as low as possible and use a 15-year loan to pay it down fast. It's working so well, we're even taking the money we were putting in our 401k and putting it into paying the loan down faster."

"In fact," Conrad continued, "we did some calculations and figured out that since our mutual funds were just going down anyway, we were better off investing in our mortgage." Conrad studied Juan's face carefully to see what Juan thought of the Soomers' plan.

Juan wasn't sure how to react. Even though he liked Conrad, he sure didn't understand him. Conrad was so successful at SCUMCO and he seemed really smart. Maybe Juan was the one who had it wrong. Then again, Juan owned several properties and his net worth had grown substantially over the years, in spite of using his properties to pay for his kids' college educations and weddings.

Conrad waited for a response from Juan. When it didn't come Conrad asked, "Why are *you* thinking about refinancing?"

Juan debated for a moment whether he wanted to spend time discussing his plans with Conrad. It wasn't that Juan was secretive. He enjoyed sharing ideas with the members of his investment club, but whenever he tried to talk with Conrad it was different. It was as though Conrad was more interested in showing off what he knew than actually listening – or even teaching. Juan had a hard time defining what it was about Conrad that bothered him. *Maybe I'm being too judgmental*, Juan thought. *Why not give it another try?*

"I refinance regularly for a variety of reasons," Juan responded. "Sometimes to improve my cash-flow, other times to reposition equity to maintain a higher equity growth rate, and sometimes to just to get money I need to pay for something large like college or a wedding!" Juan laughed. He knew Conrad could relate to paying for college and weddings. "Hap and Rich are headed off to college. Faith just finished and is planning on getting married. Joy is in her third year at Stanford. It seems I never run out of reasons to refinance my properties!" Juan chuckled again.

Conrad's mind was racing. *That's how he does it! Juan and Luv are hopelessly in debt. They must be living paycheck to paycheck. Thank goodness Connie has been disciplined to develop an emergency fund. At least we have something to fall back on.*

Conrad was feeling much better about his own situation, but now he was worried for Juan.

Conrad wanted to confirm his understanding, "So you're saying when you refinance, you replace the old loan with a bigger loan, and doing that puts cash in your pocket?"

"That's exactly right," Juan affirmed. "I don't always get cash out, but many times I do." Juan smiled. He was happy Conrad appeared to understand.

"Yeah, but doesn't that scare you?" Conrad asked. "That means your debt just keeps growing." Conrad's demeanor was one of genuine concern.

Juan was surprised by Conrad's statement. *I thought he was tracking with me,* Juan thought. *More mortgages mean more real estate, and more real estate means more appreciation, cash-flow and tax deductions. I guess Conrad doesn't understand that.*

"Conrad," Juan asked, "were you ever able to get together with Grant Deeds like you talked about way back when? I know Connie and Mrs. Deeds were friends when Simon was playing soccer. Did that relationship ever develop?"

Conrad was surprised by the sudden turn the conversation had taken. He was really more interested in explaining the dangers of debt to Juan.

"Well, actually, no," Conrad answered, "we didn't get together. We played phone tag a few times and the only time he was available to meet we had already scheduled another meeting. In fact, now that I think about it, we were getting together with one of our advisors, Don Nojak, our mortgage guy. Don was worried interest rates were going to spike up and he wanted to get us in to sign our papers. As it turned out, rates did jump up a quarter of a point the next day, even though they came back down a few days later. So I guess it was a good thing we did it when we did. But we never were able to get together with Grant Deeds. To be honest, I think he probably thinks he's too important to get together with us. His schedule was always too full – and with my busy schedule we just couldn't get together. But that's okay. There are lots of other people out there who do real estate and financial planning."

Juan stared blankly. After a few moments, the silence became awkward, so Conrad continued, "Anyway, since he was so busy, we decided to work with our own advisors. Don might not be a 'big shot' like Grant Deeds, but at least he's available and willing to work around our schedules. Freddy Katz, our tax guy, is pretty good, too. He said even if we bought investment property, we wouldn't be able to get the write-offs because we make too much money."

Conrad felt a sense of accomplishment by inserting that last comment. It wasn't as though he didn't make a good living and he sure didn't appreciate Juan's attitude about their home loan decisions. Besides, Conrad had heard about some of the problems he and Luv had experienced with their properties. They actually had the police kick down the door of one of their rentals and arrest a tenant who was dealing drugs – and the whole thing had been on a reality TV cop show!

Conrad was on a roll, so he kept going, "Yeah, so our CPA said we needed another tax deduction. He suggested I get a new car. Because I'm in sales, I can write off the lease payment. I got a great deal on it, too! It's a brand new BMW and the payment is only seven hundred bucks a month. Can you believe that? With the tax break, the new Beemer only costs me four-fifty!" Conrad was feeling very full of himself now.

"What about investment property?" Juan countered, "I thought you were interested in getting into a rental property. Have you changed your mind?" Juan was hoping to get the conversation back to real estate.

"You know," Conrad answered, "after that investment seminar way back, I was really interested for a while. I bought several books and even read some of them. I took a class at the community college and went to a free seminar on foreclosures by some guy...Warren Peace, I think it was. Anyway, I bought his course when I saw him on TV one night. I listened to the first CD. It was pretty good, but I wasn't sure what to do. Our mortgage guy, Don Nojak, got us pre-qualified, and Connie found a guy on the internet, Random Agent, who's the #1 real estate agent on his website. Randy took us out and we looked at some places with him. We made a few great offers – way below the asking price, but some fool would always offer more than us, so we never got any deals. Besides, Connie was pretty committed to this 'Debt Free Blows' plan or whatever it is with that lady on TV, Ivana B. Padov, so we didn't have much for a down payment anyway. The only properties we could afford were small and kind of crappy."

Conrad watched Juan to see if there was any agreement or sympathy. Juan sat silently.

Conrad rambled on, "Since we didn't have much luck with Randy, we found another agent who said he would show us properties and write up our offers. We shopped for a long time to find this guy. He said he would give a 25% referral fee to Don Nojak, our mortgage guy, on any deal we did with him. Don said he would give us the money since he was doing the loan anyway. We figured that would give us a better profit margin on our deal!"

Conrad was pleased to be providing evidence of his skills as a negotiator. He didn't think Juan had negotiated such favorable terms, but he wanted to be sure.

"Do your real estate agents give you discounts?" Conrad asked Juan.

Juan pondered his answer for moment. "Well…no, actually they don't," Juan answered.

I knew it! Conrad thought to himself. *I get better loans with no fees that build up equity faster. I can negotiate lower commissions and rebates with my real estate agents. I'll always offer 40% below the asking price on every property. Once I get going, I'll be doing much better than Juan! But I better be careful not to tell him all my secrets or he might use them and do better than me.*

"You know, I have over twenty-five years experience in sales, Juan," Conrad proclaimed proudly. "I'm a professional negotiator. If you ever need help getting discounts from your vendors, maybe I can give you some tips." Now Conrad was feeling back on top again. He was sure Juan could see he would do much better in real estate investing – once he got started.

"Thanks, Conrad," Juan said. "I appreciate your offer. Right now, I have a team I work with and they're pretty good." Juan didn't want to get into a philosophical debate about business relationships. Conrad obviously had an opinion, one with which Juan did not happen to agree.

Conrad didn't want to let this go. Maybe he wanted to feel more "even" since Juan hadn't been approving of his loan choices. Maybe he felt a little insecure since Juan's collection of properties was growing and Conrad's wasn't. Maybe he wanted to salve his ego because Juan's kids attended better schools than the Soomers' did. For whatever reason, Conrad continued on, "But you said your people aren't giving you discounts on their services. There are so many real estate and loan people around. Take advantage of the competition to drive down your 'cost to do'. It's a technique we use at SCUMCO all the time. If your vendors won't play, fire them and get someone else. These people are commodities. It's not personal. It's just business." Conrad felt like a shark among minnows.

Juan responded, "I understand, Conrad. You probably are a much more skilled negotiator than me. I don't really look at the people I work with as vendors. I think of them more as partners or teammates. We all want the same thing. I want to buy a property. They want to sell a property. I want to get a loan. They want to make a loan. We all need the deal to happen for each of us to get what we want. Since I plan to make most of my money from *owning* the property over time, I don't worry too much about saving every penny when I buy it. I want everyone to walk away happy they did the deal and anxious to help me do another one."

Juan concluded, "I don't ask my agents to give me discounts. I ask them to get me into properties and loans that make me money. I heard Grant Deeds say once 'How much money do you make on a property you *don't* own?' That has stuck with me ever since."

Conrad was stunned. What Juan said actually made sense, but was contrary to everything Conrad had been taught and practiced.

Juan could only smile. "Why don't you get together with my real estate agent and mortgage broker? They might have some ideas for you. What could it hurt? In the worst case, they won't show you anything new, but at least you'll affirm what you're already doing.

You might even find out they can help you get more out of what you have to work with. Either way, you win."

Juan took two business cards from his wallet and handed them to Conrad. Juan encouraged Conrad, "These men both provide professional services and they are active investors themselves. They've helped me tremendously. Perhaps they can help you." Juan smiled and added, "Only, please do me a favor. Don't ask them to discount their fees."

Conrad took the business cards and looked them over. The names looked familiar.

"Hey," Conrad said, "aren't these the guys you met at that Grant Deeds seminar way back?"

"That's right," confirmed Juan. "I've been working with them ever since."

• • •

"How soon until you leave?" came the tinny sound of Connie's voice through the speakerphone on Conrad's desk at his SCUMCO office. Conrad looked at his "To Do" list. He looked at his watch. *Eight o'clock! Where did the day go?*

Conrad replied, "I'm just packing up my desk. I'll be on the road in about fifteen minutes. Okay?"

"Okay," Connie answered. "I have all of the information together for the wedding and I want to review it with you before we commit to anything. We're really tight on time, so we need to make our decisions tonight. I thought you were going to be home early. What happened?" Connie had been frustrated with Conrad for the last several weeks. Ever since the blow up over the catering proposal, Conrad had been working late. It was as though he didn't want anything to do with his own daughter's wedding.

"Just the usual stuff," Conrad explained. "You know how it is around here these days. I'll be home soon. Put on a pot of coffee and we'll go through everything. Okay? I'll see you in a bit." He clicked off the speaker and sat back in his chair. He laid his head back, ran his hands through his hair and stared at the ceiling for a moment. *I feel like I'm on a treadmill that just won't stop.* Then he sat forward and gathered himself. He stood up and scraped all the papers on his desktop into a box and then stuffed it into the knee space under his desk.

As he drove home, Conrad tried to prepare himself for his meeting with Connie. It seemed like every time they talked finances they were doomed to fight. *Need, need, need. Want, want, want. Spend, spend, spend. We haven't been boating but maybe two or three times in the last few years,* he opined. *If I can just hang on until the kids are through college and out on their own, then we'll be able to start saving again.* He comforted himself momentarily with these thoughts.

As he rounded the corner to enter the neighborhood where he and Connie lived, his thoughts started up again. *Every year I make more money than the year before, but every year, the amount of money going out grows faster than I can earn it. Even with Connie working, we just don't seem to be able to save enough to keep up. The monthly bills are okay, but it's the big stuff that kills us. College tuition, weddings, new furniture, and appliances — the list goes on and on! Every time we save up a chunk of cash, something comes along to gobble it up.* Frustrated, he mused, *Maybe someday they'll invent a way for me to clone myself — then "I" could work five jobs!*

Conrad pulled up to the house and parked his car. Connie greeted him at the door. She ushered him into the kitchen and sat him down to a re-heated plate of leftovers. Grabbing a pile of papers off the kitchen counter, she sat down across from him at the dining table.

"Here are all the quotes on everything from the reception hall to the wedding cake. I got three quotes on everything, just like you asked." Connie spread the papers out on the table for Conrad's perusal.

"This looks great, honey," he said through a mouth full of meatloaf. "You've done a great job." He wanted to stay on as positive a note as possible.

"Thanks," Connie said. "This is a lot of work!"

Conrad nodded in agreement. "Yes, our lives are a lot of work right now." He looked over the papers. There would be no cheap way to do this. "What do our finances look like?" he asked. "Do you have any idea how we can pay for all of this?"

Connie looked at him and smiled. "That's where I need your help," she said. "Did you get any ideas from Juan? He's been finding some way to pay for his kids' college and weddings."

Conrad winced at that comment. It still bothered him that Juan made so much less at SCUMCO, but was still able to do so much more for his kids.

"I spoke with him," Conrad replied. "Basically, he borrows to pay for everything."

"Borrows?" Connie repeated in amazement. "Really? How do you know that?"

"We talked at work," Conrad said. "He was working on some spreadsheets a while ago and I asked him what he was doing. He explained the whole thing to me." Conrad watched Connie carefully for her reaction.

"I don't think borrowing is a good idea," Connie said. "My grandma always said 'Interest is like cancer. It eats away at you until you die.'

Do you remember when we ran up our credit cards in the early years?" she asked. "We had to take out a loan on your 401k to pay it all off!"

"But at least we were paying the interest to ourselves," Conrad reminded her.

Connie continued, "Once we got rid of that debt, we were able to build up our emergency fund and start saving again. I know it's been a sacrifice, but now we have a whole year of income set aside for emergencies. And with Don Nojak's help, we've been able to re-do our home and cabin loans several times to reduce our interest rates."

"I thought our home and cabin loans were going to be paid off by now?" Conrad inquired. "How much longer do we have?"

Conrad's last comment made Connie feel a little defensive. She was worried he would start criticizing her. "We still have fifteen years," she answered, and then added quickly, "but that's only if we only pay the required amount. We pay extra, so it should take less time. What's nice is that if we need extra money on some months, then I only need to make the minimum payment."

"What about my 401k?" asked Conrad. "Didn't we stop putting money into that?"

"We did for a little while so we could pay off the house faster," Connie answered. "But when we took out the loan to pay off the credit cards, I took the payment we were using to pay off the credit cards and used it to pay the 401k loan every month. That's why I had you get your paycheck adjusted. When the loan was finally paid off, I thought it would be good to start back on the 401k, since SCUMCO matches 50% of your contribution."

"That sounds good," Conrad agreed. He was impressed. It seemed like Connie really knew what she was doing. "How's the 401k doing?" he asked.

Connie hesitated. She was afraid this question would come up.

"Well," she started, "it's doing…okay. When the stock market went down, the 401k went down too, but only about 30%, so we didn't lose any of the money we put in."

Conrad was taken aback. "Down 30%? How can it go *down* 30% and we don't lose any money?"

"It only went down by the amount that the company put in," Connie responded plainly. "All the money deducted from your paycheck is still there. After that happened, I moved it all into a money-market account to protect the principal. It's been growing steadily!" Connie was pleased with her defense and hoped Conrad was too.

Conrad thought about all of this for a moment. He was getting lost in the details.

"Just give me the bottom line," he said. "What are our options for paying for this wedding?" He was trying to stay focused on the purpose of their discussion.

Connie sat quietly for a moment. Then she looked up at Conrad and said solemnly, "I don't know." She felt sad.

Conrad looked back at her. He looked at the pile of quotes. He sat back in his chair and glanced up at a picture of Sara and her fiancé, Beau. He encouraged himself that he was an intelligent, hardworking guy. *There's an answer here. I just need to find it.* He shuffled through the papers, grabbed a pad of paper and pen from the table, and then began to write:

Resources:
1. Emergency Fund: $101,300
2. College Savings: $ 18,700
3. Wedding Fund: $ 9,200
4. 401k: $127,600

He looked at the paper. *No wonder I always feel poor,* he thought. *She's been squirreling away all this money while I've been eating peanut-butter-and-jelly sandwiches.*

"Why can't we use the emergency fund for the wedding?" he asked Connie. "We don't have to pay any interest and we'll just build it back up again." He looked up from his scribbling and waited for her response.

"Oh, no!" Connie rebutted energetically. "Conrad, it took years to build up that emergency fund. In *Debt Free, as Free as the Wind Blows,* Ivana B. Padov says you should only use the emergency fund for true emergencies like unemployment or a medical crisis. I don't think Sara's wedding qualifies."

"It seems like that money is just sitting there doing nothing!" Conrad argued.

Connie thought about it, "But what about Susie and Simon? It took years to build up that fund. Even if we use it for Sara, what will we do for them?"

One crisis at a time, thought Conrad, but he could see Connie's point. "We wouldn't use all of it," he contended, "just some of it."

He looked at her, but he knew this woman's face well enough to know this emergency fund was sacred ground.

"I *really* don't feel comfortable eating into our security," she said. "There must be another way!"

"All right," Conrad agreed, deciding the better part of valor was to back off and pursue the emergency fund option only as a last resort. He looked back at his paper, "What else do we have...the wedding fund? I assume we're using all of that, right?"

Connie nodded. She didn't want to mention how long it had taken to save the wedding fund. Susie would need to wait several years if she wanted to have as nice a wedding as Sara...and Sara's wasn't looking too good.

Conrad continued, "College fund?"

"That money is already committed to Susie," Connie answered. "Simon's schooling is inexpensive now because he's at Se Nada, but the college fund isn't even enough for Susie to finish this year and next. Then Simon will be starting at Okayfer U right after her. I don't think we have anything to spare from the college fund." Connie sat quietly while Conrad absorbed all of this. She could see he was discouraged.

"What about this?" Connie suggested enthusiastically. "Why don't we borrow from the 401k just like we did with the credit cards? We don't need the 401k money for a while and even though we have to pay interest it all goes to us!" She smiled proudly at Conrad. It was as though she had just discovered the cure to the common cold.

"How do we pay it back?" countered Conrad. "Even though we pay ourselves interest, we still have to make the payment. Can we afford to do that?"

Connie's smile dipped, but her initial excitement still had her mind racing. Undeterred, she answered, "I think we can afford it. Here's what we'll do: First, I'll pay for the wedding with my 1-1/2% cash-back credit card. Then we'll get a big rebate! Then, I'll arrange a 401k loan to pay off the credit card so we don't pay any interest to the credit card company. Since Sara will now be Mrs. Beau Dipity, she'll be living with him. I'm sure the money we save on groceries and electricity will make a chunk of the 401k loan payment. Just to be sure, I'll call Don Nojak and get our home loan re-done again so we have a lower payment." If she cured the common cold before, she just discovered how to end world hunger!

Something Connie said reminded Conrad of a conversation he'd had with Juan Tunavest.

"Connie, you just said something that made me think. What if we kept our house payment the same? If a new loan would lower our payment, then wouldn't that same payment mean a bigger loan? You know what I mean?"

Connie looked confused, so Conrad continued, "If we got some cash back on the refinance, but still had the same payment, couldn't we use the extra cash to pay for the wedding?"

Connie frowned, "We can't increase our loan amount, Conrad. Debt is like cancer. Besides, with my plan we save more money. Why would we want to pay the bank interest, when we can pay ourselves?"

"Yes," Conrad rebutted, "but the payments on the 401k loan will be much higher because the loan term is only five years. That puts a lot more pressure on me to earn more money to cover the payment each month." He felt weak and exposed. Conrad had taken pride in climbing the corporate ladder and steadily increasing his income. He was confident in Connie's ability to budget and save. He thought for sure by now they would be comfortable and established, but he just felt tired and defeated. Where was the joy? *No wonder men my age buy red sports cars, get a girlfriend, and run away from their responsibilities,* he thought.

"Don't worry, honey," Connie reassured him, "I'm working too!

Between the two of us we can make the payments. Once the kids are all out on their own, we can just buckle down, work hard and save, save, save!" She smiled encouragingly.

Conrad did not look encouraged, so Connie kept trying, "Please don't worry. We have so much to be thankful for! Think of all the people at SCUMCO that don't make as much as you do. Of all the people there, you have more reason than most to hope!"

Connie's words rang in Conrad's ears. His thoughts raced. *SCUMCO...hope...hope? Hope! That's it,* Conrad thought. *Of course. Hope!* A smile slowly grew upon his face.

"Connie," he said. "I think Juan might be holding out on me. Do you remember Hope Tunavest's wedding? I talked to Juan about how he paid for all that. He said he used borrowed money, but how can he have that much debt if he makes less money than me? There must be more to it than that. He gave me the names of two of his advisors. I'd like us to go visit with them. Maybe they can give us some new ideas."

"Sure," Connie replied, "but what do I do about the wedding?"

"Go ahead with your plans for now," Conrad answered. "We'll sort it out after we see what these two guys have to say."

● ● ●

"Mr. and Mrs. Soomer? Mr. Prosper and Mr. Smart are ready to see you now."

The receptionist escorted Conrad and Connie to a large conference room with glass walls. Inside sat two professionally dressed men. As the receptionist approached the door, the men broke off their conversation and stood up to greet the Soomers.

The younger man reached out his hand and smiled, "You must be Conrad and Connie Soomer! I'm Barry Smart. I'm a real estate financing specialist." He shook Conrad's hand firmly and continued, "This is my associate Will Prosper. Will is a real estate broker who specializes in investment property. He has been investing for decades and decades!" Conrad shook Will's hand and introduced each of the two men to Connie. Everyone took their seats around the conference table.

"Thank you so much for coming in today," began Barry Smart. "We're sorry it took us a little while to get you on the calendar, but Grant's seminars generate a lot of interest and it takes time to follow up with everyone." He smiled, "Did you enjoy the seminar?"

"Yes, very much," Conrad replied, "but it's been several years since I went. We were actually referred to you by Juan and Luv Tunavest."

"The Tunavests!" exclaimed Will Prosper. "Such lovely people! We really enjoy working with them. They are doing quite well with their investment program."

"That's actually why we're here," said Connie. "Juan works with Conrad and they talk about investing every once in a while. Juan seems to have a better handle on all of this than we do. We were hoping you could help us get on track, too."

Conrad was concerned Connie would say something embarrassing about him or their finances and he wanted to make sure they knew he was a serious player, so he took over, "Connie and I have been working diligently on our equity building plan with properties for the last several years. Even though we've raised three children and put one through college – two are still in school – we've been using acceleration programs to build up equity. At the pace we're on, we'll have both our properties paid off in about fifteen years." Conrad felt encouraged as he recounted their progress.

Connie, however, wasn't really interested in what Conrad had to say. She was there to hear Mr. Prosper and Mr. Smart, so she interjected, "Even though we've built up all this equity in our properties, we still feel so much pressure every month. A large part of Conrad's income comes from bonuses. If the company's sales aren't good, we have a very tough time paying the bills each month. There are many things we have sacrificed over the last several years to work towards becoming debt free." Connie's exasperation was apparent.

Barry Smart stepped in. "You mentioned an 'equity building plan.' Tell us more about that."

Connie and Conrad looked at each other to see who would respond. Connie began, "I've always been the one to manage the family finances. Conrad was busy earning most of the money. When the kids got older, I went back to work, but I just kept handling the finances. Several years ago, I bought a book called *Debt Free, as Free as the Wind Blows* by Ivana B. Padov. Do you know who she is? She used to do a lot of seminars on public TV."

Barry and Will both smiled and nodded an acknowledgement. "Oh, yes," Barry replied, "we are very familiar with Ms. Padov."

Connie continued, "So I started working on getting us out of debt and building up our emergency fund. The only real savings program we had was our 401k plan with SCUMCO, the company Conrad works for. We put money in, but then the stock market went way down and we lost a big chunk. It seemed to make more sense to just invest in our debt, so we stopped contributing to the 401k and used that money to pay down debt. Since our home loans were our biggest debts, we started there with a *Home Equity Accelerator Program*."

Connie stopped and waited to see if the two men were interested in hearing more. Barry prompted her to continue, "And how did that work out for you?"

"Well," Connie explained, "one thing we noticed was that when we started redirecting the 401k money into paying down our loans, we had a harder time staying on budget. But every time it seemed to get really tough, Don would help us re-do our home loan and we would lower our payments."

This last comment piqued Barry's attention, "How did this affect your HEAP loan?"

Connie was impressed at Barry's insight. It was obvious he knew his business. Connie replied, "With each refinance, we would go with a fifteen-year loan because we'd get the best interest rate. When we added extra principal payments to the HEAP plan we would pay the balance down faster. Each time, we would end up with lower payments because the new balance was smaller...but we would have a new fifteen-year loan."

Will Prosper completed Connie's thought, "So you still have fifteen years left to go even though you've been accelerating your loan for fifteen years."

"Right," said Connie, "so even though our loans are very small compared to the value of the properties, we still have a while to go before they are paid off." She paused, then added, "At least we were able to establish our emergency fund." Connie sat up and said proudly, "We have enough money in our savings to live for one year with no income."

Conrad was watching this exchange carefully. His years in business had taught him to study people's expressions for insight into their thoughts. So much of what people were thinking could be seen in the expressions on their faces. Barry Smart and Will Prosper had a quiet confidence that was hard to read. Conrad wondered to himself, *What do they think? How are we doing? We must be doing better than Juan and Luv, yet the Tunavests keep purchasing properties. Where is the money coming from? There's no way SCUMCO is providing enough income to*

Juan for him to pay his monthly bills and save up down payments on properties. Luv hasn't worked for years. Where is all the money coming from? Conrad was very interested in finding out what the Tunavests were doing and how they were doing it.

Conrad started, "Juan and I were at a seminar with Grant Deeds a few years ago. Back then, Juan only had one property plus his home. I guess now he has several properties?" He was fishing for more details on Juan's investment activities.

Will Prosper responded, "We don't really discuss the details of our client's business without their consent, but I can tell you that Juan and Luv are great people and we love working with them."

"Yes, they are," agreed Barry Smart, as he redirected the conversation back to the Soomers, "But, Mr. and Mrs. Soomer, we're here to talk about you, aren't we? How can we help you?"

"If I can be quite candid," Conrad replied, "we are really anxious to get started. I happen to know I make more money than Juan, so I'm sure whatever program he's on, we can do it also. So, to get to the bottom line, we're looking for some good deals. We have some money saved up, so if you can show us a good deal, I can write a check today." Conrad sat back in his chair trying to look confident. He wanted these two men to know he was for real.

Barry smiled, "Before we start talking about specific 'deals', I think it would be good to learn a bit more about you and Mrs. Soomer. Did you have a chance to complete the profile we sent you?"

Connie pulled out two brand new file folders. Inside each were identical stacks of paper neatly two-hole punched and secured in the file folders with fasteners. She handed one folder to Will Prosper and the other to Barry Smart.

Each man flipped through his folder and looked over the papers.

Barry looked up and commented, "Very nice! Connie, did you put all this together?"

Connie smiled proudly, "Yes. I hope it's okay."

"It's wonderful!" exclaimed Will as he looked over the carefully prepared documents.

Barry took out a yellow marker and began highlighting one of the documents. "I see a lot of potential here, folks. You should be very encouraged. There are a lot of options available to you. The real question is, 'What do you want to accomplish?' Unless you are interested in buying a football team or a small island in the next ten years, you can probably get most of what you want."

Conrad and Connie looked at each other and smiled.

Barry said, "Let me summarize where we are so far. We hear you saying you want to retire in twenty years at age sixty-eight. You'd like to have $10,000 a month in sustainable income and another $1.5 million to purchase a vacation home and a new RV. As we look at your balance sheet, we see you have a home that is worth approximately $600,000 and you have a mortgage on it for about $200,000. You have a vacation home worth $280,000 with a $43,000 mortgage. You also have $127,000 in you retirement accounts and another $118,000 in savings. Your combined income is about $108,000 per year…all from W2 sources. Conrad has some bonuses, but they aren't consistent. Your credit is excellent." He paused while he glanced over his notes one final time, "Is all that correct?"

"That's pretty much it," said Conrad. "Right, honey?" he verified, looking at his wife.

"I think so," Connie affirmed. "What do we do next?"

Will Prosper replied, "You'll want to develop a specific investment plan so you know how much equity you'll need to create over the next twenty years in order to achieve your goals. Barry and his team can help you with that. They can also help you get financially pre-approved so my team can begin an earnest search for investment properties for you."

Barry Smart added, "You also have a lot of equity sitting idle. Worse, your current loan payment is based on a fifteen-year amortization schedule. Even though the interest rate is very good, your cash-flow is not being very well utilized. When you make a payment, you are actually paying down your loan by hundreds of dollars each month."

"You say that like it's not good," Connie queried. "Isn't it good to pay down the loan? We want to build up equity, that's why we always use a Capital Resource Asset Partners *Home Equity Accelerator Program* loan. Our mortgage broker is one of the biggest Direct Underwriting Mortgage Banking Acceleration System Specialists around."

"I'm sure he is," acknowledged Barry.

Will jumped in, "What Barry is saying is simply this: every month you are taking after-tax dollars from your earned income to pay down your loan. Why is this a concern? Because earned income is the most highly taxed income you can have. While there are worse things you could do with your after-tax earnings, we would argue that putting it 'in jail' with the rest of your idle equity is not one of the better options. Frankly, we think you can do many other much more productive things with your money than convert it into equity and expose it to the market. We like it when the market *gives* us equity, but we don't like to convert earned income into after-tax dollars as a way to build equity."

Connie looked confused, but Conrad thought back to the Grant Deeds seminar and his conversations over the years with Juan Tunavest. He remembered the *Free Rental Property Story* from Grant's seminar.

Conrad ventured an explanation, "I think he's talking about using a mortgage to move equity out of our house and into another investment property. That's what I think Juan is doing."

Conrad turned to Will, hoping not only to confirm his understanding of the concept, but also to get some inside information on Juan's personal finances. "Is that right?" Conrad asked.

Will Prosper answered, "Again, we aren't here to talk about the Tunavest's personal situation. In regard to using a mortgage to transfer idle equity into a new investment property, you are correct. That is exactly what we are referring to."

Will continued, "We think you should be working to spread your equity out to gain control of more properties. As long as you invest in appreciating markets, over time the rents and the equity will grow. Then you can use the growing cash-flow to access the increased passive equity the market gives you. From a tax perspective, this is a much better way to go. Of course, we aren't tax advisors, so we suggest you talk to your own tax advisor before you do anything."

"One last thing," Barry Smart added, "in the event you find yourself worried that a market and a specific property might be vulnerable to a short term 'correction' – which essentially means property values dip temporarily – it can be advantageous to use a cash-out refinance to effectively 'withdraw' equity from your property so the market can't take it away from you. You can then park the cash in a high-yielding money-market, CD or similar safety-of-principal vehicle while you ride out the storm. The difference between the cost to borrow and the yield on the parked funds is generally very small. If interest rates rise, which is one of the more common reasons for a temporary dip in values, you will have secured inexpensive funds. The yield on the parked funds may actually *exceed* the cost to borrow! This might give you neutral or even positive cash-flow on the borrowed funds. Additionally, if property values drop and you have cash, you may be able to pick up some bargains. When the market recovers, you will own more property and will have accelerated your equity growth...in spite of the temporary value decline."

Conrad and Connie were impressed, but still a little confused. It was clear they were not going to absorb all of this in one session. Conrad wished he had been going to classes with Juan all these years. There was so much to learn!

The group talked for a little longer. As the meeting wound down, Barry once again summarized and reviewed a list of action items for the Soomers to follow up on. After exchanging some parting pleasantries, the Soomers left the office and headed home. They still felt overwhelmed, but at least they had a few clearly identified steps they could focus on to get started.

The next day, Connie called her tax advisor, Freddy Katz, and talked to him about some of the things the couple had discussed with Barry Smart and Will Prosper. Freddy confirmed her questions about 1031 exchanges, cash-out refinances, and Schedule C and E deductions. She asked him why he had never explained these things to her before.

Freddy answered matter-of-factly, "You never asked."

• • •

Connie Soomer sat staring at the stack of paperwork in front of her. Her eyes were focused on the Truth-in-Lending statement that was part of the loan documents on the table. It wasn't as though she'd never been through a loan sign-off before, but this one was different than the others. She was used to looking at loan and payment amounts much smaller than those before her now.

Barry Smart sat across from the Soomers at the round conference table. "Do have any questions?" he asked again, directing his question to both Conrad and Connie, but his eyes were fixed on Connie.

"Tell me again," Connie began apologetically, "how is it we are going to be able to make this $2,300 a month payment? I just don't see how we can afford that." Connie was feeling very uneasy and embarrassed to be the one everyone was focused on. "I'm sorry," she said timidly.

Barry smiled reassuringly. "We do this all the time," he said patiently. "We don't ever want anyone to sign these papers unless they understand and agree with what they are doing. There's no need to be sorry."

Conrad looked at his wife. "Honey, it's like this: we get a new loan…it comes to about $480,000…"

Connie's eyes got big. *Four… hundred… and… eighty… thousand… dollars! That's a lot of money,* she thought. *That's a lot of debt! We've worked so hard to have a small loan, now here we are on the verge of getting a brand new huge loan! I think I'm going to be sick.* She swallowed hard.

"Connie? Are you with me?" asked Conrad. Barry sat quietly and allowed husband and wife to work through this together.

"Honey, look here," Conrad said, pulling out a yellow pad. "Here's how it works. We take this $480,000 from the bank and pay off our current loan of $200,000. Since the new loan has an interest-only option, our payment at 5.75% is only $2,300 a month, as compared to our current loan payment of $1,688 month. That means the payment is only $612 a month more."

"But," Connie defended, "the loan Don did for us is only 5.25%. Why do we want a bigger loan and a *higher* interest rate? That doesn't make sense to me."

"I understand, but there's more to it than that," Conrad explained. "It isn't about the interest rate we pay. It's about the rate of return we earn."

"But," Connie continued her defense, "how can we afford to pay an extra $612 a month?"

"It isn't really $612 a month," Conrad countered.

She looked at him blankly. He turned to Barry. "Can you explain this to her?"

"Sure," Barry replied. "Mrs. Soomer," he began in a reassuring, but authoritative tone, "because the current payment includes both principal and interest, only a portion of it is tax deductible. Since your combined state and federal marginal tax rate is approximately 40%, it works out like this..." Barry wrote out on the tablet:

> Now:
> Total Payment = $1,688 (principal and interest)
> Principal = $ 896
> Interest = $ 792 x 40% deduction = $317 tax savings
>
> $1688 less $317 tax savings = $1,371 after-tax payment

"So," Barry said as he underlined the $1,371, "this is what it really costs you after-tax to make your current payment each month." He looked into Connie's eyes searching for a confirmation of her understanding. "Are you with me so far?"

Connie nodded. Barry turned his attention back to the tablet and began to write:

> Proposed:
> Payment = $2,300 (interest only)

Barry stopped here and said, "Now, this may get a little confusing, but stick with me and I think it will become clear." He set the pen down and explained, "Tax law changes regularly and is almost always convoluted and confusing. But as challenging as it can be, it is important to understand the basics. Interest on a *purchase* money loan for a primary residence is generally deductible up to a loan amount of $1 million. In your case, your purchase loan was only $280,000, so you are well below that. However, when you *increase* your loan amount with a cash-out refinance loan, you are only allowed to deduct the interest on an additional loan amount up to $100,000 over and above the *original* purchase money loan amount's current balance – *unless* you use the cash-out to improve the *same* house you borrowed the money from. In that case, the interest on the loan amount over $100,000 *would* be deductible."

Conrad looked puzzled. "I thought interest on a home loan was *always* 100% deductible?"

Barry answered, "That's a common belief, but as I said, tax law is convoluted, confusing and ever-changing. This is why you want to work closely with your tax advisor whenever you are making financial decisions."

"But our tax guy doesn't tell us about this stuff," Conrad complained.

Barry replied, "My experience has been that most tax advisors answer the questions you ask. This is why it is important for you to gain a fundamental understanding of tax principles, so you can go in and ask the right questions. This doesn't mean you have to be the expert. In fact, we recommend that you *always* use a professional because it is their business to stay up-to-date on all the technical details. We *highly* recommend you work with advisors who actually invest in real estate for themselves. We think it makes a big difference when the people you work with have to wrestle with the same issues you do when it applies to their *own* money."

"That makes sense," Conrad said. *I wonder if Freddy Katz owns any investment real estate?*

"Let's get back to the discussion of your cash-flow analysis, shall we?" prompted Barry. He picked up the pen and returned his attention to the tablet on the table.

Barry continued, "Your new payment will be $2,300 interest-only. You will only be able to deduct the interest on the loan amount you had before, $200,000 in your case, plus the interest on an additional $100,000...for a total of $300,000. So, at a note rate of 5.75%, your deductible interest will be $1,438 per month." Barry started writing:

Deductible interest = $1,438 x 40% tax rate = $575 deduction

New payment   = $2,300
Less deduction   = $ 575
After-tax payment = $1,725

Barry circled the $1,725 figure and then flipped back to the $1,317 from the current loan after-tax payment calculation. He used the pen as a pointer, tapped on the $1,317 figure and explained, "Notice that your after-tax payment on the $200,000 balance you currently have is $1,317 per month and the after-tax payment on the new $480,000 loan is $1,725 per month." Barry paused and watched Connie to see if she was following along.

Connie sat quietly. Barry decided to press on, "The difference between the new $1,725 and the old $1,317 after-tax payments is $408 a month or $4,896 a year. While this sounds like a lot of money, we need to put it in context. Keep in mind that the $4,896 per year is controlling an additional $280,000 in working capital. When you do the math on the cash-flow expense of funds, it looks like this..." He wrote out on the tablet:

$4,896 / $280,000   = 1.75%

Conrad couldn't contain himself. "Do you see that, Con?" he exclaimed. "We can get our hands on $280,000 for a net cost of only 1.75% per year! Isn't that unbelievable?"

Connie looked at him, but didn't appear very enthused. "Yes, but how are we going to afford another $408 a month?" she asked.

Conrad paused and contemplated her question. *She has a point*, he thought. Although Conrad was quite sure it would be no problem to earn more than 1.75% on the excess cash, they would still need to make the payment. *Where are we going to get an extra $408 a month?* he wondered.

Turning to Barry, Conrad said, "I have a question."

"Yes?" Barry responded.

Conrad asked, "Shouldn't we be able to deduct the interest on both the $100,000 cash-out limit plus *$280,000* and not just $200,000 since $280,000 was the original purchase loan amount? The only reason the purchase loan amount is now $200,000 is because we've been aggressively paying it down since we got it."

Barry smiled. "Good thinking! And that would make sense, however as we've discussed, the tax law is bizarre. Because you've paid the loan balance down, you have reduced the amount of interest deduction available to you on this particular property. This is the very reason we are not big fans of big down payments or amortized loans on a primary residence. The tax law favors debt on your primary residence. Rather than fight the tax code, we like to use it to our advantage. How? We simply place our equity in other properties. In your case, unless you care to move, your situation is what it is, so we'll just make the best of it. What's important is you are now able to control and enjoy your home and its appreciation, as well as $280,000 of the bank's cash, for an extremely low net cost of funds."

"But Connie's right," Conrad replied. "What about the $408 payment?"

Barry smiled again. "You are a wise man, Conrad," he said. "It is very important to always pay close attention to cash-flow. There are a couple of options to manage the bigger payment. In both cases, what we do is divide the working capital into two parts. One part is invested to address your cash-flow needs and the other part is invested to grow your asset base."

"That makes sense," Conrad agreed.

"So, let's go ahead and put some numbers to your particular situation," Barry continued. "For sake of discussion, let's say you segregated $80,000 of the $280,000 and invested it for cash-flow. If you could get approximately 10% on the $80,000, you would realize a cash yield of about $8,000 a year. After you pay 40% tax on the income, your net is approximately $4,800 a year. This essentially covers your $408 after-tax payment, but more importantly, it leaves you $200,000 to invest for equity growth." Barry looked at Conrad to make sure he was following.

Conrad nodded. He turned to Connie, "Does that makes sense to you, honey?"

Connie looked at him. She understood, but continued to be skeptical, "Yes, but where can we get 10%? The bank is only paying 3%, maybe 5% if we put it in a CD."

"A great question," Barry responded. "While you can look into high-yielding bond funds, we like investments backed by real estate. In this case, you might consider using a high-yield mortgage fund, or you can actually invest your money directly into real estate debt through private mortgages. The cash-flow-yields on these investments can be quite attractive when compared to bank accounts."

"I've seen those advertised in the newspaper," Conrad confirmed.

"Yes," said Barry. "There are specialty loan brokers who specialize in placing investors' funds into these types of mortgages. The point is, by investing $80,000 for cash-flow, you can cover the entire extra payment and end up with $200,000 to invest for equity."

"Before you go on," Conrad interjected, "you mentioned another way to deal with the larger payment?"

"Yes," replied Barry. "Depending on the timing of the equity investment, you might simply set aside a smaller portion of $280,000 to cover the $408 larger payment. For example, if you set aside $20,000, then you would have enough money to cover the $5,000 a year of payments for four years. Now, instead of setting aside $80,000 for cash-flow and $200,000 for equity, you would set aside only $20,000 for cash-flow and you would retain $260,000 for equity investing. Of course, it is essential have the equity investment liquid at the end of the four years so you can replenish the loan payment fund. If you don't do this, then you would have to make the $408 month payment from your paycheck – which is a very unpleasant alternative!"

Amen! Conrad thought. *Finally, we are talking to someone who understands I don't want to spend the rest of my life going to work just so I can make more monthly payments.*

Barry continued, "I know all this math can be challenging, even intimidating. But doing the math is a very important part of becoming a successful investor. With your permission, I think there are some other important things to consider. May I?"

"By all means," Conrad encouraged.

"What you are giving up with this interest-only loan is $12,000 a year in equity build-up from paying down your loan. Even when you factor in the $408 per month payments, which amounts to $5,000 per year, it adds up to about $17,000 you need to get out of the $280,000 to break even. But to do that, you only need to grow the $280,000 you took out by a little over 6% a year."

"That seems achievable," responded Conrad.

"Very much so," agreed Barry. "If all you do is get a rental property that provides break-even cash-flow at 4:1 leverage, or 25% down, and the property appreciates only 5%, then your equity growth rate is 20% – considerably higher than the 6% you need to break even."

Conrad was right at the edge of his understanding, but he remembered bits and pieces of the Grant Deeds seminar and all the conversations with Juan over the years. He was sure he could master all this with just a little more time and training. Connie, however, was completely lost.

"To summarize," Barry continued, "keep in mind that investors focus on *cash-flow* and *net worth*, whereas consumers tend to focus on *interest rate* and *debt*. In your case, we have been able to address the cash-flow concern *without* tapping into your paycheck, and we still provided a sizable amount of working capital. Even at a modest 12% equity growth rate, you would nearly triple your equity growth compared to what you are doing now. Of course, as we've discussed, we think you can do much better than that. The point is, you are in great shape. You have a lot to work with and your goals are realistically achievable." He smiled encouragingly.

Now Conrad was even more excited. At last, he was beginning to understand what Juan had been doing. He turned to Connie, "Isn't this great, honey? Without taking anything out of my paycheck or reducing our lifestyle, we will have over $200,000 to invest! It would have taken us two lifetimes to save that! This is awesome!"

Connie was anything but enthused. This was just too much for her.

"Yes , but…" Connie began.

"But, WHAT?" Conrad interrupted. He was growing very agitated with his wife. He was afraid she would resist just when they were on the verge of finding the answers they had been seeking.

How can she not see this? Conrad thought as he stared her down.

Connie's eyes began to fill with tears. "I'm sorry…I…I…" she stammered, "It's just hard. It doesn't seem right to have so much debt on our home. All the books I've read say we should strive to be debt free. This seems like a giant step backward. Even Don Nojak didn't want to give us a big loan like this because he thought it wasn't a good thing."

"Mrs. Soomer," Barry Smart interjected. "Please remember you are not *spending* the equity you are taking out of your home, you are simply repositioning it. You are using it to acquire more real estate. The new loans you get on the new properties will be paid for by the rental income. Those payments don't come from your paychecks."

"Also," Barry continued, "you may be eligible for additional tax deductions depending on how the financing on the rental properties is set up. You'll want to check with your tax advisor – and since we aren't certain because your eligibility is based on your Adjusted Gross Income, we'll assume for now that you get *no* tax benefit from owning the rental properties."

Connie sat quietly with a sullen look on her face.

Barry went on, "There are two other potential profit sources from owning rental properties. One is amortization. This is the monthly pay down of your loan balance. When you were paying down your loan on your own home, you were making those payments with your own after-tax income. In a 40% tax bracket, that means you needed to earn $100 for every $60 in pay-down of debt. This is a very inefficient way to build equity because you are paying it yourself. You are simply moving money from your cash-flow statement, that is, your paycheck via your checking account, and putting it on your balance sheet as debt reduction. While it is true this builds your net worth, it isn't very efficient because you are paying it *yourself* with *after*-tax dollars – and your ability to grow your net worth relies primarily on *your* earning ability. Unless you are the owner of a successful business or an extremely highly paid wage-earner like an entertainer, athlete, or high-level business executive, it is almost impossible to out-earn taxes and inflation."

With each sentence, Conrad's understanding and enthusiasm grew.

"Tell her about appreciation," Conrad directed Barry, as he turned back to his wife, "Honey, this is the secret! This is how Juan and Luv are doing it!"

Barry concurred, "Appreciation is truly powerful. Appreciation is the increase in value that occurs over time. In real estate, it has historically been about 5-7% per year overall. Some markets are worse, some are better. Will Prosper and his team specialize in helping investors find areas where they think sustainable above-average appreciation is probable based on a variety of economic factors."

Connie sat quietly listening to Barry. Barry took out his yellow pad and began to illustrate his points.

"Let's say you take the $280,000 cash from your refinance and you set aside $30,000 in a money-market or similar bank insured, liquid, savings account. This covers your bigger payment for about five years and gives you some emergency money. Now you have $250,000 left, right?"

Connie hesitated, but nodded in agreement.

"Now," Barry continued, "let's say you buy five separate $200,000 properties and put 25% down on each. Each down payment is $50,000. Five properties at $50,000 equals $250,000. This fully invests all of your remaining cash. For the sake of discussion, let's say the rental income on each property is adequate to cover the $150,000 mortgages on each, plus all operating expenses. Are you with me so far?" he asked.

Connie slowly nodded again.

Barry turned the yellow pad around to face Connie and asked rhetorically, "So what have we accomplished?"

Answering his own question, Barry continued, "Remember, you still have your home. The only difference is that you now have an after-tax monthly payment of $408 more than you had previously, but we've got that covered with the $30,000 cash and the cash-flow it produces, right? This should easily cover the $408 per month for well over five years, and still provide some cushion."

Barry paused to allow Connie to keep pace, "But, now you also have $1,000,000 in rental properties with $750,000 in mortgages that are being fully serviced by the rental income." He paused again and watched Connie's face carefully, looking for signs of understanding. She looked up at him and then back down at the yellow pad.

Barry went on, "If the rental properties appreciate just 5% per year, your equity increases $50,000. Why? Because 5% of $1,000,000 is $50,000. Before, when you were making only house payments yourself with your after-tax dollars, your equity build-up was only in your own home from the pay down of the loan balance. This amounted to about $12,000 per year of equity build-up, all from *your* paycheck. In the new model, you are building equity over four times faster – $50,000 per year instead of just $12,000. Plus, you still have your home, which we hope will also continue to appreciate. Best of all, the net impact on your paycheck and lifestyle is neutral." Once again, he paused to allow the Soomers time to absorb the information.

"Connie," Conrad interjected, "did you hear that? We can grow our equity four times faster without earning more money at work or cutting our personal expenses! This is the answer we've been looking for!"

"Does that make sense to you?" Barry asked Connie.

"Yes," she answered softly, "but I'm just not sure I like the idea of owing so much on our home. With a $480,000 loan on our house and $750,000 of loans on the other properties, our debt would be over $1.2 million! Worse, our interest rate would be higher than it is right now." A look of dread came over her face.

"I just don't think I'm ready to do that," she sighed. "Maybe later. I'm sorry." She picked up the pen, set it down on the stack of papers, and pushed the pile away.

CHAPTER 3
The Fifties

"**H**i, Mom!" chimed the young woman's voice through the phone. Connie Soomer could hear the chatter of her twin granddaughters in the background.

"Hi, Sweetie!" Connie replied to her oldest daughter. "How are those darling little granddaughters of mine?"

"They're great, Mom," answered Sara. "They were out late last night with Beau. He had a gig at the church and they tagged along. You should see them with their little toy guitars. They want to be just like their daddy!"

Connie smiled at the thought. "Is Beau playing again soon? Dad and I would love to go with you. We can take the girls home with us afterwards. I remember how much I appreciated those chances to be alone with your father when we were young parents!"

"Actually, Mom," Sara said, "I was calling because Beau and I would like to come over and talk with you and Daddy about something kind of important."

• • •

The tension at SCUMCO was so thick you could feel it. Sales and profits were down, and since the merger, morale had sunk to new lows. Rumors of downsizing were rampant and everyone was on pins and needles in fear of losing their jobs. Conrad was surprised he had not been asked to reduce the headcount in his department. He reasoned that executive management understood how important it was to keep the sales team whole. Reductions in the sales team would not only mean fewer people left to sell, resulting in less chance of growing sales, but those who remained after a layoff would probably be demoralized and therefore less productive. It seemed reasonable to him that his department would escape the axe this time. Still, he would rest easier when the day was over and his name was still on the door of his office.

"Knock-knock!" called a man's voice. Ben Dover's face peered around the door opening into Conrad's office. "On the phone?" Dover asked.

Conrad looked up. He had been deep in thought. "No, I'm fine, Ben. Come on in."

Conrad's boss remained outside the door and answered, "I need you to come down to my office for a few minutes." He and Conrad made brief eye contact, and then Dover's face retreated from the door opening and he headed back towards his office. Conrad got up and started after him.

Dover's office was at the end of a long hallway. On one side were private offices like Conrad's. On the other side were cubicles where the sales and customer service staff were stationed. Conrad had worked with and for Dover for over twenty years. He was a nice enough guy, but he definitely looked out for himself. When times were good, Dover was your buddy. When things were tough, you'd be well-advised to watch your back. Dover knew all too well there were only a very limited number of positions at the top and he was always careful to protect his.

Conrad felt a little uneasy on the walk to Dover's office. Halfway there, Conrad looked to his right and noticed one of his sales reps packing up his desk. *That's odd,* Conrad thought, *why is Mark packing up his desk?* Mark was a sales rep on Conrad's team. He looked up and saw Conrad as he walked by. The glare from Mark's eyes seared with rage and resentment. Conrad glanced away, confused. *I don't get it,* he thought. *How could Mark be riffed without me knowing about it?*

As he approached Dover's door, Conrad's confusion was quickly becoming a sense of dread and impending doom. He felt his heart beating a little faster and his mouth was becoming dry. *No,* he thought. *No way! Surely Ben would've given me some warning, at least a chance to make my case and defend my position. I've been with him for twenty years! Ben wouldn't just blind side me like this…would he?*

Conrad stood at the door to Dover's office and waited to be noticed.

Dover looked up and invited Conrad in, "Come on in, Conrad," he offered. "Take a seat."

Conrad settled in to the guest chair in front of Dover's enormous desk. He always felt like a little child when he sat in these chairs. He often wondered if Dover had purposely shortened the chairs to make his guests feel small. Conrad looked up over the top of the desk at his boss's face.

"Conrad," Dover began, "we've been together a long time. I know you understand these are challenging times at Stone Cold United Manufacturing Company. With this new merger, all executive and management positions at SCUMCO are being evaluated carefully.

There is tremendous pressure on me to reduce costs or I may lose my job." He stared intently into Conrad's eyes.

Conrad's hands gripped the armrests as he braced himself for what he feared was certainly coming. He could feel his face get hot and he became very aware of his lip quivering. Conrad tried to appear calm.

Dover looked at Conrad sitting there like a little boy facing judgment at the hands of a stern schoolmaster. *Pathetic*, Dover gloated. *Business truly is the survival of the fittest.*

"Your position has been eliminated, Conrad," Dover pronounced coldly. "You'll need to begin cleaning out your office immediately. Reductions in force are always difficult. I'm truly sorry."

Conrad's thoughts raced. *Sorry? Sorry?! Yeah, you're sorry all right! You're a sorry excuse for a human being! How can you do this to me? You wouldn't even be sitting in that overstuffed chair if it weren't for me. Who trained these salespeople? Who developed your distribution channels? Who negotiated those profitable contracts that made SCUMCO so attractive to that German company who bought us? ME! It was me! And now "my position has been eliminated"? How about my life? Why not just say my life has been eliminated? Who's going to hire a 50-something sales manager? I don't have time to start all over again. What am I supposed to tell Connie?* Conrad was distraught and furious.

"I'm sorry, too," Conrad said plainly as he stood up to leave. Dover rose and extended his hand. "No hard feelings?" he offered.

Conrad just looked at him with disdain, then turned and headed down the hallway towards his soon-to-be former office.

Conrad was still lost in thought, lambasting Dover in the privacy of his own mind, when suddenly he was greeted by Juan Tunavest. Juan was carrying a box full of his belongings down the hallway. *It looks like Juan got the axe, too,* Conrad thought.

"You too, eh?" Juan said with a casual chuckle as the two men stood together in the SCUMCO hallway. "It just goes to show you there is no such thing as security in corporate America anymore."

"You don't seem too concerned about it," Conrad observed. "Did you already find another job?"

Juan shook his head. "No" he answered. "No other job. I think I'm probably done with jobs from now on. I didn't even see this coming. It was a real surprise. But I guess you must have seen it from your vantage point, right Conrad? You were much closer to the top than I was."

Done with jobs? Conrad marveled. *Did he say, "Done with jobs"?* Conrad was stuck on those words. *How can Juan not need a job? I've been earning more money than Juan for over twenty-five years and I still need a job!*

Juan's voice interrupted Conrad's thoughts. "Are you okay?" Juan asked with genuine concern. "Is there anything I can do?"

Conrad lifted his eyes up from staring at the floor and looked at Juan. Juan had never seen Conrad look so vulnerable. Even though he and Conrad had never been very close friends, they had been friendly enough to get to know each other pretty well. Conrad always seemed very confident. As a Sales Area Director, he was well-respected and had one of the nicest offices and largest staffs. Judging from his clothes, his car, and the kinds of toys he had, Juan always assumed Conrad was doing very well.

Conrad thought about Juan's question as the two men stood briefly looking at each other. Finally, Conrad began to speak. His voice was not his usually friendly authoritative tone, but instead the rather meek and uncertain voice of a broken and frightened man.

"Juan," Conrad started slowly, "I'm not quite sure what to do. I've worked here for over twenty-five years. This is the only real job I've ever had. As the company was growing and my sales were growing, I felt like I was making a contribution. I felt like somebody important." He paused for a moment as various memories from the last three decades flashed through his mind.

"When I became a sales director and I started making big money, I felt like I deserved it. It was great getting a bigger house. The pool, the boat, the RV, the ATVs...all the fun we had camping together..." Conrad's thought drifted towards images of his family...and especially Connie.

"Connie..." he rambled, "I always wanted to be successful in her eyes. It was so awesome pulling up in my brand new BMW and taking her out for a night on the town. It was like she was a princess and I was her prince." He smiled for a moment at the thought.

Conrad's expression changed and his eyes came back into focus. He turned and looked at Juan and that brief moment of happiness Conrad felt remembering the good times faded into a hurting, anxious stare. "Now, they've taken it all away from me," Conrad declared angrily.

Juan considered carefully how to respond. Clearly, Conrad was down and probably very vulnerable, yet Juan had strong feelings about what he was hearing. Juan had always believed a man's destiny is more in his own hands than anyone else's. Though he felt compassion for Conrad, he just couldn't let Conrad's defeatist comments go unchallenged.

Choosing his words carefully, Juan spoke solemnly, "That's because you never really had any of it."

What? Conrad fixed his eyes on Juan as the words sunk into his mind. Conrad didn't know what he was expecting Juan to say, but he was quite sure this wasn't it.

"What do you mean?" asked Conrad, unsure where this dialog would lead. It felt odd to be in a conversation without having any idea where it was going. Conrad wasn't always right about where someone else was headed, but he always had an idea. In this case, Conrad had no clue as to what Juan would say next.

"This probably isn't the right time, but if you're really interested, I'd be happy to get together with you later. Right now," Juan said, nodding towards the box in his arms and glancing into Conrad's office, "it looks like we both have some packing to do."

"Riiiight," Conrad said with resigned sigh. "But I really would like to finish this later…if you're willing."

"Sure thing," replied Juan with a smile.

• • •

"Conrad! I'm glad you're home," Connie greeted her husband as he walked through the door into their home. "I tried to call you at the office today, but your voicemail wasn't working. You'll have to check it on Monday."

"Sara called today," Connie continued, racing around the house picking things up. "She and Beau are coming over tonight. They are going to be here any minute! Get upstairs and get changed. I'll put on a pot of coffee." She hustled into the kitchen leaving Conrad standing dazed in the entryway. His mind was busy contemplating the events of the day.

"Hurry up!" Connie exhorted from the kitchen.

Conrad walked slowly up the stairs to his bedroom. His surroundings were surreal. He noticed things about his home he was sure he'd never seen before. He saw pictures hanging in the stairwell of his children when they were toddlers. There was an audio training program and some books on real estate investing still in the shrink-wrap on the bookcase at the top of the stairs. As he walked into his bedroom there was a picture of Connie and him on their wedding day. *Were all these things here before?* he wondered. He decided they must have been, but he just didn't remember noticing them. His mind was always filled with SCUMCO business. Now, his mind just had a big void. Did he really carry so much of his work around with him that he missed seeing these things he obviously had passed by every day?

"Conrad!" Connie called out from downstairs, "Hurry up! I *need* your help. The kids are going to be here any minute!"

Conrad started into motion again. He slowly took off his coat and carefully hung it in the closet. Loosening his tie, he looked at himself in the closet mirror. *God, I've gotten old,* he thought. *But I don't feel old. It seems like yesterday Connie and I were out waterskiing with the kids. Where did all the years go?*

"Conrad!" Connie's voice rang up the stairs again, "Are you okay? Please *hurry!* Can you start a fire? The kids will be here in just a few minutes! I want the house to be nice for them!"

I don't want to see the kids right now, Conrad thought. *I don't want to see anybody. I want to have a drink and go to bed.* He felt empty and tired.

Thump, thump, thump, thump, thump. Conrad could hear Connie coming up the stairs. *Oh God,* he thought, *there's no rest for the weary...and there's no where to hide.* He took a deep breath and reprimanded himself, *Shake it off, Soomer!*

"What are you *doing*?" Connie scolded from the bedroom door threshold. "Did you hear me? I need your help downstairs! Sara and Beau are coming over. They want to talk to us and it sounded important. Can't you forget about SCUMCO for just a couple of hours and pay attention to your family?" Connie was getting more upset by the minute.

Conrad focused on Connie, "I'm sorry, honey. I'll be right there."

"Good!" she snapped and she thumped back down the stairs.

Conrad took another deep breath to clear his mind and then he focused on the task at hand, *Get downstairs, Conrad. Build a fire and try to be the wise old Dad.*

• • •

"Don't cry, Mom. Please don't cry!" Sara's eyes were filled with tears as she tried to encourage her mother, "It's not like we *want* to move away. We love you guys. The girls love you!"

Connie sat curled up on the corner of her living sofa clutching a tissue and dabbing her eyes. Conrad sat beside her, staring blankly at his feet, with one hand on his wife's back. Conrad just didn't have any emotional strength to lend his distraught bride.

"Mr. Soomer?" Sara's husband Beau said. Conrad looked up at him.

"Mr. Soomer," Beau began, "I'm sorry this has you and Mrs. Soomer so upset. I hope you understand. Sara and I just want to build our lives together. We want to have a home of our own. The prices in this area are so high. We don't see how we'll ever be able to afford anything here." He watched Conrad's face for any reaction, but Conrad just stared blankly.

Sara jumped in, "Daddy, Beau and I were out at one of his concerts. It was a cute little town. We stayed at this adorable hotel and I was looking through one of those real estate magazines. I saw the cutest house, so on a whim, I called the agent. He said the place was still available, so we went and took a look at it."

Beau took over, "We ended up liking it so much we put an offer in, and it was accepted! I called a friend of mine in the area and he said he could get me a job nearby that wouldn't interfere with my music. There's a great little church in the town. I'm hoping I can get on as Worship Pastor."

Sara and Beau watched Conrad closely and waited for a response.

"I'm happy for you, Sara," Conrad said reservedly. "I'm happy that you're excited about your future." Conrad wished he could say the same for himself, but he held his tongue. He didn't want to say anything to dump cold water on his daughter's plans. He was trying very hard to be encouraging and supportive in spite of his deep disappointment and feelings of inadequacy.

Connie sat up and looked over her shoulder at Conrad. She followed his lead and smiled, but inside she was hurt and angry. This was not at all what she wanted – and she certainly wasn't happy.

"Sara," Connie asked, "if you could afford a home in this area, would you like to stay?"

"Of course we would!" said Sara. "We love it here, but buying a home in this area seems impossible. We've looked around every so often, but we just don't see anything out there we can afford. No matter how much we save, prices just go up faster. We think moving to a more affordable area is our best chance of getting a home of our own." She paused to monitor her distraught mother's reaction.

Sara reminded her, "This doesn't mean we don't love you!" She kept trying to encourage her mother. "We'll visit all the time!" she pledged.

I just wish I were in a position to help them, Conrad thought to himself, *but I can barely take care of myself.* Conrad felt so sick to his stomach he could barely sit up. *This isn't the way this story is supposed to go.*

• • •

"Okay... yes, I understand... okay... thanks, Freddy... okay... alright... thank you. Bye."

Click. Connie Soomer hung up the phone and looked solemnly at her husband.

"What did he say?" Conrad asked his wife as she sat down next to him at the kitchen table. He felt like a stranger in his own home. It was so unusual to be home during the day on a Wednesday.

"He said that if the 401k loan isn't paid back, the amount of the loan will be counted as a distribution and will be taxed as ordinary income. Plus, there's a 10% penalty for early withdrawal." Connie punched some numbers into the calculator in her checkbook. "It looks like the penalty is nearly $5,000 and the tax will be about $20,000. So, the total is roughly $25,000," she said plainly as she folded up her checkbook and returned it to her purse.

Conrad had a knot in his stomach. He noticed his mouth was dry and his eyes felt heavy. *Why don't you just kill me, God?* he thought. *Is this my reward for all these years of hard work? Am I really such a bad guy that I'm being punished like this?* He drifted off into a sea of despondency.

"I can't believe all this is happening," Connie said, holding her husband's hand. "What are we going to do?" She looked to Conrad for encouragement, but she could tell he didn't have any to give. She realized she was going to have to be the strong one at this point.

"Why don't I just use the emergency fund to pay off the 401k loan?" she suggested. "That will avoid the penalty and taxes." She looked to Conrad for a reply, but then began talking it over with herself, "But then what would we use to live on? I guess my income will be enough to meet our necessities. Unemployment will last a little while. We wouldn't have much to build our savings back up, but at least we wouldn't go backwards." She looked up at Conrad. "You can start to take money out of the 401k without any penalty starting in about five years," she offered.

Great, he thought. *The benefits of getting old – and after that I can retire broke on social security. Maybe I could make a cardboard sign and sit at the turn signal on the corner.* Conrad placed his elbows on the table and rested his forehead in his hands. He started humming the tune *Born Free*. Eventually, he started singing, "Debt free… as free as the wind blows…" He started laughing.

Connie watched him closely. *He's losing it,* she thought. She didn't know what to say or do. She was frightened.

He looked at her and said, "Connie, you know I love you, right? I mean, you know I really love you. I love you, I love the kids, the grandkids…right? You know that, right?"

She held his hand. "I know," she said softly. She wondered what Conrad was trying to say.

"We've worked hard. I've earned good money. We paid taxes. We paid LOTS of taxes, right?" Conrad looked at her for confirmation.

Connie nodded her head. "Yes, we've paid a lot of taxes," she affirmed.

"We borrowed money out of our 401k to pay for weddings and college, right?" Conrad asked. Connie nodded.

"We did that to stay out of debt, right? We were borrowing our own money and paying ourselves interest, so we would be better off financially, right? That was the plan, right?"

"That's right, Conrad," Connie acknowledged. "What are you getting at?"

"I'm just thinking…after being so careful to save and be debt free, why aren't we better off? I'm trying to understand. Why is my paycheck still so important? I mean, we save and save and save. We have no credit card debt. We have a year of living expenses stashed in the bank. Our kids are raised and on their own. But when does any money come back *out*? What's the plan for that?" Conrad pondered the questions he had posed.

Connie looked at him blankly. She had no answers. She glanced away while she thought about it. "I guess I don't know," she finally replied. Turning back to Conrad, she said, "I just felt safer if we had a lot of money in the bank and low monthly payments. I always believed if we could get our expenses low enough we wouldn't need much money to get by on."

Conrad didn't like the answer. *Get by? I work and save my whole life so I can sail into my golden years just to "get by"?* "That doesn't make sense," he challenged. "Think about it! Even if we had no house payments or car payments or credit card payments, we still have insurance, taxes, maintenance, utilities, telephone, not to mention car insurance, gas, repairs…and what about groceries…and clothing, and hair colorings, and manicures, and Christmas presents, and family parties? What about dog food and the vet bills? Medical insurance! What about medical insurance?" Conrad was becoming agitated. "Our medical insurance is more than our house payment, for Pete's sake! How in the world can we ever be 'debt free?' Life is a debt! 'Debt free' doesn't mean no bills. We still need income. What's Ivana B. Padov's plan for medical insurance?"

Conrad sat glaring at Connie. His confusion had morphed into angry frustration. She didn't know what to say. She knew he was distraught because of the layoff. Finding out the 401k loan was due and payable upon leaving SCUMCO was an unexpected and unwelcome discovery. When Freddy Katz CPA confirmed the penalties if the loan wasn't repaid, it was like the straw that broke the camel's back. Conrad was beginning to come unglued.

Connie sat quietly, then said softly, "I don't know Conrad. I'm sorry. I don't know what to say." She thought for a moment, "Maybe we're looking for answers in the wrong places."

The wrong places? Conrad thought about that for a moment. *The wrong places? Maybe so. Maybe she's right.*

"Connie," Conrad asked resolutely, "Do we have Juan and Luv Tunavest's home phone number?"

• • •

"I really appreciate you getting together with me, Juan," Conrad commented as he walked though the front door of Juan's virtually palatial home. The tile floor of the foyer opened up to an elegant spiral staircase. On the left was a distinguished office with fine mahogany casings. To the right was a spacious living room complete with a baby grand piano.

I had no idea Juan had such a nice home, Conrad thought to himself as he looked around in astonishment. "Nice place," he grossly understated.

"Thanks," Juan acknowledged. "We waited a long time to get this and we just love it!"

I can see why, Conrad thought to himself. *This place is incredible!*

Juan ushered Conrad into a beautifully decorated family room with vaulted ceilings, perfectly color-coordinated flooring, wall coverings and furniture. A warm fire softly glowed in the marble fireplace.

"Would you like something to drink?" inquired Juan, playing the proper host.

"Sure," Conrad politely accepted. "That would be nice."

Juan walked over to a granite counter-topped wet bar and opened up a small refrigerator. He pulled out two soft drinks and two glasses, which he filled with ice. Bringing the cans and glasses over to a small round cherry wood dining table, he set them down, then he pulled out a chair and gestured for Conrad to do the same. The two men sat down at the table.

"Juan," Conrad began, "We've known each other for a while, and yet I feel like I really don't know you at all." He paused and looked around. "Here I am in your house. I had no idea you had such a nice place. I guess I'm a little surprised." *Totally shocked and envious is more like it,* he thought.

Juan smiled, "I'm not sure what you expected, but I'm glad you like our home. Luv and I spent a lot of time trying to get the plans just right. Planning it all out took more time than building it!"

"This is a custom built home?" Conrad said in awe. He and Connie had looked into having a custom home built, but the price was much too high for any serious consideration. They had really just gone through the exercise for the fun of it. They never truly believed they'd ever be able to do it.

Juan could see the surprise on Conrad's face. He resisted the opportunity to casually boast about his real estate investing success. He knew this evening would be hard enough for Conrad without Juan drawing attention to his achievements and possessions.

Juan decided to move the conversation in a different direction. "I'm glad you came over, Conrad. So, what are your plans now that we're no longer part of the illustrious Stone Cold United Manufacturing Company?"

Even though this was a difficult topic for Conrad, he was glad Juan asked. It really was what he wanted to talk about. Conrad's thoughts kept gravitating back to Juan's statement their last day at SCUMCO.

"I've wanted to finish up on the conversation we started on our last day at the office," Conrad said. "When I was upset with the company for taking away my job, you said something about me never really having it. What, exactly, did you mean by that?"

Juan took a moment and organized his thoughts. "If I remember correctly," Juan started, "you commented that the company took not just your job, but your car, your house, your pool, and all those things you were supporting with your paycheck." Juan looked at Conrad and said, "What you were really describing was your lifestyle."

"Yeah, I was pretty upset," Conrad acknowledged, "but I still feel that way. I mean, I gave that company over twenty-five years of my life – and I don't mean just any twenty-five years. I gave the very BEST twenty-five years." Conrad could feel himself sinking into a pit of resentment and bitterness, "It feels *exactly like* they took my lifestyle away from me."

"Conrad," Juan responded, "I think you need to know that SCUMCO didn't take your job or your lifestyle away from you. The truth is they couldn't take those things away from you because they never really belonged to you in the first place."

That was what he said, realized Conrad. "Why do you say that? What do you mean?" Conrad asked. Unlike so many of their previous conversation in which Conrad was more interested in sharing his own ideas, this time he genuinely wanted to understand Juan's perspective.

"Conrad, what I mean is that you are blaming the company for taking away the job, its income, and the lifestyle the income provided you. Let me ask you a question. If a man gets out of school, gets a job and rents a house, and then he lives in that house for twenty-five years, but never buys a home of his own, is it the landlord's responsibility to help that man – the tenant – buy a home of his own?"

Conrad looked at Juan. Juan's point was beginning to come more into focus, but it was still a little fuzzy.

Conrad thought about it, then answered, "No, I don't think it's the landlord's responsibility to help a tenant buy his own home. I think if the tenant doesn't want to rent, he needs to go buy a home for himself."

"I agree," said Juan. "Now, while the tenant is living in the rental property, who does the property actually belong to?"

Conrad thought again for a few moments. He had taken a real estate law class once many years ago and he remembered something about different kinds of ownership. He thought the tenant had some form of ownership, but it's not permanent. He wasn't sure what to answer.

"Is this a trick question?" Conrad asked, now feeling a little perplexed.

Juan responded, "No, it's not a trick. It's pretty straightforward. Think about it in simple terms. Who does the rental house belong to, the tenant or the landlord?"

"I would have to say the landlord," replied Conrad.

"Exactly right," said Juan. "The best test of whether you own something or not is to ask yourself, 'Can I sell it?' – or better, 'If I sell it, who gets the money?'"

That made sense to Conrad, but he still wasn't sure how it applied to his situation at SCUMCO.

Juan could see the point was still eluding Conrad. "When we worked at SCUMCO," Juan explained, being careful to include himself in this example, "we were not owners, but renters. We rented out our time, talents and efforts to the company. The company used our time, talents and efforts to build its business, right?"

Once again, Conrad thought about it for a moment and then nodded in agreement, "I suppose so."

Juan continued, "We have control over our time, talents and efforts. We can 'sell' or 'rent' them out to others if we choose, but ultimately our time, talents and efforts belong to us, right?"

Conrad nodded his head just once in thoughtful agreement and waited intently for Juan to continue.

"The office, the responsibilities, the employees, the furniture, the computer, the equipment, the supplies, the customer relationships, the accounts payable, the receivables, all of that – did any of that ever belong to us apart from our roles within SCUMCO? While it is true we were able to use all these things to perform work for the company, could we sell any of them? Could we take any of them with us if we left?" Juan was growing more passionate as he spoke. He looked at Conrad waiting for a reply.

"Well," Conrad said, "no, I guess not. I suppose all those things belonged to SCUMCO."

"That's right!" exclaimed Juan. "They didn't belong to us – and neither did our jobs. Think about it. The jobs we had, whether it was a low-level job like mine, a mid-management job like yours, or a top-level executive position like Ben Dover's, it's really all the same. Our job was nothing more than a role and responsibility within the corporate structure and we only occupied it as long as its true owner, the 'landlord' of the job, SCUMCO, allowed it. The company has the right, as the 'landlord' of the job, to sell it, or evict the 'tenant' – people like you and me who are occupying the job; or do whatever they, as 'landlords,' choose to do. Tenants don't expect to have those rights because they recognize they don't own the property. Employees shouldn't expect ownership of their jobs because they are *not* the owners."

Conrad listened in stunned amazement. It was as if he was staring at a large TV screen and the picture suddenly came into focus.

Juan continued, "SCUMCO didn't owe us a future, or a paycheck for work we hadn't done yet. The only thing that was 'ours' were the paychecks we cashed, the experiences we gained, and the personal relationships we developed. The rest of our life at SCUMCO, every bit of it, never belonged to us! We were only there at the good pleasure of SCUMCO, the 'landlord' of the job."

Conrad found himself nodding in agreement with each sentence leaving Juan's mouth.

"Unfortunately," Juan said, "most employees don't realize this and are then devastated when they lose 'their' job. But it never belonged to them, so how could they 'lose' it?"

Conrad was astonished at Juan's wisdom and insight. "With all due respect, Juan," Conrad exclaimed, "you are blowing me away! I had no idea you were so intelligent. How is it that a sharp guy like you never made it to the top? What happened to keep you from advancing?"

It took quite a bit of self-control for Juan not to laugh out loud. Conrad was so trapped in his employee/consumer paradigm that he couldn't see that Juan was on top. He had simply chosen to climb a different mountain. Juan decided to simply continue the explanation and hope Conrad would keep up.

"What's worse is the false sense of security employees lull themselves into," Juan continued, purposefully assigning the responsibility for ignorance to the employee. "So once the paychecks start coming, employees go out and use this money to rent a lifestyle by purchasing cars, boats, dream houses, vacations and the like. What they don't realize is that when they pledge their future paychecks, which don't belong to them because they are contingent upon a job they don't own, they have assigned their lifestyle to their employer."

Conrad's mind began to tilt, but Juan did not want to slow down, "When you told me the company took away your job, house, car, pool, your lifestyle – and they tried to do the same thing to me – I argued they did not take it from you. You never owned those things to start with because having them all depended upon payments from future paychecks from a job you never owned."

By now Conrad recognized the dilemma. His emotions ranged from awe at Juan's wisdom, to surprise at the new perspective, to anger at all the people he felt should have warned him. He was angry at Juan for pulling the curtains back, angry at himself for having been so gullible, angry at his parents, teachers, friends…everyone, for not having told him any of this earlier.

Conrad then asked the obvious question, "What was I supposed to do? What other choices did I have? I thought I was doing the right thing. I did what everyone thought I should do…what I was taught to do. I went to college and I got good grades. I got a job at a big company and worked hard. I was loyal and put in long hours. I thought about my work all the time!" Conrad's mind drifted back to all the late nights and missed family dinners. He thought of all the times he had only been present with his family in body because his mind was consumed with SCUMCO business. He felt a lump growing in his throat as his heart pounded and his eyes filled with tears. "What was I SUPPOSED to do?" he demanded.

"I can only answer some of that question," replied Juan calmly. "I can only tell you what I did. There are so many people who have done better, but Luv and I are happy. When the layoff happened at SCUMCO, it was disappointing, but not devastating. I realized many years ago that my job at SCUMCO, or anywhere else for that matter, was just like renting a house. I needed it for a little while so I could get established, but my goal was always to have a 'job' or business of my own."

Conrad was once again caught off guard. "I didn't know you had a business of your own! When did you have time to run a business? It seemed like all the time you weren't at SCUMCO, you were off at seminars or looking at properties."

"That *is* my business," Juan explained. "I took my paychecks from SCUMCO and used them to qualify for a loan to buy my first house. I didn't have any money, but I had income and good credit. That was enough to get our first home."

"Over the next few years, my house went up in value. I was able to enjoy living there while I received some tax breaks for paying interest on the loan. You asked me a moment ago what happened to me. The answer is 'equity'. Equity happened to me! The increase in the value of my property gave me equity. It just happened! I hadn't done anything to make the house go up in value except live there. It was about this time that I heard about Grant Deeds. Remember him? Connie knew his wife, right?"

Conrad nodded. He remembered Grant Deeds. He also remembered that first seminar all those years ago. *Is that where Juan learned all this stuff?*

Juan continued, "So when I first heard Grant talk, he taught about equity optimization. He explained how to convert equity into cash which could then be used for down payments on other properties. By then, I had already bought one rental property, but I didn't really have a plan. When I first heard Grant's *Free Rental Property Story*, it started to make more sense to me. I was able to get a new loan to take equity from my home and I bought my second rental property. The income from the tenants made the mortgage payment, while the tax write-offs on the property covered the loan on my home. After a while, all my properties went up. I refinanced again and repositioned my equity for more down payments. Once I figured out this strategy, I just stuck with it."

Juan concluded and waited for Conrad's reaction.

Conrad thought back twenty years to that Grant Deeds seminar in the Moneytree Hotel, when he first found out Juan owned just one income property. He remembered Grant Deeds talking about doing the very thing Juan had described. It remained theory for Conrad, but Juan had used the education to take effective action.

"So your business was real estate investing?" asked Conrad, stating the obvious, but trying to keep Juan talking. Now that his mind was open, humble, and eager to learn, Conrad couldn't get enough.

"Sure. Real estate investing is still my business, though it's more of a lifestyle than a job," Juan said. "I chose real estate because I knew I wasn't clever enough to invent some fancy gadget everyone would want to buy. I really didn't care for corporate politics, so even if I was inclined to move into management, I don't think I would have done very well. The truth is, on those few occasions when I was offered a management position, I always turned it down. When I looked at management, all I saw were long hours, more headaches, and less time to focus on building my real estate investing business."

"One of the most important things I realized was that I did not have to personally earn all the money," Juan said. "I didn't even have to earn very much. I know you always earned more than I did at SCUMCO, but my properties eventually earned more money than you and I combined! With every property I acquired, I got the rental income, some tax deductions, and most importantly, the appreciation. As rents went up, so did my income."

Juan smiled, then continued, "You know what it's like Conrad? When

Luv used to work outside our home and bring home a paycheck, it was great, but we decided it was better for our family to have her home with the kids. Sometimes it would get tight financially – and I'd wish we were living on a family farm somewhere so I could put the kids to work to help out." Juan laughed.

Conrad could relate. He could recall several times he wished for a way to clone himself so he could earn more than one paycheck.

Juan went on, "In a way, that's what my properties are like. It's like having a big family that goes to work every day and brings home a paycheck. It got to the point where I really didn't need to go to work for money any more."

"So why did you stay with SCUMCO so long?" asked Conrad. He was growing more and more intrigued by this way of thinking Juan described.

"In the beginning, I stayed with the day job because I needed it. After a while, I didn't need to be there anymore, but having a steady job helped me get better loans and kept my credit rating up. The job provided a little extra cash-flow that helped me use more leverage while I was aggressively accumulating properties. Besides, investing in real estate is about as exciting as watching paint dry, if you know what I mean. Once you buy a property and get the management set up, you just sit and wait until you get some more cash or equity to get another one. Once you've been at it a while, it picks up. Each round of 'optimization' or refinancing to free equity for new properties, you get more cash for more down payments. Two properties become four, four become eight, and so on. It's just like breeding rabbits! It's pretty amazing!"

"Amazing" is an understatement, thought Conrad.

"I joined an investment club to stay sharp," Juan added. "We would have guest speakers teach on different subjects from time to time. The best part was just comparing notes with other active investors. It was at one of these meetings where I became friends with the owner of a real estate investment company. It turned out to be a great relationship! He always had investment projects going and often needed funding. As I became more experienced and reached a certain financial level, I was able to get involved. A bunch of us would get together and group our money together and this guy would run the project. When it was done, we would split the profits. I used my profits as down payments on more properties."

"I have to be honest," Juan continued, "there were hassles some times. You may have heard about the time one of my properties was on a reality TV cop show? It's funny now, but back then it was a pain. But, I looked at all the hassles people at SCUMCO had every day and I just accepted the fact that *every* business has its challenges. There is no free lunch!" Juan laughed again.

"By the time this layoff came, I had several million dollars in properties," Juan said. "I was fortunate the layoff didn't come at a time when I really needed the paycheck. But I enjoyed the people and I had some co-workers I was helping to get started in real estate investing. Once you realize there is plenty to go around, you don't have to keep it a secret. One of the things I liked least about corporate thinking was 'scarcity mentality'. With so few positions at the top, it could get ugly sometimes."

"I know what you mean," agreed Conrad, reflecting back on his up and down – mostly down – relationship with Ben Dover. "How come you didn't you invite me to be a part of your real estate school – or whatever it was?" asked Conrad. "I was always interested in real estate investing."

Juan had expected this to come up at some time during the evening. He had thought quite a bit about how he would address this question. It's very cruel and unbecoming to kick a man while he's down and clearly Conrad Soomer was down. Still, it was a valid question and deserved an honest answer.

"You know, Conrad," began Juan carefully. "I really wanted you to get involved in investing. You had so much more to work with than I did. You had a better job, made more money, and to be honest, I think you are smarter than I am. But when I invited you to seminars, or recommended books, or referred you to my advisors, for some reason you just didn't get into it. I just figured you had something else going and didn't really want to do real estate. You seemed very happy with your advisors and confident about your game plan. What happened?"

The reality of what Juan said hit Conrad like a kick in the stomach. Juan hadn't said anything cruel or untrue. He said it just like it was. The pain came from the reality of knowing that he had no one to blame for his situation but himself. *Life really is short* he mused.

"What happened to me?" Conrad repeated rhetorically. "That's a good question." He paused.

"Life," Conrad answered. "I was always so busy. It took everything I had just to make a living. I didn't have time...I didn't *take* the time...to design a life. It just happened. Life happened to me. Equity happened to you and life happened to me." Conrad sat quietly reflecting on this hard reality.

Juan thought about Conrad's response, and then countered, "What life? Who's life?"

"Another good question," Conrad replied as he considered his answer. Finally he offered, "SCUMCO's, I guess...maybe Ben Dover's...but not mine, not my family's." His expression grew grim. "I feel like I just let my life get away from me. I thought I was having fun, doing the right things, but I wasn't thinking about the future. I just figured it would all work out." He sighed.

"Juan?" asked Conrad tiredly, "Is it too late for me? Can you help me?"

Juan looked at Conrad. *What a shame*, Juan thought. *Here is a bright, educated, man who's worked hard all his life and he's sitting here wondering if it's too late to have hope for a financially free future. What can I tell him?*

"I don't think it's too late," answered Juan delicately, "but you can't do it exactly the way I did because you don't have as much time. And, honestly, I'm not sure I'm the right guy to help you, but I can give you some advice. I hope you'll take it to heart."

"I'm all ears," replied Conrad eagerly.

Juan explained, "If you want to make it in real estate, I think you need to get a job. Not a dream job, but any job that lets you go to work and come home at a decent hour.

Conrad listened intently.

Juan continued, "You should absolutely start studying real estate. Go to seminars, read books, join clubs, and the like. I'll give you some ideas. Remember, you are starting a business. If you were starting a sales company or a manufacturing company, you would probably join a trade association, attend conventions, network with industry experts, develop strategic relationships with vendors and customers, subscribe to trade magazines, and all that, right? Becoming a real estate investor is no different! The people I've seen fail over the years just don't take it seriously enough. I call them real estate *hobbyists*. You are a businessman and I'm sure you'll do fine, just like you did at SCUMCO. The only difference is this time you are building your own business and not someone else's."

Juan continued, "There's a lot of hocus-pocus out there, so be careful. Get some good advisors and *stick with them*. Don't nickel and dime them for their services. Good people can make you a fortune and deserve every penny you pay them. Don't be 'penny wise and pound foolish'. Look at the big picture and build strong strategic relationships. Real estate investing is a team sport and you'll need the best efforts of great people if you want to win big."

"Remember this," Juan added, "the less time you have to work with, the more important leverage is. I know you have been very conservative most of your life, and I am not suggesting you become reckless, but there are risks when you *don't* take action, as you've already found out. The risks you accept should be well-thought-out and discussed with experienced, trusted advisors who know what they're doing. Never forget that you can't make money on property you *don't* own. Effective action is the key."

"One last piece of encouragement," said Juan. "I've had some ups and downs in life, and one thing I've learned is that we tend to grow the most as a direct result of a major setback. A 'setback' is the perfect setup for a 'comeback'. So, even though it seems like the *worst* of times, it is also the *best* of times. The lessons you are learning are painful, but life-changing. So get the lessons, enjoy the journey, and don't ever quit. I promise you, winning is worth it!"

Epilogue

onrad?"

"Conrad?" the voice repeated. Two hands reached out to shake Conrad Soomer's shoulders.

"Conrad! Hey buddy, wake up! The seminar is over!"

Conrad's eyes opened slowly. Gradually, the face in front of his came into focus.

"Juan?" Conrad asked, "Is that you? Where are we?" He rubbed his eyes and blinked. "Why is your hair black?" Conrad's brow remained furled as he struggled to remember where he was and how he got there.

"My hair?" Juan Tunavest replied. "My hair has always been black. Are you okay?" He looked into Conrad eyes and repeated, "Conrad, are you *okay*?"

Conrad sat up and looked around. The Cinderella Ballroom at the Moneytree Hotel was nearly empty. The hotel crew had begun picking up trash and stacking chairs in preparation for the next day's event. Just then, Luv Tunavest walked up with a glass of water and offered it to Conrad.

"Here you go," she said, holding out the glass and smiling.

Conrad slowly reached out and took the glass. Dazed, he stared at Luv.

Juan said, "Man, Conrad! You had me a little worried. I looked around for you after the seminar started, but I guess you were stuck in the back since you got in late. At the end, I was able to talk with Grant Deeds and some of his advisors. By the time I looked around for you, I saw you asleep in a chair against the back wall. I've never seen anyone sleep so hard in my life! You missed a great seminar. You'll have to make sure you sign up early for the next one – and make sure you get some sleep *before* the event!"

Conrad glanced at his watch and checked the date and time. He looked back up at Juan and Luv, then down at the floor near his chair. He reached down and picked up his *Rags to Riches Real Estate Seminar* workbook and clutched it tightly.

Conrad Soomer looked intently at Juan Tunavest. "Juan," Conrad said resolutely, "I'd like you and Luv to be my guests at the next Grant Deeds seminar. Connie will be there, too. Then Connie and I would like to take you out to dinner. Our treat! I have a feeling this is the start of a lifelong relationship. I want to make sure you know how much I appreciate you telling me about today's event. What I learned today is going to change the direction of my life."

"Sure, Conrad," Juan replied with mild surprise. "That would be great."

Conrad smiled and thought, *Thank God I have another chance!*

*"Be sure to live this life
as though it were your last."*

– Robert Helms

Will Equity Happen to You?

Before we conclude Book One, we want to make sure you don't miss the forest for the trees. We want to close with some important attitudes which have nothing to do with the technical aspects of real estate investing, but have everything to do with success – in real estate or anything else.

- If you want to earn to spend, you will most likely never be financially independent. Set out to earn money as evidence of your contribution to the world and use the money to make investments. At the same time, be sure to enjoy the journey because none of us know when our time is up.

- If you go to work for the sole purpose of retiring, you will most likely never be successful in business. Pick something you love to do simply for the sake of doing it, then become great at it. If it is something that adds value to the world, you will most certainly be rewarded for your excellence.

- Time marches on. You must realize you are only on this planet for a season, then "game over". There is no reset button and there are no replays. *Carpe diem*! Seize the day!

- Henry Ford once said, "If you think you can or you think you can't, you're right." Very true! A winning attitude will propel you into action. A defeatist attitude will imprison you in a cage more impregnable than the highest security prison cell on the planet. Practice the art of focusing your mind on positive outcomes. Focus on solutions, not problems.

- Always remember, "If it's to be, it's up to me." No one is going to come along and hand you a gold mine. Life will give you what you'll accept. You must take personal responsibility for your success – which means you must take personal responsibility for your failures also.

- Achievement is a team sport. There is a myth out there that "independence" is something to aspire to. Hollywood glorifies these macho mavericks that don't need to listen to or cooperate with anyone. This is a bunch of garbage. More true is the old adage, "No man is an island." Stephen Covey deals with this best in his classic book *The Seven Habits of Highly Effective People* when he talks about "interdependence" being the highest level of human relationship. We could not agree more. Aspire to become a contributing member of a dynamic, positive team of people who are like-minded and focused on goals that are similar or complimentary to yours.

- Success is a lifestyle, not a destination. We'll admit that many of these are clichés, but this doesn't diminish their truth or relevance in any way. If you find yourself saying "If only this or that, then I'll be happy," then you need to make adjustments to your mindset. Happy, positive, successful people can't stand to be around negative, frustrated, unhappy people. Since achievement is a team sport, it is essential for you to be positive while you work towards your various achievements. Your positive attitude, optimism and enthusiasm will attract people and resources to your aid. Most people enjoy helping nice people. Be a nice person!

- Be who you are becoming. This is the secret to joyful living. Your past is behind you and out of your control. Those pages in your life history are written. What matters now is your future. You should think about your future long and often. What do you want to be remembered for? How do you want people to feel about your impact on their lives? Learn to see your future in your mind's eye and begin to behave like that person. Before too long, you will become that person.

- Don't worry about people and things you can't control. There are so many bad things in life that *might* happen, but never do. Focus your energy and resources on the things over which you have direct control. You'll be amazed at the momentum you will gain by doing this one simple thing.

- Follow the leader, but lead the followers. There will be many people who will cross your path. Some will want to offer you things; many more will want to get something from you. The more clarity you have about who you are, where you want to go, how you plan to get there, and why it's important to you, the less likely you are to be taken off track by someone else, no matter how well meaning they may be. Yet, if someone comes along who is congruent with your goals and is further ahead in terms of knowledge, achievement or relationships, then go ahead and follow. The key is to know when to lead and when to follow – and to never lose sight of what *you* set out to do.

- Plan your work and work your plan. This sounds basic and it is, but we notice some people are great students, great planners, and great thinkers; however, they just don't seem to be able to take action. Others like to jump right in and attack, but are guilty of leaping before they look at what they are doing or why. Work every day at balancing the two. However, if you are to err, err on the side of action. Sydney J. Harris said, "Regret for the things we did can be tempered by time, it is regret for the things we did not do that is inconsolable." Another pearl of wisdom! The only way to avoid making any mistakes is to never do anything – which, in and of itself, would be one of the *biggest* mistakes you could make.

- Don't ever quit. The moment you give up, you've lost. This doesn't mean you don't abandon bad investments, unsalvageable relationships, or faulty plans. Changing direction isn't quitting; it's adjusting to the feedback your temporary setbacks are giving you. We like General Douglas McArthur's attitude, "We are not retreating – we are advancing in another direction." Perseverance and tenacity are appropriate and necessary when dealing with the negative thoughts and people who tell you it can't be done, that you're not smart enough or lucky enough to win. Pushing through circumstantial adversity, things like human error, lender denials, computer glitches, banking problems, and the like, is just part of playing the game. You can't let adversity dissuade you from moving forward with a happy, optimistic attitude.

We could probably go on and on. Both of us are big believers in the importance of developing, maintaining, and growing a winning attitude. Both of us are voracious learners. We love to attend seminars, read books and listen to or watch recordings of inspirational messages from expert teachers. We like to network with people who have great ideas, have accomplished noteworthy things, and are otherwise committed to the perpetual improvement of themselves and the people around them. We encourage you to work every day on developing a winning attitude.

The Victor

If you think you are beaten, you are.
If you think you dare not, you don't.
If you'd like to win, but think you can't,
It's almost certain you won't.

If you think you'll lose, you've lost,
For out in the world you'll find
Success begins with a fellow's will.
It's all in the state of mind.

If you think you're outclassed, you are.
You've got to think high to rise.
You've got to be sure of yourself before
You can ever win the prize.

You see, life's battles don't always go
To the stronger or faster man.
Sooner or later the one who wins
Is the one who thinks he can.

– C.W. Longnecker

EQUITY HAPPENS™

BOOK TWO

Your Real Estate Investing Manual

EQUITY HAPPENS™

SECTION 1

Equity Happens

CHAPTER 1
Drive a Ferrari

Imagine being entered into a two-person race on the Indianapolis Motor Speedway. Assuming you are not a professional race driver, you may find this intimidating. Suppose you are racing against one of the most successful drivers in racing history, like Jeff Gordon or Richard Petty. How's your confidence now? What if your opponent were in a 1965 VW bug with 200,000 miles on a tired 4-cylinder motor, while you were driving a brand new, freshly tuned, 8-cylinder supercharged Ferrari? Now, who do you think would win the race?

Our point is that your vehicle selection can be even more important than your skill. While you still need to be able to operate the vehicle, clearly a person of lesser skill in a superior vehicle can not only compete, but has a legitimate chance at victory. In investing, as in auto racing, the vehicle makes a BIG difference!

In our *Real Estate Investor Development Program*™, we offer real estate investing strategy consultations to students who have completed specific prerequisite training. Prior to coming into the consultation, we require the investor to complete a pre-consultation profile. This profile includes a "balance sheet" and "cash-flow statement" so we can review and discuss their cash, cash-flow and equity positions. Our goal is to give the investor ideas about how to get more out of what they have to work with.

Do you know what we see on those balance sheets the vast majority of the time? The largest single component of many people's net worth is the equity in their real estate holdings – which is often made up of only their primary residence! In most cases, these people do not consider themselves real estate investors, nor did they set out to build wealth with real estate. They just wanted a nice place to live where they didn't have to pay rent. In other words, they developed this wealth virtually by accident! You can't help but wonder, what would have happened if they actually *tried* to make money with real estate?

Many of the people we meet also have money invested in stocks through a brokerage or retirement account. In these cases, most of these folks were *trying* to build wealth with their stock portfolios. Yet their real estate "accidentally" created more new wealth for them than all their other investments combined! It wasn't their skill in real estate, or lack of skill in stocks, that gave them greater success in real estate – it was the superiority of real estate as an investment vehicle.

In our opinion, real estate is the most stable, proven and novice-friendly investment vehicle available to everyday people. Yes, there are risks and headaches associated with real estate investing. But there are risks and headaches associated with home ownership, business ownership, or even going to work every day for a weekly paycheck. The question is, at the end of the day, what is the ratio of risk to reward in real estate compared to other vehicles? We contend that real estate provides one of the very best reward-to-risk ratios available.

So what is it that makes real estate so much better than the other "equity" vehicle, otherwise known as stocks?

Advocates of stock investing point out that the historical growth of the stock market over the last 70+ years (including the Great Depression) is approximately 12% per year. Meanwhile, real estate has typically only grown about 6% per year. Additionally, the stock fans say, stock investing is less hassle than real estate because with stocks you don't have to deal with tenants, loans, legal liability and other challenges unique to real estate. Besides, they continue, you can put stocks in tax-advantaged programs such as Individual Retirement Accounts (IRA's) or 401k plans where you can keep more of your money working for you and defer, or in some cases, avoid taxation. This all sounds pretty good, right?

What many people overlook, as famed radio personality Paul Harvey would say, is "the rest of the story."

The Rest of the Story
Many authors have done an excellent job of describing the advantages of real estate over stocks, so we won't belabor the point in this book. However, there are some essential differences between real estate and stocks we believe must be addressed before we move on.

Get Real
Even though the "real" in real estate actually means "royal," the fact remains that real property is tangible and permanent. In only extremely rare instances does the dirt itself literally disappear or become completely unuseable. Massive landslides into the ocean, nuclear disasters and the like are not commonplace events!

Stocks, which are simply paper securities documenting ownership in a business venture, can become completely worthless in the event the business venture ceases to operate. When this happens, the business's remaining assets, if any, are liquidated to satisfy creditors. Whatever is left over, which is usually nothing, is divided among the shareholders. The size of the company, the type of business, and the length of time the business has existed are no guarantees it will continue to exist. Just think of some of the more notable companies whose failures had catastrophic results for their shareholders. Names like Enron, Worldcom, and Arthur Andersen come to mind. The fact is that even a large venture can disappear because of a management faux pas, a product liability lawsuit, a change in a core technology, or any number of items outside the control of the investor.

Think about this: When the business occupying a building goes bankrupt, the building remains. Would you rather own the business or the building?

Get It

Ignorance is not bliss when it comes to investing. We see so many investors come through our offices who own shares of companies whose businesses they don't understand. These "investors" don't know what these companies' business models are, who their competition is, or what risks the businesses face. They don't know who makes up the boards (or sometimes even what the boards do), nor do they have any personal knowledge of, or relationship with, the executive teams, key corporate advisors or majority shareholders. These "investors" don't have any idea what these aforementioned and incredibly influential company leaders' qualifications are. Neither do they really understand the relative financial strength or weakness of the companies whose stock they have bet their financial futures on.

We realize the prospectuses and "audited" financial statements are supposed to provide the diligent investor with this information. This is great in *theory*. What we see in the real world is that most investors don't read the prospectus. They don't or can't interpret the financial statements (assuming the statements are accurate), but instead, simply rely upon their stock broker (who in turn is relying upon the research of one or more investment analysts), unaware that both the stock broker and the analyst may have hidden financial incentives to push a particular stock. The individual investor is very far removed and insulated from the knowledge of the realities and risks of the stocks they are purchasing. Remember, ignorance is not bliss. Ignorance is dangerous and very often expensive.

In contrast, we frequently joke in our seminars about the business model of real estate, "Let's see... people live in my property and pay me rent. I get that!"

When you buy a property you can see it. You can look at the neighborhood and meet the property manager and the tenants. With very little training or experience, most people can interpret a property inspection, an appraisal, and any repair bids supplied by contractors. Reading financial statements for income properties is not unlike looking at your personal finances. You have rental income, which is your "paycheck," and you have expenses, which includes mortgage payments, insurance, taxes, utilities, repairs and a few miscellaneous items. In some cases, you'll have property management expense, but other than these basic items, real estate, especially residential income property, is pretty simple to understand and own.

My Body Guard
Some might argue that stocks are regulated, which is true. However, the reality of stock market regulations versus real estate regulations is quite different. *The Securities and Exchange Commission* (SEC) regulates the sales of stocks. Russ was once licensed as a *Registered Representative* and a *Registered Principal* and is familiar with the real-world truth of how SEC regulations work at the point of sale. SEC requirements primarily deal with disclosure and suitability. Disclosure requirements are satisfied by simply providing a prospectus to the investor. Suitability is determined through a cursory look at your balance sheet to make sure you can afford to lose money. Do you feel safer now?

Real estate regulation is much more practical because the government understands that although losing your life savings is devastating, it is less so than losing your home. Of course, many of the protections available to the principals in a real estate transaction are overlooked when buyer and seller choose to deal directly rather than through professional real estate agents. This is why we strongly recommend all parties involved in a transaction always engage the services of competent, experienced, appropriately licensed and insured professionals.

Cheap and Easy

Though we will discuss the concept of leverage (the primary benefit of financing) in greater detail later, it is important to contrast the use of leverage in real estate investing as compared to the use of leverage in stock investing. There are basically two methods of leveraging stocks: "margin" and "options". Since this isn't a book on stock trading, we won't spend much time discussing leveraged stock trading except to explain a few important differences between leveraging stocks and leveraging real estate.

"Margin" is just a different word for debt. When you buy a stock on margin, you put up part of the money while the brokerage firm loans you the rest. A typical maximum leverage ratio available in margin trading is 2:1 or 50% equity (your money). The other 50% is money borrowed from the brokerage firm. With mortgages, it is possible to purchase property with as little as 20%, 10%, 5% or even 0% down! We will cover this in greater detail later, but the point is that you can get much more real estate than stocks for the same amount of your money invested.

Also, margin interest rates are typically higher than mortgage interest rates, thus the interest expense related to investing in stocks on margin is higher than that of leveraged real estate investing. Though interest expense shouldn't be a primary focus as long as you are making a profit with the borrowed money, it is obviously preferable to have a lower interest cost than higher one, all other things being equal. Our point here is that interest on debt secured by real estate will generally cost you less than interest on debt secured by stock. The amount of interest a lender charges is higher when the risk is higher. This alone should tell you something about the stability of real estate versus stocks.

Probably the most attractive feature of real estate debt compared to debt secured by stock is that real estate offers much greater security in the event the value of the security drops. Not only are stocks significantly more prone to rapid and unexpected shifts in value, but if you happen to have debt against the stock (margin) and the value of the underlying stock drops to a price where the debt exceeds more than 50%, the broker will make what is called a "margin call". When you get one of these calls, the broker requires you to bring more cash into the account to restore the leverage ratio. For example, if you own $10,000 in stock purchased with $5,000 cash and $5,000 borrowed from the brokerage (margin) and then the stock value drops to $7,000, your "equity" is reduced to $2,000 (your original $5,000 less the $3,000 loss in value). Meanwhile, the margin remains at $5,000. Because your maximum margin ratio is 2:1, you need to have at least $3,500 equity (1/2 of the now reduced value of $7,000). Since you only have $2,000 in equity, the broker's margin call will be for $1,500. This means you must bring $1,500 cash into your account within a few days, or some or all of your stock will be sold at whatever the going rate is. Russ had someone very close to him lose an eight-figure fortune on a margin call.

Contrast a margin call to real estate. Suppose you own a $100,000 property with $10,000 equity and $90,000 in debt. You have a "margin ratio" or loan-to-value (LTV) of 90%. The first thing to notice is the significantly higher amount of leverage available to you, the powerful advantages of which we will discuss later in this book.

Suppose your $100,000 property unexpectedly dropped in value by 30% and is now only worth $70,000. Before we move on, consider the improbability of this situation. How often have you seen or heard of a property which was one day worth $100,000 and the next day was worth $70,000? Very rarely! If a real estate market begins to recede, it generally happens gradually, and if you are paying attention, you will see it coming and get out well in advance of most of the damage. Even if you didn't get out, time will usually heal most wounds in real estate. Ten years later, most real estate markets which sustained sudden and significant decreases in value have not only recovered, but have increased from their original value. If you were alert and ready, you might have been able to pick up some bargains when prices were at the low point!

Getting back to our example, if your $100,000 property's value has dropped to $70,000 and you still have a $90,000 loan, does the bank call you and ask you to cover the $20,000 shortfall? No. Does the bank ask you to cough up the cash to restore the 10% equity position of the $70,000 property, which would be $7,000 in this case?   Again, the answer is no.

Unlike debt on stocks, debt on real estate does not result in margin calls. This is another significant advantage of real estate over stocks.

What about options on stocks? Is this a safer way to gain leverage on stocks? We're not talking about stock options that employees sometimes receive from companies they work for. We're talking about purchasing publicly-traded options. An option gives the holder the right, but not the obligation, to buy or sell the underlying stock at a pre-determined price in a pre-determined timeframe.

While trading stock options offers much higher leverage ratios than trading the actual stocks, options are subject to time limitations. If you fail to exercise your option in the allotted time, it expires with no value whatsoever. We understand that 80% of options traders lose money. Need we say more?

Our contention is that real estate provides the most attractive risk-to-reward ratio of any investment vehicle available to everyday people. However, not everyone believes in real estate as strongly as we do.

The Experts Agree

We have a lot of fun in our seminars laughing about all of the doom and gloom predictions of the so-called "experts". Prolific real estate author Gary Eldred, in one of his many excellent books, *The 106 Common Mistakes Homebuyers Make (and How to Avoid Them), 2nd Edition*, recorded some of the classic predictions about how the real estate bubble will soon burst:

"The prices of houses seem to have reached a plateau, and there is reasonable expectancy that prices will decline."
– *Time Magazine*[1]

"Houses cost too much for the mass market. Today's average price is… out of reach for two-thirds of all buyers."
– *Science Digest*[2]

"The goal of owning a home seems to be getting beyond the reach of more and more Americans." – *Business Week*[3]

"The era of easy profits in real estate may be drawing to a close."
– *Money Magazine*[4]

"If you're looking to buy, be careful. Rising home values are not a sure thing anymore." – *Miami Herald*[5]

"Most economists agree… a home will become little more than a roof and a tax deduction, certainly not the lucrative investment it was…"
– *Money Magazine*[6]

---

[1] This quote was written in 1947
[2] The year was 1948, when the average price was $8,000!
[3] The rest of this quote from 1969 is "The typical new house costs about $28,000."
[4] This quote was written in 1981
[5] This quote was written in 1985. Don't you feel sorry for all those suckers who bought real estate in 1985? We bet if they own those properties in 2005, they really took a bath…an equity bath!
[6] This quote was written in 1986

"We're starting to go back to the time when you bought a home not for its potential money-making abilities, but rather as a nesting spot."
– *Los Angeles Times*[7]

"Financial planners agree that houses will continue to be a poor investment." – *Kiplinger's Personal Financial Magazine*[8]

"A home is where the bad investment is."
– *San Francisco Examiner*[9]

If you haven't already, take a look at the footnotes to see when these dire declarations were made.

How do these "expert" predictions stack up against the reality of history? Apart from your own personal experience, consider the following:

Equity Happens! Will It Happen to You?

Housing Inflation 1968-2004

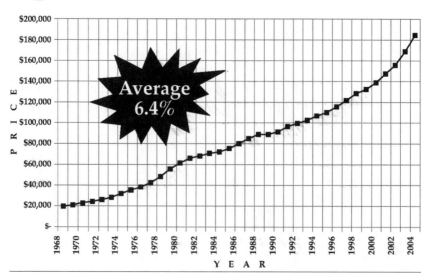

—■— Median Price

---

[7] This quote was written in 1993

[8] This quote was written in 1993

[9] This quote was written in 1996. Ironically, housing prices in the San Francisco Bay Area exploded to all time highs from 1996 to 1999. Even throughout the worst recession in Silicon Valley history, housing prices continued to rise – though at a slower pace.

As you can see, from 1968 to 2004, the median real estate prices in the United States went up 6.4% per year on average. If you are interested, here are the actual numbers:[10]

Year	Median Price	Percentage Increase
1968	$ 20,100	N/A
1969	$ 21,300	6.00
1970	$ 23,000	8.00
1971	$ 24,800	7.80
1972	$ 26,700	7.70
1973	$ 28,900	8.20
1974	$ 32,000	10.70
1975	$ 35,300	10.30
1976	$ 38,100	7.90
1977	$ 42,900	12.50
1978	$ 48,700	13.50
1979	$ 55,700	14.20
1980	$ 62,200	11.90
1981	$ 66,400	6.80
1982	$ 67,800	2.10
1983	$ 70,300	3.70
1984	$ 72,400	3.00
1985	$ 75,500	4.30
1986	$ 80,300	6.40
1987	$ 85,600	6.60
1988	$ 89,300	4.10
1989	$ 89,500	0.20
1990	$ 92,000	2.80
1991	$ 97,100	5.50
1992	$ 99,700	2.70
1993	$ 103,100	3.40
1994	$ 107,200	4.00
1995	$ 110,500	3.10
1996	$ 115,800	4.80
1997	$ 121,800	5.20
1998	$ 128,400	5.40
1999	$ 133,300	3.80
2000	$ 139,000	4.30
2001	$ 147,800	6.30
2002	$ 156,200	5.70
2003	$ 169,500	8.50
2004	$ 185,200	9.30
	Average:	**6.41**

[10] Source: National Association of Realtors

Notice that there was *never* a year where the median price went down from the previous year. Now, don't you feel sorry for all those people who "over-paid" for their real estate in 1981? We wonder if they regretted having bought their "over-priced" real estate ten years later? We suspect if anyone has regrets, they probably sound like this:

"I should not have sold!" – We call this "seller's remorse". It occurs when you sell a property, thereby relinquishing all of the future appreciation to the buyer, only to have the property go up in value! Your remorse sets in when you realize that if only you would have had a better understanding of your options *before* you sold, you might have been able to retain ownership. Then, all that wonderful new equity created by the increase in value could have landed on your balance sheet, not on the buyer's!

"I should have bought!" – We call this "non-buyer's remorse". This is the terrible realization that you missed an opportunity. Our poster children for non-buyer's remorse are Russ and his daughter Stephanie. They passed up an 8-unit apartment building in Sacramento in 2001. When Russ and Stephanie chose not to buy the property, Robert and his father Bob decided to purchase it instead. The property appreciated over $200,000 in just two years! Every time this story is told in one of our seminars, Russ and Stephanie still cringe.

One of our primary motivations in writing this book and titling it *Equity Happens* is to help you understand *why* prices go up, not *if* prices will go up. With this understanding, you can keep the doom and gloom predictions of the so-called "experts" in proper perspective. Too many people stand on the sideline in fear of the impending "bubble burst," only to look back a few years later with painful regret.

Remember this: Real estate pricing is much more strongly influenced by regional factors than national factors. This means, and history bears out, that while a specific area may experience a decline in doing well. Your mission as an investor is to identify those regional markets, sub-markets and properties that have a higher probability of performing strongly. The good news is that there are lots of them and they aren't that hard to find. The bad news is that the good deals aren't in your living room, so you will need to go out and look for them. We hope to share with you a foundational level of knowledge and wisdom, so you can be effective in investing both your time and money into finding markets and properties which will advance your goals.

C H A P T E R   2
Real Estate
FUNdamentals

This is a Football

Legend has it that Vince Lombardi, the late great former coach of the Green Bay Packers football team, and a man who probably understood winning better than any coach in his generation, would start each training camp for both his veteran and rookie players the same way. Standing before a team of champions who had just demonstrated themselves as the very best in the world at their chosen profession, he would hold up a football and declare, "Gentlemen, this is a football."

While simplistic, it drove home the importance of staying focused on the fundamentals. Once the basics were drilled over and over again, Lombardi would then start adding enhancements that produced championship results.

In real estate investment, as in football, you must understand the fundamentals. In our teaching, we like to put the emphasis on *fun*. Dudley Moore said in the movie *Arthur*, "Isn't fun the best thing to have?" Robert says, "If you don't enjoy what you do, find something else to do!" The point is, life is too short to spend time engaged in activities you don't enjoy.

With that said, and in the context that we love real estate and thoroughly enjoy our business, here's one of the truths about real estate investment you must understand: it can get a little boring! The basic activities involved in acquiring, maintaining and managing income properties are typically not what motivate the average person to invest. It's the *results* of investing that excite most people. You don't necessarily want the property, you want the *money*! But, you don't really want the money either, do you? Don't you really want the *lifestyle* the money will buy you?

As you continue to acquire properties and gain experience, be careful not to lose sight of the why behind what you are doing. Learn to enjoy the journey, embrace the people and experiences, even the difficult ones, and have fun building wealth with real estate.

Learning the basics of real estate investing is straightforward. However, like football, mastering the basics can take years. But it is in mastery that true greatness is achieved.

By way of encouragement, we want to remind you of the progression of all human achievement. We've discovered that if people do not understand this progression, they tend to quit before they get to success. This is particularly true for adults because it is easy to retreat back to something already mastered instead of pushing through the sometimes embarrassing and discouraging challenges of taking on something new. When you find yourself discouraged and wanting to quit, remind yourself of these four levels of mastery and take comfort in your *progress*, because results can seem elusive in the beginning:

Level 1: **Blissfully Incompetent** – You're incompetent, but don't even know it! Young children abide in this level. For example, consider the little boy who is going to beat up any burglar who tries to break into the home, or the child who draws an unrecognizable object and declares it a masterpiece. We see many rookie real estate investors who plan to get rich in only one year! These are all examples of blissful incompetence.

Level 2: **Discouraged Awareness** – At this level, you now realize the burglar is bigger, stronger and meaner than you are, that your picture looks nothing like the object you are attempting to draw, or that you just lost money on your first real estate deal. Most adults quit something new at this point, and to salve their bruised ego, they retreat back to something they've already mastered. Even the great Michael Jordan returned to basketball after hitting this wall in his pursuit of a career in baseball. Children, on the other hand, will usually push through because they haven't yet achieved any ego-pacifying level of mastery at anything significant. They have no choice but to push on.

Level 3: **Struggling Competence** – At this level, you have figured out how to perform the skill, but it takes tremendous concentration and effort. Sometimes people give up at this level because the rewards do not seem commensurate with the effort. The truth is, this is the level where success is almost certain. It's just a matter of time and persistence. Don't give up!

Level 4: **Mastery** – Finally, you are now extremely competent and consistently producing high-quality results with less effort than at Level 3. This isn't to say you don't work hard. There is no lasting achievement without hard work, but your success begins to compound as your motivation and enjoyment grow.

Real Estate Basics

The day-to-day basic activities and skills of a real estate investor are simple. In fact, if you want to acquire properties as a "buy-and-hold" investor, here is the magic formula:

1. Buy a Property
2. Rent the Property out
3. Repeat

If you plan to flip properties for short-term profits, the formula is a little more complex:

1. Buy a Property
2. Fix it up (or add value in some other way)
3. Sell the Property for a profit
4. Repeat

Now you have the magic formulas, so you can put down the book and go out and make a fortune! Right?

Well... not exactly!

While some "wanna-be" investors think they'll be successful if they can just get the magic formula, inside technique or secret plan, the fact is that real estate investing is really a matter of mastering a few key disciplines. To begin your journey towards mastery, you must start with the basics.

In football, Coach Lombardi identified running, throwing, catching, blocking and tackling as the basic "hard" skill set of a football player. While each player and his "hard" skills are crucially important to the team's success, there is much more to competing on the field than simply the physical aspects of the game.

Once a year we put on a free event for young people designed to show students how they can become *owners* of real estate instead of merely renters. We teach basic financial principles in a unique and fun way. Johnnie Johnson, the former football great and a first-round draft choice of the then Los Angeles Rams, talks to the kids about developing a "winning mindset". Johnnie points out that football is as much of a mental game as a physical one; and that the true secret for success in the sport begins with how you *think*. He stresses that the way you think affects the way you play. He transitions this to playing the game of life. Greatness in sports, business, or any endeavor, begins with the "soft" skills of managing your attitudes, habits and beliefs. When you add specialized knowledge, or "hard skills", to these "soft skills", you have a recipe for the foundation of success.

Likewise, in real estate investing, most of your success is based on the way you think and what you know. We have found the basics for winning as a real estate investor include:

✓ A Winning Attitude
✓ A Healthy Environment
✓ Continuous Pursuit of Knowledge through Education and Experience
✓ A Clear Personal Investment Strategy
✓ Disciplined Acquisition of Assets
✓ Knowledge of Financing Strategy and Techniques
✓ Attention to Property and Financial Management
✓ Regular Portfolio Optimization
✓ Professional Tax, Estate and Asset Protection Planning

Attitude Determines Altitude

Trite as it may be, attitude truly is everything. This may not be what you want to hear, but as famed musician Bruce Hornsby says, *"That's Just the Way It Is!"* According to noted personal development trainer Brian Tracy, *The Law of Expectation* declares that results often stem from expectations. If you expect to do well in real estate investing, you probably will. If you expect to get taken advantage of, it will probably happen. We don't know why this is true, but we have seen that it is. It's like gravity. We don't really understand how it works, we just know it does.

This idea is often difficult for many "seasoned" investors and analytical types, especially those who have been through challenging transactions in the past. At our seminars, Robert often polls the audience to see who already owns investment property, those whose only property is their personal residence, and those who own no real estate at all. He points out that the people who own *no* real estate are in the *best* position because they have not yet developed any bad habits! This is partly tongue-in-cheek to help instill hope in the "newbies," but there is also a tremendous amount of truth in it. It is easier to learn new ideas, instead of having to unlearn bad ideas. Old attitudes, habits and beliefs tend to die hard.

Experienced investors are often disadvantaged because their years at the school of hard knocks have made them skeptical, cynical and jaded. These "walking wounded" let bad experiences limit their thinking, causing them to assume that because bad things have happened in the past, then bad things are sure to happen again in the future. Unfortunately, this very expectation of failure causes them to doubt, fear, hesitate and withdraw from the very people and opportunities which can enrich them.

On the other hand, new investors often approach real estate investment from a fresh, curious, open-minded perspective. They are eager to learn and anxious to discover new ideas and to meet new people. Placed in the right environment, the rookies see evidence of success around them and believe it is possible for them to succeed, too. These "fresh" investors often find success quickly by focusing on what they want instead of concentrating on what they don't want.

Think about it. If we say, "Don't think about the Eiffel Tower," don't you find yourself *immediately* thinking about the Eiffel Tower?

Instead, if we say, "Think about oranges," then the last thing on your mind is the Eiffel Tower. If the Eiffel Tower represented failure and oranges represented success, do you see how futile it would be to concentrate on "not failing"? Learn to focus on *winning*!

A winning attitude is essential for long-term success in real estate. If you expect to win, you'll find opportunities to win. If you expect to lose, then you'll find a way to fail so you can say, "I told you so" to anyone foolish enough to listen. Don't let a bad attitude prevent you from achieving your fullest potential.

If this is your first exposure to these tried-and-true personal development concepts, be careful not to discard their importance to your quest for financial freedom. We didn't put them (or anything else for that matter) in this book just for the fun of it. Learning to manage your thoughts and emotions is essential to success in real estate investing – and in life.

If you are new to real estate investing, be sure to keep looking for the positives. Spend time with people who are excited and succeeding in real estate. Learn from the "doers" and flee from the "doomsayers" and "yeah-butters" (a "Yeah-Butter" is someone who always responds to every positive thing you say with "Yeah, but..."). We aren't suggesting you adopt a Pollyanna attitude and ignore obvious warning signs and cold hard facts. Just remember that most negativity is rooted in prejudice and fear instead of facts and experience. Consider the source, ask lots of questions, and keep everything in perspective. The solutions are out there. Make up your mind to find them. More often than not, you will.

If you are already an active investor, strive to keep an open mind. Perhaps you've had difficulty in the past. Surely you didn't think the road to riches was without potholes? Put failures in perspective. Failure is part of what makes success possible. Without failure, there is no success. Stay positive!

Once again, this doesn't mean you should stick your head in the sand, ignore adversity, and pretend things are great even when they're not. We are not professional writers or doctors of psychology. We are simply investors who live in the real world. Real estate investing can get ugly – real ugly! It would be disingenuous to suggest otherwise, but when we have a challenge in real estate, we choose to learn from it so we can do better next time. Remember, problems and failures are also where all the best lessons are. Make sure you get the lessons. After all, you probably paid full price for them.

As an investor, you should *welcome* problems. This sounds crazy, but it's by solving problems that you get good at avoiding them in the future. Often, the harder a problem is, the more you will be rewarded when you solve it.

One of the best aspects of real estate investing is you can learn not just from your own mistakes and failures, but you can also learn from the mistakes and failures of others. Robert's father, Bob Helms, often says, "You don't have to give natural childbirth to a great idea. You can adopt one!" Learning from others' experiences is one huge advantage of belonging to a fraternity of investors who are committed to sharing with and learning from one another.

Add to Your Knowledge Base

Continuous education is the hallmark of the successful investor. Brian Tracy says, "If you want to earn more, you have to learn more." How true! Real estate laws, practices, forms, techniques and conventions are constantly changing. If you are treating your real estate investing as a business, then you need to stay on top of the ever-changing landscape. Investing, like life, is dynamic. The person who fails to grow will quickly fall behind.

We believe it is impossible to know too much when it comes to investing in property. We are constantly adding to our knowledge base and sharing ideas with other investors. We study markets, monitor national and local trends, keep up-to-date with new rental laws, perform due diligence on properties, and constantly seek out other investors to learn from.

Having said this, please understand that book education by itself is not enough to bring success. You can learn all there is to learn about real estate, but if you don't use your knowledge to actually acquire property, then you will have wasted both your time and your money – not to mention the time of the people who put effort into teaching you.

Many people come to our seminars, read volumes of books, buy stacks of audio and video programs, and study all the financial formulas. These "experts" understand complex financial concepts and can crunch numbers with the best of them, yet they fail to do the single most important thing: ACQUIRE PROPERTY! One of the gigantic pitfalls of a love of education is becoming afflicted with "paralysis of analysis". Don't let this happen to you! Be sure to take a balanced approach. Education should lead to *effective action*.

There are three essential components to effective learning. A wise person will employ all three in order to obtain the deepest and most useful education:

1. **Listening** – this includes reading, watching videos, attending seminars, etc. This is a one-way delivery of information from the teacher to the student.

2. **Watching** – observing and interacting with someone else who is actually doing what you are trying to learn to do.

3. **Doing** – this is getting up out of the chair and actually doing it yourself. Think about learning to ride a bike, play the piano, drive a car, speak a language, or do arithmetic. All the lecture and observation becomes relevant and cemented into your

mind when you actually put the classroom lessons into action in real life. Nowhere is this more true than in real estate investing.

A significant portion of your education will come from hands-on experience. Once you take this to heart, you will be well on your way to developing a winning investor's mindset.

Develop Your Strategy

Building upon the foundation of a great attitude and a commitment to education for effective action, you must then decide what types of properties will work best for *you*. You must come up with a plan that supports your unique goals and capitalizes on your unique strengths, resources and opportunities.

Later, we will devote an entire chapter to showing you how to develop your personal investment strategy, but for now, suffice it to say that no two investors are identical. Each person has a unique mix of education, experiences, attitudes, relationships, and financial positioning. Additionally, each person has a different financial "destination" – the financial dream you want to achieve. You must decide what you want real estate to do for you and then devise a plan to get there. Your plan must take into account the realities of your current financial picture, timeframes, non-financial resources (the most important of which is your relationships with people who can help you), and what the marketplace is willing to give you. Too many times, we get discouraged and quit like a spoiled child because we can't get what we want, the way we want it, when we want it.

On the other hand, once over their initial fear, novice investors will jump at almost any deal put in front of them without any serious consideration of whether it fits into their strategic plan. This is usually because they don't *have* a strategic plan. Sometimes, this unguided action results in owning a "bad deal". Other times, it results in a poor reputation in the marketplace caused by signing contracts and making promises when there is no realistic means of actually honoring those commitments. We would argue the latter is the most disastrous because you only have one reputation. It's easier to recover a financial loss than the loss of a good reputation – and it's easier to recover from a financial setback when you have your reputation intact. Always remember, in the long run, a bad reputation will cost you much more than a bad deal will.

Another benefit of a clear strategy is it will help you move quickly. Sophisticated investors know exactly what they're looking for, so they recognize it when they see it. This allows them to prepare properly and act decisively. The best deals require quick action. The more you refine your strategy, the better investment choices you will find yourself making.

Building Your Portfolio of Properties

Acquiring assets is awesome! It's exciting to watch your holdings increase as you build your real estate empire. As you find new properties and structure offers, you will continue to get better at recognizing opportunity and taking action. You'll also gain the experience which only comes from real-world dealings with agents, sellers, tenants, vendors and property managers.

With any luck, the properties you add to your portfolio will continue to perform for you, on either a cash-flow or equity building basis (or both!). As your competence increases, so will your confidence. One of the signs of your development as an investor is coming to the realization that what you once thought was a great investment now seems only average.

• • •

After an exhausting day of touring markets and evaluating properties in three states, Robert and his team had seen some excellent properties. One of the team members told Robert excitedly, "Wow! If only the folks back home knew about some of the great deals out there!" Robert smiled in agreement and replied, "If only *we* knew about some of the great deals out there!"

• • •

You will find that the better *you* get, the better the deals get.

Choose the Right Financing

In his book, *The Five Rituals of Wealth*, Tod Barnhart writes, "There are no successful financial illiterates." What he means is that people who are successful in the world of money understand how money works. You need much more than a cursory understanding of real estate finance to make the most of your investments.

When contemplating an investment, you should always "run the numbers". Loans create financial leverage, which is one of your most powerful tools for creating wealth. You need to have a firm grasp on real estate financing concepts if you truly want to do well with your investing.

Loan programs and rates change frequently, as do the requirements lenders have for borrowers and properties. Unfortunately, most people buy what is sold to them, and not necessarily what is good for them. The top-selling fast foods and beverages are not necessarily what are best for people, but these products are aggressively marketed, so people buy them.

The mortgage industry is great at selling loan products, but not always great at making sure the products sold are best for the people buying them. Successful investors always have a knowledgeable financing consultant on their team to help then navigate the sea of loan programs available.

Russ created one of our more popular seminars, *Managing Your*

Mortgage for Maximum Net Worth. There are several key points Russ makes which we think all investors must understand in order to make good financing choices:

- Bad financing does not make a good property bad and good financing does not make a bad property good. Sometimes you may have a temporary situation, which makes optimum financing unavailable, but this shouldn't dissuade you from grabbing a great property when it's available. You can almost always change the financing later when your situation or the market allows.

- Financing advice handed down from generations of consumer-minded non-investors should not provide the framework for your investment financing decisions. Investors look at debt and interest rates differently than consumers do. Consumers focus on debt reduction as a means of strengthening one's balance sheet (increasing net worth) and lowering interest expense as a means of improving cash-flow. Investors, on the other hand, focus on accumulating assets that go up in value over time and provide income and tax write-offs. To an investor, interest rates are like gas prices. You like them better when they are low, but you keep filling up at whatever the going rate is so you can drive your car to work every day and earn your paycheck. As long as you are making money (increasing your net worth) with the debt and can handle the cash-flow, you aren't overly concerned with how much debt you have or how much it costs.

- Mortgages control property and cash-flow controls mortgages. We'll repeat this often. If you want to control a property long enough for it to appreciate, then pay close attention to cash-flow. Cash-flow, not interest rates or amortization (equity build-up through debt reduction), should play a major role in your financing decisions.

- Payments do not need to be made from earned income or even from rents. Cash reserves and tax credits can be used to buy time to allow a property to appreciate or rehab work to be completed, a credit problem to be cleared, or for more favorable loan terms to be sought out.

• Remember *The Golden Rule*: He who has the gold makes the rules! While there is some room for negotiation with lenders, most loans, especially on 1-4 unit residential property, will be sold into the secondary market and may have even been pre-sold before you ever sign the papers. This means the guidelines are set and if you want the money, you take it on the *lender's* terms. The good news is that mortgage money is almost always the least expensive, best tax-advantaged money you can get. Lenders make us crazy with their conservatism, but we love them anyway. Their conservative nature drives them to loan us their money at a fraction of what we can make with it. How much do you want to borrow at 8% if you are making 20% with the money? Our favorite answer is, "All of it!"

Profitable Property Management

One of the biggest keys to making money in real estate is finding good management. This is no different than owning stock in a company or a mutual fund, or running a business. In all cases, you need a good manager to tend to the daily affairs of the asset. With real estate, most of us have the basic skills required to do it ourselves if necessary. At the very least, we can understand most of what we need a good property manager to do for us. Can you imagine filling in for the CEO of a company you own stock in, or taking over for the manager of a mutual fund you own? We don't understand why anyone would want to own investments they don't understand and can't control – especially when the returns aren't as good, the assets aren't insurable, and major players can artificially move the market for personal gain.

Whether you manage your properties yourself or hire professionals to manage them for you, good management is essential to good investment performance. Robert has an investor friend, Charlie, who says, "Life is too short to manage property!" Charlie is an avid proponent of outsourcing management to a competent, professional on-site or off-site manager.

Also, depending on where your properties are located, adhering to current tenant/landlord law can be time consuming. In California and New York, for instance, many of the laws favor tenants. Landlords who don't keep up and comply with the law face severe penalties. This is one instance where an ounce of prevention is worth ten pounds of cure!

Whether you manage your properties yourself or hire someone else, we recommend you join a local apartment owner's association. Association members gain access to new forms, training classes, specialty service providers, and legal hotlines for quick answers to common questions. These are all invaluable resources to help you manage your income properties for optimum profitability.

Optimize Your Holdings

The most important fundamental concept in real estate investing is the one most investors overlook. Once you have property, you need to make sure your portfolio is optimized. This entails regularly checking on your properties and comparing their performance to your goals and other opportunities, and then making any necessary adjustments.

Just as your car runs better when you tune it up on a regular basis, so your will properties perform better when you give them the attention they need. Are you keeping your rental units in good shape? Are your rents in line with the market? Are you taking full advantage of current loan programs and interest rates to improve your cash-flow and flexibility? Have you built up enough equity to reposition into another property?

One of the great benefits of owning property is it rarely needs constant attention. People with busy lives can usually acquire real estate, get it up and running, and then let the manager deal with most of the details. However, left unchecked for too long, even the best performing property will fail to operate to its fullest potential. It may seem like a minor point, but as you will see in later chapters, the difference between "buy-and-hold" versus "buy-and-optimize" is absolutely astounding!

Plan for the Future

Most people do not like to think about death, but until someone invents a way to avoid the inevitable fate every human being faces, the prudent investor must think in terms of passing on assets to his heirs. The best way to deal with the logistics of passing assets is to think it through well in advance.

Proper estate planning is a crucial component to any real estate investment plan. Take some time to meet with the professionals on your advisory team and discuss your options. Death has serious tax ramifications and you need to know what they are and how they will affect your family. Did you know death taxes can be as high as 55%? Even life insurance proceeds can be taxed at this confiscatory rate! The use of trusts, family limited partnerships, and other vehicles can save time, money and stress for your loved ones.

The entire topic of estate planning hit home hard for us when Russ's father-in-law passed away suddenly and unexpectedly. He owned an insurance company, vineyard and several investment properties. Though his estate was somewhat complex, he had only a simple living trust. While the trust served the purpose of avoiding probate, the estate was still assessed a $200,000 state and federal tax bill. Ironically, Russ's wife wrote the check the same night we had our first *Estate Planning Strategies for Real Estate Investors* seminar. Russ opened the seminar by holding up the $200,000 check as he encouraged the audience to take the topic seriously. Being the "numbers guy", Russ pointed out that $200,000 invested at 20% down would purchase $1 million in property. If the property appreciated on average 7% per year, that

$1 million property would be worth $2 million in ten years. His point was that for the lack of investing $5,000 in estate planning, his family had lost working capital capable of earning millions of dollars! Don't let this happen to your loved ones.

Have Fun!

Now that we've covered the basics of real estate investing, let's turn our attention to the best part: having a blast doing it!

The more real estate we acquire, investors we meet, and members we add to our network, the more fun we have! In the movie *Jerry Maguire*, athlete Rod Tidwell (played by Cuba Gooding, Jr.) finds himself playing football simply for the paycheck. To get his fire back, his agent, Jerry Maguire (Tom Cruise), encourages him to go back to the reasons he started playing in the first place – not for the money, but for the pure love of the game. As the movie goes, Tidwell, a third-rate player, went on to become a superstar. Though it's only a movie, the message contains a lot of truth. There is tremendous power in pursuing your passion!

Putting together deals, finding solutions for sellers, thinking creatively, brainstorming about the highest and best use for the property, and using your skills to create win-win transactions can be tons of fun! For us, building wealth with real estate for our clients, our friends, our families and ourselves is our life's work. We are truly passionate about what we do. While you don't have to share the same vibrant enthusiasm, if you don't get a kick out of wheeling and dealing in real estate, be honest enough to realize it may not be the right wealth-building vehicle for you. If you don't enjoy what you do, it is unlikely you will stay at it long enough or work hard enough to become financially successful.

At our offices, we find ourselves laughing out loud about something or other at least a half-dozen times a day. Have you ever noticed how laughter is contagious? Making money is fun, but having fun making money is even better! We are serious when it comes to investing, but we never take ourselves too seriously. Let's face it, joyful people are simply more fun to be around!

You'll also find a fun attitude makes negotiations easier and transactions smoother. The "Godfather of Real Estate", Robert's father Bob Helms, often says, "You usually get farther with honey than you do with vinegar." Profound wisdom!

Life is short. The money you make from investing in property can increase the financial quality of your life, but the lifestyle afforded by real estate investment can add to your enjoyment level. It isn't all roses, but it sure can be fun if you let it! Even the messy parts of an activity you love are enjoyable when you keep them in context.

You'll also have the opportunity to meet lots of people, which is fascinating all by itself. Robert's mother often mused, "There's nothing like people!" If you love people, real estate investing is a great business.

Of course, one of the most enjoyable things in life is winning. Vince Lombardi proclaimed, "Winning isn't everything. It's the *only* thing!" When your definition of winning includes treating people with respect, being true to your word, and negotiating win-win, then the image of the stereo-typical self-centered cut-throat businessman goes out the window and you can get on with the business of competing. Perhaps winning isn't everything, but it sure beats losing!

CHAPTER 3
What Happened?

What is equity? Where does it come from? Why does it happen? How can you be sure it will continue? These are all essential questions for anyone considering real estate as their vehicle of choice for wealth-building. So let's examine these critical subjects...

What Is Equity?

Though it may seem elementary, for the sake of any reader who may not know, equity is simply the difference between what is owed on a property and what the property is worth. So a $350,000 property with a $150,000 loan against it would have $200,000 in owner's equity.

Where Does Equity Come From?

Equity develops in a property from two primary sources:

- **Owner's Contribution** in the form of down payment (purchase equity) and pay down of loan balance (amortization). Amortization comes from that portion of the monthly payment which reduces the balance (principal) of the loan. We call this *amortized equity*. Some people choose to make additional payments beyond what is required to simply amortize the loan. This is called "loan acceleration" because you accelerate how quickly the loan is paid off.

- **Increase of Fair Market Value** – As the market value of the property rises, 100% of the increased value adds to the owner's equity. This is true regardless of how much or how little debt the owner has against the property. We call this "new equity". It is new because the owner did not create it through a contribution. There are different categories and sub-categories of new equity, which we will cover later. For now, we will discuss equity in general with an emphasis on "passive equity", which comes from market appreciation. This type of equity is passive because, in order to receive it, the owner did not have to do anything except own the property long enough for the property to go up in value.

Why Does Equity Happen?

This is THE multi-million dollar question! History shows us that real estate values, and housing prices in particular, tend to rise consistently and predictably. Your belief or doubt that this phenomenon will continue in the future will have a profound effect on your decisions about if and how you will choose to invest in real estate. This is the one issue we don't see anyone really addressing and yet it is arguably the most salient topic related to real estate investing. The answer to why equity happens is rooted in a common sense understanding of economics and human behavior.

Rising prices are the result of two basic economic concepts: "Supply and Demand" and "Inflation". However, there is a sub-component of Demand, called "Capacity-to-Pay", which is often overlooked. Understanding how these concepts work together to affect real estate is crucial to one's belief or doubt about whether values, and thus equity, will rise.

Supply and Demand

In a free market economy, prices will tend to drop when supply is high and demand is low. In other words, when there is more than enough of something, it is said to be a "buyer's market" because sellers must compete, typically by lowering the price, to attract a buyer. Conversely, when supply is low and demand is high, prices will tend to rise as buyers bid up pricing to compete for the limited supply. This is called a "seller's market".

Think about this:

• In regard to supply, are they making any more real estate (dirt, not buildings) in the most desirable areas? In only the rarest of circumstances, such as when swampland is filled in to create more developable land, is the supply of land actually increasing.

• In regard to demand, is it likely someone might invent a technology to allow people and businesses to no longer require land on which to live, farm and operate businesses? Obviously, this is virtually impossible.

This section isn't intended to get into all of the factors affecting supply and demand for certain types of properties in specific geographic areas. We simply want to illustrate the general likelihood of consistent pricing support for real estate because of the high probability of persistent demand and an ultimately limited supply.

We realize there are vast undeveloped areas in the United States and throughout the world. It can be safely argued we are decades, perhaps centuries, away from exhausting the supply of real estate. However, people desire to be close to each other for social and economic reasons, and it takes tremendous time and effort to establish the infrastructure (freeways, water supply, power, etc.) to support a large population in an undeveloped area. So, as populations grow in specific geographic areas relative to the amount of available land or the pace of development, prices will tend to be driven up in the most desirable areas. Remember the old real estate adage about the top three criteria for determining the value of real estate: "Location, Location, Location."

Because of the enormous challenges in establishing socio-economic centers, there is a period of time during which an established center will go up in value. Even though rising prices will slow down demand, for a considerable amount of time people find paying more is still the path of least resistance. That is, it remains easier to pay more for existing properties in the desired area than to develop new properties farther out. Eventually, the high prices will force the economically weaker population out of the primary market and they must go out and fill in a smaller market or establish a brand new one. The term for this is "urban sprawl." Just think of any major metropolitan area where there is a downtown, then the suburbs, then an open area, then the suburbs of the next area, and then another downtown. Eventually the open area is consumed by the sprawl and one area blends into another. Greater Southern California in and around the Los Angeles area is a classic example of urban sprawl.

During the transition periods, there is tremendous opportunity. The trick is to identify the most desirable emerging markets, sub-markets, and properties and get in early. The good news is real estate tends to move slowly, so timing the real estate market is much more practical than timing the lightning-fast stock market.

The bigger component of understanding the mystery behind why equity happens is found in understanding inflation and the economics behind inflation. In our seminar, *Real Estate FUNdamentals for Young People*, we explain inflation and the reasons for it in very simple terms to students. If these young people can understand it, so can you. So, let's take a look at…

Inflation
What is inflation? What causes it? How does it affect real estate? This topic sounds like the purview of intellectual professors with

lots of letters after their names, but it isn't really all that complicated.

Very simply, inflation occurs when more medium of exchange, in the form of money and/or credit, is introduced into an economy faster than the growth of goods and services. Over time, this increases people's capacity-to-pay for the goods and services they desire most.

Imagine a small village where you and 99 other people live and work. Suppose the medium of exchange, or "money", is marbles and there are exactly 1,000 marbles made. The marbles are made of a very rare material, put through a difficult-to-duplicate manufacturing process, and the village government restricts their manufacture and distribution. These conditions make the possibility of additional marbles making their way into circulation virtually non-existent. So, if the marbles are distributed equally among the village's population of 100, each person would have 10 marbles in their pockets.

One day, this book, *Equity Happens*, is put up for sale, but there is only one copy in the entire village. Because of the life-changing information contained in the book's pages, there is a tremendous demand for the only available copy. Assuming no one could increase their marble supply by pooling their marbles together with or borrowing from someone else, what is the *maximum* price anyone might pay for this book if we were to auction it off to the highest bidder? The answer is 10 marbles because no one could possibly pay more than that, *even if they wanted to*. No matter how much demand or how scarce the supply, the highest price anyone could pay is limited by the amount of marbles he has. This is called "capacity-to-pay".

Now suppose everyone in the village becomes tired of carrying marbles around all the time. The marbles are heavy and make everyone's pants sag. If you should happen to develop a hole in your pocket, the marbles would quickly fall out and be easily lost.

If you left the marbles at home unattended, someone might break in and steal them. The villagers have a terrible dilemma!

One day an enterprising villager establishes a marble "bank". He hires an armed guard to protect the marbles which are stored in a burglar-proof cave sealed by a large stone. Now everyone can put his or her marbles in the bank for safekeeping. The banker gives each person "coupons" which are redeemable for the marbles whenever they need them. With this coupon system, people can exchange marble coupons instead of real marbles. Whenever a coupon-holder wanted to, he could go to the banker and redeem his marble coupons for real marbles. However, after some time the banker notices that people seldom, if ever, request their real marbles. They are quite content to conduct business using the much easier-to-handle marble coupons.

Before long, the banker realizes he can actually issue more coupons than there are real marbles. As long as everyone doesn't want their marbles at the same time, there will always be enough available to handle the occasional withdrawals.

So the banker prints up coupons for an additional 1,000 marbles and begins to use them to purchase items from other villagers. Over time, the additional coupons end up fully distributed and out in general circulation. Now, there are coupons for 2,000 marbles being used in the village – double the original amount. The first 1,000 marble coupons are those issued against the real marbles actually stored in the marble bank. The other 1,000 coupons are those printed by the banker, but have no real marbles backing them up.

Assuming the 2,000 marble coupons were distributed equally among the 100 people in the village, then each villager would now have 20 marbles (2,000/100), right? With this new increased capacity-to-pay, when *Equity Happens* is auctioned, what is the highest price anyone might bid? The answer now is… 20 marbles!

What changed to make *Equity Happens* now worth 20 marbles instead of 10? Did the book change? No. Did the supply change? No. Did the demand change? No. But because more marble coupons were now in circulation, each person's capacity-to-pay increased. This made it possible for the demand to bid the price up all the way to 20 marbles. The key principal here is that prices will go up when the demand is constant or increasing *and* there is an increasing capacity-to-pay. The more one is able to pay, the more one will pay, if the desire is strong enough.

If you had bought the book for 10 marbles and then were able to sell it for 20 marbles, wouldn't you be excited? You might spend some of your new "profit" on a bigger house or some other item you really wanted.

Meanwhile, the banker keeps printing marble coupons. He uses them to build a big fancy building, thus creating work for the villagers. He buys a fancy carriage and hires a gardener and a personal assistant. All the while he is putting these new coupons into circulation. Now there are coupons in circulation worth 40,000 marbles and people are buying and selling all kinds of goods and services. The village economy is hot! One day you look in the local paper and you see *Equity Happens* on sale for 40 marbles. Wow! You also notice other popular items are going up in price, so you decide to have a garage sale and sell all of your stuff. At the end of the sale, you add up your coupons and you have coupons for 2,000 marbles! So you head off to the bank to cash in your marble coupons for *real* marbles.

When you get to the bank and hand the banker your coupons for 2,000 marbles, he turns a little white and goes to check the marble vault. Of course, there were only ever 1,000 real marbles to back up the 40,000 in marble coupons he printed. He never expected anyone would actually come in and ask for that many real marbles. He tells you the bank is closed and you'll have to come back tomorrow. You are disturbed!

When you get home, you tell your spouse, who tells a neighbor, and before long several people in the village have heard the story. The next day when you get to the bank, you see the doors locked and a long line of people clutching marble coupons and yelling at the banker through the window. The banker has no way to redeem the coupons and now no one in the village will sell goods or services for anything except *real* marbles. Villagers will no longer accept marble coupons. Since there are now such a small supply of real marbles in circulation relative to the prices established when everyone was trading primarily coupons, prices begin to drop rapidly. Each villager's capacity-to-pay has been reduced, or deflated, to only their share of the real marbles in circulation. The village's economy is now in a great depression!

It is important to understand this depression didn't occur because people stopped wanting to buy things. The problem was they simply lost their ability to pay because there wasn't enough "medium of exchange" (marbles) to support the pricing structure created when marble coupons were the medium of exchange.

The crisis becomes so bad that the village's government steps in and outlaws the ownership of real marbles. They declare marble coupons as the only legal money in the village. The government convinces everyone the coupons are real money. In fact, the government prints on each coupon, "This coupon is legal tender for all debts, public and private" and then they have the Minister of the Treasury sign them. The government starts several major projects in the village and pays for them with the coupons they print. Since real marbles are now completely out of circulation and the only "money" being circulated are the printed coupons, people begin to accept them again – what choice do they have? After some time, the economy "recovers". However, this time the bankers aren't restricted by having to have real marbles on hand to match the number of coupons printed. As you might imagine, the banker quickly returns to printing marble coupons. Meanwhile, the village changes their economic system (with some political pressure by the banker) and introduces the concept of borrowing. With this new system, a person can get an advance on future earnings in order to obtain marble coupons now, as long as the debt is paid back later. The incentive for the lender (the banker) is to earn interest on every marble coupon loaned out. By increasing the number of coupons he prints, he can loan out the extra coupons, which have no real cost except to print, and then charge interest on them. Also, this time there is no connection between the number of real marbles and the number of marble coupons, so once again the village's economy begins to inflate.

Ironically, the people who are hurt worst in an inflationary economy are savers. People who save money when prices are going up actually lose purchasing power as prices rise.

Imagine one of the villagers places 10 marbles (or marble coupons) in the marble bank to "save" them. At the same time, the owner of the only copy of *Equity Happens* puts it up for sale on e-Bay. Another villager, looking to invest his marbles, realizes that every single time *Equity Happens* sold in the past, it always sold for more than the previous owner paid for it. The Investor reasons that this trend is likely to continue, so he decides to purchase *Equity Happens*. In this case, the starting bid is 10 marbles, which the Saver could afford if he wanted to. However, the Investor, who also has only 10 marbles, goes to the bank and borrows the 10 marbles the banker is holding for the Saver. The Investor now has 10 of his own marbles and 10 marbles which he borrowed from the bank (which came from the Saver). The Investor has doubled his capacity-to-pay and bids up *Equity Happens* to 20 marbles. Now, even if the Saver withdraws his 10 marbles to buy *Equity Happens*, he can no longer afford it!

In this new system, the economy "grows" over time and people forget all about real marbles. Everyone simply uses the printed coupons and borrowing is commonplace. Banks loan the extra coupons to people and businesses, who in turn use them to buy the goods and services they want. Over time, prices go up, so more coupons are paid to workers. As workers get more coupons, the law of supply and demand pushes prices up on items people really want. Eventually, wise villagers realize if they can buy something that is limited in supply, but high in demand, the price will rise and they can make a profit later when they sell.

Every once in a while, when prices are going up too fast, the village government raises taxes to take some of the extra coupons out of circulation. Sometimes the banks decide to slow down borrowing by increasing interest rates, thereby making it harder for villagers to borrow. In either case, capacity-to-pay is reduced, so the villagers have to slow down spending and the economy slows down. This slow-down is called a recession.

During the slow economy, the villagers focus their purchasing power only on those things they need and want *most* of all. The highest demand items in the village, after food and clothing, are for houses to live in and buildings to run businesses. The highly populated areas become the most expensive because these areas are where the majority of customers and workers are located.

If the village economy slows down *too* much, the government can put marble coupons back in circulation simply by spending them. Another way the village government might increase capacity-to-pay, would be to reduce the rate at which they took excess coupons out of the economy. In other words, the government could lower taxes so the villagers would be able to keep more of the excess coupons they earned. A third tool available to the village leaders is to have the bankers reduce the amount of interest they charged when people borrowed marble coupons. Lower interest rates mean a villager can afford to borrow more of the excess coupons for the same payment. While this reduces the amount of profit the banker makes per marble lent out, it increases the amount of borrowing, so the net amount of profit for the banker increases. The marbles don't cost the banker anything because the marbles either belong to the Savers or were simply printed, so the banker isn't too concerned if interest rates rise or fall. The banker makes money either way.

Does the story of the village people seem somewhat familiar? It should!

Whether you like it or not, the fact is that the United States is a credit-based economy. Our medium of exchange is paper "coupons" which are not redeemable for anything except goods and services. There is no longer a direct link between "dollars" and real money (gold). Through different mechanisms, the government and bankers can manufacture as many "coupons" as they choose to. The result is an ever-increasing supply of money into our economy and perpetual inflation. If you doubt it, simply look at the history of debt in the U.S. and the history of inflation. The two are inextricably linked.

Now, we don't claim to be classically trained economists. Our educational pedigrees are not very impressive. In our view, there is so much "noise" around the subject it is easy to get confused. We just try to keep it simple.

No one can deny that debt is growing. Because of the ever growing debt, more and more "coupons," or dollars, end up in circulation in order to provide enough dollars to service the debt.

When the extra dollars find their way into the hands of the people and times are "good," one of the very first things people bid up in a free market economy is real estate. Why? Because people need it and want it. So, in good times, real estate prices react quickly to the upside.

On the other hand, when the money supply is restricted, typically through a rise in interest rates or an increase in taxes, people will sell their toys and stocks, and reduce their discretionary spending, before they will sell or accept a "loss" on their real estate. Just think about how expensive, time-consuming and life-disrupting it is to move a household or a business. This is not a task people undertake lightly! We've already shown you the history of rising housing prices. Take a look at the history of average salaries in the United States, which we gleaned from Gary Eldred's *The 106 Common Mistakes Homebuyers Make (and How to Avoid Them), 2nd Edition*:

1940 Average Salary:	**$1,299 per year**
1950 Average Salary:	**$2,992 per year**
1960 Average Salary:	**$4,743 per year**
1970 Average Salary:	**$7,564 per year**
1980 Average Salary:	**$15,757 per year**
1999 Average Salary:	**$27,810 per year**
2000 Average Salary:	**$34,652 per year**
2002 Average Salary:	**$36,764 per year**[11]

Do you notice a trend? You see, over time, as people *make more* money, they can afford to *pay more* for the things they want – like real estate. Whether they own or rent, people place a high priority and spend a significant percentage of their income on putting a roof over their heads.

Once again, real estate is the first thing to attract money and the last to let it go. This creates a fair degree of stability in real estate pricing. You don't have to be a Harvard trained economist to understand this. Once you realize what actually causes real estate to appreciate and

---

[11] The year 2002 data came from the Bureau of Labor Statistics and was not taken from Mr. Eldred's book.

the high probability of those primary causes remaining in place (we call them "sustainable drivers"), it is a logical conclusion to believe real estate prices will continually and persistently rise over time. But in case you aren't yet quite persuaded...

Your Rich Uncle Wants to Help!
The Godfather of Real Estate, Bob Helms, often refers to the government as "Uncle". Though we don't always care for Uncle's involvement in our lives, we recognize the government has a vested interest in supporting real estate – and most especially residential real estate.

If you are an incumbent politician, it is awfully hard to get your constituents to re-elect you when they are living out of their car or under a bench in the city park! There is tremendous political pressure to keep housing "affordable" and available – no matter what is happening economically. In 1992, Bill Clinton staged one of the great political upsets by keeping his campaign focused on one primary issue: "It's the economy, stupid." He realized, quite accurately, that people vote with their pocket books.

Affordability, whether in housing or anything else, is a relative concept (affordable, compared to what?). In an inflationary credit-based economy like the United States, salaries and prices rise together, so affordability depends on your relationship to income sources and assets. If you have a job, you will likely see increasing income over time. This may not provide you with additional purchasing power, but at least it mitigates the effect of inflation on your standard of living. However, if you are on a fixed income, you will likely see a loss in purchasing power as prices rise. Worse, if you are depending upon bank interest rates to provide your income, you are in for a double whammy when decreasing interest rates (meaning your income is dropping) fuels a "growing economy" (inflation which produces rising prices). Decreased income combined with rising prices means serious reductions in purchasing power. Not good.

However, if you own an asset that is in demand, the asset's value is likely to go up as people's capacity to pay more for it grows as a result of their increasing income. If you don't own such assets, you will find them harder to acquire as prices continue to rise over time. This is the unenviable position many renters find themselves in throughout many of the more populous and desirable areas of the country.

Uncle recognizes housing is a primary human need and the foundation of a healthy economy and happy electorate. Uncle provides subsidized loan programs (directly or indirectly), tax credits, and other incentives to help voters afford housing.

Just as we are not economists, we are also not tax advisors. We're just a couple of guys obsessed with the subject of real estate. We have ideas and opinions formed from years of real-world activity. As such, this book is not designed to cover taxation in technical detail. With this said, you should know that real estate tax law benefits the owners of property in several ways. Some of the tax incentives your rich Uncle provides for you as an investor include:

- The $250,000 capital gains[12] tax exclusion per spouse on the sale of your primary residence when you have lived there two of the last five years.

- Deductibility of the interest expense on the purchase money mortgage for your primary residence (up to a $1 million purchase money loan amount, plus the interest on an additional cash-out refinance up to another $100,000).

- Interest and expense deductions on your rental properties (see IRS Form 1040 Schedule E).

---

[12] Capital gain is a term used to describe the profit realized upon the sale of an asset for a price higher than you paid for it. For example, if you bought a property for $100,000 and later sold it for $150,000, you would realize a $50,000 capital gain.

- Depreciation, including accelerated depreciation on certain components of rental property.

- The 1031 tax-deferred exchange, which permits the tax on a realized capital gain on an investment property to be deferred if the equity in the property is used to purchase more property according to the IRS rules.

- Owning real estate, notes and other non-traditional assets in your self-directed retirement account, thus deferring or even completely eliminating capital gains and income tax.

- Tax deductions for educational materials and training related to your real estate investment business (IRS Form 1041 Schedule C).

These are the more common of the many tax aids your rich Uncle provides to help you own and control real estate. Remember, you shouldn't act on any advice you read in a book, see on TV or hear in a seminar or on the radio. All of these sources provide potentially valuable information and ideas, but before you take action, we strongly recommend you engage the services of a professional to review your plans – preferably someone who owns investment real estate.

Will Equity Happen to You?
While nothing in life is guaranteed, there are many rational, logical, and understandable reasons to believe real estate will continue to appreciate over time. We can't think of any other investment which features universal and timeless demand, an ultimately limited supply, intrinsic value, strong governmental support, and is easy to finance, insure, understand and operate; and has a better track record. Sure, there is risk in buying real estate, but don't forget the risk of not buying!

Equity Starts at Home
Owning your own home is a foundation of the American dream.

While many people debate whether or not your personal residence is an investment, there are many compelling reasons to own the home you live in. There's the satisfaction of knowing the landlord isn't going to tell you when to move. Improvements you make to the property are not only for your enjoyment and benefit, but also help build the value of the home. More value means more equity.

Are there valid reasons for renting? Sure! Many people move into a new area and aren't sure if they want to stay or where they want to settle. It is expensive to sell a property, so if you don't hold it long enough for it to appreciate past your costs of sale, you might lose money in the short-term. In this case, it might be wiser to rent for a while and buy when you are certain you know what you want. In other cases, you might not have the financial ability to purchase right away. Remember, there is no shame in being broke – the only shame is in not making progress towards improving yourself.

Sometimes, people find themselves at a point in their lives where flexibility is important and the responsibilities and commitments associated with home-ownership are more burdensome than beneficial. However, for most people, owning will virtually always outperform renting. Of course, as Russ would say, "Do the math and the math will tell you what to do!"

Let's take a look at a typical "Rent vs. Own" scenario on the following page.

Suppose you are in a combined federal and state tax bracket of 34% and we are comparing homes with similar utility:

	Rent	Own
Monthly Housing Payment[13]	<$ 1,800>	<$ 1,800>
Property Taxes (varies by location)	$ -0-	<$ 250>[14]
Property Insurance (estimated)	$ -0-	<$ 70>
Sub-Total of Outflow	<$ 1,800>	<$ 2,120>
Debt Reduction[15]	$ -0-	$ 300
Sub-Total adjusted for Debt Reduction	<$ 1,800>	<$ 1,820>
Homeowner's Deductions		
Interest on Home Loan	$ -0-	$ 1,500[16]
Property Tax	$ -0-	$ 250
Total Deductions	$ -0-	$ 1,750
x Marginal Tax Rate	0 %	34 %
Homeowner's Tax Credit	$ -0-	$ 595
Monthly Housing Payment	<$1,800>	<$ 2,120>
Homeowner's Tax Credits	$ -0-	$ 595
After-Tax Cash-Flow	<$1,800>	<$ 1,525>
Debt Reduction	$ -0-	$ 300
After-Tax Housing Expense	<$1,800>	<$ 1,225>

The brackets simply mean subtract, as in "cash is coming out of your pocket". No brackets mean add, as in "money goes into your pocket". Simple, right?

Notice that the cost to own (apart from considering the "benefit" a renter has in pushing the costs of any major home repair back to the landlord) is actually *less* than the cost to rent. But there's more...

---

[13] This is an arbitrary number we chose to use for comparison.
[14] Based on a $300,000 property value at 1.25% annual tax (property tax rates vary by area).
[15] We are assuming a 6% 30-year fully-amortized mortgage. Consider also that the amount of the payment which reduces debt will increase slowly with each subsequent payment. This means the owner's equity will actually grow faster over time.
[16] This is the interest portion of the monthly principal and interest payment based on a $300,000 6% fully-amortized 30-year loan.

Consider that the value of the home you buy will likely appreciate as time goes by, depending on where you happen to live. This would add net worth to your balance sheet thus further reducing your overall cost of ownership. On the other hand, consider that rent on a similar home would also probably increase over time.

Why is this? Because inflation has given both the home buyer and the home renter higher incomes to spend on housing. However, in either case, the owner of the asset, either you as the home *owner*, or if you are the home renter, your landlord (the property *owner*), is rewarded by inflation. If you are not the homeowner or landlord, but are only the renter, you are victimized by inflation, not rewarded. Remember – as inflation happens, so does equity. Those who *own* appreciating property will continue to be better off that those who merely rent.

To complete our analysis, let's now take a look at the total financial picture and assume annual housing appreciation of only 5%. Remember, the average appreciation rate for the last several decades is over 6%, so we are not using unrealistic assumptions.

If the house was purchased for $300,000 using 100% financing (6% interest fully-amortized for 30 years) with a principal and interest loan payment of $1,800 per month, and the house appreciated 5% per year, then you, as the home owner, would gain new passive equity (additional net worth on your balance sheet) of over $15,000 per year:

$300,000 x 5% annual appreciation = $15,000 new equity in one year
$15,000 new annual equity
   divided by 12 months   = $1,250 per month of new equity

Not bad! That's better than many part time jobs – and also more than most people are able to consistently save from their after-tax earned incomes each month. Now let's take a look at the numbers when we factor in appreciation:

	Rent	Own
After-Tax Housing Expense		
(before appreciation)	<$ 1,800>	<$ 1,225>
New Passive Equity from Appreciation	$ -0-	$ 1,250
Net Housing Expense after Appreciation	<$ 1,800>	$ 25

Wow! The house can actually pay you $25 a month to live there! Meanwhile, the renter's housing expense continues to rise with inflation. By comparison the homeowner's loan payment is potentially fixed with a fixed-rate mortgage. (NOTE: Please do not construe this as our endorsement of 30-year fixed-rate mortgages. Proper loan selection is another topic we will explore later. Suffice it to say, the big benefit to home ownership, besides being king of your own castle, is that as a home *owner*, when equity happens, it doesn't happen to the landlord, equity happens to *you!)*

• • •

James had been renting apartments ever since he left home for college. By age thirty-five he could remember at least fifteen different landlords. Although each apartment was not necessarily nicer or bigger than the last one, his rent consistently edged up. His friend Betty had been a homeowner for two years and kept telling him he should buy a home of his own. James knew with $20,000 in the bank he was better off than many of his friends, but he still didn't see how he could get into a home without spending every cent he had saved. He also dreaded the idea of a thirty-year commitment to a loan payment.

However, Betty was persistent. She explained there were many first-time buyer programs available in the area and James could probably get a loan with as little as 3% down. She also reminded him he had been paying rent every month for the past 200 months and he had nothing to show for it! She argued that at the very least a loan payment would slowly decrease his loan balance over time and, if he had a fixed-rate loan, his payments would not continue to go up like his rent had been doing.

James was paying $1,800 per month for a two-bedroom, one-bathroom apartment in a nice complex about ten minutes from where he worked. Betty's mortgage consultant ran the numbers and showed James how, when taking his tax situation into consideration, he could afford a larger housing payment without any real change in his non-housing spending. The mortgage consultant explained that James's $1,800 rent payment, when adjusted for taxes, equated to a $2,300 mortgage payment. In other words, when taking into consideration the tax benefits of ownership, there was no substantial difference between an $1800 a month rent payment and a $2,300 per month house payment!

A loan payment of $2,300 at the prevailing interest rate would service a mortgage of approximately $275,000. With a 5% down payment, James could afford a house with a purchase price of $290,000. Working with Betty's real estate agent, James found a suitable home within five miles of his apartment.

As a homeowner, James not only enjoyed the pride and stability of ownership, but he received the benefit of rising prices. Five years later, his $290,000 house appraised for $425,000. Equity happened to James!

• • •

One side benefit of home ownership is that it helps you establish an excellent mortgage payment history (assuming you make your payment on time). Managing your mortgage and other debts wisely will increase your credit-worthiness, which is an invaluable asset as a real estate investor. Lenders base a significant portion of their approval criteria on your track record of timely payments on previous and existing loans.

Buying a home also sets an excellent example for your children and the other important people in your life. Through your actions, you will be demonstrating that home ownership is attainable. In time, they will see the benefits of owning a home by watching what happens to you. Also, developing roots in a neighborhood can have a lasting effect for generations. Home ownership exemplifies commitment. Families that rent tend to produce renters. Families that own are more likely to produce future owners. Don't underestimate the power of your example.

There's another reason you might consider buying a home. If you buy in an area which appreciates at only an average rate or better, there is a very good chance when you settle everything many years down the road, you will have lived in the home for *free*. Really!

• • •

In 1989, Robert bought a residence in San Jose, California for $172,500. Ten years later, the home was worth $385,000. As Robert considered putting the home on the market, he ran the numbers. During the ten years he owned the property, he had paid $160,321 in principal, interest, taxes and insurance. His initial down payment was $17,250 with a purchase loan of $155,250. After ten years of payments, the loan balance had been reduced to just under $130,000.

Analyzing the numbers, Robert had an epiphany that forever changed the way he looked at home ownership. He realized that every single dollar he had ever paid for the home was still sitting there in the form of equity. In other words, if he sold the house at $375,000, paid the sales costs of approximately 8%, and then paid off his now $130,000 loan, he would still walk away from the property with approximately $215,000. Yet during the ten years he lived there, he had only paid a total of $ 178,000, including his initial down payment! Essentially, he had lived there for free for ten years, received tax benefits which helped reduce his taxable income, and all the while was "saving" around $300 each month by doing nothing more than living in the house![17] Equity begins at home.

• • •

For additional perspective, imagine if Robert decided in 1989 to rent instead of purchase. Renting would have "saved" him the $17,250 down payment. Rent for a comparable home back then was approximately $800 per month, whereas his mortgage payment was just over $1,000, so renting would have "saved" him another $200 per month. Of course, rents in the area increased an average of 6% per year during over the ten years, so at the end of the period, his rent would have risen to about $1,400 per month.

To keep the math simple, assume Renter Robert had a really great landlord who never raised his rent. At $800 per month Robert would have paid $96,000 in rent in ten years. This is more than *half* of the $172,000 value of the property when he moved in!

After spending $96,000 in rent (with *after*-tax dollars) and receiving no tax breaks and no appreciation, how much would Renter Robert have to show for those ten years? Let's see…that would be *nothing*. Well, no, that's not completely true. He would probably have a very grateful landlord.

Now which do you think is better, renting or owning?

---

[17] $215,000 net new equity less the $178,000 paid in equals $37,000 of gain. This represents $3,700 per year or more than $300 per month!

CHAPTER 4
Leverage Is Super, Man!

Faster than a Speeding Bullet!
The Power of Time Leverage

Though real estate moves more slowly than most financial markets, your equity growth can still happen very quickly. Leveraging time is the critical factor. One of the best lessons an investor can learn is that "a quick nickel beats a long dime." In other words, the speed at which your money returns to you with profit can have as much impact on the velocity of your growth (rate of return) as does the actual gross profit in the deal.

Consider this: If you make $10,000 profit rehabbing a property and your friend makes $20,000 rehabbing a similar property, then who has the better return? It sounds like a trick question, right? At first glance, it seems the $20,000 profit is better. But is it?

The answer is, as is often the case, it depends! If you made $10,000 in 3 months and your friend took 12 months to make his $20,000, then even though his profit *amount* is twice yours, your speed, or *rate* of return, is actually twice as good. If you each invested $100,000, then your absolute return of $10,000 is 10%, while your friend's $20,000 is 20%. If you stop there, your friend wins.

However, your money returned in 3 months, which produces an annualized rate of return (velocity) of 40% because there are four 3-month periods (quarters) in a year. If you make 10% per quarter, your annualized return is 10% x 4 or 40%. Your friend's annualized rate of return is only 20% because it took him 12 months (1 year) to make his profit (20% x 1 is 20%). Your friend made twice the money, but it took four times as long.

It's amazing how many people will labor on a project for months, eagerly put the property on the market, but then hold out waiting for top dollar. Meanwhile, the property sits vacant month after month. Wouldn't it be better to take less and get your working capital and profit back so you can move on to the next project? Keep your money moving!

Pay attention to the velocity of your money by always calculating your annualized rate of return. It's easy:

$$\frac{\text{Profit}}{\text{Investment}} = \text{Absolute Return}$$

$$\frac{\text{Absolute Return}}{\text{\# of Months Invested}} = \text{Monthly Rate of Return}$$

$$\text{Monthly Rate of Return X 12} = \text{Annualized Return}$$

While it may seem enticing to wait for more profit, you must determine how delays may deteriorate your annualized rate of return, especially if you have other projects waiting for your investment capital – which you should!

Sometimes novice investors hold on too long for fear they won't find another deal. If your property-sourcing network isn't keeping you supplied with a steady pipeline of deals, then your problem isn't profit margin; it's inadequate inventory. Again, if your average return is 10% and you turn your projects every 3 months, you have an annualized return of 40%. Conversely, if you have a 40% profit, but it takes you 20 months, then your annualized return is only 24%. Go back and plug different numbers into the formulas to create different scenarios. You'll soon find that if you have plenty of deals in your pipeline, the 10% margin deals that turn more quickly can actually produce more velocity for your investment capital.

• • •

By most standards, Dick had done quite well finding properties in need of work and fixing them up for a profit. As he moved from one project to the next, he was getting better at estimating repair costs and finding good people to help him. He also had the benefit of a very active and appreciating real estate market. Dick found a large 3-bedroom home with a converted garage which he thought had promising potential. Robert served as Dick's real estate agent, negotiated an excellent price, and handled the transaction. After the acquisition closed, Dick and his crew immediately went to work revitalizing the property.

This house was located in a neighborhood which could definitely support a larger, newer home, so Dick set about making some major changes, including transforming the previous garage into a huge master bedroom suite and adding a brand new two-car garage. He also totally renovated the kitchen with top of the line cabinets, appliances, and beautiful granite counters. Quality touches like crown molding, under-counter lighting and a central vacuum system added much to the home. However, all this extra work also extended the project's completion time from an estimated four months to nearly eight months. Twice as long! Even though Dick thought he could get a higher resale price for the fancier home, his profit would need to be twice as much in order to simply maintain the same velocity on his money. Worse, Dick had more dollars at risk since the investment in the project was now larger. To compensate for this, Dick wanted to more than double his profit on the project.

Unfortunately, a funny thing happened on the way to market. Residential real estate sales in the area began to stall. Prices on expensive homes were actually declining as properties languished on the market. Those sellers who needed to sell were forced to accept lower prices. Because Dick wasn't an owner-occupant, it was critically important for him to sell, not only to recover his working capital and realize his profit, but to stop the monthly expenses of holding a vacant property.

Dick had worked hard on the project and even though the market was soft, he remained determined to get his price. He felt he'd built a million dollar home and didn't want to concede that the market did not currently agree. A few months earlier Dick probably could have gotten his price, but with the new market conditions, Robert, as Dick's real estate agent, suggested $899,000 was a more realistic price to get the house sold quickly.

Dick was firm, so Robert and his team listed the property at $999,999 and waited for some interest from the market. They waited…and waited…and waited. When Robert's team could no longer commit to holding open houses both days every single weekend like Dick wanted, Dick decided to hold the property open himself, sometimes enlisting the help of friends and family. Weeks went by without an offer. Dick started devising creative financing scenarios anytime someone expressed genuine interest, but couldn't afford his price.

As more time passed, Dick became increasingly desperate to sell the property. He had far too much money tied up in the project. Worse, each month he was pouring more money into debt service, insurance, maintenance, and utilities. He realized he had to do something. Begrudgingly, Dick conceded a price reduction, but refused to go below $949,000. Unfortunately, the market had continued to decline. After another month of no offers, he dropped the price to $935,000. Finally, Robert agreed to release him from the listing contract, so Dick could attempt to sell the property himself without paying any real estate commission. Dick priced the property at $899,000, but now he did not have the benefit of the mass exposure of the Multiple Listing Service.

By this time, Dick was busy working on other projects to make ends meet, so his father, mother, wife and friends all took turns holding the house open weekend after weekend after weekend. Eventually, Dick's father helped secure a buyer using a lease-to-own strategy at a price of $860,000. This deal only put $20,000 into Dick's pocket, but at least someone else would be paying the monthly expenses.

When all was said and done, Dick admitted to Robert that if he would only have listed the property at $899,000 right from the beginning, it would have probably sold faster, for a higher price, on better terms, and with a higher net profit than he ultimately realized.

How did Robert know what to price the property at? Was it his years of experience in real estate sales? Sure, experience helps, but the fact is the numbers don't lie. Robert simply performed a Comparable Market Analysis (CMA) and saw what similar properties in the area were selling for. Then, taking into consideration the temporary downward trend, he recommended a price designed to catch the attention of the local agents and buyers when it matters the most – the moment the property is first introduced to the market.

• • •

The preceding story brings up a crucial point when it comes to selling real estate: The *market* determines the price! What a seller needs or wants to get from a property is interesting and important, but only to the seller. The buyer doesn't care what the seller thinks, wants or needs. It doesn't matter how much you paid for the property, what your loan is like, how much the upgrades cost you, how much down payment you have in the deal, or how much profit you want or need. *What matters is how much a ready and able buyer is willing to pay.* This can be a hard lesson for most people to understand, especially homeowners, but the sooner you accept it, the better off you will be. In a free market economy, it is the market, not the seller's needs or the real estate agent's promise, which determines the value of a property. This is why it is always important to get a current CMA on any project to make sure you can get what you need out of it – *before* you get into it. Then leave yourself a little wiggle room in case market conditions change.

Remember, while making a profit is important, getting a property sold quickly so you can get on to the next one is more important than getting absolute top dollar. A quick nickel is better than a long dime. When it comes to investing, speed matters.

More Powerful than a Locomotive!
The Power of Financial Leverage
Earlier, we mentioned one of the greatest benefits of real estate investing is the ability to use financial leverage. Now, we want to explore the concept of leverage in greater detail.

Leverage supercharges appreciation! Take a look at the chart on the following page.

Equity	Leverage	2% Appreciation	5% Appreciation	10% Appreciation
100%	1:1	2%	5%	10%
50%	2:1	4%	10%	20%
25%	4:1	8%	20%	40%
20%	5:1	10%	25%	50%
10%	10:1	20%	50%	100%
5%	20:1	40%	100%	200%
3%	33:1	66%	165%	333%

Don't just gloss over this chart before making sure you understand what it is saying! For those of you, like Robert, who relate more to real-life examples than the geeky spreadsheets Russ likes, here's an example:

Suppose an investor has $100,000 available to invest. He might choose to buy a $200,000 property for $100,000 down and get a $100,000 mortgage for the balance. At 50% down, there is a very good chance this property will provide positive cash-flow. Positive cash-flow sounds like a wonderful thing, but before deciding, wait until we visit the topic in Chapter 9. For now, let's just look at the "equity-on-equity return" or what we call the "equity growth rate" using an appreciation factor of only 5%:

- A $100,000 down payment on a $200,000 property is 50% purchase equity. This produces 2:1 financial leverage ($200,000/$100,000 = 2:1)

- Appreciation of 5% on $200,000 produces $10,000 of new passive equity ($200,000 x 5% = $10,000)

- New passive equity of $10,000 on purchase equity of $100,000 produces a new equity on purchase equity growth rate of 10% ($10,000 / $100,000 = 10%).

- So, 2:1 leverage x 5% appreciation equals 10% growth on purchase equity, or a 10% equity growth rate.

But, what if we took the same $100,000 and made a 25% down payment on a property? Now we are controlling a $400,000 property with only 25% purchase equity, thereby gaining a more powerful leverage ratio of 4:1.

- $100,000 down on a $400,000 property = 25% down ($100,000/$400,000) or 4:1 leverage ($400,000/$100,000)

- Appreciation of 5% on $400,000 property = $20,000 of new passive equity

- New passive equity of $20,000 on purchase equity of $100,000 produces a new equity on purchase equity growth rate of 20% ($20,000 / $100,000 = 20%).

- Therefore, 4:1 leverage x 5% appreciation equals a 20% equity growth rate

Do you see how easy it is to get 20% growth on equity with real estate that "only" appreciates 5% per year?

If 25% down is better than 50% down, wouldn't 10% down be better than 25%? Let's run the numbers and see:

- $100,000 down on a $1,000,000 property = 10% down or 10:1 financial leverage

- Appreciation at 5% per year x $1,000,000 = $50,000

- Equity Growth Rate = $50,000/$100,000 or 50% (10:1 leverage x 5% appreciation)

Some investors might be concerned about using 10:1 leverage

because it can be challenging to find a property that generates enough cash-flow to cover the debt service and expenses. In other words, you might temporarily experience (gasp!) negative cash-flow. If the prospect of negative cash-flow makes you nervous, we hope to give you a new perspective in Chapter 9, so keep reading! For now, we just want you to understand that financial leverage is an important key to maintaining the velocity of your equity growth.

Able to Leap Tall Buildings –
The Power of Personal Relationships

Your ability to **L**everage **E**quity, **A**ssets, and **P**eople can help you LEAP forward and create enormous wealth in short periods of time. Combining financial and time leverage will help you acquire a larger property portfolio than you could ever hope to do simply by working at your job (trading time for dollars), paying taxes, living below your means, and then converting your after-tax savings into down payments. Because most people only think of real estate acquisition in these terms, they aren't able to accomplish much at all.

When you purchase income property, the less down payment you use, the greater your financial leverage. As we've discovered, financial leverage magnifies the benefits of appreciation and improves your equity growth rate.

The equity in the property is a combination of the purchase equity (down payment), the pay down of the loan (amortization), and the increase in the market value of the property (appreciation or passive equity). Some of the market value appreciation may be due to some effort on your part (forced equity). We will talk more in Chapter 8 about the various methods of building new equity.

The property is the asset you control. It is the thing which appreciates based on supply, demand, and the market's capacity-to-pay, thus allowing equity to happen to you. The more property (top-line real estate) you can control, the more equity will happen to you.

This brings us to the most powerful of the resources available to you – people!

Barbara Streisand once sang, "People... people who leverage people, are the wealthiest people in the world." Well, maybe that's not exactly what she sang, but she should have because it's true!

Before we go any further, we want to, as former President Richard Nixon used to say, make it perfectly clear: We are NOT advocating using people, harming people, taking advantage of people, or in any other way stepping on others to climb to the top. We are firm believers in win-win relationships. In our business, our #1 core value is "Relationships for Life". We believe our clients, members, service providers and associates are like our family. We expect to have to face them regularly for many years to come. We believe the most valuable component of any business is "good will" – positive feelings people have when they think of you and your business.

When you are an income property owner, your tenants are your customers. Providing a safe, well-maintained place to live or work is your responsibility – it's how you earn your rental income. So even if you are becoming rich using the tenant's money, if the tenants aren't yet ready to buy, is it a bad thing if they rent from you? We don't think so!

Our second core value is "**T**ogether **E**veryone **A**chieves **M**ore" or TEAM. The people who work with us aren't second-class citizens and they don't work *for* us. They work *with* us to earn a living for themselves and their families. We work together towards common *team* goals, but each individual works towards his or her own *personal* goals and objectives. Does this mean everybody likes us? No. As leaders, we sometimes have to do things that aren't fun or easy. Not everyone fits on the team or is doing their best and sometimes we have to make changes. That's true with employees, tenants, service providers and customers. When you make those hard decisions, you aren't popular, but it doesn't make you evil or wrong.

The point is that those of us who own businesses and rental properties are in a position to profit from the efforts of other people. As long as it is done fairly and with a genuine concern for others, then it is not just "not bad," but we would argue it is actually very good! You should not feel guilty if you position yourself to profit from the earnings and efforts of others, as long as you are providing fair value to the relationship.

There are two major ways to leverage people. In regard to real estate investing, when you purchase an income property, in addition to acquiring the property, you acquire the income or cash-flow. Where does this cash-flow come from? The vast majority comes from the tenants. Some of it, as we've already discussed comes from your rich Uncle.

When you own income property, the tenants go to work or run their businesses to earn a living. Then, they pay you for the use of your property to live in or operate their businesses. Think about that! These people get up every day, get dressed and go to work. You don't have to supervise them, pay for workman's compensation insurance or other benefits, or worry about paying for vacations or sick time. Yet every month you get a portion of their income in the form of the rent they pay you for the use of your property. The more of these people you have in your "employ," the more income you get!

How else do we leverage people? One of our favorite stories, and we tell it often in our seminars, is the story of Henry Ford. We're not sure where the story came from, or even if it's true, but it sure makes the point.

The story is that Henry Ford, the founder of Ford Motor Company, was getting older. The company's board of directors became concerned about Mr. Ford's ability to effectively run the company and they made a move to have Mr. Ford removed from his position as President. Through a series of legal proceedings, Mr.

Ford found himself before a judge in a hearing to determine his competency as a business executive.

When Mr. Ford was brought before the judge, the judge explained the purpose of the proceeding and advised Mr. Ford he would be questioned about his knowledge of the automobile industry. Mr. Ford acknowledged his understanding and the hearing began.

"Mr. Ford," asked the judge, "please tell us what you know about transmissions."

Mr. Ford looked directly at the judge and responded, "Your honor, my office is located in downtown Detroit at the top of one of the tallest buildings in the city. In my office, I have a large desk at which I work every day. On the right side of the top of my desk I have a wonderful device called a telephone. This is not just any telephone, but a telephone with a vast number of buttons on it. One of those many buttons is marked with the letter 'T'."

The judge listened intently as Mr. Ford continued, "When I have to make a decision that requires knowledge about transmissions, I pick up my phone and press the 'T' button. When I do, a list of the world's foremost authorities on transmissions is presented. When I call any one of them, they pick up the phone and are prepared to answer any question I may have about transmissions."

"Your honor," Mr. Ford explained, "I am a businessman, not a technician. I rely on a team of technical experts to provide me the information I need to make wise business decisions. Like my assembly line, I find this a much more efficient way to accomplish more in less time."

Mr. Ford concluded, "And that, your honor is what I know about transmissions."

Clearly, Henry Ford understood how to leverage people to do more, better and faster than he could ever do on his own. We call this having a "Power Rolodex".[18]

As a businessperson, you simply have to be a good "generalist" and "strategist". A generalist is someone who has a fundamental conceptual understanding of a technical topic. For example, a generalist would know when and why a new roof should be installed, but lacks the technical expertise to do it themselves – like a "general contractor". Another example is a doctor who is a general practitioner. He may know you need heart surgery, but lacks the technical expertise to perform it, so he refers you to a specialist.

A "strategist" is someone who knows how to take a vision (an idea, dream or concept) and distill it into "strategic objectives" – the milestone accomplishments which need to occur on the path to achieving the vision. A strategist is good at setting priorities so that the right things get done in the right order.

"Technicians" are experts at doing the tactical (hands-on) detailed work necessary to accomplish a strategic objective. In real estate investing, these are the lawyers, accountants, mortgage brokers, tax advisors, real estate brokers, construction contractors, etc. For example, you may need to evict a non-paying tenant. As a strategist, you know maintaining a "no tolerance policy" for non-paying tenants is important to the profitability of your building, but you lack the technical expertise to perform a lawful eviction. In this case, you would call on a professional eviction service, your property manager, or your real estate attorney to handle the technical details.

To be an effective real estate investor, you are best served to build strong working relationships with a team of people who can help with the technical details. This may seem obvious and elementary,

---

[18] Before there were PDAs, laptops and the proliferation of other electronic databases, people who worked in the old days (like us) had a rotary file which stored contact information – usually in the form of business cards. One of the most popular brands of these rotary files was called "Rolodex".

but we see so many people waste time (the most precious of all non-renewable resources) trying to become a "master of all". They want to know, in detail, how to do everything. The problem is that there is just too much to learn in one lifetime. If you spend all your time studying the technical details of everything, you don't have any time left for actually doing anything.

Other people's knowledge, talent, and efforts are essential to your success; therefore relationship capital is just as valuable, if not more so, than financial capital. Be sure to invest strategically and regularly in relationships, and in developing yourself as a generalist and a strategist.

The Bob Factor

You've heard the age-old adage, "It's not what you know, but who you know!" You will discover this to be absolutely true in real estate investing! As you continue your investment education, work to form relationships with people who have knowledge, expertise, or experience in areas in which you do not.

• • •

Bob the real estate broker (Broker Bob), called Bob the loan broker (Loan Bob), looking for a quick source of capital for an investment opportunity Broker Bob had found. Broker Bob was a seasoned and successful real estate investor, but most of his cash was fully deployed into other investments. Loan Bob worked regularly with a private-money lender also named Bob (Money Bob) and approached him for a quick, low-documentation loan for Broker Bob. Though Money Bob barely knew Broker Bob, he knew of Broker Bob's reputation in the real estate industry. He also knew Loan Bob had made many conventional loans for Broker Bob in the past. On just the strength of Broker Bob's reputation and his personal relationship with Loan Bob, Money Bob arranged for the financing and funded Broker Bob's loan in just seventy-two hours!

• • •

Believe it or not, the real people behind this true story are all named Bob! The moral of the story is that when you really need something to happen to pull a transaction together, you will be happy when you have a large network of competent and supportive people – no matter what their names are!

When bestselling author Robert Kiyosaki (*Rich Dad, Poor Dad*) joined us in the radio studio to do a show, he told us how his rich dad taught him, "real estate investing is a team sport." We agree! To be successful in this business, it is imperative for you to assemble a team of mentors, advisors and practitioners to help you. We call this team your Advisory Board. Your Advisory Board can help you save time, find better deals, learn more and faster, and brainstorm solutions to almost any problem that may arise. The right Advisory Board will enable you to accomplish more in less time with less risk. You don't have to know everything about real estate, you just have to know an expert in each discipline who understands your particular situation. *The best advisors have a good understanding of each other's disciplines and work well together.*

In order to assemble a truly winning Advisory Board, you will have to think differently than most people. Most investors are looking for what they can get from a relationship. You need to figure out what you can *give* to a relationship. Think about how can you add value to your advisors. When you find someone you want on your team, your mission is to discover what he needs, then commit yourself to helping him get it. We realize this seems backwards, but if you do what everybody else does, then you are likely to achieve what everybody else does. This may not sound bad until you realize the average person in America retires broke and dependent upon government and/or family to survive. On the other hand, if you want extraordinary results, then you must think and act differently than the average person. Part of this new mindset is learning to "give to get".

"Weenies" is our affectionate term for people who are always trying to get things cheaper, cut corners, and do as little as possible to get by. They pit service providers against one another hoping for the best price, but forget about value and relationship. When you go to an advisor, don't you want their very *best* efforts and advice? If they have established their pricing and you decide you don't want to pay it, then don't ask for their service. Admit that you can't afford them and go find someone cheaper. If you're right that the advisor is over-priced, then no one will engage him and eventually he will lower the price in order to attract customers. On the other hand, if other people are paying the advisor the requested rate, why should you get the same service for less? When you need service, do you want to be the most important or the *least* important client?

Successful people take into account the power of relationships. They seek the strength found in mutual commitment. Of course, successful people prudently search for the right service providers, but once they select someone to join the team, they make a commitment. Remember, commitment is a two-way street. If you want a service provider, a business partner, or even a spouse or child to give you their best effort, then you should be prepared to give them *yours*.

Suppose you need a loan. You can go to several different loan brokers and let them compete for your business based on rates or terms. Another approach is to select one loan broker based on reputation or recommendation and let them earn your business by working hard to find you the best rates or terms. Do you see the difference? If your loan broker knows you are entrusting him to find the best loan, he will work hard for your business. If he knows you are shopping your deal to several brokers, he will likely put your request to the bottom of the pile. Lack of commitment on your part is rewarded with lack of commitment on his part.

Might the loan broker use your loyalty as an opportunity to gouge you? After all, loan brokers get paid a commission. How do you know your agent isn't giving you a more expensive loan just to earn a fatter fee? The answer is based on the relationship. Sure, your loan broker could overcharge you a few times and make some extra commission dollars in the short-term. We call this "sales myopia" because it is a short-sighted business practice. But what happens when you find out? The loan broker not only loses all of your future business, but also your future referrals.

On the other hand, suppose your loan broker works hard to get you the best loan program, thereby building your confidence and loyalty. Which is a better business decision? Do you plan on using more or less financing in the future? When your loan broker invests time and effort into developing good will with you by providing a fair price and good service, he expects to earn your long-term loyalty. This builds stability and profitability into *his* loan business and into *your* investing business.

It is also important to consider what your time is worth. A friend once bragged about saving $10 on a flight. When asked how he did it, he explained he checked several travel websites repeatedly until he found the cheapest fare. When pressed, he revealed he spent more than four hours shopping. Would you work four hours to save $10? This would value your time at $2.50 per hour.

With real estate, if you want to find an investment property in a hot area, you can enlist the help of several real estate agents and hope they will all bring you prospective properties. Another option is to find the best agent you can, develop a strong relationship, and empower him to search for an outstanding property that meets your investment objectives. At first, it might seem like having many agents working on your behalf is better, but in the real world it is not. The attitude that says, "If you're the first person to find me a great deal, I'll buy it from you" will only elicit effort from desperate agents with nothing better to do.

The only commodity a service provider such as a loan broker, real estate agent, attorney or tax advisor has is their time. Like you, they want to invest it where there is the greatest likelihood of making a return. If you play the "multiple agents" game, don't you think they will be play the "multiple buyers" game? If you have several agents looking for properties for you and those agents have several buyers looking for properties, why should they send a great deal *your* way? Why not give it to another, more loyal buyer who will appreciate the opportunity and reward the agent with more future business and referrals? Commitment is a two-way street, right?

Conversely, if you'll agree to use just one agent (the right agent) in a marketplace, your loyalty will typically be rewarded. You'll get *first* access to the best properties. Once you establish yourself as a serious investor with the ability to close transactions, you'll continue to get great service and excellent opportunities.

We realize this mindset flies in the face of what many other real estate investment books say. Many other authors tell you to get lots of agents working for you. That sounds smart when you're sitting on a plane or curled up on the couch reading a book. In the real world, things are a different. Do not underestimate the power and value of good will, or the destructive power of bad will.

• • •

Stan was exceptionally bright, financially literate and eager to learn. He was also in the position of many high-salaried employees who make lots of money, but spend almost all of it. After reading some books on real estate investment, he decided to start putting some money away in anticipation of one day buying a home. A friend referred him to our mentoring clubs where he started learning more about investing. Because Stan was single and worked primarily out of his home, he had flexibility with regard to the location of the property he would buy to live in.

Each month at mentoring club, Stan watched as we presented case studies of properties. He started to wonder if it might be better for him to buy an investment property first and continue to rent his residence, rather than starting out by buying a house to live in. As always, the answer to this question is, "It depends!"

After clarifying his objectives, Stan decided to start with a small investment property. Through one of our property showcases,[19] he purchased a single family home in a low-end rental neighborhood. As with many properties in tougher areas, Stan experienced some challenges. Uncertain we were really the right team for him, Stan started to look elsewhere for investments and mentoring.

For a while, Stan was looking for deals everywhere. He called on newspaper ads, talked to FSBO's (For-Sale-By-Owner), and even sent out post cards to property owners. He eventually got into contract to purchase a house which seemed like a good fix-up opportunity, but couldn't quite pull it off. Meanwhile he was shopping lenders trying to find the "best deal" on the financing.

One night after a seminar, Stan approached each of us independently and told us he'd reached a decision regarding his investments. He admitted he'd been wasting time using a scattered approach and wanted to get rifle-like focused by committing to use our team 100% for both his property acquisition and financing. Of course, once Stan committed to us, we in turn committed our team's time and resources to helping

---

[19] Property showcases are group presentations of investment properties to pre-screened investors.

him. Soon afterwards, we helped him acquire several properties through our showcases and he was well on his way to real estate riches!

• • •

I Know You, You Know Me, Come Together, Right Now

Your success in real estate investing will be in direct proportion to the number of people who know you, like you, trust you, and know you are in the real estate investment business. The good news is you already have people in your life (hopefully!) who know you, like you, and trust you. Now you just need to find a way to let them know you are serious about real estate investing, without being obnoxious or pretentious.

Make sure people you meet know that you invest in real estate. Tell them what you specialize in, which pre-supposes you have developed a specialty you are focusing on. If you haven't developed a niche yet, we strongly recommend that you do. Rather than becoming a jack-of-all-trades-but-master-of-none, set out to "get rich in a niche". This isn't to suggest that you try to become a "master technician". You can be a generalist who specializes in a product type or area.

One benefit of specialization is you will get leads and referrals from other investors. Once others perceive you as an expert in a particular area, even those who might have considered you a competitor will seek your advice. This may open the door for joint ventures and deals from other investors who don't know how to put the transaction together. It is possible to have more than one area of specialty, but before moving on to something new, make sure you have either mastered or chosen to abandon the first area. There is power in focus. Success in any discipline is gained by mastering one skill at a time and then building up a portfolio of experience and abilities over time. Be steadfast!

Even if your investment business is part-time, have business cards printed with your contact information. Again, if you have a specific area of expertise, make sure your cards indicate this, and then pass your cards out freely! You never know where your next hot lead is going to come from. Russ frequently reminds people, "You are just one relationship away from an explosion in your business!"

• • •

Russ was doing some research for a seminar we wanted to put on. He went to Amazon.com's website and did a keyword search for books about real estate. The site returned an overwhelming list of over 2,500 titles! Undeterred, Russ patiently scrolled through the titles and about 400 books into the list, something caught Russ's eye: a book on investing in real estate using your self-directed individual retirement account. It was selling for $149.

"Interesting topic," thought Russ, "but expensive!" Suddenly, Robert's voice echoed through Russ's mind, "Compared to what?" So Russ decided to go ahead and order it.

When the book came, Russ read it. Then he logged onto the author's website and found that his office was located in Oakland, California, just about 40 miles north of where Russ was located in San Jose. He also found that the author conducted seminars on the topic.

Being a seminar junkie, Russ signed up for an eight-hour class on investing in real estate using a self-directed retirement account. At the seminar, Russ did more than simply listen. He used the opportunity to network and struck up a conversation with the author. The short of it is that Russ invited the author to conduct a seminar for our investor network. Unbeknownst to Russ, once the seminar was scheduled, the author's company posted the event, along with Russ's contact information, on their website.

One day, Russ's phone rang. On the other end of the line was a real estate agent in Phoenix, Arizona who was surfing the Net looking for information about real estate investing. He called Russ to see about attending the seminar. Russ used the opportunity to ask the agent about his business and the Phoenix market.

As it turned out, Robert was planning a trip to Phoenix for some other business, so Russ called him and suggested he try to get together with the agent. Even though he had a very full schedule, Robert (being the open-minded, opportunity seeking person he is), found time for the meeting.

Robert met with the agent, who introduced Robert to the broker the agent worked for. The broker turned out to be one of the top brokers in Phoenix, as well as an active real estate developer. He was well-connected to other valuable people, including lenders, property managers and contractors. To this day, this broker continues to be a steady source of investment property opportunities for our investor network. We have done *millions* of dollars of business with and through this broker!

• • •

We could tell you story after story of amazing opportunities which developed out of just one relationship, but you get the point.

Never forget, you are just one relationship away from an explosion in your business – and you never know where that one relationship will come from. However, one thing is certain. No one is going to come over to your house, pull you off your couch and introduce you to an important contact. You still have to get out in the real world and network with real people.

In our training programs for real estate and loan professionals, we urge them not to be "secret agents". If you want to be successful, you must tell the world what you do. Contrary to what some teach, the best deals are *not* found in the newspaper – or even the Multiple Listing Services. Often, the best opportunities come through inside information. Someone knows someone else who has a property or a project available. In the real estate profession, properties available for sale, but not yet publicly advertised are called "pocket listings". Agents who are actively building relationships with the investor community are often aware of, and sometimes control, these pocket listings. You want to be the *first* person to come to mind when these deals pop up. Have we stressed the importance of developing strong personal relationships?

Unlike the stock market, where (as Martha Stewart can tell you) it is illegal to buy and sell on "inside information", in real estate it is not only legal, but preferred! So let the world know you are a ready, willing and able buyer of investment property.

As friends and acquaintances discover what you do, they will be able to refer people who can help you. Many of the best business relationships we have came from referrals of people we know and meet in our *non*-business activities. You will find this business to be more of a lifestyle than a job. Anywhere there are people, there is opportunity.

Look for strategic alliances to leverage your time. We focus our time on developing relationships with "centers of influence" – people who have the ability to communicate with and influence a large group of people.

As you continue to add strong members to your team, you will naturally get better at what you do. Noted speaker David D'arcangelo points out, "You will become the sum total of the five people you spend the most time with." Very true! Therefore, choose your friends wisely.

Finally, guard your reputation in the marketplace. Your reputation is one of the most valuable assets you have. Like most industries, the real estate investment business is a very small world. If you plan to be in this business for the long haul, be sure that the way you present yourself in the market keeps the big picture in mind.

Do you want to be known for your integrity? Is your word your bond? Do you make good on your promises and stand by your commitments? Do you think win-win? Do you sincerely want to make a positive difference in someone's life? Do you want to make a contribution to the world?

Conversely, do you want to be known as "Louie Low-ball", the guy who is always submitting ridiculously low offers? Or "Negative Nellie", who is always complaining about how bad everything is and how everyone is out to get you? What about "Tight-wad Tim", always negotiating commissions down and trying to "nickel and dime" every tenant, vendor, and seller?

How you are perceived in the market place depends on your actions. It is what you do that matters most. Not what you say, or what you intend, or what you suppose, or what you convince people to believe at the beginning. Actions speak louder than almost anything. Robert constantly reminds us, "Time will either promote you or expose you." If you want to develop a great reputation, simply act as if the whole world is watching...because it is.

EQUITY HAPPENS™

SECTION 2

The Good Deals

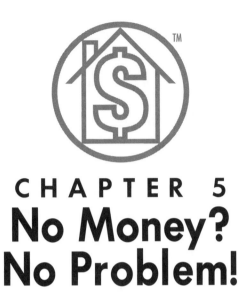

CHAPTER 5
No Money?
No Problem!

If you stay up late enough, you'll inevitably find yourself watching one of those television infomercial gurus explaining how, for a nominal charge payable in three easy payments, anyone with a pulse can make hundreds of thousands of dollars with real estate virtually overnight. At 3:30 in the morning, it sure seems like a good idea to call one of those helpful operators who are standing by. However, there are two harsh realities you must face.

First, there's an excellent chance you'll never even open the shrink-wrap. Don't feel too badly. That's just human nature. We've met many would-be investors who bought the "secret system" and are just waiting until they have a little spare time to get started. Their problem isn't lack of information; it's lack of motivation and discipline. It's one of the reasons we've included so much commentary on developing and maintaining a winning attitude.

Secondly, while there are certainly some clever ideas presented in the infomercial materials, many of them simply won't work for the average person in the real world. Writing a hundred offers a week *sounds* like a great way to utilize the *Law of Large Numbers*, but in the real world, do you have the time for this kind of approach? Finding assumable loans and owner-carry-back financing for the down payment sounds intriguing, but how many of those deals are really out there? Convincing a distraught owner to sign over their equity to you for pennies on the dollar might sound profitable, until someone threatens to punch you!

When people in our seminars ask, "Do those programs advertised on TV really work?" we say, "Sure, they work extremely well...for the people selling them!"

Please understand what we're saying here. We're obviously not against education and we certainly don't think we are the only teachers with something valid to say. The fact is, if you bought every get-rich-quick real estate program you came across, you would certainly find some great nuggets of useful information. Unfortunately, you'd also hear plenty of bogus advice that would do little more than waste your time. Our concern is that beginning investors might not be able to tell the difference.

At our live events, we make fun of the run-to-the-back-of-the-room-with-your-credit-card seminars that are designed to either sell you another pile of books and CD's, or sell you into the 3-day $5,000 seminar where you will learn all of the "real" secrets. We don't criticize because we think books, videos and seminars are bad investments. In fact, our attitude is quite the contrary! When we attend a seminar, we buy most everything they have. We think that even if we gain just one truly valuable idea and use it, it justifies the time and expense necessary to find it.

The main reason we aren't fond of "hypesters", who seem to be primarily interested in running your credit card through their machine, is that so few offer much of real value. Teachers who present once-in-a-lifetime deals as commonplace completely misrepresent the truly powerful investment vehicle that real estate is. We realize get-rich-quick sells better than get-rich-slow-and-steady, but for most people slow and steady wins the race.

When Russ taught each of his five children how to ride a bicycle, before they ever sat on the seat, he told them, "If you want to learn how to ride this bike, all you have to do is get on and pedal. After you fall off *twenty* times, you will know how to ride!" Prepared with this advice, when the children would get on the bike and fall, they weren't discouraged. They understood and believed it was normal to fall, and learning how to ride would take time and persistent effort. Imagine their delight when they were riding unassisted after falling down "only" six or seven times!

Our point is that when people enter this business by buying a get-rich-quick pitch that doesn't happen, they walk away from real estate investing convinced it doesn't work. Yet, real estate is probably the surest path to wealth for the average person. What a shame for someone to give up because the opportunity was over-hyped.

We strive to present realistic information which people can use to make educated investment decisions. Sure, we have fun and get people excited about investing in real estate, but at the core of our teaching is the idea of *Education for Effective Action*™. We've made this our slogan, because it's what our seminars, books, and radio program are dedicated to accomplishing. What we teach comes directly out of the real world, which is why it will work there. One of our dreams is to someday have an infomercial with taped success stories from some of our many investors with small print that reads, "Results *are* typical. The majority of people who participate in this program have achieved a net worth in excess of $1 million dollars." Now wouldn't *that* be refreshing?

Go ahead and attend every real estate investing seminar you can, but focus on programs created by people who actually do what they teach. Many of the people who produce those very expensive programs are experts at getting you to part with your money. Don't let go of your hard-earned dollars unless you know the people teaching walk their talk. After all, every dollar you spend on the "magic silver bullet secret formula system" is a dollar you won't have available to invest in real estate.

So, if the "No Money, No Brains, No Job, No Credit" myth really means "No Chance", then what do you realistically need to get started investing? Let's take a look…

Exactly What I Can Afford

Many gurus tell us, with the right set of circumstances, people can buy real estate with none of their own money down, and you know what? It's true! Thousands of people purchase homes with very little and sometimes absolutely no money down. United States service veterans are often eligible for 100% financing on their primary residence. Some sellers who own property outright are willing to carry the financing themselves in exchange for a good interest rate and timely payments. Many institutional lenders have conventional loan programs that provide 100% financing. A common financing arrangement, which avoids costly private mortgage insurance (PMI) and achieves 100% financing, is called a "piggy-back" loan. Piggy-backs (also referred to as "combination loans" or "combos") encumber a property with two loans – one loan at 80% loan-to-value (LTV) and another at 20% LTV. The net result is 100% financing.

There's also the "wrap-around mortgage" or "wrap". In one variation of this, Borrower A might sell a property to Borrower B using a "contract for sale" instead of a typical grant deed. This allows Borrower A to *retain* title and his original loan, while he provides owner-carry-back financing to Borrower B. Even though A has retained title, the contract for sale provides B with effective control of the property because A is contractually obligated to deliver the grant deed when the owner-carry-back financing is paid off by B.

Why would B do this? The primary reason is because he doesn't have the ability or desire to obtain conventional financing. This may be due to poor credit, insufficient or non-documented income, or a desire to keep this loan off his credit report. A's motivation could be to stop negative cash-flow on a hard-to-sell property, and/or to continue to show the asset on their balance sheet,[20] or stay in a position to repossess the property in the event of default by B. Another reason A would utilize this technique is to generate positive cash-flow using the bank's money without the hassles of land-lording.

Assuming Borrower A's payment to the bank is smaller than Borrower B's payment to Borrower A, with a wrap, Borrower B gets the property and Borrower A makes a profit on the spread (the difference between A's lower payment and B's larger payment). Wraps sound easy to do...in a book. The reality is that wraps are much more difficult (and risky) than some "gurus" reveal.

Virtually all conventional loans contain "due-on-sale" or "acceleration" clauses. This means if the lender finds out about the sale, the underlying loan to Borrower A may be called immediately due and payable. Because the property has already been sold to B, A cannot sell the property to pay the loan when it is called. This means *someone* needs to come up with a chunk of cash quickly! Many title and escrow services refuse to facilitate wraps because of the risk of inexperienced people suing everyone associated with the transaction when it blows up.

What about assumable loans? The idea of simply stepping in and taking over payments for the seller, thereby retaining the original

---

[20] While it is fraudulent, when presenting financial statements to a creditor, to claim as an asset something that you have sold, or to omit a liability you have assumed (such as financing owed to a private party which is not being reported to the credit bureaus), this is an all-to-common practice in the market place. We do not advise or condone this approach, but simply are explaining the technique and the motivation behind its use. Loan fraud is a felony, so even if the loan broker says it is okay, it isn't. When in doubt, check with your attorney.

loan, sounds attractive and simple, but the truth is that most loans are not assumable without a full credit underwriting of the assuming party. In other words, the person assuming the loan still has to qualify under the lender's guidelines. If the goal of assumable financing is for non-credit-worthy buyers to gain access to financing, while it sounds really cool in a book or seminar, it just doesn't fly very often in the real world.

It is true certain loans originated before 1989 are unconditionally assumable, but how many pre-1989 loans are out there? Even if you find one, imagine all of the appreciation (new equity) and amortization (pay down of the loan balance) that would have built up in the property since 1989! In order to assume the loan, you still have to cash-out the owner's equity – which by now should be substantial.

Theoretically, the owner could carry back the complete balance of their equity so you can assume the loan and not have to undergo a credit check. How many of those owners do you suppose are out there? Try winning the lottery. You'll probably have better luck! Robert jokes in our seminars, "Owner-carry-back financing is like sex. Even when it's bad, it's still pretty good... and more people talk about it than actually get it!" The point is that owner-carry-back financing is wonderful when it can be negotiated, but it is harder to find than many pitchmen let on.

We believe in order for a technique or strategy to be truly effective, it has to be executable and repeatable in the real world by average people with a reasonable level of education, resources, time and commitment. You don't want to invest your most precious resources, your time and hope, in trying to find a "needle in a haystack". Can it be done? Yes. Is it effective? We don't think so.

While some people purchase investment properties with no money down, the vast majority of people cannot. Once you understand the difficulty of putting nothing down, you may wonder why people are even excited about it in the first place.

In order to qualify for conventional 100% financing on a property, you will need to have (at the very least) good credit. Even if your credit score is excellent, most 100% loans are reserved for owner-occupied housing or one or two-unit residential income properties. You can purchase a home to live in without putting a big chunk down, but when it comes to investment property the lender is less likely to take *all* of the risk by loaning you *all* of the money.

Even if you can get 100% financing on a rental property by converting a previous residence into a rental or arranging owner-carry-back financing, the cash-flow of the property will be difficult to manage because of the large loan payments. In other words, the outflow for debt service, taxes, insurance and operating expenses would likely exceed the rental income and you would be "suffering" negative cash-flow. Although we don't have a problem with a property that negatively cash-flows *if* the investor has a plan for profit *and* manages the cash-flow carefully, severe negative cash-flow left unchecked puts you in danger of losing your investment. If you lose control of the cash-flow, you will lose control of the mortgage. When you lose control of the mortgage, you will lose the property – and your credit rating. Remember, you can't make a profit from a property that is no longer yours. Worse, with a foreclosure, a history of payment defaults, and an impaired credit score, you will have a much harder time going forward as an investor.

If you use 100% financing, conventional or otherwise, keep in mind that in an appreciating market, the cash-flow will almost certainly be negative, so you will still need cash reserves to cover the negative, unless you are comfortable feeding the negative from your paycheck. Our point is, in all but the rarest of circumstances, "no money down" for people with no job, no cash and poor credit is a false hope promoted by hypesters to sell over-priced "education" to gullible buyers – not that we have an opinion on the subject!

Skin in the Game

Lenders like to see buyers of property have something at stake in the property. As enticing as "no money down" sounds, we suggest you put together a plan to acquire some investment capital. At the very least, liquid cash will give you a cushion if you do stumble onto that incredible 100% financed income property opportunity. Cash reserves are important not only to protect you from unexpected expenses or a reduction of rental income, but lenders will require you to have some cash held in reserve after the transaction closes, *especially* if you have no money in the property. In fact, you should plan on most conventional lenders wanting you to have up to six months' of PITI (Principal, Interest, Taxes and Insurance) payments in cash reserves after the close.

Potential partners will also probably want you to have some of your own money in a deal. You may not need to bring the majority of the funds – you may be primarily contributing the deal, relationships, expertise, project management, or physical effort – but most partners are going to want to see you have some financial risk, even if you are just paying for the fees, materials or holding costs. The point is that you will have more options available if you have some of your own money to work with.

Buying real estate is not without sacrifice. Examine your monthly spending habits to see where you can siphon a few dollars into your investment capital piggy bank. Do you shell out four bucks a day for a double half-caf no-whip latte? Try a drip coffee with a little nonfat milk. Every time you do, you'll save two dollars or up to sixty dollars a month. Do you like soda from the vending machine? Try spring water from the water cooler. What about popcorn at the movies? Bring a snack from home. You get the idea. Little changes can add up to big dollars faster than you think. It may not seem like much, until you consider how powerful cash-flow is. Two hundred fifty dollars a month is the interest-only payment at 6% interest on a $50,000 mortgage!

Another tactic to consider for freeing up some dollars is to adjust your current payroll withholding schedule at your job. The new tax deductions you'll receive from investing in real estate can be realized on a monthly basis by increasing your withholding exemptions. Remember, in almost all cases, interest on home loans and loans used for investment is tax deductible. We suggest you invest a few dollars and some time to meet with your tax advisor and find out how a proposed real estate purchase or loan will affect your tax situation. A tax advisor can tell you how to adjust your paycheck withholding (if you are a W2 employee) or your estimated tax payments (if you are self-employed). Reduced withholding is another way to immediately improve your cash-flow for savings or for debt service.

Brother, Can You Spare a Dime?

One excellent source of down payment capital may be your friends and family. Lenders are not necessarily averse to parents, grandparents and siblings loaning you money to invest in real estate. Gifting is a great technique for owner-occupied properties, but most lenders will not allow a gift to be used for down payment on an investment property.

If you think borrowing from friends or family is a possibility, give it some thought before pursuing this option. We believe most families can successfully invest together. We have personally seen the fruits of that concept, but we also acknowledge the viewpoint some people have that you should avoid doing business with family and friends. How you choose to broach this subject will depend on your philosophy and your personal family situation.

In the late 1980's, Robert and his father, Bob, helped many people put together equity-sharing transactions. Equity-sharing agreements are essentially partnerships which allow one partner to come up with the down payment while the other partner is responsible for the monthly payments – or various combinations thereof. Back when there weren't many first-time buyer loan programs available and 20% down was the general requirement, equity-sharing was a great option for helping people get started in home ownership. Quite a few of the transactions Robert and Bob did involved family members buying property together via an equity-sharing agreement.

While equity-sharing isn't as popular for purchasing homes because of the plethora of 100% financing available today for owner-occupants with good credit, it remains a great way to acquire investment property. In fact, partnering with other people is probably our favorite way to invest.

• • •

Jenny and Paul had excellent jobs and good income, but were having difficulty saving enough money for a down payment. They were referred to Robert and Bob by a friend who had been able to buy a home with an equity-share partner. Jenny's parents wanted to help the couple buy a home, but were reluctant to simply give them the down payment. This was partially because Jenny was the oldest of three sisters and a gift of this size would create an expensive and difficult-to-repeat family precedent! Bob explained how an equity-sharing arrangement might meet their needs. Jenny's parents could provide the down payment Jenny and Paul lacked, and in exchange, share in the future appreciation of the property. Jenny and Paul could easily make the monthly payments, for which they would also gain a share of the appreciation. Best of all, each party was protected because each had a documented legal interest in the subject property.

Five years after they bought the home, it had appreciated more than $100,000 – equity happened! After selling costs, Jenny and Paul had over $35,000 for a down payment on their next home, which they were able to purchase on their own. Jenny's parents got back their initial down payment, plus a profit of $35,000, just in time to help Jenny's sister and her husband buy their first home as an equity-share!

• • •

One of the great sources of down payment capital for investment property is new equity from appreciation on a personal residence. In the previous story, Jenny and Paul used their share of the new equity to purchase another home and Mom and Dad used theirs to help the next child. However, rather than sell, had they used a cash-out refinance to access the new equity, Jenny and Paul might have stayed in the first home and both the parents and the kids might have used their $35,000 to purchase investment property.

CHAPTER 6
Size Matters

Is bigger better? In real estate investment, we think size matters in most cases. Now, as with most things in life, to be a sound and successful investor, you probably need to start small. The first deals are as much about the education as the profit. Get your feet wet and develop a comfort level with the process, but your goal should be to eventually get in on the bigger, more profitable deals.

Many investors first venture outside of the owner-occupied world of real estate with a rental house or multi-unit property. In case you don't have one yet, we've included our popular *Free Duplex Story* for you later in this book.

Russ's first real estate transaction was to purchase a single-family house, do some minor upgrades, and sell it for a profit less than two years later. Robert's first real estate purchase was a two-unit residence. He lived in one unit while renting out the other unit. From there, Robert moved into a townhouse and kept the two-unit property, renting out both sides. Keeping a house and choosing to rent it rather than sell can be a great way to start. One to four-unit residential rental properties make great initial investment vehicles due to their relatively low cost and liquidity, and because they are easy to sell and refinance. However, once you have a few rental properties under your belt, it's time to consider moving up the property ladder.

What's the Big Deal?

Bigger Dollars

The first reason we like bigger deals is the absolute dollars in the transaction are bigger. If you make a 10% profit on a $100,000 condo, you make $10,000. If you make the same percentage of profit on a $1 million building, you make $100,000, but it probably didn't take you ten times the effort, time or energy to do it. However, it did take more investment capital.

Because our program began in Silicon Valley, many of our members live in the San Francisco Bay Area. They are used to seeing average-size homes sell for a half-million dollars or more! People from other areas don't understand why anyone would pay $750,000 for a three-bedroom, two-bath, 1500 square foot home on a sixth-acre lot.

While we often go to less costly markets to find good buy-and-hold properties, we think there is excellent potential in rehabbing properties in more expensive areas. The average single-family home fixer-upper project will yield an 8-12% profit margin. If you rehab a home and sell it for $200,000, you'll probably make $16,000 to $24,000 for your trouble. But if you sell a rehabbed home for $600,000, then your profit could be more like $48,000 to $72,000! If the only difference between the homes is geography, then your cost, time and effort are probably similar. This is called "economy of scale".

Less Competition

It's been said that the ladder of success is only crowded at the bottom. In other words, there are far more people competing for the entry level properties. The more competitors for available profits, the lower the profit margin because the competition bids the acquisition price up. Yet, when fewer people are competing because of the higher barrier to entry (an expensive project), there are higher potential profit margins. This is the main reason to go bigger when you can.

Also, the types of people who buy larger properties tend to be seasoned, sophisticated investors. This generally means less emotion, less irrelevant inquiries, and less game playing. Larger deals can actually proceed more smoothly than smaller deals and the purchase prices are not as likely to get bid up to where a professional investor can't make an acceptable profit. When you are an investor competing for properties with potential owner-occupants, the profits are harder to realize because owner-occupants will not consider their labor as an expense when bidding for the property. They are willing to work for free because the property will be their home.

Another nice thing about bigger deals is the agents involved in the transactions are often more experienced and professional. There are exceptions, but it's difficult to stay in the multi-housing, retail or commercial brokerage business if you're not competent. When you are a professional, it is nice to work with other professionals. True professionals are appreciative of the benefits of win-win, so they avoid "majoring in the minors" when negotiating.

Less people vying for larger properties can occasionally work *against* you when you need to sell, which is why you want to buy right and always have your exit strategy in mind *before* you buy any property. This is especially true with rehabs, conversions and new development. Think about the types of buyers you will need to attract, what they are looking for in a property, and how they can pay for it. Sometimes a novice investor will get overly creative by adding something which isn't properly permitted, installing high maintenance landscaping, and otherwise creating a "fixed up" property which is less attractive to a potential buyer because it is hard to finance or expensive to maintain.

Better Financing

As you own more real estate, getting loans becomes increasingly difficult for one to four-unit residential properties. Lender guidelines and programs for one to four-unit residential properties focus primarily on the borrower's financial ability and qualifications, including credit history, income, and assets. Rental income from the subject property will also be considered and the property will need to appraise at the sales price or higher, but these types of loans are more dependent on the borrower and less so on the collateral (the subject property). In fact, if the borrower is strong enough, the bank will lend – even if the property is vacant and generating no income at all!

Once you cross over into the world of commercial financing (five-or-more residential units, industrial, office or retail units), everything is different. The lending criteria are based more on the *property's* income and less on the investor's individual financial strength. Commercial income property loans depend on the condition and operating history of the property, verifiable rents, current and anticipated expenses, occupancy rates, and appraised value. The borrower's credit score and investment experience are also considered, but if the property doesn't interest the lender, then the buyer's profile is irrelevant.

• • •

One of Robert's first group investments was a large rehab project in Las Vegas, Nevada. The group purchased 151 residential units comprised of 18 separate buildings on one street. Five investors put up between $250,000 and $350,000 each to raise the 25% down payment required, while Robert and an investment partner applied for a commercial loan for the balance.

Complete financial packets were prepared on each investor and submitted to the bank. There was so much paperwork! For weeks, the loan officer called almost daily asking for further information and additional clarification. At last, the application was ready to go to the loan committee. After pacing around the office like expectant fathers, Robert and his investment partners finally got the call from the bank. The loan had been approved! Even better, the committee decided *not* to require guarantees from any of the minor investors. They liked the property and its very strong cash-flow.

Only Robert and one partner, as managers of the project, were required to guarantee the loan. Ironically, of all the investors in the group, they actually had the *lowest* credit scores, but the bank was more interested in the cash-flow of the property and the *experience*, not the credit rating, of the project managers.

• • •

A quick, but very important aside: if you plan to use loans as part of your real estate investment strategy, make sure you are diligent about always paying every one of them on time. Your past performance will continue to dictate your future ability to obtain financing. If you have been a notoriously bad bookkeeper, invest the money to hire a professional. If you have been poor about managing your finances in the past, change! Remember, in order for your results to change, you will need to develop new attitudes, habits, beliefs and skills.

Better Performance

Larger projects allow investors to capitalize on economies of scale. The more rental units over which you can spread the cost of maintenance, utilities, advertising and management, the better! For example, supplies can be purchased in bulk and service contracts may be eligible for volume discounts. When you are a bigger customer, you get better service. Even vacancies have less effect because your income is coming from multiple units.

Part of the reason insurance companies, pension funds and Real Estate Investment Trusts (REITs) invest in large properties is that these professional investors understand large properties tend to have less fluctuation in their performance. Many veteran investors continue to trade up to larger properties to take advantage of the more stable and reliable cash-flows of bigger buildings.

CHAPTER 7
Raising Your Average

While there is more to real estate than just housing, housing tends to lead the market. When housing is up, all other forms of real estate will usually follow. Since 1968, housing in America has appreciated an average of 6.40% per year.[21] But do you want to settle for only average? We hope you want to beat the average! So, other than magnifying appreciation through the amazing power of leverage, how can you improve *your* average?

Just as there are areas where real estate appreciates below the average, there are areas that appreciate *above* the average. If you're willing to invest some time and money into doing some research, you'll probably be able to identify the current and future markets which are well-positioned to outperform the average.

One of our most popular seminars is called *Analyzing Markets and Properties: The Due Diligence Process*. In a fast-paced, information-

---

[21] Source: National Association of Realtors for years 1968 - 2004

packed sixteen hours over two days, Robert provides comprehensive education on what to look for and how to find it when seeking a market poised for hyper growth. Using these techniques, Robert has consistently gone into markets the year *before* they became the #1 appreciating market in the United States. Coincidence? Perhaps, but there is more than dumb luck at work. Hot markets, like success, leave clues. If you know what to look for, you can improve the odds of finding yourself in the right place at the right time. Are you ready to get lucky?

While the topic of identifying the next "hot market" could probably (and someday might!) provide enough content for an entire new book, let us share with you some of the basics.

It's the Economy, Stupid

If the only jobs were in the Mohave Desert, where do you think America's highest priced real estate would be? The Mohave Desert! You see, people like to go to exotic parts of the world on vacation, but they always come home to the place where they can make a living. People will always want (need) to live where the jobs are. If all you did was concentrate on areas with a strong local economy, you would do well.

As long as politicians understand this basic concept, they will always do whatever is in their power (which, good or bad, is considerable) to create a political and economic environment to stimulate job growth. Where do you suppose they will focus their efforts? Is it in Smallville USA with a population of 43, or do you think they might favor Metropolis USA with a population (that is, "voter base") of millions?

If a given geographic region is a frequent stop for presidential candidates and state politicians, there is a good likelihood political muscle will be supporting that region's local economy. A strong local economy means jobs, and jobs mean demand for real estate.

Follow the Leader

Before major corporations like McDonald's, Wal-Mart, or Costco invest millions of dollars in establishing a new location, do you think they do any research? Of course they do! Organizations like these have entire departments dedicated to market research, demographic trends analysis and government relations, all to determine where the next new population base will be. None of these organizations open up an operation where there are no people...or do they?

Have you even seen a McDonald's restaurant pop up in what seems like the middle of nowhere? Invariably, a few months later other businesses move in. Soon, houses are being built and people are moving in. Sometimes following a market leader is a simple way to place your investment dollars in the path of progress.

Follow the Concrete

An important growth indicator is infrastructure. When you see or hear about a major freeway, bridge or airport being built, this tells you the local planners are preparing for growth. Most of these events are not secret. It's just that novices don't recognize the signs until the best opportunities are gone. Pay attention to what is going on in the markets you are interested in. How? Visit the area regularly, build relationships with locals and stay in touch. Subscribe to the local newspapers. Even if you are far away, you can get a good feel for a market if you put some effort and creativity into it.

Speculation or Investment?

There is a huge difference between speculation and investment. When an investor speculates, they are making a purchase hoping to catch a trend. Stock traders call this "technical analysis". It really doesn't matter what is driving the movement as long as you catch the wave and ride it. Sometimes people make a lot of money doing this. Often times, novices get wiped out because they aren't experienced enough to notice a "change in the wind", and when the trend changes, they are late to exit. This is especially true with the stock market, which trades at lightning speed.

True investors watch for sound fundamentals which are not only supporting a trend, but have the staying power to sustain it. Stock traders call this "fundamental analysis". In stocks, things like growth of sales and profits, investment in research and development, debt and liquidity ratios, and return on equity are all part of a fundamental analysis.

In real estate, fundamentals include economic strength, job growth, educational and transportation infrastructure, amount of remaining developable land, and other factors affecting Supply, Demand and Capacity-to-Pay. When the fundamentals for job and income growth and the resulting high demand for real estate to house people and businesses is combined with some limitation on the local market's ability to keep up with this demand, then the stage is set for aggressive appreciation. Appreciation is a manifestation of both speculation and sound fundamental growth. Therefore, a trend, in and of itself, is not necessarily sustainable. The overall real estate market "bubble" may never burst, but *yours* might. Be careful not to let an unsupportable trend leave you holding the bag!

For example, Russ taught a class to a group of real estate agents in a small Northern California retirement community. The agents were very excited about the rapid appreciation of housing prices their community was enjoying at that time. They asked Russ if we had any plans to invest in the area. When he inquired about what was driving the surge in demand, the agents told him there were lots of retired Silicon Valley residents buying homes for themselves.

Hmmm…think about that for a moment. If the appreciation is being created by retirees who are bidding up the price of homes to retire in, are they going to be interested in renting from you? Probably not.

Are these retirees upwardly mobile with growing families and rising incomes, thereby pushing up through the market to buy bigger and better homes? Not likely. Are they starting businesses and creating jobs? No.

What does the influx of these retirees do for the local economy? Sure, they'll purchase gas and groceries. They'll probably eat out regularly. They'll surely add business to the local healthcare providers. But will the jobs their presence creates be the type likely to push up real estate prices consistently for an extended period of time? We aren't so sure. Yes, you can make money in a speculative market where there is a temporary spike in demand and prices, but you need to get the timing right. However, when you invest in areas with a well-established economy and a large population, you have a higher likelihood of getting strong and steady appreciation over the long haul. Slow and steady wins the race!

As we worked through the final edits of *Equity Happens*, there was a lot of noise about the real estate bubble "bursting". On its face, the idea the bubble might burst is ridiculous. When an actual bubble bursts, it is gone forever. It explodes into nothingness. The reason the term "bubble burst" gets applied to stocks, is because companies can and do go completely out of business, never to be seen or heard from again. Russ knows. When the dot-com bubble burst, his shares in Mortgage.com became worthless. Why? The company disappeared from the face of the earth. Ironically, the building they were in is still sitting there. That, as Robert would say, is a *clue*.

Because real estate is real and the need for it is universal and eternal, the probability of a global "burst" is ludicrous, unless the entire economy collapses. If this happens, then where are you safe? At worst, there are times when a bubble passes a little gas. It burps. Seldom does it belch. After a while, free-market forces balance out supply and demand, while an inflationary economy provides ever-increasing capacity-to-pay in terms of absolute dollars. In other words, the real estate bubble goes back to inflating.

However, fear sells newspapers and magazines, so whenever the market is doing well, the doomsayers come out with ill-thought-out commentaries. Our problem with this is that when these fears are stoked by journalists seeking ratings, everyday people suffer from inaction caused by paralyzing fear. One of our biggest motivations for writing this book, teaching our seminars, broadcasting our radio show, and expanding our *Real Estate Investor Development Program*™, is to help people cut through the media banter and reason through the facts.

When the newspapers started to liken real estate investing to the "irrational exuberance" of the stock market in the late 90's, Russ wrote an article to help investors deal with what he called *The Speculation Specter*. Below is an excerpt from that article:

The Speculation Specter

Some thoughts not only relevant to the topic of equity arbitrage,[22] but to the entire concept of equity investing, have to do with the argument raised by some that this type of investing is purely speculative and therefore more dangerous than other types of real estate investing. The author agrees with the notion that equity investing is "speculative," but would also argue that, to a large degree, *all* investing is in fact speculative.

In the common vernacular, "speculation" is a euphemism for "gambling". The idea is that a gambler has no control over the outcome, thus the game at hand is one merely of random chance. In certain types of gaming, such as slot machines and dice, the author would tend to agree. We do not see "professional" slot machine players. There is no skill involved in simply dropping coins in a machine and pulling a lever.

---

[22] Arbitrage is just a fancy word for making money on the spread between two similar financial instruments. "Equity arbitrage" is a term we use to describe the technique of borrowing money against a property for one interest rate and then investing that same money into another investment at a higher rate.

However, one of the more popular "sports" today is poker. There is even a world series of poker! This is because the game of poker is not one of random chance, but one of pursuing target outcomes based on one's skills in determining and responding to probabilities. In other words, as Kenny Rogers sang, "you've got to know when to hold 'em, know when to fold 'em, know when to walk away, know when to run..." A skilled poker player, while subject to the "luck of the draw", also has the ability to manage probabilities and make decisions about how to react to a variety of ever-changing variables as they manifest. Is this to suggest that equity investing is akin to playing poker? Not at all. Poker requires far greater skill to be successful than does real estate investing. The point is that there are varying degrees of risk, based on probabilities and one's ability to react appropriately to them.

Before we proceed, let us examine the technical definitions of "speculation". From an English dictionary, we find the following definition:

spec·u·la·tion[23]
> 1.
>> a. *Contemplation or consideration of a subject; meditation.*
>> b. *A conclusion, opinion, or theory reached by conjecture.*
>> c. *Reasoning based on inconclusive evidence; conjecture or supposition.*
> 2.
>> a. *Engagement in risky business transactions on the chance of quick or considerable profit.*
>> b. *A commercial or financial transaction involving speculation.*

---

[23] Source: *The American Heritage® Dictionary of the English Language, Fourth Edition* Copyright © 2000 by Houghton Mifflin Company. Published by Houghton Mifflin Company.

From a financial dictionary, we get a somewhat different definition:

speculation[24] – *The taking of above-average risks to achieve above-average returns, generally during a relatively short period of time. Speculation involves buying something on the basis of its potential selling price rather than on the basis of its actual value.*

It appears the thought is that it is "risky" to buy something based on something you hope will happen as opposed to something which has in fact already happened. Just as a poker player places a bet "hoping" for a favorable card, so a speculative investor buys hoping for a favorable return in the form of future income and/or capital gain.

If one stops and applies this same logic to "investing" in obtaining a college degree, one might conclude that it is risky to go to college. Is not the student paying for a degree based on the *hope* of getting a better paying job? There is no guarantee the graduate will earn more income as a result of having a degree. In fact, there is no guarantee the graduate will even be able to find a job at all. The graduate (or his or her parents) will have invested a large sum of money, not to mention time and effort, into obtaining the degree based purely on the hope of a yet unknown future job with presumably more income than that of a person without a college degree. Yet, most people would not consider this speculative because the probabilities are favorable. The common argument in favor of the substantial investment of time and money into obtaining a college degree is, "Sure, there is no guarantee, but historically people with college degrees earn more than those that don't, and the chances are

---

[24] Source: *Wall Street Words: An A to Z Guide to Investment Terms for Today's Investor* by David L. Scott. Copyright © 2003 by Houghton Mifflin Company. Published by Houghton Mifflin Company.

good there will be a job out there somewhere waiting for the graduate." Could not this same line of reasoning be applied to purchasing a luxury condominium or any other property based on the probability of appreciation? "Sure, there is no guarantee. But historically nice properties in nice areas tend to appreciate above average – and the average is over 6% which includes all the properties which don't appreciate at all. The chances are good that someone of means will be willing to pay a premium price for a premium property in a premium area – especially since there aren't as many premium properties and premium areas as people who want them and can afford them."

In terms of conservative real estate investing (investing in existing properties for cash-flow from current market rents), an investor makes a down payment, secures a purchase money loan with a personal guarantee, and then hopes the property will generate sufficient rental income to service the debt, pay all operating expenses, and produce an acceptable level of profit to the investor. Of course, there are no guarantees the units will rent, or that rents will be sufficient to cover the debt service and expenses. There are many factors outside the owner's control, such as income tax rates, depreciation schedules, mortgage interest rates, property insurance rates, local economic factors affecting employment (demand for housing and capacity-to-pay), and of course, the tenants themselves. There are no guarantees the tenants will not do more damage to the property than the value of the rental income they contribute. In other words, even with a "conservative" approach, there are a host of unknowns outside of the individual investor's control. In truth, there is no such thing as "risk free".

This isn't intended to sour you on investing in real estate, but simply to break the paradigm that cash-flow investing is not speculative. The truth is there are many factors outside of the investor's control and the best one can do is to make wise decisions based on probabilities. Evaluating and managing the probabilities is the essence of being a successful investor, whether for cash-flow or for equity.

This author would argue that there are many identifiable factors which contribute to appreciation. In any given market place these factors should be identified and evaluated for their probability to continue. If the factors that caused a market place and property to appreciate in the past remain active and healthy, does it not seem reasonable that these factors, or drivers, might continue and therefore drive further appreciation in the future?

Perhaps the best definition of what causes the "speculation specter" is *reasoning based on inconclusive evidence, conjecture, or supposition.* Fear of the unknown causes many investors to pause, stop and sometimes retreat. Just as charging forward blindly is foolish, so is retreating blindly. A wise investor will reason through the evidence, evaluate the options and their probabilities for success, utilize appropriate safeguards to mitigate risk (insurance, cash reserves, emergency exit strategy, etc.), take appropriate action, monitor progress and results, and make adjustments accordingly. The good news is that of all the various types of investing, not the least of which is the ubiquitous technique of buying and holding stocks, real estate investing (including that of acquiring luxury condominiums for equity growth) is among the most easily understood and controlled by persons of average skill and intelligence. When one considers how many people "bet" their future on pieces of paper (stock) representing ownership in businesses they don't understand, can't control, and the shares of which trade at lightning speed in a worldwide exchange inhabited by ruthless, nameless, faceless professionals, then the notion that purchasing world class real estate in highly desirable areas based on the "hope" it will go up seems like the safer bet. But that is just this author's opinion and you must form your own. After all, it's your money and your future.

The preceding excerpt came from a special report titled *Luxury High-Rise Condominium Investing Strategies*. It was written as part of a fun seminar we did in 2005 called *Vertical Living / Vertical Profits – Investing in the New Boom in Real Estate*. If you'd like a copy of the complete report, please visit www.equityhappens.com/reports.

Base Hits

Everyone loves the grand slam. In baseball, there is nothing more thrilling than watching a batter slug one out of the park when the bases are loaded. But how often does this really happen?

We love it when we end up in a market, like we did in Sacramento in 2002, Las Vegas in 2004, and Phoenix in 2005, where we get more than 25% annual appreciation. We have one investor who turned $30,000 into over $300,000 in just eighteen months using just two two-unit residential rental properties! Even though we are happy for him and love to tell the story, we could never in good conscience suggest these results are typical. This is just evidence that if you are in the game long enough, every once in a while you'll hit a home run.

The point we want to make is that many games are won when teams put together a long string of base hits. Base hits aren't as glamorous as grand slams, but if they put points on the scoreboard and you win the game, isn't that what matters?

For example, imagine you were able to find markets where the appreciation was averaging 8% or more annually and all the fundamentals were in place to suggest the trend was sustainable. If you did nothing but reposition your real estate holdings from lower appreciating market to higher appreciating ones, you'd do better than average.

By using the power of leverage, you amplify the benefit of finding the better market. Just as we learned in Chapter 4, the additional appreciation is magnified by the amount of leverage. So, if you find a market that appreciates at 10% instead of 6%, then the extra 4%, at 10:1 leverage, could accelerate your equity growth rate by an *additional* 40%!

By simply finding areas with better than average appreciation and utilizing leverage to control property, you can *easily* beat average returns. You don't have to hit a home run and find the number one market every time. Even markets that are slightly above average can make a big difference. Base hits score points!

Step Up to the Plate

Another way to increase your "hitting percentage" is to make sure you are ready, willing and able to invest. This may sound simple, but it is a very powerful and important concept.

The very fact you have invested your time and money in this book, tells us the chances are good you are "ready" to invest. Rarely do people who aren't serious about making a change in their thinking, action and results make it this far into a book like this one.

Whether or not you are "able" to invest depends primarily on your financial situation. A good real estate financing consultant can help assess your borrowing power and qualify you for loans based on the resources you have to work with. How much cash do you have available for a down payment? What is your monthly cash-flow? What is your credit rating? Do you have equity in property to pledge as collateral?

If you do not yet know your borrowing power, we recommend you engage the services of an experienced real estate financing professional. Even though there are many websites offering to "prequalify" you for free, the problem with these types of online calculators is they simply analyze the numbers you put in. There is an old adage regarding computers, "garbage in, garbage out". But, you say, isn't that all a financing consultant would do? If you thought that, then you *definitely* need to work with a pro.

Many people do not realize lenders (banks, not mortgage brokers) look at your finances much differently than you do. Lenders establish rules by which they approve or deny loan applications. These rules are called "underwriting guidelines". The guidelines dictate how much of your income is "qualifying income" and how much of your cash is from "approved sources". If you don't know what income and cash qualify, how do you really know how much loan you qualify for? The answer is: you don't. If you are serious about being truly "able" from a financial perspective, take the time to get a professional borrowing power analysis. For more information on financing pre-approval, visit www.equityhappens.com/reports and request a copy of Russ's article, *The Truth About Pre-Approval.*

The biggest hurdle we see most people trip over is being truly "willing" to take action. We often find people in our program who are clearly "ready" (motivated, educated, and believe in the vehicle of real estate), completely "able" (have cash, solid income, great credit, and are pre-approved), and yet still have a terrible time pulling the trigger on a transaction. Our experience is that this unwillingness to act is usually the direct result of fear, uncertainty and doubt. These ready and able people are afraid to make a mistake, are not convinced the risk will be worth the reward, and therefore find they are *unwilling* to move forward.

The best way to become willing to take action or increase your level of activity is to study the results of those who have come before you. Lots of investors have been exactly where you are, whether you are brand new and excited about investing, but terrified to take the first real step; or you are slightly experienced, but nervous about how to move up to bigger properties, projects or new markets. Talk to others to see what they did to overcome their fears. Ask if they are glad they did. Don't allow yourself to focus on finding reasons *not* to invest, look for reassurances and evidence of success to help your mind reason with your emotions so you can take effective action. It is natural to fear the unknown, but if you want to change your life, it is necessary to do things you've never done before.

In our investor consultations, Robert's father, Bob, is often introduced by Russ as the resident "gray hair" whose role in the consultation is to lend perspective from his decades and decades of investing experience. Though this introduction is tongue-in-cheek, there is actually a lot of truth in it. Think about it. Bob began investing in 1957 and is still aggressively investing well into his seventies! Is there anything Bob hasn't seen? What if there's a war? He's seen several. What if we suffer a terrorist attack? It's happened. What if the President gets assassinated, threatened with impeachment, or resigns? Been there, seen that. What if interest rates go through the roof? What if interest rates drop to forty-year lows? What if Congress increases taxes? What if they reduce them? What if there is a budget surplus? What if there's a huge budget deficit or an oil crisis? What if the government freezes prices and wages? What if there's high inflation? What about low inflation? What about a recession? A stock market crash? Stagflation? A savings and loan collapse? A Republican President and Congress? A Democrat controlled Congress and President? Political gridlock? An earthquake? What if the Asian economy crashes? What if the technology bubble bursts? Yeah, yeah, yeah....seen it all.

Get the picture? At the end of the day (in this case, the century – sorry, Bob!), real estate just keeps on going. Why? Because no matter what occurs, people need places to live and work. As long as individuals are permitted to own property, those individuals who own real estate will be the wealthiest. If the right to ownership of private property is taken away, then it really won't matter if your property is paid for, or how much you have in the bank, because our entire economic system would be in disarray. In other words, we will have much greater problems to deal with. Short of that, there are few more stable places to build and store up wealth than in real estate.

Please don't misunderstand what we are saying here. There are very real risks in owning real estate. Just ask any homeowner. Building wealth with real estate is like owning a home; you just have more of them – more property, more debt, more equity, more cash-flow, more expenses, and more responsibility. You don't get more equity and cash-flow (the good things) without accepting the rest (the "risky" things). So, risk free investing is a fallacy.

Remember "risk" exists everywhere and in everything. In a practical sense, "risk" is relative and based significantly on *your* perception of it. The first time you encounter a property with termites, it can be scary. The tenth time it's no big deal. Risk is relative to one's education, experience, and expectation. With that said, risks can be classified into two categories: genuine and perceived. We concentrate on putting perceived risks in perspective and then using risk-mitigation tools and strategies to manage the genuine risks.

Mitigating risk does not mean ignoring potential problems. Risk mitigation starts with acknowledging the risks and then considering the likelihood of them occurring. People get killed every day in automobiles, so you could say riding in a car is risky and you'd be right. Yet you probably spent some time driving or riding in a car this week. Why would you do that when you know people get killed in cars every day? The answer is that you felt the benefit (getting where you needed to be) outweighed the risk (the very slight chance you would be involved in an accident), and you are familiar with the risk, so it didn't bother you. We don't mean to belittle the severity of car accidents, but we merely point out the concept that risk must be viewed relative to reward, probability, and experience.

To be willing to move ahead with a property purchase means you have considered the relative risks and decided the potential rewards outweigh them. We suggest you make a list of all of the things that concern you about real estate investing. Take your time and get it *all* out. If you are a newbie, we promise you that all of them will jump out and cloud your mind when the purchase contract comes out. It's best to get them out of the way early! Once you have your list of concerns, then create a second list right next to it and write down all of the risk mitigation tools and strategies available. This list would include things like insurance, education, professional representation (and the errors and omissions insurance that comes with it), etc. As we suggested earlier, take counsel with other active investors and get ideas from them. There is very little you will face or fear that someone else hasn't already worked through. A strong network of experienced investors and advisors is one of your greatest risk mitigation tools.

The Right Coach

Even professional athletes at the highest level have coaches. So do many successful businesspeople. In order to refine your skills, you often need the encouragement and guidance of experts.

Where do you get your investment advice? From Joe down at the market? From your hairdresser? From Sally at the PTA? Shouldn't you get your investment advice from people who are actually investing?

We believe that no matter what their intentions, people who do not actively invest in real estate have not *earned the right* to give you advice. Everyone has an opinion. Next time someone is making you aware of theirs, simply consider the source. If they are a successful real estate investor, then listen respectively to their opinion. You don't have to heed their advice or even agree, but at least consider it. If, on the other hand, they have no real-world investment experience, take anything they say with a grain of salt. It doesn't mean they don't have something useful to say, but keep it in perspective. There's a lot of noise out there, so one of the most important skills you will develop is the ability to filter input so you can focus on the ideas and opinions which matter most. A good mentor and network will be invaluable in this regard.

Realistically, finding quality advisors can be very challenging. Solving this problem was one of our motivations in creating Advisor Financial Alliance (AFA) and our *Real Estate Investor Mentoring Clubs*. AFA is an association of financial services professionals and companies who are dedicated to helping people build and preserve personal wealth with real estate investments. The affiliated advisors are required to be real estate investors themselves, abide by the AFA's code of ethics, and contribute their time and content to the educational programs AFA produces *without* hard-selling their products or services. In exchange, they have the opportunity to present their expertise to a target rich audience in the hope of attracting new clients. If you are a financial services professional who actually invests, and you like what you read in *Equity Happens*, please contact us. We'd love to hear what you have to offer.

Our *Real Estate Investor Mentoring Clubs* were formed to bring active and aspiring investors together in an environment designed to foster learning through open sharing, relationships and professional input. At each club meeting, a professional presents a lecture on a specific topic related to real estate investing. Several case studies of properties from different areas are analyzed and discussed. Lastly, there is an "open forum" where virtually anything related to real estate investing can be discussed under the protection of a non-disclosure, non-solicitation and non-compete/circumvention agreement. In each club, there is a Facilitator who keeps the conversation orderly, a Secretary who records meeting minutes and handles club logistics, and a Mentor. The Mentor is an active investor and/or financial professional who brings expertise about a specific area related to real estate investing.

The result of the Program is an environment where investors are able to coach each other and learn from everyone's experience. Properly organized, investment clubs can produce a similar result. It is one of the best ways we know to find advice from real life investors. If there isn't a club in your area, consider starting one. You might even consider using *Equity Happens* as one of your textbooks.

Just Chew It

Someone in our office used to have a sign above her desk that said, "Bite off more than you can chew. Then chew it!" It became one of our favorite sayings. Many of the successes we have had personally, as well as those we have witnessed from our investors, have come from a propensity for taking action. As we watch beginning investors transition into experienced veterans, one thing is clear, the winners are being rewarded for *doing*, not for just learning, planning and analyzing. All of these are important, but nothing is more important than taking action.

Brian Tracy says in order to be successful, you simply have to act "as if" you already are. It's as much about your mindset as the actions you take. In fact, the actions you take grow out of your mindset. If you think like a winner, you will find yourself doing the things winners do. If you do the things winners do long enough, you will eventually accomplish the things winners accomplish. When you think about it, it makes perfect sense.

Winners simply refuse to lose. They are convinced there is an answer to every problem. Believing the solutions are out there, winners just keep optimistically seeking until they find the answer. If you are unfamiliar with the lives of men like Thomas Edison, Harlan Sanders and Abraham Lincoln, go look them up. Edison went through 10,000 failed experiments to finally find a filament to work in his light bulb. Sanders took 1,000 rejections before someone said "yes" to his recipe for Kentucky Fried Chicken. Several times, Lincoln was defeated for public office and failed in business before becoming one of the greatest leaders in U.S. history. Winners refuse to lose.

All of this may sound like motivational mumbo jumbo, but this might be the single most important section of this book! A commitment to winning, to finding solutions, to not quitting until the goal is attained, to taking a big bite, and then chewing and chewing and chewing until you succeed, is the mentality of all high achieving people.

Who is it that you really want to be? Take some time with a pen and paper and describe the person you need to become in order to have everything you want in life. Then COMMIT to become that person. We say, "Be who you are becoming." In other words, play the role to the hilt. Go all out. Believe 110%. Don't hold anything back and don't let anyone hold you back. Be tenacious.

Do you remember the movie Rudy? It's a true story about a young man named Rudy Ruettiger and his dream of playing football at the University of Notre Dame. Rudy was a person who wouldn't quit. He wanted to play football for Notre Dame more than anything in the world. More than meeting other people's expectations, more than playing it safe, more than being comfortable, more than anything.

Everywhere Rudy turned, he faced rejection. Year after year he was turned down, but he never gave up. Every step of the way it looked hopeless, but little by little he made progress. From simply getting admitted to the school, to earning a position on the practice squad, to eventually suiting up and stepping onto the field for the last game of his last year at the school, and then finally, playing in a real game. Every step of the way he endured ridicule, hardship, and setbacks, but he kept on chewing. He refused to lose.

Now, by many standards, Rudy wasn't successful. For all that hard work and sacrifice, all he got was a single play in a single game. Some might say he was a complete failure. However, Rudy's success wasn't in playing football for Notre Dame, it was in who Rudy became as a human being in the process of pursuing his dream.

Robert had the opportunity to meet Rudy in person and heard him speak to a large audience. His advice was simple, "When you find yourself in a difficult situation and you feel like quitting, ask yourself, 'What would Rudy do?' and with luck, you'll find the answer!" You will find it very helpful to have heroes whose examples inspire you when the going gets tough.

You have a vested interest in the person you're becoming. No one will care more about you and your real estate investments than you do. What happens to you is often based on the effort you put forth and the attitude you embrace when faced with adversity. You can't control what life does to you, but you must choose on a daily basis how you will respond to it. Our advice is, when in doubt, just chew it!

Celebrate Good Times, Come On!

What does a sports team do when they win a championship? They jump up and down, hoot and holler, and dance across the field congratulating each other. This outward celebration relieves stress, builds morale, and recognizes their accomplishment.

When you have a "win" in your investing business, make it a point to celebrate! Enjoy the moment. Do something memorable. Heck, spend some money on yourself and your family. Bob Helms is fond of a billboard he saw which said, "Save your pennies, but every now and then have a gumball." The more successful you become, the bigger your gumballs get! One of Bob's recent gumballs was a brand new jet-black Mercedes-Benz SL500.

In the beginning of 2005, our network of companies embarked on a very ambitious schedule of seminars. Because many of our events are nights and weekends, but all the preparation and follow-up is done during regular business hours, it seemed like all everyone did was work. As much as we love what we do, we were all getting tired and a little cranky. By the end of May, our team was at their wits end. We promised them we would lighten up at the end of June, but then a funny thing happened.

One of our companies was given an exclusive right to advance market one of the premier real estate developments in the world. With next to no notice, we had just a few weeks to organize and implement an aggressive marketing plan. So much for a light summer!

In just four weeks, we put together a plan that helped investors acquire many millions of dollars of real estate. Most of the work happened in the last ten days. To celebrate, we took the entire team to Las Vegas. When the check came, the tab was well into five-figures. Was it worth it? You bet!

Celebrating the victories gives you incentive to go on and do more. Most people make a much bigger deal of their failures than they do of their successes. It is important to acknowledge failure and learn from it, but don't forget to acknowledge victory and celebrate it! Celebration puts all of the hard work in perspective and reminds you why what you do is important.

EQUITY HAPPENS™

SECTION 3

Helping Equity Happen

CHAPTER 8
Equity Growth Strategies

We know equity happens because it has happened to us, hundreds of people in our program, and millions of property owners in great markets across the United States – and around the world. We want equity to happen to you! Our goal is that this book will help by motivating you, stimulating thought (and action), and organizing ideas and strategies in a practical, useable way. Growing equity is an essential part of wealth building with real estate.

In Chapter 3, we discussed equity in two broad categories: New Equity and Owner's Contribution. For purposes of this section, we want to go into greater detail.

In our program, we classify equity into six primary types: 1) Found Equity, 2) Forced Equity, 3) Passive Equity, 4) Phased Equity, 5) Purchase Equity, and 6) Amortized Equity.

As you should know by now, we like the equity that doesn't come from our paychecks, but is given to us by the market. These include found, forced, passive and phased equity. Let's take a closer look at what we mean by these terms:

Found Equity happens as a result of helping the current owner of a property that has equity in it. By finding ways to solve the current owner's problem (the need for a quick close is a common one), you can sometimes get a discount on the price. The difference between what the property is worth in the open market and your discounted price is "found" equity. The equity is yours simply because you purchase or otherwise gain control of the property, however you don't have to develop, repair, convert or otherwise improve it. NOTE: Found equity doesn't necessarily have to result from opportunistically preying upon distressed sellers. Always try to be fair.

Forced Equity happens when you proactively add value to a property in such a way as to create equity without having to wait passively for market appreciation. The three basic ways of doing this are:
- New development – building something that wasn't there before.
- Re-development – repairing or improving something that is already there.
- Conversion – changing zoning and/or entitlements to a more profitable use.

Passive Equity happens when you follow Mark Twain's advice, "Don't wait to buy real estate, buy real estate and *wait!*" If you hold on to a property long enough in the right market, you'll probably experience increases in both market value and income.

Phased Equity happens when you purchase a property in a new development and, as subsequent phases of the development are released at higher prices, your property is pulled up in value. A variation of this is when you purchase very early in the pre-construction phase of a development and gain control of the property without actually having to fund or occupy it for many months. In an appreciating market, your property might go up in value before it's even built!

Amortized Equity happens when you pay down your loan using the rental income from the property. This is good because it is profit to you. We like this. You can also get amortized equity on your personal residence when *you* go to work, earn money, pay taxes and then pay down your own loan. But, as you might guess, this latter type of amortized equity doesn't get us very excited.

Purchase Equity doesn't really happen, but rather is a form of owner's contribution. In other words, it's money you earned by going to work. Technically, when you do a cash-out refinance and use the cash as a down payment on another property (something we like to do!), it would be considered purchase equity. However, since in this case, the purchase equity really came from another property (presumably from the appreciation on the first property) and not from your paycheck, we don't refer to it as purchase equity. It's really just a repositioning of new equity.

If you are making a short-term investment in a market that is potentially over-heated, meaning you are concerned about the market's ability to sustain short-term appreciation, you would be wise to focus on *forced* and *found* equity. With these strategies, you are not dependent upon passive appreciation for your equity.

Obviously, you can combine any or all of these strategies on a single investment. Suppose you acquire a two-unit residential building in poor condition on a large lot from a seller who wants to close quickly. If you were to come in with a strong offer to close fast, you may get a discount (found equity). Once in, you could fix up the existing structure (re-development forced equity), change the zoning to permit the construction of a second two-unit structure (conversion forced equity), and build the new structure (new development forced equity). Once built, you could raise the rents based on the nicer buildings (more forced equity), then hold the property for the next ten years and let appreciation add passive equity.

I Found It!

Keeping your eyes open for potential equity is an essential skill for success in real estate investment. As you research and analyze properties, be on the lookout for opportunities to take advantage of hidden equity waiting to be found.

• • •

Mac was a seasoned real estate broker in another state who was always on the lookout for properties with excellent upside potential. Through his relationship with a local builder, Mac found a new development deal that would produce six brand new two-unit residential properties on one street. He had a copy of the architect's conceptual drawings in his office, and Robert indicated his interest in one or two of the buildings.

Mac mentioned he already had some preliminary interest, but would let Robert know when he had more complete financial information. Robert joked about wanting to take all six buildings.

Well, guess what? A week later, Mac called and asked if Robert was serious about taking all six buildings. Mac said the builder might be willing to offer a discount because by taking all six buildings at once, Robert would be eliminating the builder's marketing risk and expense. The builder was anxious to close this project out and get on to the next one.

Robert confirmed his interest, so Mac put the deal together in just a couple of days. Mac arranged a price that was 8-10% below what similar units in the area were selling for, simply because Robert was willing to buy all six at one time.

By purchasing the entire inventory of the builder (twelve rental units in six buildings), Robert was able to get a great price, thereby creating "built-in" equity for the investors in our program who ultimately bought the buildings. We "found" equity by helping the builder convert his assets (buildings) back into cash more quickly and at a lower cost. Most importantly, everyone in the deal walked away happy.

• • •

Cash Is King

Investors must learn to recognize a "good deal" when they see one, but finding the deal is only one part of the equation. Successful investors take fast action on good deals because the best properties sell quickly!

Money talks. In fact, it shouts! While not necessarily a plan for the beginning investor, having enough cash to take advantage of an opportunity is an important key to gaining found equity. Although we are *huge* fans of leverage because it magnifies appreciation, arranging financing using conventional loan programs takes time. Unfortunately, time is not your friend when you find a hot opportunity.

One way to put yourself in position to make deals fast is to keep a lot of cash or credit readily available for this purpose. Ready cash makes deals happen. This doesn't mean you have to keep the mattress stuffed with twenty-dollar bills. Cash or cash equivalents (liquid assets) come in all shapes and sizes. Home equity lines of credit, money-market accounts, even credit card advances are all tools to access cash on short notice. People who can get their hands on cash quickly will always have an advantage over people who cannot. Motivational speaker Les Brown says, "It's better to be prepared and not have an opportunity, than to have an opportunity and not be prepared." When you have cash, opportunity will eventually find you.

We all like the idea of no-money-down strategies because everyone qualifies to make those offers! But think about it. If you're selling a property, do you want an offer from someone with zero money in the deal, or would you prefer someone who can give you all cash quickly? Sorry for the reality check, but cold hard cash wins hands down every time.

Keep in mind "cash" doesn't necessarily mean *all* cash. Sometimes a large down payment can be just as effective. A strategy we have used successfully to get the nod in a multiple offer situation is to write a large earnest money deposit check. While the average person includes an earnest deposit of just one to three percent of the purchase price, we might write an initial deposit check of ten to forty percent of the offer price. This makes the offer appear stronger without necessarily having to be the highest bidder.

"Best offer" is not synonymous with "highest price". Good agents know the best offer is the one *most likely to happen*, not just the one with the highest price. High price is nice, but it won't overcome poor credit, unrealistic loan parameters, a prolonged closing, or an insufficient appraisal. Sellers and their agents don't profit from deals that don't happen.

● ● ●

Robert and one of his investment partners were on a trip looking at a property that an associate of theirs had found through networking with other investors. Since the property was located several states away, Robert decided to fly to town the night before to have additional time to walk the property and the neighborhood. As they were checking in, Robert noticed the local real estate magazine in the hotel's information rack. Looking through the magazine that night, he noticed that all but two of the listings were for single-family homes. There was also one listing for an undeveloped lot and one listing for a multi-unit residential building.

Intrigued by the multi-unit property, Robert called the listing agent. The building was already under contract to another buyer.

The listing agent offered to show Robert and his partner the building just in case they might be interested in submitting a back-up offer. The next day, the walk-through of the first property they originally came to see took less time than budgeted, so Robert called the listing agent of the multi-unit building and made an appointment to look at it.

In viewing the property, it was discovered the building needed quite a bit of work, but the asking price seemed very reasonable. However, rather than submit an offer, Robert simply told the agent they would be interested in writing an *all-cash* offer in the event the original buyer was not able to close the transaction. Sure enough, three weeks later the listing agent called Robert and said the sale to the other buyer was looking shaky.

Although Robert and his partner were willing to pay the seller's full asking price, they had a hunch a cash offer might result in the seller's acceptance of a lower price by the seller, especially since the first buyer had been in contract for over ninety days and failed to close. Robert and his partner immediately submitted an all-cash offer with a ten-day close at approximately 18% below the asking price. The agent responded almost instantly with an acceptance from the seller. The seller had a problem he needed solved – and he was willing to discount the property to get the deal done. Apparently a quick (and practically guaranteed) close was worth more to the seller than getting full price. You will find this to be true in many instances. When someone wants to sell, they want to sell. Offers are interesting, but cash talks loud and clear.

• • •

Another strategy we sometimes use is to write an all-cash offer, but include the following language in the contract: "Buyer reserves the right to obtain a loan to purchase the property, but this is not a contingency of the contract."

Now you must use caution when using a gambit like this, because if you cannot obtain financing, you must have the cash to close the deal. However, this tactic often allows you to get a loan on a property while still utilizing the strength of an all-cash offer. Be sure to consult your real estate agent or broker (and your bank account) prior to including such language in any offer.

• • •

Gordon is a general contractor who remodels homes. He came across a dilapidated house on a nice lot in a great neighborhood. He was excited about this property because the lot was easily big enough to put two homes on, and the house immediately next door had been knocked down and replaced with a brand new 3,000 plus square foot home. Gordon's plan was to tear down the dilapidated house and build two, or perhaps three, beautiful houses like the one next door.

The estimated land value in the area was easily $900,000. The seller's asking price was $875,000 and the real estate agent Gordon worked with discovered there were at least three offers coming in. But Gordon had an ace up his sleeve. He had just finished a large remodel job and had collected almost $100,000 for the project. He also had a line of credit on his personal residence for $200,000.

Gordon had his agent write an offer for $800,000 and included an earnest money deposit check for $300,000. Although all three other buyers each offered a higher price than Gordon, his large cash deposit got the attention of the seller. One buyer had deposited only $1,000 and another only $5,000. The third buyer didn't even include an earnest money check with the offer, but said he would deliver a check for $20,000 if his offer was accepted. To the seller, Gordon appeared much more serious and able than the other would-be buyers, and accordingly his offer was accepted over the others. Once again, cash talks.

• • •

"But," you say, "I don't have any cash!" We agree this is a big "but", however, there are ways to compensate – and most of them are based on the adage, "Good deals will attract good money."

The first place to search for cash is your own balance sheet. Many people we work with *think* they have no money, but in fact they have quite a lot – they just don't know how to see it, access it and use it. Later, we will discuss in detail how to use cash, cash-flow, equity and credit, but for now let's just consider a few ideas about how to scare up some funds from your own balance sheet.

One tremendous asset is your good credit rating (assuming you have good credit). Perhaps you can apply for a line of credit which can then be used to get cash. Also, good credit is really just a form of reputation. Do you have a good reputation with friends and family? Perhaps you can borrow or co-invest (equity-share) with someone you know.

Get creative! This is where our previous discussion of *Rudy* applies. After all, if you needed the money badly enough, you'd find it, wouldn't you? Imagine your spouse or child was diagnosed with a terminal illness, but an expensive medical procedure would save their life. Is there anything you wouldn't do to find the funds? Suppose you were offered the opportunity to purchase a $250,000 car for $20,000, but you needed the money in a week. Who would you call? What would you do?

When you find a great deal on a property and there is money to be made, people who have money will help you – especially if you share the profit. And why wouldn't you? After all, something is better than nothing, right? If you have good credit, some assets, and/or have a good reputation and healthy personal relationships, then getting the money shouldn't be difficult – whether from banks or friends or family. If you have no assets, no credit, a poor reputation, and no friends, then you don't need a book on real estate investing – you need a book on character development and personal relationships.

The reason most people won't ever be able to come up with the cash to snap up a great property is they've simply resigned themselves to "the fact" they don't have the money. Henry Ford once said, "Whether you think you can or think you can't, you're right!" Don't let limited thinking control your future. Don't say, "I can't afford it." Instead, ask, *"How* can I afford it?" Then go figure it out. The solutions are out there. Focus on pursuing solutions, instead of observing the obstacles.

It may sound like more positive-thinking hype, but you bought this book looking for answers. Did you think we would provide a step-by-step treasure map? There are people out there right now who are going to become successful in real estate – without a treasure map! The answers aren't in this book. They are in the real world. We're here to tell you that you must train your brain to focus on opportunities and solutions. When the opportunities are bigger than the obstacles, you will find the way.

HINT: Focus more on *people and relationships* and less on information.

If you are already doing this, great! Keep it going. If you are cynical, please do not make the mistake of discounting this important concept.

• • •

After securing two excellent land parcels, both of which were ideal for development in a high-growth area of a new market, we had forged some great relationships with local service providers. Through our growing network of contacts, we began to hear about investment opportunities *before* they reached the public. One of the major landowners in the area became aware of the types of projects we were planning in the area, and the landowner offered to sell us another attractive parcel at a very reasonable price.

After performing some basic due diligence, Robert determined the land was easily worth $400,000 more than the price we were offered. Nonetheless, this price would still net the seller a handsome profit. More importantly, the community would benefit from the much-needed development. Our challenge was that our assets were already deployed, so we lacked the cash to close the deal in a reasonable timeframe. Knowing the direction of the land values in the area, Robert was determined to make the deal happen, but believed we needed to move quickly – and for cash.

Working with a real estate attorney, a plan was devised to organize a group purchase of the land by several individual investors. While none of the investors had the ability to purchase the land on their own, by teaming up they were able to move quickly, close the purchase for cash, and thereby secure a sizeable amount of found equity. The seller was happy, the investors were happy, and we were happy. When the project is completed, we trust the community will also be happy. But none of this would have happened if we would have simply looked at our checkbook and said, "We can't afford it." Instead, we chose to say, "*How* can we afford it?" and then set about finding a solution in the form of people who could help us.

• • •

What's Your Problem?

Another way to find equity is to look for people who have it locked up where they can't get to it. Some investors look for situations where a property owner has gotten into financial trouble and needs help to avoid losing their property. Foreclosures, bankruptcies and tax-liens are examples of distressed situations where a little help from the right investor can lead to a win-win situation for everyone involved.

How you approach a distressed situation depends on your mindset. While some people are like vultures just waiting to take advantage of people who are down, many investors who work these types of properties really do want to help people. While you may be able to gain some equity for yourself, if you get involved early enough, you also may be able to help someone save their credit and possibly get out of a difficult situation without losing all their money and most of their dignity.

The secret to helping people who are in desperate circumstances is to take a fair and balanced approach. Depending on your personality, you will be faced with two temptations. First, if you lean towards greediness, you will be tempted to leverage the owner's desperation to squeeze every penny of profit out of them. Our definition of success includes adding value to the world, so it is hard to for us to consider someone successful who exploits another person, no matter how profitable it is. The other temptation will be to be overly sympathetic and work for free or not get enough return based on the effort and risk you are taking. Be fair and think win-win. You will sleep better at night and your business will be profitable.

Owner's distress comes in a lot of packages. There might be a death, illness, divorce, job loss, drug or alcohol problem, gambling addiction, or a bad business decision. Sometimes, bad things happen to good people, so not everyone who is in dire financial straits is a loser. Be careful not to forget the humanity and dignity of the distressed owner.

Also, distress situations can be emotionally supercharged. People who are desperate are not always rational. Sometimes they can be mean – even violent. If a desperate person thinks you are trying to rip them off, you could not only lose the deal, but you may find yourself in a dangerous situation, so use good common sense.

There are two common categories of severe financial distress: foreclosure and pre-foreclosure. With foreclosure, the lender has already taken the property back, so you will be dealing with the trustee or his agent. The former owner is out of the picture. Because the foreclosure process is closely regulated in almost all jurisdictions, there is not a lot of flexibility in the process. Basically, you show up and bid. Our observation is that this is a difficult game to play successfully and is not something we personally engage in. Rather than take up time discussing the details of how to work foreclosures, if this is something you are interested in, there are many books and seminars on the subject. Take them all in, then head to the courthouse steps and observe a few auctions. Interview people who are really doing it (or trying to), and find out how it's going for them in the real world.

The other category is pre-foreclosure. There are a lot of things that happen on the way to foreclosure – and in most cases, great properties with good equity don't ever get to foreclosure. Someone will come along and save the owner. It's just a matter of who, when, and how. The key is getting into relationship with the owner before there is a lot of competition. If you wait for a "Notice of Default" to be publicly filed, you will have lots of people involved. Better to build a strong network of "bird dogs" – people who will let you know when they hear about a situation where an owner is in trouble financially. These "bird dogs" might include mortgage brokers (especially "hard-money" brokers) and real estate agents, because a distressed owner will look to borrow or sell to get out of trouble. Make sure you keep in mind the mortgage or real estate broker's motivations. The mortgage broker wants a loan and the real estate broker wants the listing. If your involvement threatens their opportunity to get a deal, they won't help you. Make sure you paint a picture that includes them getting some business if you can cut a deal with the owner. For example, if you get the property, and you choose to sell it or refinance it – make sure that business goes to the person who brought you the lead.

In regard to working with the owner, the key to success is to identify the owner's needs and desires. Sometimes owners just want out with some money and no foreclosure on their credit report. Other times, they very much want to stay in the property so the kids don't have to leave their school or friends, or if it is a business, so they can stay in business and get back on their feet. Find out what they want and try to find a way to help them get it while still making a profit yourself. When the owner sees your concern for his needs and desires, he will be more likely to open up and work with you to find a mutually beneficial solution. If you aren't greedy, owners will not resent you making a profit for helping them. It's all in your attitude and approach.

Let's say you find someone with significant equity in a property, but his credit or cash-flow is so bad he can't get to it. The problem with equity is it isn't liquid. Depending on the situation, there are several things you might propose:

1. Loan them money through a hard-money loan broker.[25] You can get a high yield on your capital and you are first in line to foreclose if the owner doesn't get himself turned around.

2. Offer to buy the property quickly for cash at a discount. You can then refinance it to get much of your cash out, then rent the property out to cover the loan payment.

---

[25] A hard-money loan broker is a mortgage broker who specializes in matching private party lenders with borrowers who are willing, for whatever reason, to pay premium interest rates and fees, and have substantial equity in the subject property. Not all people who borrow money through hard-money brokers are in financial trouble. Sometimes, private money can be obtained much more quickly and easily, and when speed matters more than cost, private money can be a great source of investment capital.

3. If the original owner wants to stay as your tenant, you might arrange to have him pre-pay his lease (with the proceeds of your purchase). Meanwhile, you have the benefit of the appreciation. After the purchase "seasons" 6 -12 months, you can refinance based on the fair market value and potentially get even more cash out.

4. If the original owner wants to keep the property, you might offer him a lease with an option to purchase. Now, even though he sold the property to you, he gets to stay and has the opportunity to buy the property back (at a profit to you) when he is in better financial condition. If he doesn't exercise the option, then you keep the property, and any option premium you may have collected.

In any of these or other scenarios, it is really just a matter of trying to find a solution to the owner's problem that makes you a fair profit for the value you add. Do the math and work with a licensed real estate agent and/or real estate attorney to make sure your creativity doesn't violate real estate law. Remember, you earn your money for solving problems.

If you choose to look for distressed property situations, keep in mind you'll need to be careful to learn the intricacies of the markets you select. Bankruptcies, foreclosures, short sales and other defaults are highly specialized transactions and one wrong move can devastate everyone involved. Take the time to really learn the game if you expect to be a serious player. While there are lots of seminars, books and CDs on this subject – and you should probably review them all – as we've said, the best way to learn is to find someone who is successfully doing it and have them mentor you.

Why would someone be willing to teach you? This really depends on the individual, but if you find a likely candidate take him out to lunch and find out what his needs are. Perhaps you bring something to help him and together you can achieve more. Believe it or not, some people genuinely like to teach. Perhaps this person needs cash and you have some (be careful). Maybe you have a contracting, legal or financial background or you are good with landscaping or design. The basic principle here is you must give to get. More often than not, if you help other people, they will be willing to help you.

May the Force Be With You!

One of the most financially and emotionally rewarding experiences in real estate is that of adding value to a property, thereby creating equity for yourself, while simultaneously contributing to the neighborhood and community. "Forcing" equity is the process of finding an under-utilized property and bringing it up to its highest and best use.

"Highest and best use" is a term we borrow from appraisal and often involves seeing beyond the obvious. For example, a two-bedroom home with a dining room, family room and two bathrooms might be more marketable as a three-bedroom home. While it is nice to have a dining room, if the dining room were converted to a third bedroom you'd likely gain more value.

Sometimes zoning is a factor. A single residence on a lot zoned R2 (two residences) might provide the opportunity to build a second unit, which would significantly increase the cash-flow and potentially cover the loan you take out to do the construction. Sometimes, the current zoning is not ideal and you have to try to change it. Though a zoning change can be an expensive and time-consuming undertaking, it can also pay handsome rewards. For example, an older house on a busy street might make a nice small office or retail space. This is where a good personal relationship (have we mentioned the importance of relationships in this business?) with the folks in the city planning office can be a tremendous benefit. You'll need their support to push through a request for re-zoning. Take a trip downtown and visit the city planning office in every market place you choose to be active in.

Invest the time to get acquainted with the policies and procedures. Familiarity will give you extra confidence when you are looking at a potential project and think you will need to work with the planners. This way the whole process won't seem so mysterious to you.

If you don't have any personal experience with construction, then make sure you have a good contractor on your team. You should still read some books and attend classes on construction so you will be familiar with the terms and various possibilities. Like any profession, you need to invest time in learning your trade. It's a safe bet Donald Trump knows something about construction even though he probably isn't raising a hammer on the job site!

• • •

Russ bought a single-family house shortly before it went to auction. It was in need of extensive renovation. At the time, he had no appreciable construction experience, but decided to take the project on as a learning experience. For the first two weeks after taking possession, he simply walked up and down the aisles at the local home improvement store just looking at everything there was. He read several books on remodeling and attended some of the store's do-it-yourself seminars. Most of the information you need is readily available, but no one is going to hand it to you. You must seek it out!

After the rehab project was planned on paper and it came time to actually do the work, Russ elected to act as the General Contractor (something you can do when you are the owner) and selected all of the sub-contractors. He befriended the contractors (it's amazing how much good will you can get from a few boxes of pizza) and worked right alongside them. Though the project took longer than Russ anticipated, the extra time was part of the price he paid for the education. He learned about plumbing, electrical, flooring, doors, framing, windows, roofing, painting, cabinetry, and finish carpentry. The result is that Russ is no longer intimidated to talk to contractors and can now look at a rehab project with a much more realistic sense of how much time and money it takes to get it ready to market. He also learned he doesn't ever want to get tactically involved in a rehab project again!

• • •

Another note on befriending contractors: Do you think contractors ever come across distressed properties and serious "don't wanters" (someone who has a property they really want to get rid of)? Of course they do! Is this information you can use? Absolutely! Make sure people you know are aware of your desire to buy properties, and then reward the people who actually help you find deals. When you invest strategically in relationships, you can truly compress time frames.

A very profitable, but sometimes mysterious method of forcing equity through a zoning change is called "conversion". For example, it is possible to purchase a multi-unit apartment building and, through a zoning and parcel map change, sell each individual apartment to separate investors or owner-occupants as condominiums. Investors have found these "condo-conversions" to be extremely profitable because individual owners will pay a much higher price per unit ("per door") for condominiums than investors will pay for apartments.

If you decide to take on a condo-conversion there are certain caveats you should be aware of. Besides the zoning and map change, you'll need to make sure the way the utilities are set up are conducive to individual ownership. You may also need to establish a Home Owners Association (HOA), which will involve working closely with an experienced attorney and the state department of real estate.

One of the most important items that many converters overlook is to carefully monitor how many non-owner-occupants (investors) are allowed to purchase into the project. If you fill the project up with renters, it may make the units less desirable for owners. If your owner-occupant ratio falls too low (typically less that 60%), then your buyers may have severe difficulties securing conventional financing. You won't realize a profit if you can't sell the finished product. Because of this, you should work closely with an experienced mortgage broker to make sure your target buyer will be able to obtain purchase money loans to buy your condos. A purchase contract is only valuable if the transaction closes and you get your money.

Whenever you are looking at a rehab or conversion project, we recommend you enlist the help of the real estate agent on your local team to provide you insight into the potential resale value of various proposed changes. It is essential to remember your resale price is dictated by the market, *not* by your need to make a profit. Always start from the resale price and work backwards to see what you should be paying for the property and budgeting for the conversion. If you start from the purchase price and go forward, your target price may be completely out of touch with the reality of the market. It sounds simple, but we see people get this wrong all the time.

Lastly, this segment is titled "May the Force Be With You" as a reference to "forcing" equity, but if you've seen the *Star Wars* movies, you know the Jedi masters are able to use "the Force" to influence other people's thoughts. There isn't anything mystical about developing strong personal relationships with influential people, but it sure can help you when you want a decision to go your way or you need someone's best effort or advice. When you are frustrated and tempted to give someone a piece of your mind, consider carefully how "venting" may adversely affect your relationship. Make sure whatever you do or say is edifying to your relationship or you might fall victim to the "Dark Side" and the very people whose help you need not only won't come through for you, but they may actually look for ways to undermine you! Don't *ever* be rude to your waitress while your food is behind the counter.

Long Live the King

While we still love leverage, sometimes forced equity transactions involve properties which are not desirable as collateral by lenders. In English, this means the more upside to a "fixer" property, the less likely you'll be able to get a conventional loan on it. Lenders don't care what you *plan* to do to make the property wonderful. They only care about what is true right now. Appraisers are constrained by this same perspective. For that reason, cash remains "king" when it comes to fixer-uppers.

You should know there are specialty lenders who like to make "rehab" loans. On bigger projects, commercial lenders will make "construction" loans. On development projects, you can get "acquisition and development" loans. This is another reason to get an experienced financing person on your team. Remember, you don't have to know all the details, you just need to know someone who does. If you are a newbie, you will have a hard time getting these types of loans because the banks want to make sure they are giving the funds to someone who knows what they are doing. Unfortunately, they don't give aptitude tests you can cram for. You actually have to have a track record, or partner with someone who does.

For ugly properties and a rookie investor, cash is still king. Remember, "cash" doesn't have to be actual cash – at least not yours. Cash can come from the bank in the form of proceeds from a loan against another property you own. Cash can be a private loan from a family member, a group of friends, or other investors as we discussed earlier. In other words, "cash" can still be 100% borrowed money. You are simply trying to avoid getting rejected for a conventional loan from an institutional lender because your collateral (the subject property) is in poor condition at the time of purchase.

Another caveat is to remember your acquisition price establishes the most current comparative sale for the property. If your flip project is scheduled to take less than six months (we hope so!), then your buyer may have an issue getting an appraisal to come in at the sales price. The buyer's lender will want to know why the resale price is so much higher than your acquisition price, regardless of what the other comps are. In anticipation of this, make sure you are prepared with photos, receipts, and contractor's invoices to help the appraiser see *all* the value you forced into the property.

If the appraisal comes up short, even if the buyer agrees the price is fair, he will need to come with cash to make up the difference between the purchase price and the appraisal. This might kill the deal! One option in this scenario is for you, as the Seller, to carry back the difference and suggest the Buyer use a short-term loan.[26] Refer the Buyer to *your* mortgage broker. Why? Because your mortgage broker understands your strategy, is on your team, and sending the business his way will help you build additional good will with him. Your mortgage broker can then be proactive (because he wants another deal) in following up with the buyer to refinance six to twelve months later, so you can get your money. When the refinance is complete based on the higher purchase price, the buyer will have cash to pay off the loan you carried back and everyone is happy. The buyer has the property, the mortgage broker got a deal, and you got your money!

El Dumpo

The typical rehab scenario involves taking a poorly maintained or outdated property and performing upgrades and repairs necessary to realize a gain. While not every "flip" involves making repairs, all "fixer-uppers" are flip opportunities. Some gurus suggest that with just a little carpet and paint, an ugly duckling property can be magically transformed into a beautiful swan and sold at a sizeable

---

[26] A "short-term loan" is not an actual loan program, but rather the concept of using a loan whose costs are very low at acquisition and for approximately the first twenty-four months. Long-term interest volatility and expense are a much lower consideration of loan selection because you don't plan to have the loan long term.

profit. The reality is that most properties with enough profit margin to be worth your time will require more work than simply "lipstick and hairspray".

If you have skills in construction, painting, plumbing and the like, small fixer-uppers may be the perfect investment vehicle for you. Even people without such skills can make a profit by finding properties with good potential and hiring out the work. Keep in mind, however, that your initial profit margin will have to be greater if you expect to hire competent help to complete the project. Even if you choose to do the work yourself, you should place a value on your own time. Too many people think they have a profitable project until they factor in their own time and realize they really only earned $2.50 per hour. They'd be better off flipping hamburgers than houses!

One reason we really like fixers is that everyone in the neighborhood appreciates having the worst property on the block transformed into one of the nicest. One of the things our investor group gets involved in is going into neighborhoods with deferred maintenance and upgrading several properties at once. Our team looks for properties in markets where there is solid upside potential. By getting several individual investors involved in a target area, we can often positively affect an entire block or neighborhood – plus, every investor is a beneficiary of not just their own efforts, but the efforts of each other.

• • •

Arnold liked to work with his hands. In high school he would spend his weekends working around the house with his father and working on projects for his neighbors. After high school, Arnold went to work for a contractor and before long was running teams doing high-end remodels. After a couple of years of witnessing the transformation of these homes and realizing how the renovations affected value, Arnold was convinced he could make more money by doing the projects himself rather than working for someone else.

After approaching his parents and several friends and relatives, Arnold was able to raise sufficient capital to purchase a rundown property in Sacramento, California. It was a single lot with two small houses in fairly poor cosmetic condition, but it had "good bones" (structurally sound). One house was a one-bedroom with one-bathroom, and the other was a two-bedroom, one-bathroom house.

The one-bedroom house was vacant, so Arnold and his crew (two other friends he had met in the construction business) started there. They actually stayed in the house during the renovation.

Once the two-bedroom house was vacant (the tenant was in the process of moving out when Arnold bought the property), Arnold and company turned their attention to it. Within just six weeks, both homes were beautiful and the neighbors were ecstatic!

Derek, who was a mutual friend of Arnold's and Robert's, had heard about how great the Sacramento market was. He wanted to purchase a rental property there, so before Arnold had even completed the rehab, Robert put together a pro-forma analysis of how the property would cash-flow once the work was completed and new tenants were found. Derek liked the numbers and entered into a contract to purchase the property from Arnold. Derek's loan was being processed even as the rehab work was in progress. Derek was able to close escrow just a few days after Arnold and his crew completed the work. Derek got an inside deal and Arnold leveraged time to create a faster velocity of his money.

• • •

Dirt to Dollars

Another excellent and exciting way to force equity is to create something where there is currently nothing. Developing bare land into housing or a commercial building can be lucrative and quite fulfilling. Profit margins on real estate development usually far exceed those on rehabilitation projects. There is also much satisfaction in watching a bare piece of land become a contributing asset to a community.

Real estate development sounds like a difficult and expensive game to get into – and it is! However, the rewards can be similarly spectacular. So how does a newcomer break in to the business?

First, as with anything in life worth doing, you will need to invest time and money learning the business. We suppose somewhere out there, there's a college of real estate development, but we aren't sure it would be your first choice. Colleges are great at teaching theory, but perhaps not so effective at teaching what works in the real world. We believe in the mentor/apprentice model. Learning what works in the real world is found at the side of someone who is effective in the real world. If you have the opportunity to work with an active real estate developer, take it – even if you have to work for free. How much did you get paid to go to college? Nothing? Then why did you go? Get the point?

People work hard every day and *pay* the institution so they can learn. Why should an apprenticeship program be any different? Besides, would you rather learn from an academic who teaches only theory – or from an active, successful real-world practitioner? So what if the developer makes millions from your efforts? Aren't you planning on making millions with the education? Always be careful of your mindset – the wrong one will cost you many millions in lost opportunity.

Another perk of working with an active developer is the opportunity to build relationships with bankers, contractors, and other people who will be important to your future success. Treat those relationships with respect and always remember where they came from. No one likes a backstabber.

You don't have to wait until you get into a relationship with a developer to begin to learn the business. Start small. Do small fixer-uppers. Learn basic construction terms and procedures. Get used to looking at blueprints, talking with contractors, inspectors, city planners, and architects. Later, you'll be dealing with civil and structural engineers, commercial bankers, and more sophisticated contractors. Even if you don't make tons of money on your first several transactions, remember that it's the education you're after. You have to learn to walk before you can run.

Another important part of getting into the development business is financing. Understanding commercial and construction lending are important components of your education. Until you are able to find a developer to work with, try finding work in commercial lending. At the very least, befriend someone in the profession and spend time "talking shop" with him. Subscribe to trade magazines and go to lending conventions. Learn the lingo. Find out what types of loan programs are out there and what lenders look for in borrowers and projects.

Remember, you are working on an "extreme makeover" of your financial life. When a banker looks at you they want to see experience, track record, and assets. It will take you time to develop these things, but you can get a long way by "borrowing" credibility from others. You might take on strategic partners from time to time because they bring an area of strength to your overall presentation. In time, you will learn from them (and they from you) and even if you choose to part company, you will have established your own credibility and reputation during your time together. Also, parting does not have to be a bitter experience. Take the high road and be gracious – even if the partnership didn't end on a high note. You can bet all your contacts will be watching your behavior carefully. You want to paint a picture of professionalism and class. These qualities are attractive and reassuring to the people whose help you will need to be successful. Of course, the opposite is true, so always be on your best behavior. As we've said, act like the world is watching everything you do – because it is.

Even as you are re-inventing yourself as a credible real estate investor and developer, you should work on understanding what the market needs. A basic success principle in business is to identify a need in the market place and find a way to meet that need. For example, if you have a particular geographic area you are interested in working in, go to the city planning office and review the General Plan. Attend any public meetings related to city planning and try to get a feel for what the government and the public are looking for in the area. Ultimately, as a developer, you must build projects people want to buy, lenders want to fund, and the local government and community is willing to approve.

Does this all sound like a lot of work? That's right. Did you think someone was going to come along and hand you a winning lottery ticket? "Get rich quick and easy!" sells great on late-night TV, but not in the real world. Successful people get up every day and go to work to achieve their dreams. The thing that makes them successful is not just that they achieve financial rewards, but they get to spend every day doing what they love to do. They are pursuing their passion. Passion provides the power to keep you pushing forward in spite of obstacles. You can't win if you quit and you won't quit if you're passionate about what you're doing.

The best shortcut we know is to get very clear about what you need to do and then stay focused on doing it until you've won. Learn from other people's successes and failures, be patiently persistent as you advance toward your dream, and pay close attention to your reputation and relationships. Remember, the key to big results is leverage. Take the time to organize your "tools". Learn how to use them, and then get to work – and stay there – until you are done. If there is a magic formula, this might be it!

NOTE: By now, you've probably noticed we have repeated certain themes throughout the book. HINT: There's a reason for it.

Jump in the Pool with Flipper

Suppose you like the idea of "forcing" equity, but aren't sure where to start. Perhaps you feel the risk and uncertainty is too much at this stage in your development as an investor. This is understandable. The idea of taking on a complete renovation or new development project can be very intimidating when you are just getting started.

What if there was a way for you to participate in the wonderful world of forced equity without having to contribute 100% of the money, time and effort, and without taking all of the risk by yourself?

Many investors realize excellent profits from flipping properties by pooling their resources with other investors. By leveraging the financial power of the group with the expertise of experienced investors, everyone benefits from access to the larger, more difficult, and therefore potentially more profitable projects.

There are a variety of ways to pool funds and organize responsibilities. Once again, this topic alone could be the subject of an entire book. For now, we will give you some fundamental ideas and encourage you to seek out experienced counsel before organizing or participating in any type of syndication (group investment).

The most fundamental difference between various types of structures is determined by the roles of the people putting in the money. If all the investor contributes is money and has no active role in the investing activity, the investor is considered to be "passive". If you are the organizer of an investment pool and have passive investors, we *strongly* urge you to work closely with experienced legal counsel or you might find yourself on the wrong end of securities laws.

If all of the investors have some degree of decision-making responsibility, they are considered "active", and it is less likely you will be in violation of securities laws. Nonetheless, you should *always* have an experienced lawyer involved in the organization of any group investment.

With the securities law caveats out of the way, let's discuss the actual organization of the investment. Once again, we divide the organizational structure into two broad categories: *direct* ownership and *indirect* ownership.

Direct ownership is where each of the investor's names appears on title (the grant deed) to the property. The most common arrangement is "Tenants-In-Common" (TIC). There are other ways to hold title to real property and you can usually get a very useful guide to these from your local real estate broker. The two primary advantages to the investor in direct ownership are a) having your name on title provides an indisputable claim to ownership of the property, and b) capital gains on direct ownership profits are generally eligible for tax-deferred exchange into new properties (assuming the property is held for the production of income). The disadvantages are that there is some liability exposure for anyone whose name appears on title, the owners' names are a matter of public record (for those concerned about privacy), and everyone whose name is on title will generally be required to personally guarantee any financing.

Indirect ownership is where the investors form an entity such as a limited liability company (LLC), limited partnership (LP) or corporation with which to hold the property. In these cases, the investors do not own the property directly, but rather they own the entity that owns the property. The reason for doing this is to put a liability shield between the property and the investors and/or to keep the investors' names off of title for privacy or financing purposes.

Now that you've organized your structure and gathered up the money, what's next?

The main purpose of pooling funds is to be in position for everyone in the deal to get a higher return on the time and money invested than is possible on their own. If this isn't the case, there is no reason to go through the trouble of putting it all together. However, this isn't to say that the return is strictly financial. You may decide to participate with a more experienced investor as much for the experience as for the financial return. You might decide the reduced risk and hassle of being in the deal with others is a better overall value to you than taking on the project all by yourself even though you have the funds, the time and the skill. Value isn't simply financial.

• • •

Robert found an interesting property in Phoenix, Arizona that seemed like a great candidate for a flip. The seller, Edward, liked to buy underutilized properties, fix them up over time, get the rents up, sell them and then do a 1031 tax-deferred exchange into another similar opportunity. Robert had purchased one of these "finished" properties from Edward and was very pleased with the quality of work Edward had done and the performance of the property once the work was completed.

Because he was familiar with the quality of Edward's work, Robert was very interested in taking a look at another property Edward was working on. This particular property was unique because it comprised of sixteen rental units on three separate, but contiguous parcels. There were two four-unit buildings, three two-unit buildings, and two single-family houses. Ed had rehabbed most of the units, and was working on one of the houses when Robert made an offer on the property. The other house was in livable condition, but would probably have to be torn down at some point in the near future.

While the property would make a great buy-and-hold, Robert's exit strategy was to acquire all the units, work with an agent to subdivide the three lots into four lots, and then sell the four individual properties to investors. At their original purchase price, Robert would be able to sell the individual parcels to separate investors at an attractively low price and still realize a healthy profit on the flip.

Rather than tie up his personal capital, Robert decided to involve other investors. Robert's attorney set up a limited liability company, and the LLC was capitalized through the contributions of the individual investors. The LLC then used the funds to acquire the property and complete the work required to subdivide, upgrade the properties and improve the cash-flow.

Once the project was completed, the LLC sold each of the four parcels to four individual investors and closed the transactions within six months of the initial acquisition. The investors in the LLC earned a good return, and each of the buy-and-hold investors ended up with great long-term rental property. Win-win!

• • •

Another important principle of investing with others is to make sure the individual's investment objectives, timelines, and target returns are aligned with the management's objectives, targets, and timelines. There are few things worse than being in a relationship (business, investment or otherwise) where a mismatch in vision exists. The best inoculation against this is for each person to have a reasonably clear personal investment philosophy and communicate it clearly to potential co-investors. If there is a match, you have a good foundation for a successful investing relationship. If not, then no matter how interesting the deal may seem, proceed with caution. As action prone as we are, we don't recommend jumping into "partnerships" without significant forethought, communication and counsel. Unfortunately, we speak from education gained at the school of hard knocks.

Another word of caution: Have you ever noticed some of the books and tapes hawked at free seminars tout the "secret" even your attorneys and accountants don't know? If someone gives you information and suggests that you NOT involve your attorney or accountant, run (don't walk) to the nearest door. With that said, we also want to comment here about working with attorneys and accountants. Our experience is that most attorneys and accountants are conservative by nature. They view their primary responsibility as keeping you out of trouble, not helping you become wealthy. As such, they tend not to give *strategic* advice, but rather they focus on tactical technical information such as which forms to fill out or how to write up agreements. Don't get us wrong; these are very valuable services. However, we think a little "healthy tension" between you and your advisors is also very useful.

What do we mean by "healthy tension?" We think you should be looking for aggressive ways to build wealth by thinking outside the box and pushing the envelope. Your advisors should be pulling you back from the cliff while you are pushing to try to fly. In time, you'll learn to work well together, but don't make the mistake of expecting the attorneys and accountants to coach you on aggressive strategies. Most of them won't. Use them for what they are good at, but stay connected to active, aggressive investors for the best strategic thinking. Then, run your tactical plans past your advisors to make sure you don't make an innocent, but stupid and costly, mistake.

Know When to Hold 'em
One of the most popular styles of real estate investments is to "buy-and-hold". We've mentioned this term several times up to this point, but never really explained it because its meaning is somewhat obvious. However, for the sake of clarity let's go ahead and define exactly what we mean.

Simply stated, buy-and-hold is the strategy of buying a property and holding it over the long-term. Obviously, this is much easier when the property is producing income, so rental properties are the most likely candidates for buy-and-hold, though we've seen some supposed flips that looked more like buy-and-hold based on the snail's pace at which the rehab or development took place!

The profit on a buy-and-hold comes from the cash-flow on operations (rental income plus tax credits less operating expenses and debt service) and equity build-up (amortization of the loan and appreciation of the property). Always remember, there are two categories of profit: a) cash-flow on operations and b) appreciation. If all you do is look at cash-flow, you will almost certainly miss the largest component of your return – and perhaps be inclined to walk away from a profitable property. On the other hand, if you focus solely on appreciation and neglect cash-flow, the property may go up in value over time, but you run the risk of losing it in foreclosure (assuming debt is involved) and never realizing the profit. Cash-flow controls the mortgage, the mortgage controls the property, and the property provides appreciation and cash-flow. Pay attention to cash-flow!

Buy-and-hold isn't as glamorous or as immediately rewarding as forcing equity through development, rehab or conversion, but the equity that accrues to the owner over time simply for holding the property for "passive equity" can be substantial.

As we've discussed, in most real estate markets, property values increase steadily over time. This is the reason an equity investor uses buy-and-hold. If you buy a property right, manage it well, and monitor its performance, you can own a passive real estate investment that provides cash-flow, appreciation and tax benefits. Part of effective management is making sure rents are current based on the local marketplace. Striking the delicate balance between high-paying occupancy and top-of-the-market rents is one of the critical areas for you and/or your property manager to stay focused on. If the rent is too high, you will drive your tenants (your customers) to the competition (other rentals in the area). If your rents are too low, you sacrifice valuable cash-flow *and* equity (more on that when we discuss "gross rent multipliers" and how income property is valued).

• • •

Ted and May knew real estate had the potential to grow in value and provide a steady stream of income. In 1984 they put a down payment on a five-unit building in a small city just south of San Jose, California. At the time, the property had a HUD Section 8 (a government-subsidized housing program) contract, which guaranteed the rents in exchange for making the units available to low-income tenants.

While the California real estate market had its ups and downs during the period they owned the building, Ted and May were careful to treat their tenants fairly and provide a safe, comfortable place for them to live. One of the things their tenants asked for was a laundry room. Ted converted a storage room on the property into a nice laundry room with one washer and one dryer. Before long, the coin-operated machines were in constant use. It turned out the tenants from the buildings on either side of Ted and May's building had discovered the laundry room and found it more convenient than going to the local Laundromat. As the use of the laundry room grew, so did Ted and May's income!

Ted decided investing in another washer and dryer would make sense. For the next ten years, the monthly income from the laundry room exceeded $250 each month. Some months the income was as high as $400! Ted and May were able to recover the cost of the laundry equipment in just a few months and enjoy the extra income for many months after that – all without raising the rents.

• • •

NOTE: Many companies will provide coin-operated washers and dryers to landlords for a portion of the revenue. These companies maintain and service the machines, and take care of the collection and disbursement of the income. However, make sure you run the numbers. Depending on the unit mix and tenant base, you may find buying and servicing your own machines will be more profitable.

Hurry Up and Wait

A variation on the buy-and-hold strategy is what we call "flip-and-hold". At first glance, this seems like an oxymoron, but flip-and-hold refers to the situation where you flip the financing, yet hold onto the property. For example, suppose you buy a property that needs work. Rather than do the rehab and sell the property (incurring sales costs and relinquishing the asset), you simply cash-out refinance the property after the work is done and the value has been raised. Then keep the property as a long-term investment and let appreciation and leverage work for you.

• • •

Wanda was excited about investing in real estate, but like many young single professionals she did not have the resources to do much at first. In fact, she didn't even own a home. Wanda decided to focus on leveraging her modest resources with the power of her support team to do a small rehab project and generate a quick profit. Her plan was to use this profit as a down payment on another property.

Through our network, Wanda found a two-unit residential property in Sacramento, California. It needed a considerable amount of cosmetic work, but was structurally sound. Even though the property represented an excellent buy, because of the property's poor condition, the lender wanted to see Wanda come up with at least 30% down. She didn't have enough cash to put such a sizable amount down, so Wanda turned to a private investor who agreed to loan her 90% of the purchase price at a very competitive interest rate in exchange for a portion of the profits (this type of financing arrangement is called convertible debt). Wanda was obligated to repay the loan with interest whether she made a profit or not, but the investor held the option of taking an equity position in the property so he could share in the profits – if there were any.

With the help of a local general contractor, Wanda was able to arrange the work needed to get the property in shape. To her surprise, both of the tenants in the property agreed to remain in their units during the construction period. This pleasant, but unexpected turn of events alleviated some financial pressure because the rental income offset some of her carrying costs. While the market conditions may have allowed her to raise the rent a little, Wanda decided not to do so, because if the current tenants left, any incremental increase in the monthly rent from new tenants would have been consumed by the vacancy. For example, if her units were renting for $500 per month and she thought the market would give her $550, her potential increase would be $50 per unit x 2 or $100 per month. If raising the rent caused just one of the tenants to leave and it took her one month to find a new tenant, she would gain $600 over six months ($100 month increase x 6 months or $600), but lose $500 in vacancy, plus advertising and cleaning costs. By agreeing to keep the rent at the current rate for six months, Wanda retained both of the current tenants, who were paying below market rent, and Wanda had no disruption in rental income during the rehab. Win-win!

Although Wanda's original plan was to sell the property once it was fixed up, after the work on the property was complete, she ran the numbers again and decided to see if she could keep the property. With the improved condition, and two stable tenants, she was able to get a new loan on the property based on its new value, pay off the private investor along with his share of the profit, and keep the property. She was able to "flip" the financing to get her money back out, but "hold" the property for long-term appreciation. As it turned out, Sacramento became the #1 appreciating market in the country the following year. Good job!

• • •

For years Robert was a strictly buy-and-hold investor, mostly because he had watched his father successfully build a nice portfolio of income properties over a period of many years. After being exposed to several of the flip projects their clients were doing, Robert and Bob decided to try their hands at a fixer-upper. They located a four-unit property in an up-and-coming neighborhood and arranged for a 70/20/10 loan. This means Robert and his father came up with a 10% down payment, asked the seller to carry back 20%, and got a new first loan for 70%.

Neither Bob nor Robert are very mechanically inclined, so they hired one of their contractor clients to do the work necessary to fix the property up. After four months and just over $30,000 of rehab expense, the units were ready to go and were rented at then-market rates. After performing a new market analysis on the property, it looked like they would probably make close to $80,000 in profit on the project. Not bad for their first flip!

Then a funny thing happened on the way to market. Bob and Robert started talking about how nice the property looked, how great the new tenants were, and how the neighborhood had really improved since they first acquired the property. So they approached the property from a different angle. How would it look if they simply kept it?

They decided to keep the property a while longer and use the cash-flow to hold the property while the value continued to increase. After another year, they sold it as part of a 1031 tax-deferred exchange at a net profit of $120,000 – much better than the $80,000 originally budgeted.

• • •

The power of flip-and-hold is in recycling your working capital by forcing equity and then pulling your investment capital back out so you can move on to the next property. Meanwhile, you are building a portfolio of income and equity producing properties. The net result is you build more equity faster. We like it.

The problem most people have with real estate investing is coming up with down payments. This is why the "no money down" programs all sell so well. But what people really need is a game plan for creating a "down payment machine". Unfortunately, average people try to be their own down payment machine by getting up every day and going to work, paying taxes, living below their means, and putting their savings in the bank at an interest rate typically at or below inflation. There are very few people with the income earning ability and personal discipline to do this successfully.

Flip-and-hold is one of several different strategies we use to make our properties create down payments for other properties. While the concept of flip-and-hold is simple, there are some technical items you should be aware of.

Lenders are more skittish about cash-out refinance loans than they are with purchase loans. This is especially true with investment properties. The more equity remaining in a property, the happier the lenders are. It makes them feel safe. So when you apply for a cash-out loan, they charge a little extra. When you want piles of cash out, they charge more, or sometimes they refuse to do the loan. They also have certain rules about how fast "forced" equity can be taken back out.

When you buy a property, fix it up, and attempt to refinance it based on a higher appraisal, the lender may decide they will only loan based on the original purchase price, if the purchase is less than one year old. Of course, this sabotages your flip-and-hold plan and ties up your working capital for far too long. However, there are some things you can do to work around this.

When you are doing your rehab, make sure you take before and after pictures – lots of them! Include close ups and captions. These pictures will help satisfy both the appraiser and the loan underwriter and prove you actually did add significant value to the property. Unfortunately, there are scam artists out there who attempt to defraud lenders by faking fix-up projects and taking cash out of properties to which they added no real value. A picture, as they say, is worth a thousand words – and in this case, thousands of dollars!

Also, make sure you keep copies of all the receipts for labor and materials. Most lenders will allow you to bump up the value of the property for a cash-out refinance based upon the actual hard dollars you invested in the fix-up. This is good enough to get back most of your invested capital, but wouldn't it be great to be able to take out some profit without having to wait a year for the purchase to "season"?

If you plan to be a serious Flip-and-Hold investor, you may want to set up your own construction company. It must be a legitimate company, properly licensed and should be incorporated. When you do the rehab project, have your construction company do the work and issue legitimate receipts at fair market value for the work performed. Your pricing should include a reasonable operating profit to the construction company.

Now, when you submit your loan package and include copies of the receipts, pictures, and an appraisal showing the true cost and market value of the rehab work performed by your construction company, the lender is more likely to allow a greater amount of cash out to reimburse you for the expensed incurred. The profit ends up with the construction company and ultimately with you, but it was done honestly and in a manner acceptable to the lender.

Now that you have your cash, you are on to the next project to repeat the process. Effectively, you are able to "churn" out down payments by flipping your cash while you build your income property portfolio by holding over the long-term.

Dial 10-10-1031 to Save Money

While there are plenty of investors who do very well with buy-and-hold investment properties, many miss out on opportunities to optimize their returns. In fact, it is very common for an investor to allow a property to go "unchecked" simply because it is bringing in positive cash-flow. Why would this be bad?

Successful buy-and-hold investors know that by monitoring the performance of their income properties, they can achieve much better than average returns. Earlier we spoke of methods you can use to beat the average rate of appreciation. If you are a buy-and-hold investor, paying particular attention to the key indicators in your markets, as well as other markets, helps you make effective decisions on how to manage your portfolio.

In our educational program, we teach a concept called "optimization," which we will discuss at various times throughout the book. Optimization is simply the process of getting the most out of your investment portfolio in the long-term without undue risk to your finances or reputation. In regard to equity optimization, it is likely you will make regular use of what is called a "1031 tax-deferred exchange" to re-deploy idle equity and maintain an optimal equity growth rate.

Put Off Today What You Can Compound Tomorrow

A 1031 tax-deferred exchange is simply a process by which an investor who is holding an investment property can sell it and defer paying any capital gains tax due on the profit. "1031" refers to the section in the Internal Revenue Code which permits this. There are specific rules about how a 1031 must be executed in order to defer the tax and you must follow them carefully. However, there are many great publications on all of the technical details of 1031 tax-deferred exchanges, so we aren't going to cover them here. We'll assume when your time comes to do a 1031 you will be wise enough to engage the services of a competent 1031 tax-deferred exchange intermediary (the facilitator who handles the funds for you) and a real estate agent experienced in 1031 tax-deferred exchanges. For now, we'd like to discuss the strategy behind using a 1031.

A 1031 tax-deferred exchange is a tool investors use to transfer equity from one or more currently owned properties to one or more new properties which presumably promise better financial performance. For example, you might own several small properties in appreciating areas, but as you move towards retirement you'd rather own just one large apartment building that hemorrhages positive cash-flow. If you were to simply sell the smaller appreciated buildings, you would be faced with federal capital gains taxes. If you had been deferring gains for many years, this tax might be substantial!

The federal capital gains rate at the time of this writing is 15% of the net gain. For example, if you owned a property with a cost basis of $100,000 and you sold it later for $215,000 with $15,000 in sales expenses, you have realized a capital gain of $100,000. At 15%, your federal tax would be $15,000. If you live in a state which compounds your misery by tacking on state taxes, you'll pay even more. When you take into account something called "depreciation recapture" you will potentially pay even more still. Since we plan to organize our investing to avoid these taxes, we aren't going to get into detail as to what they are. For more information, visit with a qualified and experienced tax advisor.

Using the 1031 tax-deferred exchange, the IRS permits you to sell the appreciated properties, pay no current capital gains taxes (taxes are deferred), and apply the cash proceeds (your net equity) to the purchase of new property(s). The advantages of this are several.

First, the tax you did not have to pay is now available to help you control more property. For example, if you had a capital gain of $100,000 on the property you are relinquishing (selling), then you would owe a capital gains tax of $15,000. Once you give it to Uncle Sam, it is gone forever! If you then used the remaining $85,000 to make a 10% down payment on a new property, you could buy an $850,000 property. However, if you didn't have to pay the $15,000 in tax, you would have the full $100,000 to invest. If you used $100,000 to make a 10% down payment on a new building, you would be able to get a $1,000,000 building. Do you see how the $15,000 in tax just cost you $150,000 in real estate?

It gets worse. What if the new property appreciated a little over 7% per year for the next ten years? This means the value would approximately double during that time. Now the $850,000 building would be worth $1,700,000, but the $1,000,000 building would be worth $2,000,000.

Now, this might seem difficult, but stick with us because it is important you understand this! Here we go...

Scenario A (Pay the Tax) – The $850,000 property had a 90% loan or $765,000. The balance was the $85,000 purchase equity which came from the after-tax gain on the previous property. If the property doubled in ten years, it would be worth $1,700,000. When you subtract the $765,000 loan balance (assuming you didn't pay it down), you have $935,000 in total equity. Subtract from that your purchase equity of $85,000 and you have $850,000 of *new* equity. Great!

Scenario B (Defer the Tax) – However, if you had deferred the tax, you could have used all of the $100,000 from the original property as 10% purchase equity on a new $1,000,000 property and you would get a $900,000 loan. If this property doubled in ten years, then it would be worth $2,000,000. When you subtract the $900,000 loan, you have $1,100,000 of total equity. Subtract from that the $100,000 purchase equity you started with and you have $1,000,000 in *new* equity. *Really* great!

The difference in new equity between the $850,000 in Scenario A if you had paid the tax and the $1,000,000 on Scenario B if you had deferred the tax is $150,000. This means that little capital gains tax of $15,000 ten years ago actually cost you $150,000 in equity. Ouch! But, it gets worse...

An $850,000 building on a residential property depreciation schedule would provide approximately $27,000 a year of depreciation. The beautiful thing about depreciation is it is a non-cash expense. It sounds like an oxymoron, right? "Non-cash" and "expense" are two words that don't seem like they go together. It's like "reliable" and "copier". We just aren't accustomed to using those two words in the same sentence. But in this case it's true! Depreciation is a "loss" the tax code permits you to deduct from your income – even though you didn't really pay anything out. So, in the real world, depreciation can actually *improve* your cash-flow. As a professional investor, you can apply those "phantom" losses to your other income and eliminate large chunks of tax liability. This is a good thing.

If you owned the Scenario B $1,000,000 building instead of only the Scenario A $850,000 building, your depreciation would be more like $32,000 per year, instead of the $27,000. This is an extra $5,000 per year of deductible losses. Over ten years, the bigger building would provide an additional $50,000 of write-offs. If you were in a 35% tax bracket, that's another $17,000 missed opportunity from failing to use a 1031 tax-deferred exchange. Yuck. But, it gets even worse...

Which building do you think generates more cash-flow – the smaller $850,000 building or the bigger $1 million dollar building? That's right, the bigger building. If each building was generating cash at a rate of 1/10 of the purchase price annually (a gross rent multiplier of 10), the $850,000 building would generate $85,000 per year while the $1,000,000 would generate $100,000 a year. The difference is $15,000 a year. Ten years later, this difference is another $150,000! Yowza! But, before you get too worked up, remember the bigger building also has a bigger loan, so most of that greater income goes to pay the bigger loan...at least at first.

You see, over time, rents tend to go up. If rents rise an average of just 3% per year, the $85,000 per year rents on the $850,000 building would have climbed to $114,000 per year in ten years, while the rents on the $1,000,000 building would have climbed to $134,000. So after ten years, your cash-flow going forward on the bigger building would be an extra $20,000 income per year.

Of course, if the properties continued to appreciate at 7% per year, then at the end of ten years, the now $1,700,000 building would be adding new equity at a rate of $119,000 per year, but the now $2,000,000 building would be adding new equity at a rate of $140,000 per year. The difference is another $21,000 equity per year.

Now do you see the power of the 1031 tax-deferred exchange to preserve investment capital?

• • •

Lloyd and his longtime friend Harry had a common interest in real estate and found themselves looking at a potential fixer-upper in a tougher area of Oakland, California. They decided between the two of them they had what it took to go for it. After learning much about the business of rental rehab, they completed the project and found themselves the proud owners of a rental property that cash-flowed.

However, Oakland has a rent control policy. The problem with rent control regulations is they effectively discourage property owners from improving their properties. When an owner cannot raise rents enough on an improved property to provide an attractive return on investment (ROI), the only other way to improve ROI is to reduce expenses. As time went by, Lloyd and Harry noticed an increasing amount of deferred maintenance in many of the properties in the neighborhood. The area was beginning to look pretty ratty. They also found the caliber of tenants they were attracting was not as desirable as it once was. Although their property had appreciated in value, they were not seeing the healthy cash-flow they once enjoyed. Lloyd started to do some research on other markets to see if there were better areas to invest in.

After attending our mentoring clubs for a few months, Lloyd was intrigued by the Sacramento market and suggested to Harry that they consider selling their building in order to 1031 tax-deferred exchange into a property in Sacramento. While they both felt buy-and-hold was the right investment strategy for them, they made the decision to transfer their equity to Sacramento. It seemed to them to be a much better market place than Oakland.

While they didn't get quite as much for the Oakland property as they hoped, they were able to exchange into an excellent property in Sacramento with much upside potential. In fact, they bought a building on a street on which four other investors from our group also bought properties. After just six months, they had better cash-flow, less turnover, and a better equity position. Even though they incurred sales expense to sell the Oakland property, they didn't have to pay capital gains, and now their equity was deployed in a hot market rather than in a cooling one.

• • •

The previous true story illustrates another motivation for doing a 1031 tax-deferred exchange. When you buy a property in one area and decide later another area offers better investment performance, you can use the exchange to transfer the equity into one or more properties in the better area. While selling expenses are not to be taken lightly, if you find yourself in a declining area and know of an emerging growth market elsewhere, it is usually best to take the sales expense hit and get into the hotter market. Much of the expense can be mitigated by increasing your leverage ratio when buying the new property. This doesn't mean you don't pay the sales expense, but the expense is quickly justified by the better equity growth in the new property.

For example, if you owned a $500,000 building in a flat or declining area, and have a loan of $300,000, you would have $200,000 in equity available to exchange forward. If you sell, you might incur a total sales expense including commissions, transaction costs and repairs of 8-10% of the sales price. In this case, let's say the sales expenses are $50,000. Now after our last illustration of how bad it is to pay $15,000 in capital gains, we're sure the idea of incurring $50,000 in expenses is not attractive.[27] However, in this case, your property is in a poor performing market and you want to get to a better one. If the appreciation in the new market is enough, it justifies the $50,000 expense. Let's do the math and see.

After paying the $50,000 selling expenses, you exchange your remaining $150,000 forward at 5:1 (20 % down) by buying a $750,000 building in an appreciating market. If the property appreciates 7% a year, your net worth is now growing by over $50,000 per year. Compare that to the previous $500,000 property in a flat or declining market. $500,000 x zero equals zero. You don't have to be a rocket scientist to see that spending $50,000 to get into a better market can make good financial sense. The 1031 tax-deferred exchange helped you avoid compounding your pain by paying capital gains on the relinquished property. So even though you incurred sales expenses, the 1031 still provided a significant benefit.

---

[27] Remember, that whether you use an exchange or not, when you sell you will have expenses. The prior illustration involving deferring the $15,000 tax simply showed the impact of paying the tax, all things (including sales expense) being equal.

• • •

Pete was a general contractor who specialized in remodeling high-end homes. When his business expanded, he purchased an industrial building with a large garage area and a roll-up door. A few years later he rented the building to a painting contractor he had worked with for quite some time. When the contractor moved out, Pete was having difficulty renting the building, but came across someone who was interested in buying it.

It was about this time Pete decided to come to one of our educational events on investing. Robert's father, Bob, met with Pete and his wife, Mary Jane, after the seminar to discuss ideas about using the proceeds from the sale of the industrial building to further their real estate holdings.

Pete and Mary Jane decided a tax-deferred exchange made sense for them. They were in their early forties, had stable income, and didn't need the proceeds from the "relinquished" building. They did, however, want to structure their "replacement" properties so they would have cash-flow of $3,000 to $4,000 per month.

Beginning with the end in mind, Robert and Bob identified several candidate properties that would meet Pete and Mary Jane's requirements. The two best opportunities were a fourteen-unit apartment building in Las Vegas which Robert had secured the rights to, and four individual parcels containing four rental units each in Phoenix. Pete and Mary Jane would be coming out of the relinquished industrial building with approximately $590,000 in net equity forward.

After running the numbers, it appeared either the Las Vegas or Phoenix properties would meet the parameters of the exchange and provide the cash-flow desired:

Scenario 1:

Las Vegas 14-Unit Building:

Purchase Price	$ 730,000
Down Payment (~79%)	$ 575,000
New First Loan (~21%)	$ 155,000
Annual Gross Scheduled Income (8 GRM)[28]	$ 91,200
Less Vacancy Allowance (7% of GSI)[29]	$ 6,384
Gross Effective Income	$ 84,816
Less Expenses (36% of GSI)	$ 32,832
Net Operating Income	$ 51,984
Annual Debt Service (loan payments) at 6%	$ 11,152
Annual Before-Tax Cash-Flow	$ 40,832
Monthly Before-Tax Cash-Flow	$ 3,403

Scenario 2:

Phoenix 16-Unit Complex:

Purchase Price	$1,126,500
Down Payment (~50%)	$ 567,500
New First Loan (~50%)	$ 559,000
Annual Gross Scheduled Income (10 GRM)	$ 112,600
Less Vacancy Allowance (4% of GSI)[30]	$ 4,504
Gross Effective Income	$ 108,096
Less Expenses (32% of GSI)	$ 36,032
Net Operating Income	$ 72,064
Annual Debt Service (loan payments) at 6%	$ 40,218
Annual Before-Tax Cash-Flow	$ 31,846
Monthly Before-Tax Cash-Flow	$ 2,654

---

[28] GRM stands for Gross Rent Multiplier. See the Glossary for more information.
[29] We used 7% as an estimated vacancy factor based on the average vacancy in this particular neighborhood. Vacancy factor estimates are an inexact science at best. A good source for fairly accurate data is an informal poll of property managers in the area.
[30] Although the units were currently fully rented, we used 4% vacancy factor based on the average vacancy in that area of Phoenix.

Comparing the two scenarios, the Las Vegas property seemed to fit the couple's cash-flow requirements better. However, by purchasing the Phoenix properties, Pete and Mary Jane would be controlling almost $400,000 more real estate than if they chose the Las Vegas property. The benefit of $400,000 more real estate in an appreciating market could be considerable. If the Phoenix properties and the Las Vegas properties both appreciated just 5% per year, the Phoenix properties would be going up in value $56,000 per year, while the Las Vegas properties would be going up in value only $36,000. The difference would be $20,000 per year in greater appreciation on the bigger portfolio; plus, as we learned in the last section on 1031 tax-deferred exchanges, there are several other factors that make controlling more "top-line" real estate very attractive.

However, choosing to acquire the Phoenix properties in order to gain more top-line real estate would come at the expense of diminished cash-flow when compared to the Las Vegas properties. This might be a valid trade-off to gain more appreciation, especially if Phoenix appreciated faster than 5%. At the time, Phoenix had been appreciating at nearly 10%! Cash-flow or appreciation? Hmmm…decisions, decisions.

Then Pete had an idea. He asked, "What if we purchased *both* properties?" Interesting thought! So, we ran the numbers:

(See Scenario 3 on the following page)

Scenario 3:

Purchase BOTH Properties	
Combined Purchase Price	$1,856,500
Down Payment (~30%)	$ 556,950
New First Loan (~70%)	$1,299,550
Annual Gross Scheduled Income (9.1 GRM)	$ 203,800
Less Vacancy Allowance (~5% of GSI)	$ 10,888
Gross Effective Income	$ 192,912
Less Expenses (~34% of GSI)	$ 68,864
Net Operating Income	$ 124,048
Annual Debt Service (loan payments) at 6%	$ 93,498
Annual Before-Tax Cash-Flow	$ 30,550
Monthly Before-Tax Cash-Flow	$ 2,546

As you can see, if Pete and Mary Jane acquired *both* properties, their monthly before-tax cash-flow of $2,546 is only $108 less than the $2,654 they would have if they went solely with the Phoenix property. Think about that. For only $108 less cash-flow, Pete and Mary Jane would control $1.85 million in real estate versus only $1.12 million if they had bought the Phoenix property only (scenario 2). The difference, of course, is the $730,000 Las Vegas property. Another way to look at it is the $730,000 Las Vegas property only cost them $108 per month! If the Las Vegas property appreciated at 5% per year (at the time, Las Vegas had been over 10% for 13 consecutive years), the new passive equity growth would be over $36,000 per year or $3,000 per month. Would you invest $108 per month of cash-flow to obtain $3,000 a month in increased net worth? We would!

Now that we know buying *both* properties is only $108 less cash-flow than buying just the Phoenix property, let's compare buying only the Las Vegas property (Scenario 1) versus buying both (Scenario 3). The estimated BTCF on only the Las Vegas property was $3,403, while the Las Vegas and Phoenix combined purchase projected cash-flow of only $2,546. We see that the combined purchase produces $857 per month less than the Las Vegas property by itself.

Giving up $857 in potential income is a bigger sacrifice that merely foregoing $108, so once again, Pete and Mary Jane had a decision to make. Did they want to give up $857 BTCF to obtain $3,000 per month (or more!) of new passive equity?

After talking through each scenario, and discussing how much cash-flow they *really* needed each month, Pete and Mary Jane elected to purchase both properties. As it turned out, over the next few years, both markets did very well. In fact, Las Vegas went on to become the #1 appreciating market in the history of tracking U.S. appreciation!

Though this story is primarily intended to show the power of optimizing your equity by using a 1031 tax-deferred exchange, there are other lessons to point out. Positive cash-flow is nice, but if you don't need it, you will often do better investing for equity. In this case, not only did Pete and Mary Jane increase their net worth, but they also diversified their risk by securing more income sources (tenants) and not being exposed to only one real estate market.

• • •

NOTE: This simplified example concentrated on the cash-flow *before* taxes. When analyzing income property, tax considerations fall primarily into two categories: tax due on income generated and tax credits for depreciation. Often the "after-tax" picture is very different from the "before-tax" picture. However, each person's tax situation varies, so we elected not to make tax bracket assumptions in this case study. But make sure you involve your tax advisor when determining how any proposed transaction might affect *your* tax liability and after-tax cash-flow.

Pay particular attention to the passive activity loss rules.

Also, keep in mind that while tax benefits can often help the performance of your real estate investments, you should not make investment decisions based solely on tax considerations. This is because the only thing certain about tax law is that it will change! Make your decision to invest in a property on the before-tax numbers, and consider any additional tax benefits a bonus.

By continually keeping your eyes open for up-and-coming markets and by monitoring the performance of your income properties, you can be poised to take advantage of opportunities to strategically upgrade your investment portfolio. The 1031 tax-deferred exchange is one tool in your toolkit which can be used to reposition your equity to maintain optimum velocity.

C H A P T E R   9
Positive Cash-Flow Sucks!

Positive cash-flow *sucks*? That's a little strong, don't you think? Are you confused, or worse, offended? Before your mind closes, let us explain.

"Positive," "Cash," and "Flow" are three words most investors like to use together. Positive Cash-Flow occurs when a property's rental income is greater than all of its expenses. At first glance, this sounds like a really good idea. After all, shouldn't you strive to have more income than expenses with your rental properties? Aren't we in this business to make a profit? Have Robert and Russ totally lost their minds?

In our personal consultations, we ask investors to help us understand their investment objectives. Time and time again we hear, "We *need* positive cash-flow!" But you know what? Most of the time it isn't true. Most people don't really *need* positive cash-flow, not right now, because they have jobs or businesses which provide adequate cash-flow. We realize you can always use more cash-flow, and what you have never seems like enough, but the truth is most people are getting by. In fact, these same people who say they need cash-flow from their real estate are making enough money to pay all their bills, over-pay on their taxes and, beyond that, they pay into retirement accounts, pay down "good debt," and save money each month. In other words, they have extra cash-flow and are using the excess to strengthen their balance sheet. But is this the most effective use of the cash-flow available after their consumption needs have been met?

The reason for such a strong title for this chapter is that the positive cash-flow paradigm is one of the hardest to break. There are so many teachers and investors preaching cash-flow investing, it is hard for people to understand equity investing. Yet, most all of the really great success stories in real estate, even the ones touted by cash-flow teachers, are based on wealth created from equity: found, forced, phased or passive.

So, assuming we are accurate (we will prove it mathematically) that equity investing is preferable to cash-flow investing for most people, why are so many people convinced they should be focused on cash-flow?

Many people pursue cash-flow simply because it is how they have been trained to think of money. Go to school, get a job, get a regular paycheck, obligate yourself to monthly payments for housing, transportation, insurance, etc. Then set up a budget and plan your life around monthly cash-flow. Does this sound familiar?

If you earn $5,000 per month or $60,000 per year, would it be okay to get a $120,000 paycheck every two years? It seems weird because we are trained to think about monthly income and expenses, so we prefer our money to come in monthly. We don't need money to come in monthly, but we like it to. It just feels right.

Many people pursue cash-flow because they think if they can get enough cash-flow from their properties to replace their earned income, then they can quit their day job. This is true, but if you try to build towards retirement through cash-flow, it takes longer to retire. It almost defeats your purpose. It's like trying to save your way to retirement. This may sound wacky, but if you do the math (which we will do shortly), you'll find it to be true.

Most people are better off focusing on investing for future benefit (equity), not current benefit (cash-flow). This concept may sound off the beaten path when it comes to real estate, but when you think about it, people commonly defer cash-flow for future benefit with other conventional investments.

For instance, perhaps you have a 401k retirement plan at work and you put money into it every month. How much current cash-flow does it provide you? Zippo. Then why are you okay with this? Is it because you understand you are not investing for cash-flow, but rather for net worth? In fact, to make these 401k contributions, you have money flowing out of your income, effectively creating "negative cash-flow" in your investment program. Doesn't this disturb you?

Obviously, people contribute to their 401k plan, retirement programs, children's college education funds, and other long-term investments, not for positive cash-flow today, but for the *future* value of the investment. Their hope is the investment will grow in value over time, so the money will be there down the road when it is truly needed.

Couldn't the same be said for your real estate investments? In fact, *shouldn't* the same thing be said for your real estate investments? Consider that people take money out of their paychecks to buy stocks or mutual funds which do *not* pay dividends (cash-flow), have no protection against losing value, and have no guarantee of future appreciation. Worse, the investor typically has very little understanding or control of the companies they've invested in! Yet, conventional financial planning wisdom says this is the path to financial independence. No wonder so many people retire broke!

Isn't real estate a superior investment for all the reasons we've already discussed in previous chapters? If you don't think so, you probably should put this book down right now. But if you believe, like we do, that real estate equity happens, then think about what you really need to do to make equity happen to you in a BIG way.

Simply stated, new equity (the kind you didn't get from going to work, earning money, paying taxes, and using what's left to pay down a loan) happens to people who own appreciating real estate. It's simple. The more appreciating real estate you own, the more equity happens to you. If you own $100,000 of real estate and it goes up 10%, then your equity grew $10,000. If you own $1,000,000 of real estate and it goes up 10%, then your equity grew $100,000. The last time we looked, $100,000 is better than $10,000, don't you agree?

Based on this, it is obvious the key to big equity growth is to own as much appreciating real estate as you can reasonably control.

We control property with cash-flow. When we buy a home and get a loan, we use our earned cash-flow to service the loan, thus controlling the property. When we own an income property, we use the rental income to service the loan, thus controlling the property. If the rental income isn't enough to cover the loan payment, our cash-flow on the property becomes negative. If we use income from some other source, including our job, savings, credit, tax credits, or another income property, we are able to service the loan and continue to control the property.

We submit that owning a property with a slightly negative cash-flow each month is very similar from a philosophical perspective to putting money into your retirement plan each month. "Feeding" your appreciating property some cash from other sources on a monthly basis is really just another incremental investment in the property. Technically, the money doesn't go from your checking account to your balance sheet, but as long as your net worth grows, isn't it essentially the same thing? You invest cash-flow each month based on the expectation the property will be much more valuable in the future than it is today. The cash you invest into the property isn't to pay off the property, but rather to control the property while it appreciates.

Again, cash-flow is the tool we use to control a piece of property while it appreciates. If we consume the cash-flow, then we aren't using it to control property. If we save it, it doesn't add up to much very fast. In either case, it is taxed. We aren't interested in going to work, paying taxes, living like a pauper, and piling money up in a bank account or mutual fund somewhere so we can live off the reserves some day. We are interested in gaining control of appreciating, income-producing assets, so the new equity created over time adds net worth to our balance sheets. Later, we can reorganize those now asset-rich balance sheets into a powerful income producing machine – a goose that lays golden eggs.[31]

Before we continue, let's step back and review the big picture so we can put all of this commentary in proper perspective. This may seem redundant, but we would rather over communicate than have you miss these important concepts.

The entire purpose of investing is to develop a performing and optimized balance sheet. "Performing" means the assets on your balance sheet are generating cash that can be consumed. It doesn't have to be monthly, but sooner or later your balance sheet

---

[31] If you are not familiar with "the goose that lays the golden eggs," it is a phrase taken from an old fable of a farmer who discovered he owned a goose that laid eggs of pure gold. After a short time, the farmer became greedy and impatient, so rather than wait for the goose to lay the next gold egg, he cut the goose open, thereby killing it, in order to get to all the eggs at once. Of course, there were no eggs – and now the goose was gone, along with its ability to produce golden eggs.

has to produce cash to support you. When your balance sheet is capable of producing enough cash to meet your spending needs, adjusted for inflation, *without* consuming your assets, you have reached what is called "Critical Mass".

"Optimized" means you are getting the *most* out of what you have to work with after taking into account taxes, inflation and sustainable asset growth. The topic of optimization is lengthy, but the essential concept is that there is a significant difference between "maximum" and "optimum". In short, "maximum" comes at the expense of something else. For example, if you have $1,000,000 of assets and you wish to maximize safety of principal, you might put it all in savings accounts or government bonds at low interest rates. You would have maximized safety, but compromised yield and growth. The low yield and slow growth would sacrifice cash-flow and make you vulnerable to inflation.

An optimized balance sheet would produce adequate income (consumable cash) to meet current needs, a growing income to compensate for inflation, with the highest after-tax yield and a growing asset base. A recipe for disaster is to consume assets. Don't eat the goose that lays the golden eggs.

If you have indeed achieved Critical Mass, then you are probably ready to begin optimizing your balance sheet for cash-flow. Our experience is that most people who read this kind of book are not yet at Critical Mass, or if they are, they don't know it. Consequently, most of our discussion is centered on helping people get to Critical Mass as quickly as prudently possible.

If you are not yet at Critical Mass, meaning you don't have enough assets to generate adequate sustainable after-tax consumable cash to meet your needs without decreasing your net worth, then the only reason to invest for cash-flow would be if cash-flow investing created the most rapid growth of assets. So the pivotal question is, does cash-flow investing build assets the fastest?

Great question! But before we go there, we need to cover some essential concepts.

The Amazing Power of Cash-Flow

We have seen how time leverage converts effort into equity "faster than a speeding bullet" and how loan-to-value ratios makes down payments "more powerful than a locomotive" by magnifying appreciation over time. As wonderful as these things are, the power of cash-flow is even more amazing. However, before we delve into the amazing power of cash-flow, you must have a fundamental understanding of how mortgages convert...

Streams into Oceans

As we explore the topic of mortgages, let's begin by establishing a clear understanding of what we are talking about. In many states, the technical term for a loan against real estate is "trust deed," though in the real world everyone tends to call it a "mortgage". Technically, there is a difference, but for purposes of real estate investing the two terms can be used interchangeably. In our discussion and throughout this book, we will almost always use the term "mortgage" when discussing a loan secured by real property.

The purpose of a mortgage is the conversion of cash-flow into lump sums of cash and vice-versa. When you create a mortgage you have signed a promissory note, which is essentially a promise to pay to the lender a series of monthly payments (cash-flow) over an extended period of time. You have pledged a *stream* of cash-flow to the lender. In exchange for this pledge, the lender gives you an *ocean* or lump sum of cash you use to purchase the subject property or cash out equity. To secure your promise, you pledge the subject property as collateral for the loan. If you fail to pay the lender according to the terms of the promissory note, the lender takes your property away from you and sells it in order to get their money back. This process is called "foreclosure" and it is *not* a good thing.

Simply stated, mortgages are paper agreements, which convert "streams of cash-flow" into "oceans of cash". You can literally create hundreds of thousands of dollars (and much more!) with the stroke of a pen!

With this fundamental understanding of mortgages, we can now explore the variations on this simple theme to help you control more real estate by using other people's money. Then, when equity happens, it will be happening to you.

Let's now return to the amazing power of cash-flow. When you think of becoming a real estate investor with millions of dollars in property, do you feel a little overwhelmed? Most of our beginning investing students do, but if you take it a little bit at a time, it all starts to build. Just like the answer to the old question, "How do you eat an elephant?" One bite at a time!

If you think back to buying your first new car, didn't the price tag seem out of reach? Remember how the salesperson helped you "get into this fine automobile?" It normally starts with a discussion of how much monthly payment (cash-flow) you feel comfortable with, then a trip to the friendly finance manager. When that $20,000 price tag was broken down into a digestible bite-size $400 per month, it didn't seem so bad. Now, here you are in a brand new $20,000 car for only $400 per month! This is the power of cash-flow.

Most people don't think about the power of cash-flow much beyond converting their earned income into the things they want, like houses, cars, boats, home theaters, college education, etc. However, the power of cash-flow goes far beyond such simplistic "consumer" thinking.

Now, before you read any further, you need to stand up, stretch, take a deep breath and say to yourself, "Math is good. Math is fun." and, "It's all about the numbers!" The fact is that real estate investing is a business. Financial analysis (math) is an important part of making good business decisions. Fortunately, real estate investing is somewhat forgiving, so you don't have to be a rocket scientist to do well, but it is important to pay attention to the numbers and optimize your positions so you can get the most out of your cash, credit, equity and cash-flow. Failure to optimize can cost you millions of dollars in missed opportunity! Just ask Bob Helms (sorry, Bob)!

Before we explore the power of cash-flow from the perspective of what it means to you and how you can use it, let's just take a look at the power of cash-flow in general and how even small amounts of inflating income create huge amounts of equity.

Imagine you own a single-family residence in a neighborhood of many similar properties, and the house adjacent to yours goes up for sale. Two different buyers are competing for the home, but one potential buyer can afford to pay $300 per month more than the other. The buyer who is able to afford $300 a month more for the home can afford to bid $50,000 more for the property. Why? Because a $300 per month payment on a 6% fully-amortized 30-year loan means the stronger buyer can get a $50,000 larger mortgage. The mortgage converts his $300 per month stream of payments into a $50,000 ocean of cash to bid up the property. This means the buyer's $300 per month just created $50,000 of cash for the seller!

So what does this mean to you? After all, it isn't your property being sold. But, because you own the house next door to the one that just sold for $50,000 more, your house just became worth $50,000 more based on a comparable sales method of appraisal. Essentially, your new neighbor's $300 a month mortgage payment (cash-flow) just became your $50,000 new passive equity – and not only yours, but every other comparable house in about a one-mile radius. Think about that for a moment. If there were 1,000 comparable houses[32] in a

---

[32] A one mile radius would encompass an area of 87.5 million square feet / 43,560 (square feet per acre) = 2,010 acres / 2 houses per acre (allows for roads, etc) = 1,000 homes.

1 mile radius and every single one of them could use this sale as a "comp" to establish value, the buyer's modest $300 per month mortgage payment just created $50 million in new equity! WOW! How many of those 1,000 houses do *you* want to own?

Now do you see why, "It's the economy, stupid"? If you invest where people have rising incomes, equity is certain to occur over time. The incredible thing is it doesn't take that much income to create massive amounts of equity. This is one of the amazing powers of cash-flow – and it doesn't even have to be *your* cash-flow!

Compared to What?

Why would Robert say, "Positive cash-flow sucks?" The answer is found in one of his favorite questions, "Compared to what?" After each seminar, people line up to ask him questions and to share their comments:

"Yeah, but Robert…your educational events are too expensive!"

Compared to what? Compared to not learning? Compared to financial illiteracy?

"Yeah, but Robert…the numbers are too hard for me!"

Compared to what? Compared to making bad financial decisions and losing hundreds of thousands of dollars in unnecessary costs and lost opportunities?

"Yeah, but Robert… investing in real estate is too scary for me!"

Compared to what? Compared to watching inflation destroy your purchasing power? Compared to watching the stock market take away half your net worth with no warning? Compared to retiring in poverty like 65% of Americans over age 65? Isn't poverty scarier?

"Yeah, but Robert…all that information about landlord/tenant law at Landlord Boot Camp gives me a headache."

Compared to what? Compared to ignorantly breaking the law and getting fined or sued?

"Hey, Robert! Russ sure is smart…and handsome!"

Compared to what?

"Robert! My properties are generating positive cash-flow! Isn't that good?"

Compared to what?

Our point is that you can't make good decisions in a vacuum. You need a frame of reference. When someone says, "I want positive cash-flow", what are they really saying and what do they really want? How does positive cash-flow compare to alternatives?

Here are the important points to consider when looking at positive cash-flow:

1. Are you referring to before-tax or after-tax cash-flow?

2. What is the positive cash-flow worth in terms of converting equity into cash or transferring equity from one property to another? In other words, how much good debt could the positive cash-flow service?

3. What are the tax ramifications of the cash-flow in its various uses?

4. What am I *really* trying to accomplish?

If you are struggling with these questions, hang in there! We'll go through them in detail.

Let's look at a simple example and then we'll go back and compare negative cash-flow real estate investing to negative cash-flow stock investing.

Assume you buy a $200,000 property which produces $600 a month positive cash-flow. At 20% down, you would need $40,000 to acquire the property. $600 a month produces $7,200 per year, which is an 18% cash-on-cash return on your original $40,000. Most investors would consider this very attractive. Good luck finding very many of these, but that's a different discussion.

How many of these $600 per month positive cash-flow properties would you like to have? All of them? Ten properties like this would yield $6,000 per month cash-flow. Sounds good! But right now, you only have one, so what does it take to get the second one? Another $40,000! At $600 per month (before tax), you would be saving $7,200 per year.

At $7,200 per year, it would take you over 5-1/2 years to save up $40,000 to buy the second property. Of course, once you had two, it would only take 2-3/4 years to save up for the third one. With three, it would take another just less than 2 more years to save up for number 4. With four, it would take another 1-1/3 years to save up for number five. With five, it would take just over one year to save up for the sixth property.

At this point, you have been at it for 12-1/2 years, you have not enjoyed spending even $1 of your rental income, but you have six properties producing $43,000 per year in positive cash-flow *before* taxes. After taxes, it might be much less. This isn't bad, but there might be a better, faster way to get to the next down payment than trying to save it up from cash-flow. We will explore this shortly.

Meanwhile, let's get some perspective by looking at what we call "negative cash-flow stock investing". Suppose that you contribute $300 a month into a mutual fund, which you hope will go up 12% per year on average over time. The $300 contribution is made with after-tax money, so in a 35% tax bracket, you would actually need to earn $460 to net the $300 ($460 less 35% tax equals $300 take-home). On an annual basis you would need to earn $5,520 ($460 x 12) and then pay $1,920 in tax, just so you could get $3,600 into your mutual fund. Are you with us so far? You earned $5,520 to save $3,600.

At 12% annual growth, your $3,600 would add $432 of new wealth to your balance sheet each year, assuming you had the entire $3,600 invested on the first day of the year. Of course, you wouldn't have it all in on the first day, so your actual growth would be less, but for sake of this discussion, let's suppose you had it all invested on the first day. At 12% annually, your $3,600 principal plus $432 of growth would be worth $4,432 at the end of the first year. To gain this, you earned $5,520. So, to summarize, you earned $5,520 to end up with $4,432. Are you ahead? Not really. In fact, you're still negative by $1,088! Ouch.

Instead, what if you had purchased a property and used the $5,520 of earnings to get a bigger loan, thus controlling more real estate? At 6% 30-year fully-amortized, the $460 per month ($5,520 for 12 months) would get you a $75,000 mortgage. If the property appreciated just 6% (which we know is below average), at the end of the year your new equity on just the extra portion of real estate you purchased with the bigger loan ($75,000) would be $4,500. This is slightly better than the $4,432 mutual fund scenario because with real estate, you earned $5,520 and ended up with $4,500. However, there is more to consider.

Do you remember amortization? Each month when your tenants make your mortgage payment, they are retiring a small portion of debt. The pay down of your debt adds additional net worth to your balance sheet of $75 a month. This adds up to an additional $900 in a year of increased net worth through debt reduction (amortization). So now, $4,500 in new equity (6% of $75,000) plus the $900 in amortization is $5,400 in net worth for the $5,520 in earned income. You're not ahead yet (though it's already better than the mutual fund), but wait, there's more!

What about depreciation? Based on an 80% improvements ratio,[33] the extra $75,000 in real estate (acquired through the extra $75,000 loan) would contribute an additional $763 ($75,000 x 80% = $60,000/27.5 years[34] = $2,181 x 35% tax rate = $763 per year) in tax credits against your other passive income. When you add this $763 to the $5,400 you have now improved your results to $6,163 for $5,520 invested. At last, a truly positive result! But, what is your actual rate of growth?

$6,163 (total aggregate value at year end)
Less $5,520 (amount of earned income invested)
$ 643 gain

$ 643 gain / $5,520 invested = 11.7% gain on investment

How does that compare to the "12%" on your mutual fund?

$4,432 (total value of mutual fund at year end)
Less $5,520 (amount of income earned to fund the investment)
<$1,088> gain

<$1,088> gain / $5,520 invested = <19.7%> gain on investment

This is a *negative* 19.7% growth on your earned income! Whether this money came from your job or your positive cash-flow property, even if you invest it in a mutual fund and get a growth rate of 12%, the tax is killing your total wealth-building program.

Now, apart from the preceding example, consider that your income from a rental property is likely to increase because people's income rises (inflation) over time, and thus they bid up housing values, both

---

[33] This is the percentage of the acquisition price that is attributed to improvements (the building) and not the dirt. It helps determine the depreciable basis. For more information on these terms, see the Glossary.
[34] As of this writing, the current tax code depreciation schedule on residential real estate is 27.5 years straight-line.

rental and purchase. When the rental income rises, a property which was "negative cash-flow" at the start might actually become positive – or at least less negative.

Our point with all of this is that even if you "lose" money on a property because you have to pay extra each month and those extra payments don't end up directly in a savings or investment account, those dollars are still working for you. Cash-flow controls mortgages and mortgages control real estate and real estate appreciates, provides tax benefits, and tends to increase in both value *and* income over time.

While positive cash-flow doesn't really "suck", it sure isn't the one-size-fits-all solution when it comes to real estate investing. Cash-flow, while powerful, is only one part of a much bigger picture. *Total growth* should really be the focus of every serious investor, particularly during the asset phase (when you are building toward Critical Mass) of one's investment career. Total growth encompasses cash-flow, tax credits, amortization and appreciation.

Analyze This

It is critically important to stay focused on what you are investing for (equity or cash-flow) and to compare investments based on their total return, a major portion of which will be the equity growth rate (remember Chapter 4?). However, there are other ways to compare income properties. In order to be an effective investor, you will need to be able to assess and compare income properties in a variety of ways.

The different methods we use to compare cash-flow on income properties are:

- Gross Rent Multiplier (GRM)
- Capitalization Rate (Cap Rate)
- Before Tax Cash-Flow (BTCF)
- After-Tax Cash-Flow (ATCF)

These methods are mathematical calculations designed to provide a statistical comparison of income properties. The first two are represented numerically; the last two are represented financially.

Ready? Here we go:

That's Gross

Gross Rent Multiplier is determined simply by taking the purchase price or Fair Market Value of the property and dividing it by the annualized Gross Scheduled Income (GSI). The GSI is what the property is supposed to rent for without taking into consideration any vacancy allowance, expenses or debt service. For example, a 10-unit building in which each unit was renting for $500 per month would be generating $5,000 per month or $60,000 per year in GSI. If the property were selling for $600,000, the GRM would be 10. Why? Because $600,0000 divided by $60,000 is 10.

$$\frac{\text{Property Value}}{\text{Annualized Gross Scheduled Income}} = \text{Gross Rent Multiplier}$$

GRM is useful when making a quick determination of value between two or more properties. The lower the GRM, the better the value, because you are buying more income for less purchase price. For example, suppose you were comparing two properties:

	Property A	Property B
Purchase Price	$600,000	$1,200,000
Gross Scheduled Income	$60,000	$60,000
Gross Rent Multiplier	10	20

As you can see, with Property B you are paying twice as much for the same income as Property A. Now there is a lot more to evaluating an income property than simply calculating GRM, but it is a quick and easy way to do a preliminary comparison.

Before we move on to Cap Rate, let's consider how your understanding of GRM can help you evaluate a found / forced equity opportunity.

Suppose you find a $1,000,000 property in a market that is selling for ten times its gross income of $100,000 and this seems reasonable compared to other properties in the market. However, upon inspection you realize the rents are below market and could be raised. Additionally, you see an opportunity to convert storage space into rental units. The net effect is you can raise the gross income by $2,000 per month. Watch how doing this affects your equity:

	Before	After
Gross Scheduled Income	$100,000	$124,000
Gross Rent Multiplier	10	10
Property Value	$1,000,000	$1,240,000
New Income	—	$24,000 per year
New Equity	—	$240,000

Once again we see the amazing power of cash-flow. By increasing the monthly income by $2,000 you have increased your equity by $240,000! If you were a cash-flow investor, you would pay taxes on this new $2,000 per month income and then save what's left to build up a down payment.

If you were inclined to optimize for equity, you might consider investing the new cash-flow into a larger mortgage and then transferring the new equity to a new property. With a 7.5% 30-year fully-amortized loan, you could get $200,000 cash out for only $1,400 per month. This would leave you $600 per month before-tax positive cash-flow, but also provide you with $200,000 cash *now* to make down payments on more property. Wow!

But if you were trying to save up $200,000 from your positive cash-flow, how long would it take? Well, even if you only paid 17% in taxes and could save $20,000 per year, it would take you TEN years! Do you see how much faster equity investing is?

Getting back to the subject at hand, let's now discuss Cap Rate.

Nice Cap!

Capitalization Rate, or Cap Rate takes into account expenses, but not debt service. It is a way to compare the financial performance of two or more income properties irrespective of how much debt is involved in the acquisition. Essentially, Cap Rate shows you the rate of cash-on-cash return if you were to buy property for cash.

To determine Cap Rate, you need to understand the Basic Income Formula and have insight into the actual expenses of the subject property. Obviously, a 100-year-old Victorian house is going to have different operating results than a brand new condominium. The maintenance expenses in the older property will be higher. In the real world it is sometimes difficult to get accurate expense details from the seller, so you may be forced to guesstimate. If so, be realistic about the condition of the property. In any case, once you have the estimated expenses, plug them into the Basic Income Formula:

	Gross Scheduled Income (what the property should generate when fully rented)
Less	Vacancy Allowance (a percentage of GSI based on local market realities)
Less	Expenses (an amount, if known, or a percentage of GSI based on guesstimate)
Equals	Net Operating Income

Once you have the Net Operating Income (NOI), you divide it by the purchase price or value of the property to determine the Cap Rate:

$$\frac{\text{Net Operating Income}}{\text{Property Value}} = \text{Capitalization Rate}$$

For example, a $600,000 property with a $5,000 a month GSI, a local market vacancy factor of 5%, and guesstimated expenses of 35% would look like this:

	Gross Scheduled Income	$60,000 ($5,000 a month x 12 months)
Less	Vacancy Allowance	$ 3,000 ($60,000 x 5% estimated vacancy)
Less	Expenses	$21,000 ($60,000 x 35% expense factor)
Equals	Net Operating Income	$36,000

$$\frac{\$36,000}{\$600,000} = 6\% \text{ Cap Rate}$$

In the case of Cap Rate, a *higher* number is better because it means more net operating income relative to purchase price. If this confuses you, stop now and plug in different numbers into the preceding formula and look at the results. We know it isn't entertaining, but if you want to master the material you must DO THE MATH.

Got it? Good. Now, let's discuss cash-flow calculations. Determining Before-Tax Cash-Flow is simply a matter of deducting annual debt service from the Net Operating Income. In order to do this, you will need to know what your monthly payments will be on a given loan amount at a given interest rate. There are many handy calculators, spreadsheet programs, and printed tables to help you calculate fully-amortized payments. Interest-only payments are much easier to figure out:

> Loan Amount
> **x** Annual Interest Rate
> ---
> = Annual Interest
> ÷ 12 Months
> ---
> = Monthly Interest-Only Payment

Example:
> $100,000 Loan Amount
> **x** 6%　　　Annual Interest Rate
> ---
> = $6,000　Annual Interest
> ÷ 12　　　Months
> ---
> = $500　　Interest-Only Payment

Calculating *After*-Tax Cash-Flow is a bit more complicated and will involve determining your marginal tax bracket, your eligibility for Passive Activity Loss,[35] and the depreciation schedule of the particular property. Within the area of depreciation, there may be certain parts of the particular property that are eligible for accelerated depreciation. Income property taxation could be an entire book in and of itself, so we aren't going to delve into it in great detail. Suffice it to say, you want to become familiar with IRS form 1040 Schedule E and spend time with your tax advisor to determine how your tax status will affect your after-tax cash-flow.

There are different ways of looking at cash-flow. Each is valid, but different. Most of us live and work in the real world, so we tend to look at money in real-world terms. If you receive a check for $5,000 and put it in the bank, you have $5,000 on deposit and you can write checks against it all the way up to the full $5,000. That seems simple, right? Well, it isn't.

For example, for purposes of loan qualification, a lender will not consider all real-world income as "qualifying income". If you own a four-unit building that brings in $2,000 per month in rent, most lenders will only count $1,500 as qualifying income. Yet in the real world, you are receiving $2,000. The formula commercial lenders use is even more complicated, but the result is the same: you don't get credit for all the rental income. Even though there is a perfectly valid reason for this, it still seems odd, doesn't it? Maybe. It depends on what you're used to.

If you go to work as an employee and receive W2 wages of $5,000 per month, is your check really $5,000? No. In almost all cases, your employer is deducting payroll and income taxes from your gross pay. So even though you earn $5,000 for taxable purposes, you don't get $5,000 in the real world. This is the difference

---

[35] See the glossary for a description of Passive Activity Loss

between the way your employer looks at your pay and how you look at it. In the real world, you pay the most attention to real money you can spend, that is, your "net" take-home pay. This seems very normal to most people because it is what they are used to.

When it comes to income from real estate, there are different ways to look at the cash-flow. We've already touched on how a real estate lender would look at it, but are there other ways?

Here is a very simplistic cash-flow analysis based solely on cash actually received or disbursed:

Actual Rental Income	$2,000
Property Management	<$ 180>
Mortgage Payment	<$1,000>
Utilities (landlord's portion)	<$ 50>
Insurance	<$ 70>
Cash-Flow	$ 700

Looks good, right? Positive cash-flow! We're sure you can see there are some things missing, like vacancy allowance, repairs, etc., but in the real world of cashing and writing checks, this is what it would look like, *if* the units were fully rented (no vacancy) and no repairs were needed for that particular month. HINT: In the real world, it won't work like this very often. You would be foolish to buy a property based on this analysis and expect it to consistently deliver $700 per month of consumable money.

From an *operating* point of view, you must consider several other items that don't necessarily impact real-world cash-flow, but impact both your cash-flow statement and your balance sheet. For example:

Actual Operating Income	$2,000	Received in current month
Property Management	<$ 180>	Paid out in current month
Mortgage Payment	<$1,000>	Paid out in current month
Utilities	<$ 30>	Paid out in current month
Insurance	<$ 70>	Paid out in current month
Cash-Flow	$ 700	
Vacancy Allowance 5%	<$ 100>	Placed in savings as a contingency
Operating Expense Fund 30%	<$ 600>	Placed in savings as a contingency
Cash-Flow	$ –0–	

Your "operating expense fund" includes set-asides for things like annual property taxes, turn-over (preparing the property after a vacancy for the next tenant), repairs, etc. These expenses don't happen each month, but we account for them anyway, because we know they are certain, or least very likely, to occur and we want to be ready. Notice how the money for these contingent expenses (vacancy and non-current operating costs) flowed off your cash-flow statement and onto your balance sheet (your savings account). It seems sensible to do this, and it is, but there's still more to consider.

So far, we have touched briefly on *qualifying* income (the way a lender views income for purposes of qualifying for a loan). We looked in more detail at *actual* cash-flow (counting only those funds actually received or disbursed) and *operating* cash-flow (actual cash-flow plus set-asides for contingencies). Now, we want to look at cash-flow from a tax perspective.

One of the more challenging aspects of bookkeeping for rental properties is figuring out after-tax cash-flow. Even though we don't deal with income taxes on a monthly basis, like our other contingencies, we want to account for it monthly so that when the bill inevitably comes, we aren't unprepared.

For *tax accounting* purposes, income property is viewed this way:

	Actual Operating Income Received
Less	Actual Operating Expenses Paid (excluding debt service)
Less	Loan Interest Paid
Less	Depreciation
Equals	Taxable Passive Income (or Loss)
Less	Income Tax
Equals	After-Tax Income

Please stick with us through this. We are almost done. There are two ugly parts to real estate. One is property management and the other is accounting. But these are the two most important areas of owning real estate. When you neglect one or both, your ownership experience will be more painful. Hang in there!

Getting back to our previous example of how income property is viewed from a tax perspective, notice that the formula yields "after-tax *income*" and not "after-tax *cash-flow*". Most people, including us, use the terms "income" and "cash-flow" interchangeably. Actually, they are different.

In most cases, the IRS collects "income" tax, not "cash-flow" tax. So the formulas we use to figure out our tax liability are different than the ones we use to calculate our after-tax cash-flow. Your tax accountant needs to be expert in accurately determining your income tax, but (with your tax accountant's help) you need to get good at determining your "after-tax cash-flow" because this is what matters most on a month-to-month basis in the real world.

In the tax accounting formula we previously showed, there was no direct provision for amortization. Remember, amortization is the amount of your monthly mortgage payment which pays down your outstanding loan balance. It is a very real part of your monthly cash-flow (because it flows out to the lender each month), but since you can't deduct it, it doesn't show up in the tax formula as a separate item. Rather than further complicate your understanding of the tax side, let's get back to figuring out what really matters: "real-world after-tax cash flow". You can work with your tax advisor for a better understanding of calculating tax liability (have fun).

In the real-world, we want to figure out how much comes in and how much goes out on a monthly basis and then adjust it for certain-to-happen non-monthly items, like income and property taxes, which are likely to impact our cash-flow. Be aware, there are tax ramifications which do not affect your cash-flow, but accrue and will be dealt with at the time of sale. Right now, we only want to focus on things that directly and currently affect your cash-flow.

So how do we figure out real-world after-tax operating cash-flow?

Here you go:

	Actual Operating Income Received	(current month)
Less	Actual Operating Expenses Paid, inc. mortgage	(current month)
Equals	Actual Monthly Before-Tax Cash Flow	(current month)
Less	Projected Property Tax Expense	(set aside monthly)
Plus	Useable Tax Credits[36]	(anticipated annually, accounted for monthly)
Equals	Real-World After-Tax Cash-Flow	

Remember, this will look better to you than it should because we are not making provision for repairs, vacancy, turn-over, etc. These are all very real and important, but most of the time you don't have to deal with them on monthly basis – and they aren't certain-to-occur like tax, mortgage and insurance payments. Further, if you are willing to

---

[36] Useable tax credits are not realized on a monthly basis, but will usually be realized on an annual basis. They are included here because they can be accurately anticipated and therefore accounted for on a monthly basis.

rely upon other cash-reserves and/or credit lines to protect you if something large and unexpected comes up, then you can run cash-flow pretty tight (allowing maximum leverage) while the property value and rents increase over time. NOTE: You should always maintain some cash and credit reserves to make sure you can deal with unexpected expenses or interruptions of income.

Lastly, don't think that any of these cash-flow analyses are used for purposes of determining return on investment. Total return will include amortization and appreciation, which both affect equity and not cash-flow. For an equity investor, the purpose of cash-flow is primarily to control the property while it appreciates; therefore cash-flow plays a very minor role, if any, in directly contributing to ROI.

Oil & Vinegar

Before we continue, we want to warn you against a common and costly mistake we see people make when they have, as Bob "The Godfather of Real Estate" Helms says, "just enough information to think they are qualified to remove their own appendix!" When someone hears, "Leverage is good, positive cash-flow is bad", and then goes out and buys a property using 10% down in a cash-flow (non-appreciating) market because the property can operate at break even cash-flow, what do they have?

A mess! Why? If all the cash-flow is going into operational expenses and debt service, then is there any profit from cash-flow? No. If the property is in a non-inflating market, then how much profit is there from appreciation? None.

In the scenario of high loan-to-value financing in a non-appreciating market, the only ways left to make money are amortization and depreciation. While these are nice to have, they are also a *very* slow path to increasing wealth. But if the owner decides to get out of the property to invest in a better property or market, what do they have? Not much! Why? Because the selling expense will be 8-10% of the sales price. Without appreciation, the sales price will be very near the purchase price, so an 8-10% selling expense will consume 60-80% of the original purchase equity. Check it out:

Purchase Equity	$ 10,000
Purchase Mortgage	$ 90,000
Purchase Price	$100,000
Sales Price	$100,000
Sales Expense (8%)	<$ 8,000>
Loan Pay-off	<$ 90,000>
Net Proceeds	$ 2,000
Starting Capital	$ 10,000
Ending Capital	$ 2,000
Change $	<$ 8,000>
Change %	- 80%

Ouch! Please don't make this mistake! It is very costly to mismatch markets and financing strategies. Make sure you think through your entrance, holding and exit strategies, and then run the numbers using assumptions which are most likely based on history and probabilities. As distasteful and boring as many people find number crunching, it is an absolute necessity to do the math on every deal.

Returning to our discussion of real-world cash-flow in the last example (before "Oil & Vinegar"), notice how "useable tax credits" (most of which came from depreciation) show up as a "plus", thus actually improving real-world cash-flow. This means it is literally possible to have a property that "loses" money for tax purposes, but actually makes money in the real world.

Wait. Did you get that? A property can lose money for tax purposes, but actually make money (positive cash-flow) in the real world!

Is this a good thing? Say "yes" because that's the answer! How many of these "losers" can you afford to own? A lot more than those that actually lose real money in your real world.

Our point is, you must take into consideration your individual tax situation and know what you are referring to when you say "positive cash-flow". While it is important to know how the lender, the IRS, and your balance sheet look at cash-flow, make sure you pay attention to cash-flow in your real world.

Thanks a Lot, I Really Depreciate It!

As we discussed when we looked at 1031 tax-deferred exchanges, depreciation is a "non-cash expense". This non-cash expense, or "phantom loss", results in a tax credit against other passive income, and *lowers* your cost basis on the subject property. Your "cost basis" is what is deducted from the final sales price to determine your realized (received) capital gain. When you realize this gain, you will be taxed at the then-current federal capital gains rate. If you happen to live in a state with a capital gains income tax, it will be worse.

If you sell the property without taking advantage of a 1031 tax-deferred exchange, the depreciation is "recaptured" because your realized capital gain is higher based on the now lowered cost basis. Some people think this is a negative, but we don't worry about it for two reasons. First, there is nothing you can do about it. People who worry about things like this are more concerned with paying capital gains tax than making profitable investments. This is like those people who think not making income is the answer to paying income tax! Another term for this is, "cutting off your nose to spite your face". While we encourage you to do everything you legally can to reduce your tax, when all is said and done, be thankful you have income and profits to be taxed on. Besides, if you structure your affairs correctly, you can avoid paying most of the tax anyway. This isn't a book on advanced tax strategies and estate planning, but we recommend you take the time to become knowledgeable in this area. One of Russ's favorite tax books is the *Ernst & Young Tax Guide* which they publish each year. As you continue to understand the power of cash-flow, you will realize taxes are a much greater form of negative cash-flow than an income property you need to "feed" each month.

The second reason we don't stress out about depreciation recapture is we think it is well worth the price. Depreciation can provide so much help with cash-flow early when it is the most difficult to control the property. Cash-flow is always more challenging in the early term of your property ownership because you haven't had time to raise rents. Once again, cash-flow controls mortgages and mortgages control properties (have you noticed we've repeated this a few times?). Income properties provide income, appreciation, and tax breaks. You cannot make money on a property you don't own. If depreciation helps you control the property, we suggest you use it!

Positively Negative

Way back in Chapter 3, we learned when a loan balance is reduced with each payment the loan is being "amortized". When your monthly payment is insufficient to pay off the current interest, the unpaid interest is added to the unpaid loan balance. This causes the loan balance to increase. This is called "negative amortization". As we know, the difference between your loan balance and the fair market value is your "equity". Theoretically, a growing loan balance is eating into your equity. In the equity-building phase of your investing career, while you are still working towards Critical Mass, your goal is to grow your equity. A negative amortization loan adds to your loan balance, so it would appear to be decreasing your equity. But is it really?

If the property is appreciating *faster* than the loan balance is growing, then your equity is actually growing even though your debt is growing also. Study the following chart:

Negative Amortization Analysis

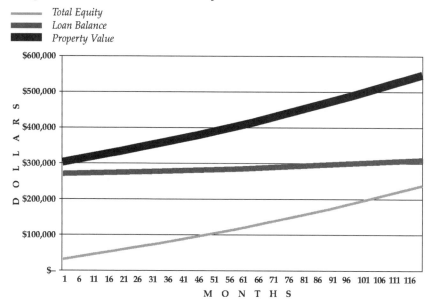

This chart is based on a $300,000 property purchased with $30,000 purchase equity (down payment) and a $270,000 loan at 6%. A fully-amortized payment would be $1,619 per month, but in this illustration, the investor uses a negative-amortization loan and pays only $1,119 per month. This means his monthly payment is not enough to pay the interest. He is short (negative) by $500 per month or $6,000 per year.

However, the benefit of this lower payment is that it improves the investor's real-world cash-flow by $500 per month. On the other hand, it causes the loan balance to go up over time as the unpaid interest is added to the outstanding loan balance. The investor is effectively continuing to borrow against the property in order to help make the payments.

The chart assumes the property appreciates at just a 6% annualized rate. Notice that even though the loan balance is growing, the property value (new equity) is growing even faster. The result is a growing net worth. Go back and look at the chart. Make sure you understand.

But there is even more to this story.

If you aren't using the $500 per month to pay all the interest due on the loan on the $300,000 property, but you have the $500 per month available, then what else might you do with it? If you have available equity in another property, you might use the $500 per month to access $100,000 in idle equity with a 6% interest-only loan. If you then took the $100,000 and used it as 20% purchase equity (down payment) on another $500,000 property and the new property's cash-flow covered the debt service on a new $400,000 loan and all expenses, you would now have control of *another* $500,000 in real estate. All for just $500 per month!

If this new $500,000 property appreciated at 6% it would add $30,000 per year, or $2,500 per month, to your financial position. Consider that $2,500 per month on a $500 per month investment is a 500% growth rate! If you can get 500% on your money, why wouldn't want to "borrow" the $500 each month from the first property by short paying the interest? Yes, your debt is growing, but your net worth is growing much faster!

Remember, investors focus on cash-flow and net worth, *not* interest rate and debt. If our cash-flow is good (meaning we can control all of our mortgages) and our balance sheet is growing, we are happy. Some people build their net worth by fixating on debt reduction and savings. We can prove mathematically and anecdotally that this is a slow and often elusive path to financial independence. It isn't bad if it is your only option, but the purpose of this book is to show you another way.

Flow, Flow, Flow Your Boat

Remember, mortgages convert streams of income into oceans of cash and vice versa. This is where the true power of cash-flow resides.

For example, a 30-year fully-amortized mortgage with an interest rate of 7.5% converts a stream of $700 per month into a $100,000 ocean of cash. This can be in the form of a purchase money loan on a new property or a cash-out refinance to reposition equity out of a currently owned property for investment into another property.

When someone comes up to us in a seminar and brags about their $700 a month positive cash-flow on their $500,000 property with a $250,000 loan and then asks Robert if that's good, Robert says, "Compared to what?" Then, Russ's brain goes into spreadsheet mode, and this is what he thinks:

Scenario A: I ♥ Positive Cash-Flow

	$700 per month taxable positive cash-flow
Less	$252 taxes (36% marginal tax rate)
Equals	$448 a month consumable money

A $500,000 property at 2:1 leverage (50% equity) provides 10% equity growth rate, assuming an average 5% annual appreciation rate (if this confuses you, go back and review Chapter 4).

When you add in your gross income of $700 per month, or $8,400 per year, your equity growth rate is 13.36%

$500,000 property value x 5% appreciation	= $25,000 new equity
$700 gross positive cash-flow x 12 months	= $ 8,400 new gross profit
Total new profit	= $33,400

$$\frac{\$33,400 \text{ new profit}}{\$250,000 \text{ invested equity}} = 13.4\% \text{ before tax growth on equity}[37]$$

---

[37] Please remember, this isn't the same as total return, which would include profit from amortization and tax credits and takes into account the effect of income tax (shown above). We're simply trying to compare cash-flow to equity growth to see which provides the highest percentage growth of net worth.

Is this good? Hmmm…compared to what?

Scenario B: Positive Cash-Flow Sucks!

Instead of taking the $700 per month in positive taxable cash-flow (which would yield only $448 in consumable cash at a 36% marginal tax rate), what if you used the $700 per month to borrow another $112,500 against the property, using a 7.5% interest-only loan? This makes the $700 effectively non-taxable because it no longer "positive cash-flow". It is now an expense (interest on a loan for investment purposes).

Meanwhile, the lender wire-transfers the $112,500 in cash to your checking account. If you were willing to accept $448 per month of net consumable money ($700 per month positive cash-flow less income tax of $252), then go ahead and set aside $26,880 in a savings account and draw out the $448 per month for the next 60 months. After all, you deserve a little bit of reward along the way, right?

Now, take the remaining $85,620 and make a 25% down payment on a $340,000 rental property. Use rents to cover the new mortgage and operating expenses. If the property goes up in value 7% per year on average, the property will be adding approximately $23,800 of new equity to your balance sheet each year instead of only $8,400 from positive cash-flow – and you still get to spend the $448 per month for 60 months!

Review the chart on the following page and compare the two scenarios after five years:

	Scenario A I ♥ Positive Cash-Flow	Scenario B Positive Cash-Flow Sucks
Number of Properties	1	2
Combined Starting Value of Properties (top-line value)	$500,000	$840,000
60 months net spending money (assumes no rent increases)	$448 x 60 = $26,880	$448 x 60 = $26,880
New Equity at 7% appreciation each year after 5 years	$500,000 x 7% = $35,000 x 5 years = $175,000	$840,000 x 7% = $58,800 x 5 years = $294,000

By reinvesting taxable positive cash-flow into converting idle equity into purchase equity on more income property, you
    a) own more real estate,
    b) build more equity faster,
    c) still get to spend $448/month for 5 years.

Because of inflation, there is a probability that after five years your rental income on both the first and second properties has gone up. You may well end up with positive cash-flow again. Do you want it? Perhaps. Or maybe you want to repeat the whole process and go out and get more top-line real estate.

Consider this real-life story…

• • •

Bob's Big Investment!
Bob and his brother purchased a 3-story apartment building one block from San Jose State University in 1976 for $235,000. After operating the building with a resident manager and renting primarily to students for twenty-five years, they sold the building in 2001 for $2,600,000.

WOW! Equity happens! Now that's a real estate success story. Or is it?

Let's take a look at what *might* have happened if they had paid a little closer attention to the optimization of their equity...

Acquisition 1976 ↓	Sometime in Between ↓	Sometime in Between ↓	Sale 2001 ↓
Value: $235,000 Loan: $200,000 Equity: $ 35,000	Value: $800,000	Value: $1,500,000	Value: $2,600,000

The preceding timeline shows that some time between acquisition in 1976 and the sale in 2001, the building was worth $800,000. At some time after that, but before 2001, we know the building was worth $1,500,000. It doesn't really matter when – we just need to know it happened. Obviously, it did.

What if, instead of holding onto the building as they did from 1976 to 2001, the brothers looked for opportunities to optimize their equity? For example, when the building was worth $800,000, they could have sold it, paid off the loan (at which point the loan would have been close to $200,000), and carried forward the remaining $600,000 of equity (using a 1031 tax-deferred exchange) to use as a down payment on another building.

The following chart illustrates that at 20% down (5:1 leverage), they could have bought a building for $3,000,000 using the $600,000 as down payment and getting a loan for the remaining $2,400,000.[38]

---

[38] For simplicity's sake in this conceptual illustration, we are not accounting for cash-flow, taxes, and transaction expenses. The purpose of the story is to show the power of equity optimization.

Acquisition 1976 ↓	Sometime in Between ↓	Sometime in Between ↓	Sale 2001 ↓
Value: $235,000 Loan: $200,000 Equity: $ 35,000	Value: $800,000 Loan: $200,000 Equity: $ 600,000	Value: $1,500,000	Value: $2,600,000
	New Property Value: $3,000,000 Loan: $2,400,000 Equity: $ 600,000		

Now, from the time the value of the first $235,000 building increased from $800,000 to $1.5 million, what do you think the value of the $3 million building went to? If it went up at the same rate as the first building, the $3 million building would now be worth $5.6 million!

If at that time, they sold the second $5.6 million building, they could have paid off the $2.4 million loan and exchanged $3.2 million of equity into another building. At 20% down (5:1 leverage), Bob and his brother could have purchased a $16 million property using the $3.2 million as down payment and getting a new loan for the remaining $12.8 million:

Acquisition 1976 ↓	Sometime in Between ↓	Sometime in Between ↓	Sale 2001 ↓
Value: $235,000 Loan: $200,000 Equity: $ 35,000	Value: $800,000 Loan: $200,000 Equity: $ 600,000	Value: $1,500,000	Value: $2,600,000
	New Property Value: $3,000,000 Loan:$2,400,000 Equity: $ 600,000	Price:$ 5,600,000 Loan:$ 2,400,000 Equity:$ 3,200,000	
		New Property Price: $16,000,000 Loan: $12,800,000 Equity: $ 3,200,000	

So, from the time the original $235,000 building went from a value of $1.5 million to $2.6 million, what would the $16 million property have gone up to if it had appreciated at the same rate as the first building? An astounding $27 million! Now, if they sold the $27 million building, they could pay off the $12.8 million loan and still have $14.2 million pre-tax cash remaining:

Acquisition 1976 ↓	Sometime in Between ↓	Sometime in Between ↓	Sale 2001 ↓
Value: $235,000 Loan: $200,000 Equity: $ 35,000	Value: $800,000 Loan: $200,000 Equity: $ 600,000	Value: $1,500,000	Value: $2,600,000
	New Property Value: $3,000,000 Loan: $2,400,000 Equity: $ 600,000	Price: $5,600,000 Loan: $2,400,000 Equity: $3,200,000	
		New Property Price: $16,000,000 Loan: $12,800,000 Equity: $ 3,200,000	Price: $27,000,000 Loan: $12,800,000 Equity: $14,200,000

Holy equity, Batman! By simply doing only *two* 1031 tax-deferred exchanges over a period of twenty-five years, they might have had $14.2 million instead of the $2.4 million they made by holding on to the original building all that time!

BUT...what if Bob and his brother had carefully managed their cash-flow and equity and optimized even more effectively? We've done projections on various scenarios on several occasions and the numbers get huge, but we always have to stop because Bob starts having heart palpitations and can't catch his breath.

• • •

The preceding story, which we have re-named "Bob's Big Boo-Boo" shows what *might* have happened with optimization and illustrates the important difference between investing for cash-flow and investing for equity. By holding onto the original building and letting the cash-flow improve, the two brothers gave up the opportunity to exchange into more property which would have ultimately resulted in much more appreciation. Remember, as equity builds up, your leverage ratio declines, thus lowering the magnification of appreciation (once again, if you are struggling with this concept, go back and review Chapter 4).

Meanwhile, here is something else to contemplate. Which scenario would have resulted in the most cash-flow over those twenty-five years?

Obviously, in the non-optimized buy-and-hold model (the one Bob and his brother actually did), the cash-flow increased substantially as the loan was paid down and the rents increased over time. Also, consider that in the hypothetical optimization model, each time a new building was acquired at only 20% down, the brothers would have been taking on substantially more debt, along with a substantially higher mortgage payment. The result would be very little, if any, positive cash-flow immediately following each exchange. In fact, based on the financial models Russ created using gross rent multipliers of 8 to 10 and the actual historical average mortgage rates (which got as high as 16%!), the brothers would have actually "suffered" a few years of negative cash-flow.

So what do you think? Which scenario produced higher aggregate cash-flow over the entire twenty-five years?

Even though the optimization scenario created bigger mortgages and higher mortgage payments, it also provided a much larger building with substantially higher gross income. Over time, as rents rise, the increase would be across a much larger number of rental units. Always remember, in terms of absolute dollars, a fixed percentage of a bigger number will always yield a bigger number. It is true with equity and it is true with cash-flow.

Simply stated, a $10,000,000 property at 10 GRM is grossing $1,000,000. A $1,000,000 property at 10 GRM is grossing $100,000. Even if the smaller building was at a 5 GRM, it would still only gross $200,000. The point is, no matter what you do in terms of management, financing, or expense control, you will *never* get as much top-line income from a $1 million building as you will from a $10 million building.

If your net income, after expenses and debt service, is 3%, your $1 million building will give you before-tax cash-flow of $30,000 per year. Your $10 million building will give you $300,000. Even if you could increase your net income rate as much as 20% (good luck!), your $1 million building would only produce $200,000.

If you were to increase your before-tax cash-flow just 1% on a $10 million building, the net result in absolute dollars in your pocket is $100,000. To match this with a $1 million building, it would take a net change of 10%. At the end of the day, bigger buildings, even those with more leverage (and debt service), will end up flowing more cash than a smaller building with less debt. Admittedly, there will be temporary dips in cash-flow at each optimization, but these are easily recovered from the larger cash-flows on larger buildings as rents increase over a broader base.

It can be confusing, can't it? We understand. For those of you with college degrees, you probably took some courses that were confusing. Do classes like Calculus, Chemistry and Physics come to mind? Yet, many of you pushed through to your graduate degree, maybe even to a Masters or Doctorate! Why did you work that hard? Presumably, because you believed higher education would improve your earning potential, right? Well, we've got good news and we've got bad news.

The bad news is there is no magic get-rich-quick real estate investing formula that will work predictably for large numbers of lazy, uneducated people. Even though the hope of this pie-in-the-sky sells millions of dollars of books, audio/video programs and expensive seminars, the truth is most people can't make it happen. We are sorry to burst your bubble. Fortunately, it's the only bubble related to real estate that you should be worried about anyway!

The good news is that virtually anyone reading this book can take the lessons from Bob's Big Boo-Boo, apply the concepts, and go on to build significant wealth over the next 15 to 25 years – without any highly unusual or fortuitous circumstances. However, (more bad news), you can't be afraid of crunching numbers. When you do the math, the math will tell you what to do. Then, you must *do it*.

Okay. We're off the soap box temporarily, so let's get back to the question at hand. Which scenario produces more positive cash-flow?

The answer is (drum roll please)…

Scenario B! The optimized model produces *substantially* more positive cash-flow – in addition to creating millions of additional dollars in equity!

How do we know? Come on, how do you think we know? We crunched the numbers! We even factored in transaction costs, variables in interest rates (based on the actual average interest rates for the period, including rates over 16%), and changes in the rental market.

We know there are only a handful of readers who powered through this last section and really tried to track with all of the math. Those types of people will probably (and should) break out a calculator and figure it all out for themselves. So, rather than take up more pages in the book for those few readers' sakes, here is the summary of the math:

Scenario	Equity	Cash-Flow	Total
Non-Optimized	$ 2,527,281	$1,632,228	$ 4,159,509
Optimized	$12,564,538	$4,134,816	$16,699,354

Not only did the equity increase by a whopping 500%, but the total cash-flow was up 400%. Do you think numbers like these make a difference in people's real-world lives? Yes, they make a HUGE difference!

Robert says "positive cash-flow sucks" all the time just to shock people out of a paradigm. We aren't suggesting you don't look for ways to generate as much income with as little expense as possible. In fact, this is exactly what you should be doing because (have you heard this before?) cash-flow controls mortgages and mortgages control real estate. When you can control an appreciating property using the bank's "ocean of money" and the tenant's "stream of cash-flow," then you are well-positioned to have equity happen to you!

Remember, almost no one will save their way to prosperity! Taxes and living expenses consume virtually all of the average person's income. Even if you manage to earn a superior income and live consistently below your means so you can squirrel away the excess in a nice "safe" place like a bank account, you will still have inflation (the consistent and persistent increase in the cost of living) eating away at your purchasing power. When you combine inflation with the increasing lifespans we are enjoying as a result of better medical technology, you can see the challenge a saver faces! Why fight inflation when you can make it work for you?

There is no way to get off of the "trading time for dollars treadmill" (your job), unless your businesses, investments and properties produce *consumable* profits. However, there are different ways to get profits out of a property. We are suggesting before you simply consume the positive cash-flow as your livelihood, you might consider other alternatives, especially until you reach Critical Mass.

Robert says, "Equity growth is the best path to cash-flow." Of course, this will only be true if you truly believe equity happens. On the other hand, if you think real estate will no longer go up in value over time, then equity investing is not for you. However, keep in mind, even at a modest appreciation rate of 2-3% per year (less than half the historical average), a property at 20% down (5:1 leverage) will provide an equity growth rate of 10-15% per year (Have we mentioned how important it is for you to understand the concepts in Chapter 4?).

C H A P T E R   1 0
The Free Duplex Story

We've already spent considerable time exploding the myths of the late night TV infomercial hypesters. Even though we've blown up the ubiquitous no-money-down pitch, we actually have one of our own! The only difference between our *Free Duplex Story* and the typical no-money-down story is that our *Free Duplex Story* is realistic, easily duplicated, and not dependent upon some esoteric or outdated financing, an ignorant or desperate seller, or any other rare or difficult-to-find occurrence.

The *Free Duplex Story* was developed during a mentoring club meeting specifically to explain the four ways of profiting with income property. By way of review, those four ways are:

1. Cash-Flow
2. Depreciation
3. Amortization
4. Appreciation

The *Free Duplex Story* describes the process of using a cash-out refinance mortgage to reposition equity from a currently owned property to a new income property, then using the rental income and tax credits to offset the expenses of the increased debt.

Suppose Ima Homeowner has a $500,000 home with a $250,000 mortgage on it. This means Ima has $250,000 of equity. She is comfortably making the monthly payment and life is fine.

NOTE: Before we go further, keep in mind that in Silicon Valley, at the time of this writing, the median home price is just above $700,000. For this price, you can get a 3-bedroom, 2-bathroom, 30-year old, 1400 square foot home on a 6,000 square foot lot. Unless you live in a highly appreciated market like New York, Boston, the San Francisco Bay Area, or Southern California, our example might seem shocking. Don't let this throw you off. You can adjust the numbers up or down to match your market. The numbers are much less important than getting the concepts. Once you understand the strategy, you can work out the numbers for your particular situation. Now back to our friend, Ima...

After attending an *Equity Happens Real Estate Investing Seminar*, Ima gets excited about buying an investment property, but she doesn't have any down payment, so she goes to the *Managing Your Mortgage for Maximum Net Worth* seminar and decides to have a follow-up consultation with a financing consultant.

In her financing consultation, Ima discovers she can replace her $250,000 loan with a new, larger $300,000 loan. The old loan was at 6% interest with a $1,500 per month fully-amortized principal and interest payment. The new loan is also at 6% fully-amortized over 30 years, so the new payment is $1,800 per month. The new bigger loan payment means Ima's net outflow increases $300 per month. However, the new $300,000 loan pays off the old $250,000 loan thereby leaving Ima with $50,000 cash left over. Effectively, she is paying $300 per month to convert $50,000 of her equity into cash.

Let's stop here and assess her situation.

	Before	After	Change
House Value	$500,000	$500,000	No Change
Loan	$250,000	$300,000	$50,000 more debt
Equity	$250,000	$200,000	$50,000 less equity
Cash	$–0–	$ 50,000	$50,000 more cash
Cash and Equity	$250,000	$250,000	No change
Out Flow	$1,500 per month	$1,800 per month	$300 more outflow

Notice that Ima's Cash and Equity position hasn't changed. In other words, even through she has more debt, her net worth hasn't changed. The mortgage simply converted some of her equity into cash. What changed is her cash-flow. She now has a $300 per month bigger payment.

Ima's financing consultant shows her a 30-year amortization table for her $300,000 loan at 6% interest. He points out that $300 of the $1,800 monthly payment is actually a principal payment that is reducing her debt. She finds out her loan provides her the option of not paying the $300 to reduce the loan balance. The financing consultant points out that if she goes ahead and pays the $300 principal reduction this month, the following month she saves a "whopping" $1.50 in interest.[39] This extra "savings" is applied to reducing her loan amount.

When Ima discovers that her $300 larger payment was only saving her $1.50, she decides to exercise her interest-only payment option. This makes her payment only $1,500 per month.

"Wow!" exclaims Ima. "I have the same house I was in before and the same monthly payment, but I have $50,000 in cash! That's amazing!"

---

[39] You can verify this yourself simply by using an amortization calculator and doing the math. If you don't have one, visit www.EquityHappens.com/calculators. Have fun!

Ima's financing consultant explains that Ima's new $1,500 payment is entirely interest. The financing consultant explains that interest on one's primary residence is generally tax deductible. He refers Ima to a tax advisor to verify her personal tax situation. When she visits the tax advisor, Ima discovers she is in the 25% federal and 9% state tax bracket for a combined marginal income tax rate of 34%. Her old loan was only $1,250 in interest, so she actually has more interest deduction with the new interest-only loan than she did before. Ima learns she will be able to get an additional tax credit of $85 per month because the extra $250 in interest she is now paying (the difference between her new all-interest $1,500 per month payment and the $1,250 interest portion of her previous payment) is tax deductible. Based on this, Ima goes to her employer and changes her withholding allowances to reduce deductions from her paycheck by $85 per month.

In calculating her after-tax cash-flow, Ima finds herself $85 a month better off than she was before. Although her $1,500 per month payment is the same, she is getting an extra $85 tax credit. So her actual tax adjusted outflow is $1,415. Meanwhile, she has $50,000 cash to invest!

Ima's financing consultant refers her to an investment property real estate agent who locates a nice two-unit residence (a duplex) priced for sale at $250,000. Ima uses the $50,000 as purchase equity (down payment) and obtains a $200,000 purchase mortgage. Each side of the duplex is rented for $850 per month, so Ima uses this rental income to help her qualify for the loan. At 7.5% interest, the monthly principal and interest payment on the $200,000 loan is $1,400 per month. Taxes on the property work out to $250 per month, while insurance runs $50 per month.

Let's stop and do a quick cash-flow analysis:

Rental Income (2 units at $850 each) $1,700

Expenses:	
Mortgage ($200,000 at 7.5%)	<$1,400>
Insurance	<$ 50>
Taxes	<$ 250>
Outflow	<$1,700>

It looks like, from a cash-flow perspective, this property is close to break even.[40]

"WOW!" Ima exclaims again. "Now, I still have my same house, with my same payment, but I now have a $250,000 rental property that pays for itself! This is so amazing!"

In her next conversation with her tax advisor, she learns the $1400 a month mortgage payment on the duplex has $150 of amortization (reduction of loan balance). The tax advisor tells her this amount is not deductible. He says because the payments are being made with the rental income, the amortization is actually profit to her. Her net worth is growing by $150 each month as the loan gets paid down – using the tenant's money!

"It gets better," explains the tax advisor. "Are you familiar with depreciation?" he asks. Ima shakes her head, so the tax advisor continues, "Depreciation is a calculation used to provide an accounting for the wear and tear on the building. The government allows you to take this as an expense against the property even though you don't actually spend any money out of pocket. It's called a non-cash expense."

---

[40] We realize there are operating expenses we have not accounted for, but the purpose of this story isn't to get into a detailed Annual Property Operating Data (APOD), but simply to illustrate the concept of repositioning equity from one property into another and utilizing rental income, tax credits, and amortization to cover the costs of controlling the property while it appreciates.

The tax advisor goes on to explain that the current depreciation schedule on residential income property is 27.5 years straight line. In the case of Ima's duplex, the tax advisor says that 85% of the purchase price would be the depreciable basis, since the property's value is mostly in the building and not the dirt.[41] So now the numbers look like this:

Purchase price	= $250,000
x 85%	= $212,500
÷ 27.5	= $ 7,727 in depreciation expense
x 34% tax rate	= $ 2,627 per year or $219 per month

"So," explains the tax advisor, "you actually receive a tax credit of $219 per month against the taxes you owe on your earned income."[42]

Now Ima is very excited. She grabs a sheet of paper and starts laying everything out. "Let me see if I have this right…" she says.

"I get $50,000 from the bank as a loan against my equity. This adds $300 per month to my house payment, except I used an interest-only loan, so my payment was the same as when I had only a $250,000 loan. Because the new payment is 100% deductible, I changed my withholding and got an extra $85 a month tax credit. Is that right?"

"That is correct," the tax advisor replies. "However, you need to consider that you are now no longer paying down your home loan."

Ima is confused. "What do you mean?" she asks.

---

[41] There is no formally established ratio between dirt and improvements. It will vary by property. Work closely with your tax advisor on a case-by-case basis to determine what is the highest depreciable basis you can reasonably justify to the IRS.

[42] Caution! The tax rules change regularly and vary depending on your individual circumstances. In this hypothetical example, "Ima" has less than $100,000 per year Adjusted Gross Income (AGI). In this case, Ima is able to take up to $25,000 per year Passive Activity Loss credit. We recommend you visit www.irs.gov and read publication 925 to become familiar with Passive Activity Loss rules – then visit your tax advisor to find out how the PAL rules may apply to your unique situation.

Ima's tax advisor clarifies, "Your $250,000 loan had a payment of $1,500 per month. $250 of this payment was principal reduction. When you decided to stop paying down your home loan, you stopped 'saving' money in your home equity. Your paycheck is no longer adding $250 per month to your net worth through debt reduction."

"However," he continues, "you are getting an $85 larger tax credit on the new $1,500 interest-only payment, so the net difference is really only $165."

Ima concentrates carefully on what he is saying. "Okay, so I am 'behind' by $165 a month, but you said the $150 pay down on the rental property loan was profit to me, right?"

"That's right," responds Ima's tax advisor, happy to see that Ima is beginning to grasp the concepts.

Ima perks up, "Then, if I am 'behind' by $165, but 'ahead' by $150, then I'm really only 'behind' by $15. Is that right?" Ima looks at her tax advisor for confirmation. He nods in agreement.

Ima smiles and continues, "Now are you telling me I get another $219 per month in tax credits from passive activity loss and this actually helps my real-world cash-flow? So, I'm not really 'behind' by $15 a month, but I'm really ahead by over $200 a month! It seems like this duplex isn't costing me anything to own. In fact, it's making me money. Is that right?"

"That's exactly right, Ima!" the tax advisor confirms. "But it gets better still!"

"Better?" Ima asks. "How can it get better than this?"

Ima's tax advisor smiles and explains, "Here's how: The duplex you bought is in an area where property tends to go up in value over time.

Even though you paid full price for the duplex, it has actually gone up since you bought it. In fact, it has gone up over 5%. I know it may not seem like much, but 5% of $250,000 is $12,500. In other words, the property is now worth $262,500. The extra $12,500 is yours as new equity."

"Wow!" Ima exclaims as she summarizes her situation. "I had a house with a $1,500 per month payment. Now I still have the *same* house with the *same* payment. But now I have a rental property that pays for itself and has gone up in value over $12,000! That really is AMAZING!"

Ima is right. It is amazing. That's why we call this the *Amazing Free Duplex Story*.

But, as you might guess, there is more to the story…

If all Ima did was hold on to the duplex, at 5% annual appreciation over time, her equity and positive cash-flow would continue to grow. In ten years, her property could easily be worth $375,000 and her rental income could go from $850 per side to $1200 per side, which would be an increase of $350 per month per side or $700 per month for the entire property. This is an additional $125,000 in equity and $700 per month in positive cash-flow.

However, since attending the *Equity Happens Real Estate Investing Seminar*, Ima purchased a copy of *Equity Happens* and found out that positive cash-flow…well, it sucks. She decides to refinance the duplex and take $100,000 cash out. Her loan payment at 7.5% interest[43] is $700 per month, but it is covered by the increased rents. When the loan funds, she has $100,000 cash wired directly into her checking account.

---

[43] Interest rates on non-owner-occupied properties tend to be higher than those of owner-occupied because the lender considers rental properties to be riskier.

WOW! Ima calls her real estate investment planner to see what to do now. Her advisor tells her about "Rabbit Investing".

Rabbit Investing

There was a credit card commercial being aired some time ago featuring a man who went into a pet store to buy a pair of rabbits for his daughter. The clerk was delayed while checking the man's identification to authorize his purchase. Meanwhile, the rabbits did what rabbits do. Before long, there were rabbits everywhere!

"Rabbit Investing" is the idea of transferring equity from one property and putting it into another investment property *vis-a-vis* the *Free Duplex Story*. Then, every few years, as appreciation allows, repeat the process with every property owned. One property becomes two, two become four, four become eight, eight become sixteen, etc. The resulting multiplication adds millions of dollars in new real estate to your portfolio!

Let's take a look at how it might work…

Suppose you have $100,000 in available equity sitting idle in a property you own. If you were to convert the equity to cash using a 6% interest-only loan, your payment would be $500 per month. This $500 per month is deductible interest, so if you were in a 35% tax bracket your after-tax expense to free up this $100,000 is only $325.

Now take the $100,000 and use it as 20% down payment on a $500,000 rental property. Let's say the rental income and tax deductions cover the operating costs and loan payment. Now you have two properties: the one you started with and the one you just acquired.

We know the average annual appreciation of residential real estate in the United States is over 6%. Do you suppose with some research and effort you might find markets that perform above average? Let's say you get an average of 7% appreciation per property per year.

Based on 7% annual appreciation, at the end of five years, your $500,000 property would be worth approximately $700,000. If you were to refinance at an 80% loan-to-value, you would have a new loan of $560,000. You would use the proceeds to pay off the original loan of $400,000, leaving you with $160,000 to make a down payment on another (your third) property. At 20 % down, $160,000 would buy you an $800,000 property. Once again, we assume the rental income and tax deductions on the new property are sufficient to cover all operating expenses and mortgage payments. Also, your rents on the first rental property have risen to cover the new larger mortgage.

After another five years, both rental property #1 and rental property #2 have appreciated. For that matter, so did the first property you started with, but let's say this was your personal residence and you don't want to reposition any more equity from your home. You only did it the first time to get started.

Now, rental property #1 has grown from $700,000 to $980,000. Rental property #2 has appreciated from $800,000 to $1.1 million. Rents have also gone up over this time, so you decide to reinvest the new rental income into repositioning more equity to buy yet another property (your third rental property).

You obtain an 80% loan on rental property #2 (now worth $1.1 million) for $880,000. Like before, you use the loan proceeds to pay off the old loan of $640,000, leaving you with $240,000 to invest. But before you proceed, you decide to refinance rental property #1.

Rental property #1 is now worth $980,000 and has a loan remaining of $560,000, so you get a new 80% loan of $784,000 and pay off the old $560,000 loan. This leaves you with cash to invest of $224,000. Combined with the cash proceeds from rental property #2, you now have $464,000 to invest. At 20% down, $464,000 will get you rental a property (#3) at a value of $2.3 million!

Another five years pass and each of your three rental properties have appreciated by 7% per year:

- Property #1 went from $980,000 to $1.3 million, but has a loan remaining of $784,000.
- Property #2 went from $1.1 million to $1.5 million, but has a loan remaining of $880,000.
- Property #3 went from $2.3 million to $3.2 million, but has a loan remaining of $1.84 million.

Guess what you decide to do? That's right! Do it again:

- A new 80% loan on Property #1 yields another $256,000 of cash to invest.
- A new 80% loan on Property #2 yields another $320,000 of cash to invest.
- A new 80% loan on Property #3 yields another $720,000 of cash to invest.

Now, you have a total of $1.296 million to use as a down payment! At 20% down, you could get a $6.48 million property!

After another five years, all four properties appreciate, and you've been at this for twenty years. What do you have?

- Property 1 went from $1.3 million to $1.9 million, but has a loan remaining of $1.04 million.
- Property 2 went from $1.5 million to $2.2 million, but has a loan remaining of $1.2 million.
- Property 3 went from $3.2 million to $4.5 million, but has a loan remaining of $2.56 million.
- Property 4 went from $6.48 million to $8.9 million, but has a loan remaining of $5.18 million.

Wow! After twenty years, starting with only $500 a month of tax deductible payments used to reposition $100,000 of equity from your home, you have built up a real estate portfolio of $17.5 million with equity of $7.5 million. And if you chose not to continue breeding equity, your cash-flow on this portfolio would become substantially positive. Isn't that worth struggling through a little math?

Here's the best news. This entire scenario is based on an average appreciation rate of 7%. Historically, the national average over decades is 6.4%. We think with education, diligence, and key relationships, it won't take once-in-a-lifetime luck to average 7% over the long haul. You can pad your numbers by using forced equity strategies along the way. Also, there is a lot of 80% LTV financing available. The point is, this scenario is based on assumptions which are *realistic and repeatable* for the average investor.

Rabbit investing isn't complicated, but you must be diligent to track your properties' appreciation, as well as changing tax laws, mortgage rates and fair market rents. The most important factor is to be disciplined to reinvest cash-flow streams into oceans of cash-out refinance proceeds from equity so you can make down payments on the additional properties. This is called *Equity Growth Optimization*.

Remember this: If you have a choice between paying interest or taxes, pay interest. When you pay interest, you get a loan (lump sum), which controls real estate, which in turn provides rental income, depreciation, and appreciation. When you pay tax, what do you get? Hmmm… we're not sure either.

EQUITY HAPPENS™

SECTION 4

Education for Effective Action™

CHAPTER 11
Get Ripped

RIP is a term we borrowed from bodybuilding to create an acronym for Real estate Investment Planning. A bodybuilder exercises incredible self-control to shed all extraneous body fat to get "ripped". This elimination of body fat provides the judges with a clear look at the impressive muscle development the athlete has achieved. This clear look is called "definition".

In any form of human achievement, developing clarity of objective is a critical step towards the formation of a successful strategy and tactical plan. Remember, you can't hit a target you can't see. Russ often teaches at our educational events, "When one has clarity of vision, strategy and tactics become self-evident."

Of all the topics we address in this book, from our educational events, to the mentoring program, to our daily professional activities, the topic of vision clarity is the most personal to Russ:

• • •

From the time I first got married (less than three months after my 18th birthday), I had a strong desire to be successful. I wanted to enter the fraternity of men who provided well for their families. Young and insecure, but very competitive, I was determined to be financially successful. Both my father and my father-in-law were businessmen, and it was very important to me to make them proud of me as a businessman.

Unfortunately, I was poorly qualified to do much of anything. I hadn't done well in high school, didn't have any significant amount of college education, and though I had been working on and off since I was 14 years old (which only amounted to four years at age 18), I didn't have much experience in anything other than making donuts and pumping gas. Ill-prepared for adult life, my first job was as an entry-level warehouse worker at Hewlett-Packard. I worked in the receiving department auditing incoming shipments to make sure the contents of the packages matched the packing slip. I must have counted millions of keycaps, integrated circuits, and other various and sundry electronic components! I hated every day.

Every so often the "big boss", the division manager, would come to visit us in the warehouse. He worked in another, much fancier building – one that actually had floor coverings! I was in a warehouse with a bare concrete floor. All I ever saw of any of the other buildings were the receiving docks as I moved boxes of materials from warehouse to production line.

When the division manager visited, he would talk about the vision of the company, the goals for our group, and the important role those of us in the warehouse played in the company's success. He did his best to make us feel important, but I didn't feel important at all. I wanted to move up. I wanted to be financially successful.

In the warehouse lunchroom, we had a bulletin board with clipboards hanging on it. They had the internal job listings which described all of the different openings in the company. These postings provided a salary range for each position, so it was easy for me to see where the money was – and where it wasn't. I quickly discovered there was no money working in the warehouse! The highest position I could see from my vantage point was the division manager job. It paid over $50,000 a year, which seemed like a fortune back in 1978!

The job listing for the division manager job said the position required a college degree, which I didn't have. As an alternative to a degree, the company required a minimum of a certain number of years experience in the position just below that of division manager. So I would look up the position just below division manager to try to figure out how to get to that job. I continued to trace backwards down the corporate ladder until I finally got to my position, Material Handler 1. This was one level above amoeba in the corporate food chain.

Maybe this is where I drew my first flow chart, but I sat down and traced my way to that coveted division manager position. Based on the number of years of experience required at each of the myriad levels on the road to Division Manager , my calculations showed I would be nearly 1,200 years old before I would reach my goal of being a division manager!

What do you do when you're 18 years old and your life looks like its over before you even get started? I was depressed for a little while. I began to understand why so many of my co-workers lived for the weekend and the end of month "beer busts" the company would host. We would hate life 40 hours each week, then "celebrate" for 3 hours, only to go home and sleep it off until the dreaded alarm clock went off on Monday morning and it started all over again.

Eventually, I snapped out of it. I realized I wanted more out of life than sleep-walking through the week so I could get to the weekends. Besides when I got to the weekend, I never had enough money to do anything anyway.

As I tried to figure out how to get my life on track, I did a few things right and a lot of things wrong, but deep inside I was driven by an insatiable desire to become successful.

I was smart enough to know I couldn't care less about being a division manager. I only wanted the $50,000 a year. I also knew I needed options, but I didn't see any. I needed a bigger perspective, so I did what a lot of young people do. I went to dad.

My father happened to be a plant manager for a technology company. Coincidence? Perhaps. But it is very common for young people to head off into life and pursue the things their parents have. We tend to aim at the things we see, which is why the company you keep and the vision you have are so essential to your success. My father suggested I go to school and get in position to work my way up the corporate ladder faster. I found this ironic and perhaps even hypocritical, since he didn't have a college degree. Now that I am a father myself, I understand better where he was coming from. I find myself giving my most passionate advice about the things I have the greatest regrets about. I've done well without a degree, but I also wasted a lot of time as a young man – time that could have been invested in gaining knowledge and experience, and in building important strategic relationships.

Though I listened to what my father said, I didn't like it. I didn't really care for school and I wasn't interested in climbing the corporate ladder. I was looking for a shortcut and was discouraged when my father didn't have any magic formula to offer me.

Falling into an even greater depression, I decided to go with my wife to Southern California , visit my uncle, and ride roller-coasters at Magic Mountain and Disneyland. I've always been an adrenaline junkie and I just wanted to escape the confines of a life with no apparent palatable options.

What happened next was profound.

(Side note: I've learned that as your life goes along, every once in a while you will have what I refer to as a "moment of reflection". This is a time where you stop thinking about the future and you simply look back on your life and reflect on where you came from, where you are and how you got there. This can sometimes be encouraging and sometimes not, but it is always enlightening. History, even our own, has many lessons waiting to be discovered. Invariably, as you look back, you will see certain experiences, dates, people, lessons or other profound events that have had significant impact on your life. The day I met Robert Helms was one of those "dates with destiny" for me. In many ways, so was my "escape from reality" vacation to Southern California.)

When I went to Southern California to visit my uncle, I was discouraged about my future. Because I was looking for answers, I looked at his life very carefully to see if there might be something there I could draw from. I needed a new vision.

My uncle was an outside salesman for a commercial office supply company. As my father's younger brother, he was only twelve years older than me. He was a fun-loving guy, so I related to him pretty well. He had a nice new home with a swimming pool, a pretty wife, horses in his back yard, and he drove a Porsche! He seemed happy and was really fun to hang out with.

I couldn't help but ask him what he did and how he got there. He didn't have a college degree and was making a six-figure income. That was a lot of money back then. Even more amazing to me was this was more than twice as much as the division manager job I had dreamed of. Naturally, I interrogated him about his job.

I ended up quitting my job at Hewlett-Packard in Northern California and I moved to Southern California to apprentice with my uncle. I went to work as a "sales trainee" at the same company my uncle worked for. At the time, I was extremely shy and introverted. It took me years to overcome my shyness, but I realized I needed to change if I wanted my life to change. As painful as personal growth was for me, the prospect of a life of below average income and unfulfilled dreams was worse! If I wanted to change my circumstances and future, I knew I would need to change myself.

Within a few months, at barely 19 years old, my wife and I purchased our first home. It was a brand new three-bedroom, two-bathroom tract home in Rancho Cucamonga. Shortly thereafter, my uncle, his friend and I started a small business. I put in $500, which was a huge amount to me back then. I also agreed to work for a very low wage.

Over the next few months, these two older men taught me business and sales. Looking back, I realize they weren't great businessmen at the time (though my uncle was and is a great salesman), but they were smarter and more experienced than me. We made all kinds of mistakes and had a variety of personal problems that were painful for all of us. In spite of all that, a year later, I sold my interest in the business for $5,000 and sold the house for $17,000 more than I paid for it. Back then, my wife and I only earned a combined gross income of less than $1,500 per month. This was only $18,000 a year! I made more on the capital gains on the business and the house than both of us did working full-time for a year!

Do you see the lessons here?

First, I was determined to be successful and I didn't give up. Even though I didn't know exactly what I was looking for, I was alert to opportunity. When it came, I didn't hesitate to make a move, even though it meant moving away from friends and family – something that was particularly difficult for my new wife.

Second, I relied upon mentors to take me where I couldn't go by myself. Though I am a mentor to many people today, I also continue to seek out the wisdom and experience of other people. Today, many of my mentors are actually younger than I am, but they are certainly smarter and more experienced than me in their particular areas of expertise.

Third, I was willing to grow and change to become whoever I needed to be, in order to achieve the success I was after.

Fourth, I found out sales was a shortcut to big income. I found out straight commission or business ownership was the best way to go because now it was 100% up to me. I didn't have to work my way through artificial, subjective standards like college degrees, aptitude tests, or arbitrary time requirements. If I worked hard and smart, I could compress timeframes and receive immediate rewards.

Fifth, I found out there were more ways to make money than simply trading time for dollars. When I was a business owner, I not only made money for doing my daily job, but I built up equity in the business itself – equity I could get if I chose to sell the business later. When I was a property owner, inflation didn't hurt me, it helped me! I actually was making money by living in the house.

In spite of all these great lessons, I went on to make a number of huge mistakes. Probably the biggest was the mistake of forsaking my game plan to follow another man's dream.

After my experience in Southern California and my struggles with a number of personal problems, I put together a game plan to achieve my financial goals. I moved back to Northern California and got a job as a sales rep for a commercial office supply company. I worked hard and went on to develop a high personal income. In time, I bought another home, which I eventually turned into a rental. I began studying financial planning, but couldn't really find anything of substance about real estate investing.

The man I worked for at the office supply company was a big believer in personal development and exposed me to variety of excellent training programs. One of my favorites was Tom Hopkins' "How to Master the Art of Selling". In that program, I was taught a very healthy perspective on failure, which helps me push myself into new growth to this day.

I learned never to see failure as permanent or personal. Failure was simply an experience one goes through as a natural, normal part of growing through pushing the limits of one's abilities. Failure provides the feedback necessary to adjust one's course and perfect one's performance. Prior to this life-changing paradigm shift, I had viewed failure as personal, as an integral part of my being, as my destiny and lot in life. I often felt doomed to fail.

By changing my attitude toward failure, I learned to believe I was destined to succeed, not doomed to fail. You can imagine how liberating this new truth was for me!

Hopkins also talked on his tapes about a formula for getting rich using real estate. It was very simplistic, but it resonated with me. He simply advocated working hard and smart, living below your means, saving money, and then using the savings to buy assets which go up in value and pay you income and tax credits to own them. Wow! What a concept!

One of the other great concepts I learned had to do with goal setting and time management. I learned how important it is to "Plan your work and work your plan". Even though I had co-founded a small company as a very young man, we never had a plan. We just got up every day, worked hard and did the best we could. It wasn't until many years later I became familiar with the structure and importance of a clear business plan.

So, even though I didn't have a formal investment plan, I decided I was going to buy one house per year for five years, financing each one with a 15-year loan, and then use the rents to pay the loans off. This way, by the time my kids were grown, each child would have a house free and clear of debt. Of course, knowing what I know today, I wouldn't do it this way, but it seemed right to me at the time. At any rate, now I had my plan.

Because I didn't know any real-life real estate investors, I started buying books and going to seminars. I asked around among people I knew to see if anyone knew anything or anyone who could help me to learn more. A friend from church who sold me my car insurance referred me to another man who had a business selling life insurance.

When I met this life insurance salesman, I found out the life insurance I had from my father's insurance agent was a rip-off. Not only did I not have enough coverage, but I was also paying ten times too much for what I had! As a young father and sole breadwinner, it was important for me to have adequate coverage. I ended up replacing my old insurance with a much larger and cheaper policy.

I also found out my new life insurance agent had been a mortgage broker and a real estate investor. In fact, he told me he had become a self-made millionaire seven years earlier at age 27, but had lost it all through some factors outside his control. I didn't really understand all he said, but I was excited because I had finally found someone experienced who might be willing to mentor me in real estate investing.

This life insurance salesman asked me if I was interested in selling insurance to make some extra money. I was already doing well with my office supply sales job, but I certainly didn't mind having extra money. Besides, I believed in the product, since I had bought it myself. Mostly, what I wanted was the opportunity to get close to him and learn his mortgage and real estate secrets for success. I figured if I helped him, he might help me. If selling a little life insurance is what it took to get me into a relationship with the right mentor, I was up for it.

The life insurance salesman never taught me anything about mortgages and real estate. In fact, he wasn't very interested in my goals at all. He was a charismatic leader and I was young, eager and impressionable. Before too long, I was so excited about the insurance business, I sold my rental property, quit my six-figure sales job and opened my own insurance office. I forgot all about my plan to build a portfolio of income properties. After a few years of frustration, with the help of some Tony Robbins tapes on goal setting and lots of prayer, I woke up one day to the realization that I didn't care for the insurance business at all. My health, my finances, my self-confidence, and my marriage were all in disarray because I lost my focus. I got caught up in another man's vision and it cost me dearly.

I don't blame the life insurance salesman or anyone else for my mistakes. I just want to make sure you can learn from them! I paid full price for my lessons. I hope to give them to you for the bargain price of the cost of this book and the time you've invested reading it.

In our educational events, Robert and I often talk about the importance of developing a personal investment philosophy along with a personal investment strategy. This emphasis is important because you will have many people and opportunities competing for your money, time, affection and efforts. How do you know what to invest in?

Remember, every decision has to be evaluated in the light of your plan. This, of course, pre-supposes that you have a plan, you believe in your plan, and you stay focused on your plan.

I hope I have made the point. You will dramatically improve your chances of success by having a well thought-out game plan to follow.

· · ·

The Daily Plan It

The first step in developing your personal real estate investment plan is to establish what we call your "compelling why". This is not a financial goal, but rather it is a lifestyle goal. Just as Russ did not necessarily want a job as a division manager at HP, neither did he really want $50,000 per year income. What he wanted was the lifestyle he thought the $50,000 a year income would pay for.

Similarly, you probably have at least a vague idea of what you want life to look like at some particular point in the future. This future date may be retirement, or when the kids are out of school and on their own, or some other future season in life. Perhaps you are deferring certain things while you are fulfilling your obligations or getting yourself in a better position. Russ is looking forward to writing and painting, learning to play the piano and fly a plane, doing volunteer work, and riding dirt bikes with his children and future grandchildren. He'd like to have a horse ranch with several acres of open space for his children and their families to enjoy. Robert wants to spend more time playing music, attending concerts and traveling abroad. As a new husband and father, Robert is looking forward to investing time into his new family life. Something we are both passionate about is raising financial awareness and literacy, especially among young people. To some, these are lofty dreams, to others they might be considered modest. In any case, they are highly personally motivating. Our point is that there are financial considerations to achieving them.

Perhaps you want to travel, or own a yacht or plane, or retire to Hawaii. Whatever it is you are aiming at, if it is compelling enough and you have a game plan to achieve it, you will get up every day and push through the inevitable obstacles you'll need to face to get there. Proper planning can help shorten the distance between where you are and where you want to be. It's like planning a trip. You can head off in the general direction or you can get out a map and chart your course. Obviously, the well-planned trip usually goes much more smoothly.

Once you have itemized the components of your compelling why, you must put a budget to it. How much cash will you need to "buy" that life? How much cash-flow will you need to maintain it? What date do you want to "cross over" into your new life? The answers to these questions about cash, cash-flow and target date become your Strategic Objective. It is the target you will point all of your investing at.

The process for developing a plan looks like this:

Compelling Why?
What is it I want to achieve and why is it important to me?

Strategic Objective / Compelling What?
How much cash and cash-flow do I need to pay for my
Compelling Why and when do I want it?

Strategy / How
How can I use my current cash, cash-flow, equity, credit, knowledge,
skills and relationships to achieve my Strategic Objective?

Tactics / Specific Actions
What do I need to do on a daily, weekly, monthly and yearly basis
in order to implement my Strategy?

Obviously, it isn't possible in a book to prescribe a specific action plan that is suitable for every reader. We don't believe in a one-size-fits-all solution. You are as unique as your fingerprint. Your starting point, destination, and timeframes are unique to you. Our goal here is to provide you with the fundamentals of real estate investment planning and encourage you to find a support group (what Napoleon Hill refers to in his classic book *Think and Grow Rich* as a "mastermind group") – a team of advisors, mentors, service providers, and fellow investors who can help you refine, implement and successfully execute your plan. We call these people, "Your Personal Financial Advisory Board".

Here is a homework assignment to guide you through the process of developing your Strategic Objective:

Determine Your Strategic Objective

1. Choose a date in the future (10 to 30 or more years from now) by which time you want to arrive at your Compelling Why lifestyle. This is your Date Target. You can make the date sooner, but you must understand it takes time to develop substantial wealth with real estate investing for all but the most aggressive investor.

2. Imagine Your Future
   - Who and what are most important to you?
   - What do you want to have in terms of possessions and lifestyle?
   - What do you want to spend your time doing?
   - Be specific and itemize the list!

3. Budget Your Future
   - How much cash do you need on your target date to buy the things you need to have to outfit your future life? This is your Cash Target.
   - How much monthly income do you need to pay all of your monthly living expenses in your future life? This is your Cash-Flow Target.

Once your Strategic Objective is clearly defined, you are ready to being working on your preliminary strategy.

Develop Your Preliminary Strategy

1. Clearly identify your Strategic Objective (from the previous exercise):

   Example:
   Target Date: 30 years from today (currently age 35, future age 65)
   Target Cash: $1.5 Million
   Target Cash-flow: $10,000 Before-Tax Cash-Flow per month

Ideally, both the Cash and Cash-Flow targets should be inflation adjusted when the time horizon is this long, but for simplicity's sake, we will leave the numbers as they are.

2. Determine your Current Reality:
   - Balance Sheet (Assets minus Liabilities equals Net Worth)
   - Cash-Flow Statement (Income minus Expenses equals Cash-Flow)
   - Borrowing Power (credit rating, available credit lines, cash-flow after current living expenses that is available for additional debt service)
   - Knowledge and Relationships – Who and what do you know, who and what do you need to know, and who and what are missing?

Before we examine what Current Reality might look like from a financial perspective for a hypothetical aspiring investor, let's cover a few very important basics:

- "Inflation adjusted" means taking into account the lost purchasing power caused by inflation. For example, if inflation were to cause prices to rise by 5% a year, then something which cost $100 at the beginning of the year would cost $105 at the end of the year. Worse, each year the inflation factor compounds because the item which now costs $105 at the beginning of the second year goes up not only by $5 on the original $100 price, but also another 25 cents for the 5% inflation on the previous year's $5 of inflation. This causes the third year beginning price of the item which was originally $100 to now be $110.25.

- For purposes of investing, we do not consider personal property such as automobiles, boats, recreational vehicles, jewelry, consumer electronics, furniture and the like as "assets". In most cases, these items were not purchased with wealth enhancement as the primary objective, they tend to go down in value over time, and they often add expenses to your cash-flow statement without adding any income or tax benefits. When in doubt, ask yourself if the asset is adding useable wealth to your financial statements. If it adds income, it is probably an asset. If it adds expense, it is probably a liability, with one exception: if an item is adding net worth to your balance sheet faster than it is adding expenses to your cash-flow statement, you might consider the item an asset. Just make sure you have a viable plan for converting the asset into useable cash when needed.

- Consumer debt ("bad debt") is money owed for consumable and non-appreciating, non-revenue producing items such as vacations, groceries, cars (not used in business), pleasure boats, recreational vehicles, etc. Debt on anything that doesn't provide cash-flow or an increase to net worth is bad debt. We might debate whether a personal residence is an asset (makes money) or a liability (costs money), and we think the answer depends on whether the house is appreciating and the new equity is used to invest. In that case, you might consider it an asset. On the other hand, if you are simply living in the house and paying it off, it is probably a liability because it isn't providing you with any *useable* money. Of course, this debate could easily occupy an entire chapter on its own, but we trust you get the point.

- From a real estate lender's perspective, "housing expenses" include the principal and interest on all mortgage payments, property insurance premiums, and property taxes on your primary and secondary residences. These payments are called PITI (Principal, Interest, Taxes and Insurance) payments and are used to calculate your housing debt-to-income ratio.

- "Debt service" is the total of all payments on non-housing related debt, such as credit cards, auto loans, etc. Lenders add this to the PITI payment to calculate your *total* "debt-to-income ratio". As a guideline, real estate lenders like to see this number at 40% or below (including the new loan being applied for).

Now, let's take a look at our hypothetical investor's Current Reality:

Balance Sheet

Assets

Cash	$ 10,000
Stocks	$ 20,000
Retirement	$ 80,000
Real Estate	$500,000
Total Assets	$610,000

Liabilities

Consumer Debt	$ 7,000
Real Estate Debt	$200,000
Total Liabilities	$207,000

Net Worth (Assets Minus Liabilities) $403,000

Cash-Flow Statement

Income

Earned Income	$	7,000
Investment Income	$	200
Tax Credits	$	390
Total Income	$	7,590

Expenses

Housing Expenses	$	1,700
Non-Housing Debt Service	$	500
Personal Expenses	$	2,100
Total Before-Tax Expenses	$	4,300
Taxes	$	2,500
Total After-Tax Expenses	$	6,800
After-Tax Cash-Flow	$	790

Up to this point, most people will have no problem figuring out their Current Reality. It might take a little time and research, but there is nothing mysterious about setting up a Balance Sheet and a Cash-Flow Statement. However, when it comes to determining one's Borrowing Power, it is best to solicit the help of a professional. A Borrowing Power Analysis can be complicated when it comes to income-producing real estate. This is not like a routine pre-approval for a personal residence. With a personal residence, the total amount of income is a known quantity because the homeowners will be making all of the payments from their earnings and known investment income. With a residential income property, the income from the subject property remains unknown until the actual property is identified. It isn't the purpose of this book to train you in the nuances of residential investment property lending, so we won't go into detail here. Suffice it to say that because leverage (debt) is such a powerful tool for magnifying appreciation, your Borrowing Power is something you will be paying significant attention to as you build your property portfolio. You will want to have an experienced real estate financing professional on your team to keep you up-to-date on the latest loan programs, interest rates, and underwriting guidelines.

All Four One

Cash, cash-flow, equity and credit are the four things we use as investors to gain and maintain control of real estate. A summary of our hypothetical investor looks like this:

- Real Estate Equity $300,000
- 401K $ 80,000
- Unsecured Credit Lines $ 20,000
- After-Tax Cash-Flow $ 790 per month
- FICO Score (Middle)[44]   735

---

[44] FICO is an acronym for Fair, Isaac & Company. FICO created the "secret formula" for placing a numeric rating on a borrower to help lenders assess credit risk. The score is generated by running a borrower's credit history (obtained from one or more of the three major credit bureaus). Because the data from each bureau varies, the FICO scoring engine creates a unique score for each bureau. Lenders typically throw out the high and low scores and use the middle score, hence the term "FICO middle score".

My Assets in Jail

As is the case with the vast majority of people that come through our offices for consultations, our hypothetical investors have most of their wealth in the equity in their home. We realize this isn't true in every community because not all real estate everywhere appreciates. If you happen to live in one of these areas where real estate prices don't move up very fast...move. No, we're just kidding. If you happen to live in an area which doesn't appreciate or doesn't have good sustainable appreciation potential, you may want to make it your goal to acquire investment real estate in an area with a good history of appreciation and solid indications of continuing. While there is much more to identifying a likely marketplace, a good starting point is a large population, a strong local economy, a reasonable "desirability" factor, and some potentially limiting factor to continued new housing development. In our seminar *Analyzing Markets and Properties: The Due Diligence Process*, Robert explains what he and his team look for when seeking the next potentially hot market. Though no one has a crystal ball, there are several key indicators you can watch for. Robert trains his team and members of the mentoring club on how to watch these important indicators of appreciation.

In the case of our hypothetical investors, they have $300,000 equity in their real estate. Thanks to their great credit score (anything over 700 is considered very strong) and the wonderful loan products available today, there is a good probability they could access nearly all of this equity and use it to purchase additional properties.

Notice also that our hypothetical investors have $80,000 in their 401k plan with their current employer. Most companies do not allow you to transfer your 401k funds into a self-directed Individual Retirement Account (IRA) without terminating employment. However, many people who have left a company don't realize they can transfer their 401k funds to one of several retirement plan custodians who allow the purchase of real estate and other non-traditional assets. In the case of our hypothetical investors, they are limited to borrowing against their 401k plan in order be able to invest their retirement money elsewhere.

One caveat: If you terminate employment by choice or otherwise while any loan from the 401k is outstanding, you will either need to repay the loan immediately or be faced with having the IRS re-characterize the loan as a withdrawal. The danger is that early withdrawals are subject to taxes and penalties. This should be avoided at nearly all costs as the penalty and taxes could take as much as 50% of the loan amount. Ouch! Another point to consider is that 401k loans typically have relatively high payments. This is because the loan is typically amortized over only a 60-month period. All things considered, we like to see people get as much of their real estate equity repositioned before they consider a 401k loan. For those with available equity, using a cash-out refinance to convert equity to cash which can then be invested into more properties is a much more effective use of cash-flow. Why? Because with a real estate loan, you can get more lump sum for less monthly payment than with almost any other form of borrowing.

Another important point for a real estate investor to consider is that 401k funds can help satisfy lender guidelines for after close-of-escrow cash reserves – just by sitting there. Lenders will typically require that sufficient liquid cash reserves remain on your balance sheet after close-of-escrow in an amount equal to six months of PITI payments on the subject property. When your goal is to remain as fully invested as prudently possible, the lender's cash reserve requirement can really hamper your ability to put your money to work, especially when you are first getting started. Since many lenders will allow 70% of vested 401k funds to count as cash reserves, these funds provide a valuable Borrowing Power purpose, even when they can't be invested directly into real estate.

Credit Where Credit Is Due

We are not advocates of using unsecured credit, such as personal lines of credit and credit cards, as a tool to acquire and control real estate for the long term. The interest rates on credit cards are typically high and volatile relative to mortgage rates. Also, high amounts of credit card debt on your credit report will damage your credit score. A high credit score is hard enough to maintain once you start adding several mortgages without adding the additional burden of large amounts of credit card debt. Nonetheless, credit lines can be a very useful tool to take advantage of short-term investment opportunities, such as flips, or in making short-term high-yielding bridge loans to other investors. The key to successfully making money with credit lines is getting a high enough yield on the investment to make a profit, and then getting back to cash fast so you can pay the credit line(s) off again.

For an aggressive investor, credit lines are useful for providing short-term liquidity so available cash can be put to work, instead of simply sitting idle in a low-yielding savings account. Most credit has very little expense if unused. For less than $50 per year, you might have a $20,000 credit line. In contrast, $20,000 in cash held in a passbook savings account might earn a taxable annual return of 2-5% as of this writing, but what do you lose by doing this? Consider that $20,000 invested at a 20% growth rate would produce $4,000 per year in new wealth. Isn't that worth $50 a year in a service fee to keep a credit line open for emergencies?

You see, when you think like an investor, it makes no sense to allow assets to sit idle just so you can get a free checking account or avoid a service fee. We call this jumping over dollars to save pennies! If cash is sitting idle on your balance sheet in order to provide security for a "rainy day", you might consider keeping a dedicated credit line available for that unlikely rainy day. Then, keep most of your cash fully invested. If the rainy day actually comes and you have to use the credit line, you can look at selling or refinancing your investments in order to pay it off. The amount of interest you would pay for the time you had drawn on the credit lines will pale next to the amount of profit you can gain from staying fully invested.

In case you are concerned about where the 20% growth on your investment comes from, remember that we learned in Chapter 4 about how leverage magnifies appreciation. If $20,000 were used to purchase a property at 20% down, you would now own a $100,000 property. Using rents and tax credits to cover the $80,000 mortgage and operating expenses, you would have break-even cash-flow. If the property appreciated a modest 4% in a year, your growth on purchase equity is 20% because you control the property at 5:1 leverage. If you do the math, you'll find that 4% of $100,000 is $4,000 growth and $4,000 / $20,000 = 20%. See? It all pencils out.

Go with the Flow

Our hypothetical investors have quite a bit of cash-flow from their earned income, although they probably don't feel like it. Even after paying a hefty $2,110 ($2,500 liability less $390 credits) in taxes, they still end up with $790 of discretionary income left over each month (refer back to their Cash-Flow Statement). If they are like most people, the money is gone at the end of the month and they have no idea where it went. This is an argument for budgeting and having a good recordkeeping system, but this is a soap box we will stay off of for now. As we said in Chapter 6, if you know you are a poor bookkeeper, don't kid yourself into thinking you'll change (though you could); just hire someone to do it for you and get busy making money. Even if you are a good bookkeeper, is bookkeeping the best use of your time? Might not you invest your time, talent and attention towards more profitable activities?

One option would be for our hypothetical investors to take most of their $790 in discretionary cash-flow and use it to access the $300,000 in idle equity in their real estate via a cash-out refinance. This is heresy to many consumer-minded financial planners, but for many beginning investors this is the only sizable amount of money they have to work with. Admittedly, there is risk in borrowing against a property, BUT there is also risk in *not* investing. As Clint Eastwood once said, "If you want a guarantee, buy a toaster." The fact is, if you want to make money you will need to take some risks. Just be smart about it by having a plan.

Please keep in mind, we are not telling you, our reader, what you should do in your specific and unique situation. Remember, we believe "prescription without diagnosis is malpractice". We are simply sharing ideas and strategies to help you understand some basic real estate investment planning concepts so you can work more effectively with your own personal financial advisory board.

The challenge you face as an investor, and one which all investors must work through, is how to best reorganize your cash, cash-flow, equity, and credit in order to develop enough wealth to fund your Strategic Objective. One of the most challenging aspects of financial planning for the non-professional is determining how much equity is necessary to generate the desired monthly cash-flow through real estate. This is much more complex than simply buying a CD, bond, annuity or some other traditional income producing investment. We would argue that the extra trouble of working through an investment plan built around real estate is worthwhile because of real estate's relative stability and high growth potential, the likelihood of long-term growth of both equity *and* income over time, and the favorable tax treatment which real estate provides to both cash-flow and equity investors.

Choose Your Weapon

Cash-flow vehicles are those used at your Target Date (some time in the future) to provide cash-flow in the amount targeted. Equity vehicles are those used to reach Critical Mass. To help you keep these straight, remember there are two major phases in a real estate investor's life:

1. **Equity** phase (a.k.a. asset accumulation phase) – this is where your investment decisions are primarily focused on building

your net worth. In other words, you are using your cash-flow (income less expenses) in a way that optimizes your equity growth. As we learned earlier, there are two ways to build equity: amortization (pay down of debt) or appreciation (build up of new equity, which can be "passive", "found", "phased" and "forced" – as we discussed in Chapter 8). We believe the best and fastest results come from focusing on accumulating *new* equity as opposed to paying down loans with your after-tax earnings.

2. **Cash-Flow** phase – this is where you have accumulated sufficient equity to control enough income producing assets to meet your cash-flow requirements. At this time, and preferably not before, equity is repositioned to those investment vehicles which will consistently produce the required amount of cash-flow – *without* reducing equity. Ideally, the portfolio would also continue to grow equity to protect you from the purchasing power eroding effects of inflation.

Cash-Flow Vehicles
In the following charts, we compare stocks (paper equities), mortgages and bonds (paper income), and income property (income and equity producing real estate).

Cash-Flow Vehicles

	Stock Market	Mortgages or Bonds	Income Real Estate
Invested Equity or Capital	$1,500,000	$1,500,000	$1,500,000
Annual Cash Return on Investment Required	8%	8%	8.5% Cap Rate (65% LTV, 7% 30 year note)[45]
Potential for Equity Growth	Yes	Negligible	Yes
Volatility	High	Low	Low
Potential Cash-Flow Growth	Yes	No (except for reallocation)[46]	Yes
Taxes Due at Reallocation?	Yes, except IRA or QP[47]	Yes, except for IRA or QP	Not with 1031, IRA or QP
Management Responsibility	Yes (can be delegated to advisor)	Yes (can be delagated to advisor)	Yes (can be delagated to property managers and/or advisors)

Why do we use $1.5 million investment capital for our comparison? We determined the invested capital requirement by working backwards from the income target. Our hypothetical investors want $120,000 per year of sustainable income. We calculated that $1,500,000 x 8% is $120,000 of annual income or $10,000 per month BTCF (before-tax cash-flow). Each of these cash-flow vehicles will provide this target cash-flow stream based on the assumptions shown. Naturally, sellers of each type of investment vehicle might claim

---

[45] The capitalization rate (cap rate) shows the cash return on acquisition price and is based on the Net Operating Income (NOI). NOI does not take into account debt service, so for purposes of this illustration we are assuming debt of 65% at 7% fully-amortized over 30 years.
[46] Reallocation means selling all or part of the portfolio and buying other investments in order to modify portfolio performance.
[47] QP = Qualified Plan – this is a tax advantaged arrangement allowed under IRS code.

their investment vehicle of choice can perform better than illustrated, but each is represented in an equally conservative fashion. Remember, when setting up your real estate investment plan, you must base your assumptions on *reasonably repeatable* results. It's always more acceptable to make *more* money than anticipated, while the reverse can be quite distressing!

When we compare real estate investment planning with traditional financial planning, we find important differences. With traditional financial planning, assets are allocated into a diversified mix of paper-based investments like stocks, bonds and mutual funds in order to mitigate some of the risks associated with each of the various individual vehicles. For example, a young person is much more susceptible to losing purchasing power over time due to the compounding effects of inflation. Therefore, traditional financial planning wisdom places a greater emphasis on stocks (equities) in the early part of an investor's life. The accompanying volatility of the stock market is generally accepted as part of the price one pays to take advantage of the inflation of the stock's price over time. If the stock's value grows faster than inflation, the investor realizes a net gain in purchasing power.

Later in life, traditional financial planning wisdom advises the re-allocation of one's portfolio with a greater percentage invested in "blue chip"[48] stocks, general or "broad" market mutual funds and high-yield bonds.[49] The reason for this re-allocation is to shelter the investor from the volatility of the stock market when a significant reduction in value could be devastating (when would it not be?). Later in life, when there is insufficient time for the value of a portfolio to "come back" from a sharp decline, the

---

[48] A "blue chip" company is mature and financially strong, often with a track record of paying out part of their operating profits to shareholders in the form of cash payouts known as "dividends".

[49] Bonds are debt obligations (securitized IOU's) of major companies, municipalities and governments. They typically pay a specified amount of interest income to the bond holder (the investor).

investor relying upon investment income may need to accept a significant reduction in standard of living (yuck!). Consider when a stock drops 50% (half) in value, it must grow 100% (double) in order to just "come back" to where it started. We question the wisdom of ever putting yourself in a position to take such a hit! We suppose if buy-and-hold stock investing is the only option available, it is better than trying to out-earn and out-save taxes and inflation. In our opinion, taxes and inflation are the greatest threats to every wage-earner's financial well-being. We like real estate because it allows us to *benefit* from inflation while enjoying tax advantages.

In real estate, the relationship between appreciation and income is different than it is with the stock and bond market. Over time, real estate goes up in value because of inflation, just like stocks. Over time, the income (rent) goes up for the same reason – and at the same time! No re-allocation is needed. It happens automatically! Remember, income property is valued by the income it produces. More income equals more value. More value equals more equity. If a=b and b=c, then a= c, right? So, if more income equals more value and more value equals more equity, then more income equals more equity, right?

Coming back to the graph we are using to compare different choices for creating cash-flow for our hypothetical investors, you can see that no matter which cash-flow vehicle our hypothetical investors choose (you know our preference), they still need $1.5 million to get the $10,000 per month cash-flow that their Strategic Objective calls for. Now the big question arises: how do they get from Current Reality to Critical Mass, which for them is $1.5 million?

Equity Growth Vehicles
Just as your choice of career should be made with careful consideration and wise counsel, so should the decision about what type of investment vehicle you choose to stake your financial future on. Therefore, let's once again compare real estate to stocks and bonds:

Equity Growth Vehicles

	Buy-and-Hold Stock Market	Buy-and-Hold Real Estate
Leverage	1:1	4:1
Historical Average Annual Growth	12%	6%
Beginning Invested Capital	$100,000	$100,000
Tax Credits	Realized Losses Only	Passive Activity Loss (Depreciation Is Not Realized)
Annual Tax on Growth	Dividends and Realized Gains	After-Tax Depreciation Income Only (Realized Capital Gains Can Be Deferred via 1031)
Optimization	N/A	5 Years
Time	20 Years	20 Years
Ending Net Equity	$1.8 Million	$3.06 Million
Additional Capital Required at Beginning to Achieve Target of $1.5 Million on Time	$184,000	$ –0–
Additional Time Required to Achieve $1.5 Million without Additional Capital Investment at Beginning	10 Years	–0–

It is very difficult to explain these concepts in a live seminar. It is even harder in a book. However, we will do our best to simplify this so you can get the concepts. Once you understand the concepts, doing the math is really quite simple.

"Math?" you say. "I hate math. It's boring and it's hard!"

We know it's hard. Don't give up! The easiest thing to do is to fold this book up and not do anything. Quitting now won't change your future! You picked up this book for a reason. We trust that you wanted to learn, not simply be entertained. No one promised it would be fun or easy, but how hard do most people work to get a college degree so they can get a job? Isn't real estate investing better than a job? It is! So stay with us! A "degree" in real estate is much faster and cheaper to get than an MBA – and you'll probably make much more money in real estate than in some fancy corporate job with your MBA. That is, unless you use your income from that fancy job to invest in real estate. So, here we are again. You need to learn to do the math!

Let's get back to our hypothetical investors. We know they want $1.5 million in cash and $10,000 per month in cash-flow. Our cash-flow vehicle analysis says we need $1.5 million invested at an annual yield of 8% to generate $10,000 per month in income:

$1,500,000 x 8% per year = $120,000 per year = $10,000 per month

This means our investors need to take the cash, cash-flow, equity and credit in their Current Reality and use them to build up at least $3 million of equity over the next twenty years. This would give them $1.5 million of consumable cash and $1.5 million to invest to produce $10,000 per month before-tax cash-flow.

With $100,000 in available cash and/or equity to start with, using realistic assumptions, the Equity Growth Vehicle comparison charts show us that real estate at 4:1 leverage clearly outperforms the stock market in terms of growth of net worth over time. Notice in our chart that $100,000 invested in the stock market compounding yearly (un-taxed) will grow to $1.08 million.

How did we figure this out? Actually, it's very simple. Just take $100,000 x (100%+12%) and then multiply the product times 112% and repeat until you have done it 30 times. The $100,000 is your starting capital (principal) and the 100% is the return of principal. The 12% is the growth. So it looks like this:

Starting Principal: $100,000
Annualized Return: 12%

Year #	Principal	Growth	Balance Forward
1	$100,000	$ 12,000	$ 112,000
2	$112,000	$ 13,440	$ 125,440
3	$125,440	$ 15,053	$ 140,493
4	$140,493	$ 16,859	$ 157,352
5	$ 57,352	$ 18,882	$ 176,234
6	$176,234	$ 21,148	$ 197,382
7	$197,382	$ 23,686	$ 221,068
8	$221,068	$ 26,528	$ 247,596
9	$247,596	$ 29,712	$ 277,308
10	$277,308	$ 33,277	$ 310,585
11	$310,585	$ 37,270	$ 347,855
12	$347,855	$ 41,743	$ 389,598
13	$389,598	$ 46,752	$ 436,349
14	$436,349	$ 52,362	$ 488,711
15	$488,711	$ 58,645	$ 547,357
16	$547,357	$ 65,683	$ 613,039
17	$613,039	$ 73,565	$ 686,604
18	$686,604	$ 82,392	$ 768,997
19	$768,997	$ 92,280	$ 861,276
20	$861,276	$103,353	$ 964,629
21	$964,629	$115,756	$1,080,385

Not to continue to beat up the buy-and-hold stock market investing approach (but we will), remember how little control the average individual investor has over their stock market investments. With real estate, the investor selects property management or may elect to self-manage. The investor decides on tenants or sets policy for the property manager, decides on repairs and improvements, and in general has considerably more ability to directly increase the value of the property.

Now let's look at using the same $100,000 we used to grow $1.08 million in the stock market, and see how we would invest in real estate in order to beat the stock market.

If we take the $100,000 and make a 25% down payment on an income property where rents will cover the mortgage and operating expenses, then we could buy a $400,000 property. If the property appreciates 6% per year, then five years later, this $400,000 property will have appreciated to $535,000:

Property #1 appreciating at 6% per year:

Year	Starting Market Price	Ending Market Price	Loan Amount	New Equity (from Appreciation)	Total Equity (Purchase and New)
1	$400,000	$424,000	$300,000	$24,000	$124,000
2	$424,000	$449,440	$300,000	$49,440	$149,440
3	$449,440	$476,406	$300,000	$76,406	$176,406
4	$476,406	$504,991	$300,000	$104,991	$204,991
5	$504,991	$535,290	$300,000	$135,290	$235,290

At the end of the fifth year, we would refinance the now $535,290 property with a 75% cash-out loan: $535,290 x 75% = 401,467 new loan. The new loan is used to pay off the original $300,000 loan with $101,467 cash left over. We can take this $100,000 and make another 25% down payment on another $400,000 property and repeat the process over the next five years:

Property # 2 appreciating at 6% per year:

Year	Starting Market Price	Ending Market Price	Loan Amount	New Equity (from Appreciation)	Total Equity (Purchase and New)
6	$400,000	$424,000	$300,000	$24,000	$124,000
7	$424,000	$449,440	$300,000	$49,440	$149,440
8	$449,440	$476,406	$300,000	$76,406	$176,406
9	$476,406	$504,991	$300,000	$104,991	$204,991
10	$504,991	$535,290	$300,000	$135,290	$235,290

Meanwhile, what happened to the first property?

Property #1 appreciating at 6% per year:

Year	Starting Market Price	Ending Market Price	Loan Amount	New Equity (from Appreciation)	Total Equity (Purchase and New)
6	$535,290	$567,407	$401,467	$32,117	$165,940
7	$567,407	$601,451	$401,467	$34,044	$199,984
8	$601,451	$637,539	$401,467	$36,088	$236,072
9	$637,539	$675,791	$401,467	$38,252	$274,324
10	$675,791	$716,339	$401,467	$40,548	$314,872

Now let's look at the numbers when we put both Property #1 and Property # 2 together.

Property #1 and Property # 2 Consolidated

Year	Starting Market Price	Ending Market Price	Loan Amount	New Equity (from Appreciation)	Total Equity (Purchase and New)
6	$ 935,290	$ 991,407	$701,467	$ 56,117	$289,940
7	$ 991,407	$1,050,891	$701,467	$ 83,484	$349,424
8	$1,050,891	$1,112,765	$701,467	$112,494	$412,478
9	$1,112,765	$1,180,782	$701,467	$143,243	$479,315
10	$1,180,782	$1,251,629	$701,467	$175,748	$550,162

Notice that by starting with only $100,000, we now have $550,162 in Total Equity. This means we have grown our net worth by $450,162 in ten years. Not bad! But we aren't done yet! Let's take a look at what happens if we refinance *both* Property #1 and Property #2, each with a 75% cash-out loan, use the proceeds to pay off the old loans, and then use the cash to make a down payment on a *third* property:

$1,251,629 x 75% = $ 938,721 less old loans of $701,467 = $237,255 cash out.

Let's use this new cash to make a 25% down payment on Property #3:

$ 949,000 Purchase Price
$ 237,250 25% down payment
$ 711,750 75% loan

Property # 3 appreciating at 6% per year:

Year	Starting Market Price	Ending Market Price	Loan Amount	New Equity (from Appreciation)	Total Equity (Purchase and New)
11	$ 949,000	$1,005,940	$711,750	$56,940	$294,190
12	$1,005,940	$1,066,296	$711,750	$60,356	$354,546
13	$1,066,296	$1,130,274	$711,750	$63,978	$418,524
14	$1,130,274	$1,198,090	$711,750	$67,816	$486,340
15	$1,198,090	$1,269,976	$711,750	$71,886	$558,226

During Years 11-15, while Property #3 is appreciating as shown above, what are Properties #1 and #2 doing? They are also going up in value. Take a look:

Properties #1 and #2 appreciating at 6% per year:

Year	Starting Market Price	Ending Market Price	Loan Amount	New Equity (from Appreciation)	Total Equity (Purchase and New)
11	$1,251,629	$1,326,726	$938,721	$75,097	$388,005
12	$1,326,726	$1,406,330	$938,721	$79,604	$467,609
13	$1,406,330	$1,490,710	$938,721	$84,380	$551,989
14	$1,490,710	$1,580,125	$938,721	$89,442	$641,431
15	$1,580,125	$1,674,961	$938,721	$94,809	$736,240

Let's consolidate all three properties together onto one spreadsheet and look at the aggregate portfolio now:

Properties #1, #2 and #3:

Year	Starting Market Price	Ending Market Price	Loan Amount	New Equity (from Appreciation)	Total Equity (Purchase and New)
11	$2,200,629	$2,332,666	$1,650,471	$132,037	$ 682,195
12	$2,332,666	$2,472,626	$1,650,471	$139,960	$ 822,155
13	$2,472,626	$2,620,984	$1,650,471	$148,358	$ 970,513
14	$2,620,984	$2,778,242	$1,650,471	$157,258	$1,127,771
15	$2,778,242	$2,944,937	$1,650,471	$166,695	$1,294,466

Wow! We started with only $100,000 and built it up to nearly $1.3 million in fifteen years! Of course, we aren't done yet because we still need $3 million to fund our hypothetical investor's Strategic Objective. So, let's go ahead and refinance all three properties in the portfolio at a 75% loan-to-value:

$2,944,937 x 75% = $2,208,702 new loan. Pay off the old loans of $1,650,471, which leaves us $558,232 in cash. Once again, we will use this new cash to make a 25% down payment on yet another property:

> $2,230,000 **Property # 4**
> $ 557,500 **25% Down**
> $1,672,500 **75% Loan**

Property #4 appreciating at 6% per year:

Year	Starting Market Price	Ending Market Price	Loan Amount	New Equity (from Appreciation)	Total Equity (Purchase and New)
16	$2,230,000	$2,363,800	$1,672,500	$133,800	$ 691,300
17	$2,363,800	$2,505,628	$1,672,500	$141,828	$ 833,128
18	$2,505,628	$2,655,965	$1,672,500	$150,337	$ 938,465
19	$2,655,965	$2,815,323	$1,672,500	$159,358	$1,142,823
20	$2,815,323	$2,984,243	$1,672,500	$168,919	$1,311,743

Of course, while Property #4 is going up to $2.9 million, Properties #1, #2 and #3 are also still appreciating:

Properties #1, #2 and #3 appreciating at 6% per year:

Year	Starting Market Price	Ending Market Price	Loan Amount	New Equity (from Appreciation)	Total Equity (Purchase and New)
16	$2,944,937	$3,121,633	$2,208,702	$176,696	$ 912,931
17	$3,121,633	$3,308,931	$2,208,702	$187,298	$1,100,229
18	$3,507,467	$3,507,467	$2,208,702	$198,535	$1,298,765
19	$3,717,915	$3,717,915	$2,208,702	$210,448	$1,509,213
20	$3,940,990	$3,940,990	$2,208,702	$223,074	$1,732,288

Now , let's add up the Year 20 Total Equity from Property #4 and the Year 20 Total Equity from Properties #1, #2 and #3 and see where we are:

Year 20 Total Equity from Property #4:	$1,311,743
Year 20 Total Equity from Properties #1, #2, #3:	$1,732,288
Year 20 Total Equity from Properties #1-4:	$3,044,031

Look at that! We did it! Our hypothetical investors have taken their $100,000 and invested it based on using 25% down payments on properties appreciating at 6% per year, refinancing faithfully every five years, and then investing the liquid equity (cash out) into additional properties. This is a very conservative approach to real estate investing based on only the historical average appreciation (not wishful thinking) and only 25% down, but it got the job done! You can imagine what might have happened with a more aggressive approach including greater leverage, disciplined cash-flow management, and careful market and property due diligence.

Most importantly, we used the real estate portfolio to come up with all the down payments! Can you imagine what you would need to earn to save up enough to buy this much property?

Consider also that even if both stocks and real estate "only" perform to their historical averages, it is clear real estate is the winner by nearly $2 MILLION! What makes the difference? Leverage! Have we mentioned Chapter 4?

We trust we've adequately made the case for real estate over buy-and-hold stocks as the equity-building vehicle of choice! So now, let's go to work on...

Philosophically Speaking

Once you have set your Strategic Objective (Cash Target, Cash-Flow Target, and Date Target), how do you decide what kind of properties to invest in? The key is to develop your personal investment philosophy.

Remember, there are no problem properties, only problem ownerships. One person's dream property is another person's nightmare property. There are many types of properties and many types of investors. Your mission is to figure out what type of investor you are and what types of properties and markets will work best for you. We call this "getting in touch with your inner investor".

One of the challenges we've had in writing this book comes from our belief that every investor is unique. We don't believe there is a one-size-fits-all magic formula that is guaranteed to work for anyone willing to pay for and follow it. Whenever people ask us to tell them exactly what they need to do, we smile and remind them, "Prescription without diagnosis is malpractice."

As educators and mentors, we focus on helping people learn how to think, and not simply on telling people what to do, because what to do changes depending on a host of variables too numerous to formularize. These variables are both external and internal. External variables include national items such as interest rates, tax law, banking practice, loan programs, underwriting guidelines, and more. Other external variables include local items like regional economic trends, population and demographical trends, property taxes, landlord tenant law (e.g. rent control), city planning guidelines, etc. As you can see, the list of external variables a real estate investor must navigate is long and constantly changing. This alone makes a magic formula difficult to implement in real life, no matter how easy it sounds in a seminar or television commercial.

In addition to the external variables, there are a number of "internal" investor-specific variables, which make it impractical to design a magic formula. Some of these variables pertain to an individual investor's financial position: items such as cash, cash-flow, equity, credit rating, and relationships. Many of the internal variables pertain to the individual investor's attitudes, habits, knowledge and beliefs. Negative attitudes, unproductive habits, and limiting beliefs are the things which hinder most people's investment potential, yet we see so few real estate educators addressing these essential issues of mindset and emotional control. Technical knowledge is only useful when you have the emotional fortitude to take action.

In our educational events and mentoring clubs, we strive to help people develop a clear personal investment philosophy. This clarity helps guide their decision making as they respond to the myriad of external variables real-world investing brings. To facilitate the process of developing a personal investment philosophy, Robert developed a series of "continuums" to assist people in thinking about where they see themselves as investors:

Primary Objective Continuum

Equity   **Cash-Flow**
$$\longleftarrow\!\!\!\!\!\!\!-\!\!\!\!\!\!\!-\!\!\!\!\!\!\!\longrightarrow$$
Primary Objective

Your Primary Objective has to do with what you want the property to do for you financially. On one end of this continuum is Cash-Flow and on the other is Equity Growth. Getting clear on your Primary Objective is very important because it will dictate not only what types of properties you buy and how you finance them, but also what market places you choose to focus on.

While there are certainly markets and properties which provide both cash-flow and equity growth, we have found that properties which produce superior cash-flow at loan-to-values above 80% typically provide relatively little appreciation. Conversely, properties that tend to appreciate quickly often require large amounts of purchase equity (down payment and therefore, loss of leverage) in order to achieve a break-even or better cash-flow. Why? If a property is appreciating well, investors focus on total growth (of which appreciation is a major contributor) and are willing to bid the property up to where the cash-flow return is smaller. In other words, investors are willing to pay more for the same cash-flow when they think the appreciation will more than compensate in terms of total return. In markets where properties do not appreciate well, investors don't bid up pricing beyond the point where the property still provides an acceptable cash-flow because the investors don't anticipate augmenting their cash-on-cash return with appreciation.

Again, the question of Primary Objective is foundational to many other decisions, so it is important you are clear on what you want your properties to do for you financially. Are you still in pursuit of Critical Mass? If so, you probably want to emphasize investing for equity. If you have reached the point where you have enough equity to generate the kind of income you want, then you should allocate your equity into markets, properties and financing arrangements that will optimize after-tax cash-flow, even if your total return is not as high. If you've already reached Critical Mass, then equity growth becomes secondary to after-tax cash-flow. As long as you keep a little leverage in it, even if you are in cash-flow markets that don't appreciate as well, you'll probably have no trouble outpacing inflation. Consider that 3% appreciation at 3:1 leverage still produces a 9% equity growth rate.

Risk Tolerance Continuum

Conservative   **Aggressive**

$\longleftrightarrow$

Risk Tolerance

Determining how much risk you are willing to accept is both personal and difficult. Are you more conservative by nature or are you more adventurous? As with all of our continuums, there is not a right or wrong answer. Consider also that "risk" is a highly relative term. As we discussed in Chapter 7, there are a variety of risks – some of which are genuine and others simply perceived.

One of the biggest risks we see people pass over every day is the risk of inaction. Inaction is often caused by procrastination, fear of the unknown, or paralysis from over-analysis (which is really the fear of making a mistake). Sometimes an investor must accept the risk of action because there is greater risk from inaction. These are challenging issues to reconcile, but putting it off will not help your situation. In fact, it will exacerbate the problem. Indecision is a decision. People buy books, audio and video programs, seminars, and work with advisors, to try to find the foolproof, risk free, no effort, smooth highway, but the truth is this "Holy Grail" doesn't exist. If it did, everyone would have found it by now and would be on that yellow brick road to real estate riches. We wouldn't need to write this book and ask you to do all the hard work of clarifying your vision, organizing your resources, and assessing your investor personality.

However, we presume you bought the book because you are looking for real-world answers that work for ordinary people with an average amount of resources and time. Well, here you go: if you want to be a happy, successful investor, you will need to "get in touch with you inner investor" – and a huge part of the process is determining your risk tolerance. So review Chapter 7 and think about where you are at right now. But remember, your risk tolerance will change as you gain more education, experience and financial strength.

Property Type Continuum

Single Family Homes　　　　　　　　　**Larger Buildings**

◄───►

Types of Property

What types of properties are you interested in? While this may change over time, it is important for you to identify your current targets of opportunity – especially if you are a beginner. Do you feel more comfortable with single-family homes since they are relatively liquid and easy to understand? Are you intrigued by *The Free Duplex Story* and want to focus on acquiring two-unit rentals? Would you rather benefit from the economies of scale offered by larger buildings or development projects? Are you more interested in retail or other commercial property? Perhaps you'd like a lower maintenance income property like a storage center or mobile home park?

As your investment experience grows, you will find that different types of property provide different types of opportunities and challenges. Evaluating opportunity is an inexact science at best, and more probably, an art. The best way to learn is to analyze a wide variety of properties in the markets you are interested in. We always include real-world case studies as part of each and every mentoring club meeting. We've looked at conversion projects, raw land, mobile home parks, large apartment buildings, single-family houses, residential condominiums, pre-construction high-rise towers, office buildings, and much more. There's no substitute for looking at lots of deals, but it does take time.

If you have the ability to join an investment club, or start a group of your own, make it a habit to analyze many different properties. This can be a very efficient way to get a feel for how certain property types tend to perform financially – and how much effort is required to acquire and manage them. As you gather information and experience, keep notes and try to index property types to financial outcomes. This will help you evaluate properties more quickly and accurately with an eye toward how any specific property might affect your lifestyle and your portfolio's financial results.

Investment Duration Continuum

Flip Properties   Buy-and-Hold

$$\longleftarrow\hspace{6cm}\longrightarrow$$

Duration of Investment

How long you choose to hold a property will depend partially on where you want the property to take you financially, how quickly you want to get there, and how involved you are willing to be. Typical "flippers" (people who buy a property, fix it up or otherwise add value, and then sell it immediately for a quick profit), are seeking big money fast and are willing to work hard to get it. This style of active investing is best suited for a full-time investor because, as we have discussed, time leverage is the key to high returns on non-income properties. If you are only part-time, it is hard to keep a project moving forward aggressively enough to make a great return. On the other hand, someone who can't or won't work that hard may be perfectly content to buy a property, hold it for the long-term, and take a slower, but potentially larger gain through buy-and-hold appreciation, cash-flow, amortization, and depreciation.

Some people choose to flip when they first get started simply so they can build up enough capital for down payments and cash reserves on buy-and-hold properties. Then, as the buy-and-hold property goes up in value over time, the investor pulls equity from Property A to make a down payment on Property B (the "free" duplex concept). Once the passive equity of the portfolio is growing fast enough to provide a steady stream of down payments, it may no longer be necessary or desirable to continue to flip. Again, your philosophies and strategies will continually change as your education, experience, relationships and resources grow.

Property Profile Continuum

Lower End	Pride of Ownership

←——————————————————————————→

Property Profile

A property's profile has to do with the quality of tenants and area. This can be a sensitive issue for many investors. Pride of Ownership properties are those units that look beautiful and are in great neighborhoods. While they may appreciate nicely, it is typically difficult to get them to cash-flow without a large down payment. The types of people who can afford to pay high enough rent to cover your big loan on a nice property are the kind of people who will go buy their own property rather than rent from you. This can be true of both residential and commercial tenants. So in order for you to have low enough debt service to prevent excessive negative cash-flow, you often need a larger down payment. Remember, however, the larger down payment diminishes the benefits of leverage.

On the other end of the spectrum, lower-end properties can often provide better cash-flow and total return (primarily through better leverage), but some investors are not comfortable dealing with properties in these neighborhoods. It is important to carefully consider your tolerance for tougher properties and weigh the risks against the rewards. Remember, there is no right or wrong answer. It is simply a matter of personal preference. The good news is that people have built tremendous wealth with all different types of properties, and so can you!

Property Management Continuum

Self-Managed	Professional

←——————————————————————————→

Property Management

How involved do you want to be in the day-to-day operations of your properties? Many people are too busy to manage their properties themselves. They like the idea of outsourcing property management. Conversely, hands-on investors prefer to get very involved with the management so they can stay close to their investments. These people tend to feel no one will look out for their interests as well as they will. While this is probably true, the downside is that you just can't get very big if you are doing everything yourself. However, when you first start out, it can make good sense to be hands-on so you can learn the details of the business. We find most investors eventually decide to utilize outside management when their portfolios reach a certain size because there is just too much work to do by themselves, even if they wanted to. Once the decision is made about whether or not to self-manage or outsource, it is important to account for the additional cost of professional management. If your personal investment philosophy calls for professional management, you will need to add approximately 8-10% or more to your monthly expense factor.

Investment Proximity Continuum

Your Neighborhood   **Worldwide**

⬅━━━━━━━━━━━━━━━━━━━━━━━━━━━━━━━━━➡

Investment Proximity

Where you choose to invest will be one of the most important decisions you make. There are many things to consider when choosing areas to invest in. Do you plan to self-manage? Are you willing to travel to investigate markets and properties? A major factor will be whether or not there are properties in your neighborhood or local marketplace that are suitable for meeting your investment objectives, and whether or not you can afford the properties in your area.

Where you fall on the Investment Proximity continuum may simply be a result of where you landed on the other continuums. Sometimes the reverse is true and your investment proximity decision drives many of your other decisions because you are restricted to only the types of properties available in your market. It's simply a matter of getting clarity on your value hierarchy –

what matters most to you. We have a friend whose father is a long time real estate investor, but has a very strict proximity rule. He will only buy properties within a 20-minute drive of his home. Being near his investment properties is one of the single most important considerations shaping his personal investment philosophy. All of his investment choices must fit inside this "20-minute rule".

On the other side of the spectrum, Robert has a simple saying that is part of his personal investment philosophy, "Live where you want to live, but invest where the numbers make sense!" In Robert's value hierarchy, financial return is more important than avoiding travel, working with only a single regional team of service providers, the ease of learning only one market, or any desire to remain personally involved in managing all of his properties. As you might guess, Robert travels constantly, has teams of service providers in several marketplaces, and can no longer be actively involved in the management of all his properties. For some people, this lifestyle would be completely unacceptable. To Robert, a 20-minute rule is far too confining. Do you see how getting clear on what you really want and are willing to do is important to achieving balanced success? This is why there can never be a one-size-fits-all magic formula. People, properties and markets are just too diverse for a universal prescription.

The Power of the Pen

Virtually every book written on success stresses the critical importance of putting plans in writing. Yet, so many people refuse to do it. Why is this? Legendary business philosopher Jim Rohn responds, "Nobody knows!" What we do know is that the act of writing down your personal investment philosophy will help you gain clarity and remain focused. Just do it!

Here's how to get started:

1. Review each of the continuums and write a brief statement about how each relates to your investment objectives, personality type,

and your current resources in terms of finances, time, talent, experience, education, and relationships.

2. Rank your responses to each continuum in order of importance to you. Simply pick any two and ask yourself which one is more important than the other. Take the winner and put it up against the next one. Which is more important? Then take the winner and compare it to the next. When you get through them all, you should have a clear #1. Then start the process again until you have a #2. Repeat until all continuums are ranked first to last. As you go through this process, you will raise new questions and discover new answers. Sometimes you will need to conduct research, which can be technical (i.e., a call to your CPA for tax advice) or anecdotal (i.e., a call to a more experienced investor for their thoughts).

3. As new ideas and feelings emerge, edit your responses accordingly, and then re-rank them. Repeat the process until you are very clear about your personal investment philosophy.

Keep your written personal investment philosophy in a handy place and review it regularly. Take it with you when you look at properties, meet with advisors, or attend real estate meetings and seminars. Your personal investment philosophy is one of your greatest tools to inoculate you from "herd mentality" (simply doing what everyone else is doing without thinking much about it), and will help you avoid getting caught up in hype. When you act without thinking, you run the risk of ending up with a problem property. Remember, there are no problem properties – only problem ownerships. Don't buy something you don't want. It might be great for the guy or gal next to you, but if it conflicts with your personal investment philosophy, then you'll likely be sorry if you end up owning it. Your personal investment philosophy will help you be more decisive with less remorse – whether you say "yes" or "no". You'll also find everyone will enjoy dealing with you much more. Your clarity will make it easier for them to help you in the way you want and need to be helped.

We have one more important warning. Your personal investment philosophy will change regularly. As you learn and do more, you will find it appealing and necessary to modify your thinking. In other words, your personal investment philosophy is not static, but dynamic and fluid. Don't let this frustrate or discourage you. It's normal! The fact that you are re-thinking your philosophy means you are thinking and learning, which is a wonderful thing. Besides, circumstances change. Tax and tenant law, interest rates, loan programs, demographic and economic trends, and a host of other items that affect your investment decisions, will form an ever-changing landscape that you will need to continually navigate in order to be and remain successful.

With all this said, consider that if you have a personal investment philosophy which doesn't result in property ownership, then your criteria may not be very realistic. The purpose of your personal investment philosophy is to guide your investment actions, not prevent them! As we've shared earlier, you don't want to get caught standing at the plate waiting for the perfect pitch. You must swing the bat in order to get a hit. There are no walks in real estate investing.

CHAPTER 12
Opt to Be a Miser, but Not to the Max!

Many so-called "investors" attempt to squeeze every single dollar out of every deal they do. They push the market and make sure they always have the highest rents. They negotiate, haggle and connive to get the absolute lowest price on everything they buy. They try to cut fees and commissions, resist making any deal-sweetening concessions, and look for every opportunity to cut corners in order to "save" money – as if money and profits were the only things of value in their business!

We believe strongly (can you tell?) that you will do much better in the long run by seeking to "optimize" your return instead of attempting to "maximize" your return. It's a subtle, but profound difference, and one worth noting, hence our devotion of an entire chapter to this subject. Unless you enjoy upsetting people, burning bridges, and leaving anger and bitterness in your wake, you will not be happy as a "maximizer" – and neither will the people whose help you need to be successful.

A Maximizer is obsessed with getting every penny of profit on every deal.

An Optimizer wants to get all he can, but not without leaving something on the table for the other party.

A Maximizer looks out for Number One and negotiates hard to gain an advantage on every point, steadfastly refusing to make concessions.

An Optimizer keeps the other parties' interests in mind, negotiates fairly and seeks win-win relationships and transactions.

A Maximizer looks at prosperity as a zero-sum game and thinks the only way to get more is to take it from someone else.

An Optimizer has "abundance mentality" and believes there is more than enough for everybody.

A Maximizer goes for the home run on every try, but lets lots of opportunity go by while waiting for the perfect pitch.

An Optimizer understands the power of consistency and focuses on hitting solid base hits, thereby getting on base more often, scoring more runs, helping others score, and hitting the home run more often.

A Maximizer is greedy, self-serving, and uses people to serve money.

An Optimizer is generous, community-focused, and uses money to serve people.

A Maximizer wants everything or nothing – he would rather lose than let someone else win too.

An Optimizer thinks something is better than nothing and is genuinely happy when other people prosper.

A Maximizer is always in a hurry to make money, and is willing to compromise his integrity and reputation to get it with as little effort or contribution as possible.

An Optimizer is patient, steadfast, willing to work, plans carefully, takes calculated risks, and understands that direction is more important than speed.

A Maximizer looks to take advantage of others' hardships and attempts to profit regardless of the expense to others.

An Optimizer finds opportunities to serve others and trusts that he will be rewarded for doing so, but doesn't try to force the issue.

A Maximizer is a taker – someone who thinks it is clever and shrewd to extract service from another without paying for it, leaves small tips, takes an unfair share of free samples, and always wants the most for the least.

An Optimizer is a giver – someone who understands you must give to get, is generous in rewarding people and organizations which have added value, and considers "cost" in the proper context of value received.

We've had multitudes of people come to our educational events, mentoring clubs and strategy consultations. We continually preach the importance of building good will, how real estate investing is a team sport, and that success will be based largely on the number of people who know you, like you, trust and respect you, and know you are in the business. In spite of our exhortations, people continually do stupid things that diminish, if not completely obliterate, their chances for success. Profiting with real estate is very much dependent on having good relationships with people who have access to the knowledge, products and services, and opportunities you need. When you do things which agitate, infuriate, or otherwise irritate your partners, service providers, tenants, employees, and advisors, you lessen their desire to help you – and if you are really a jerk, they may consciously or unconsciously seek to undermine you. Who needs that?

We've worked hard to create a network of service providers who are committed to upholding a set of values in doing business with members of our clubs. We despise hidden agendas, so we are open with our club members about our business motives. They know exactly how we make our money, so they can put our advice and comments in proper context. At the beginning of the relationship, we place our value proposition on the table and ask people to accept it or reject it. It is no secret we cannot and will not spend our time or the time of our associates helping people who are not willing to pay for the services they are requesting or refuse to accept responsibility for their own successes and failures.

Unfortunately, we have a small percentage of people who will attend several educational events, come in for a free consultation, and tell us they are committed to supporting our network of companies. They get all their questions answered, and then go off and take their business to other companies because they can save a few dollars on a transaction – or worse, they attempt to secretly capitalize on our business relationships in an attempt to "save" money or gain an advantage over other investors in our program. Of course, this behavior is their prerogative. No one is obligated to do business with our companies just because they come to our educational events, read our books, or join our clubs.

What amazes us is how shocked these "takers" are when no one will take their calls, answer their questions, or feed them inside deals and information. What did they expect? Just as it is their prerogative to look for freebies or exploit our program, so it is our prerogative, and that of our alliance of providers, to avoid being taken advantage of. Please understand this isn't retaliatory; it's just business. How long would you go to work if your employer didn't pay you? How long should a business provide services to "customers" who aren't willing to pay? How long would you work for a boss who mistreated you? The funny thing is that "takers" literally do not understand this because they only look out for themselves.

We certainly agree you should always be mindful of your bottom line, but we believe it is best to always look out not only for your own interests, but also for the interests of others. Optimize your relationships and you will optimize your success.

Pay Full Price

Consumer-minded people place a high priority on saving money. A big part of this mentality is an emphasis on reducing expenses. We argue that making a profit should be your *first* priority. When it comes to real estate, simply stated, you won't make a profit on property you *don't* own. This sounds like common sense, but we see person after person attempt to save money by offering less, only to walk away empty-handed. They fail to realize that the amount of money "saved" pales compared to the amount of profit available. Don't major in the minors!

Making a return on your investment pre-supposes that you actually make the investment in the first place! Part of investing is becoming "ready, willing and able". Beyond this, you must make offers, and more importantly, get your offers accepted. It shouldn't surprise you to know that there are other people out there who have discovered the wealth-building potential of real estate, and they want some, too. In other words, you have competitors for the best properties!

At one of our *Real Estate Investor Development Program*™ orientations, a woman asked about our offer strategy. "You all seem to be active investors," she said. "So I want to know – do you offer 10% below market value or is it more like 20%?"

We smiled. Obviously, she'd sent away for one of those late-night TV real estate programs. It sure *sounds* easy to go around making low-ball offers hoping to find some ignorant or desperate seller who might be willing to sell you his property for 20% less than it's worth. Because it sounds easy, people who buy these programs figure they can make low-ball offers and have success. While low-balling might work occasionally, it will be very difficult to build a good reputation, much less a sizable portfolio, when most of the offers you make are being rejected by insulted sellers represented by frustrated real estate agents. No one likes to feel like the prey of an unskilled opportunist.

When we compete in a hot marketplace, our offer may represent one of a dozen or more offers. While we don't get every property we offer on, we win more often than not. Do you imagine that we get our offers accepted because we offer 10-20% below the asking price? The truth is, many times we offer *above* the asking price just to have a chance of getting the property. The way we look at it, if we don't get the property, how much will we gain from it? While we don't want to pay more than necessary, we do want to win the contest for the property. Additionally, we believe it is important to invest in developing a solid reputation in the real estate community.

Before meeting Robert, Russ bought a property that was about to be foreclosed on. It was a 5-bedroom, 3-bath, two-story home on a cul-de-sac with a view of the foothills. He paid $224,000 for it. Ten years later it was worth nearly $600,000, even though he only invested $60,000 in rehabbing it. Some people thought Russ put too much into the rehab. How significant is the $60,000 put into the property in comparison to the $350,000 in new equity ten years later?

About a year after he bought this property, a similar property in similarly poor condition came on the market for $215,000. Russ decided he was only willing to pay $180,000. Then some "idiot" bid $220,000 and Russ didn't get the property. Ten years later, that "idiot" who "overpaid" owns a $700,000 property. So who's the idiot? Is it the guy who "overpaid" and received $480,000 in appreciation in ten years or the "shrewd" consumer who was "smart" enough not to overpay for the property and consequently has nothing? Russ still suffers from non-buyer's remorse on that one!

In 2002, Sacramento California had the highest appreciation of any city in the United States. In 2001, Robert led many investors into properties in Sacramento. A year later, virtually all of those investors had at least 20% additional equity, some as high as 40%. In almost all cases, our investors paid at or above the asking price. But they got the properties – and the equity growth that came with them! Do you think there were other competing offers submitted below the asking price? Of course there were! Did those low-bidding "investors" get any of the properties they offered on? Very few. If your offer is not accepted, how much profit do you stand to make? Remember, you cannot make money on a property you don't own (have we said this already?)!

Some people argue you shouldn't count on future appreciation for the majority of your profit in a real estate investment. We agree that if you don't believe real estate values will increase over time, then you shouldn't use a lot of leverage (high loan-to-value loans) on properties you pay full price for. However, as we approach the end of this book, we want to remind you of the alternative.

If you don't buy properties with an expectation of long-term appreciation (remember, with time and leverage, it doesn't have to be unusually high appreciation, just 5% to 8% a year can make you wealthy), then you must focus on "finding" equity by paying less than fair market price, charging more than fair market rents, cutting back on maintenance and upgrades, and squeezing all your service providers to cut their fees, all in order to make the property profitable for you.

When you look to increase your profit by squeezing others, you create several unproductive outcomes:

1. You make the seller your adversary because you are trying to pay less than fair market price.

2. You make the real estate agent, the loan broker, the property manager and every other service provider your adversary because you are trying to pay them less than the going rate for their services.

3. You make the tenants your adversaries because you are trying to charge them more than fair market rent for the use of a property, which you are maintaining at the lowest possible level.

4. You make the community your adversary because your property and tenants are not improving the area, but are actually degrading the area. If it goes on too long, the government will get involved – either directly through police action or indirectly through political action.

5. You are working harder because fewer people are on your side. Most of the people involved with you resent you and want to see you fail.

6. You are depending upon your ability to find rare circumstances in order to "find" equity vis-à-vis an ignorant or distressed seller who will sign over his equity to you.

We believe true success in real estate investment is the result of structuring win-win transactions, not by taking undue advantage of other people.

So again, following some arbitrary formula for writing hundreds of low-ball offers is not the key to success in real estate investment. A successful offer takes into consideration how well the property is priced to begin with, what the trends are in the marketplace, and what the seller's true motivation is. To be successful in negotiating a good purchase, you must carefully analyze all the factors involved and take the advice of the people who know the area and the market best. If you are paying them a fair rate for their services, they will be happy to help you. And if they help you succeed, you should be happy to pay them!

This may sound like common sense (because it is), yet there are still people who write 50 or more low-ball offers every month at 20% (or more) below asking price in the hope some fool will be stupid enough to sell his property far below what it's worth.

Do you like wasting time and money? Of course not! Then why waste your time and the time of the various professionals involved by writing offers that go nowhere? Sure, you may occasionally get one, but it probably won't turn out to be the super deal you imagine. Very seldom will a prize property land in the hands of a well-known low-baller because a) you are known as this type of "investor," and b) most professionals will not only refuse to help you, but will advise others to stay away from you. No one in the industry wants to encourage this type of time-wasting behavior. Granted, you will always be able to find some rookie real estate agent who doesn't have anything better to do and will chase around for you, but only for a little while. It won't take long for the agent to figure out he is wasting time and worse, ruining his own reputation by being associated with you.

Can you tell we have a strong opinion on this? This is VERY IMPORTANT.

Do yourself a big favor. If you're serious about acquiring wealth with real estate, learn what it takes to structure successful win-win transactions. Some great resources are the classic books *How to Win Friends and Influence People* by Dale Carnegie and *The Seven Habits of Highly Effective People* by Stephen Covey.

If you plan to be in this business for the long run, be mindful of your reputation in the marketplace. Build it carefully and protect it jealously. If you develop a reputation for fair dealing and negotiating win-win deals, then investors and service providers will line up to do business with you. If you have the reputation of scraping every last dime off the table and screwing people over every time you're given a chance, you'll have a long, hard road ahead of you. As always, the choice is yours.

One caveat: Abraham Lincoln said, "You can't please all the people all the time." He's right. In spite of your best efforts, there are people out there who will blame you for their problems. Listen to what they say, then look in the mirror and ask yourself if there is any truth in it. If so, make the necessary apologies and adjustments. If not, then forget about it, and them, quickly.

Pay for Service

You may be familiar with the saying, "You get what you pay for!" In the world of real estate, you can often get more than you pay for. For example, what does it cost to retain the services of the very best real estate agent in any area? It's about the same as it is to hire the worst agent. A great real estate agent can easily make you far more than what they charge, whereas an average agent can actually cost you more money! The same is true for your mortgage broker. Don't just shop the interest rate – shop for service, expertise, reputation and commitment. It takes about as long to shop rates and reduced commissions as it takes to find the right service provider, but only one activity is truly a good investment of your time and effort.

We once read a survey from one of the state associations of Realtors® and it said that approximately 95% of real estate agents will never sell more than one multi-unit property in their entire career. Most real estate agents in America sell houses to people who live in them. Please understand, there's nothing wrong with this. We salute these hard-working agents who are the purveyors of the American dream to homeowners. When you need to buy or sell a home, you should *always* engage the services of a professional real estate agent.

However, when it comes to *investment* property, your local residential agent may not be your best choice. Brokering investment property requires specialized knowledge and experience, so make sure you find an agent who is familiar with the types of properties and markets you want to invest in. Your best choice will generally come from those agents who personally invest in real estate for themselves. The first question you should ask a potential agent (or any service provider who will be an integral part of your advisory team) is, "Do you own any investment property?" A great follow-up question is, "What percentage of your practice is devoted to investment property?" Beyond this, you'll want to know how well connected the agent is to sources of investment property, especially out of the area. Unfortunately for the average real estate investor, the real estate profession is practiced on a highly regionalized basis. Therefore, if you are interested in out-of-area investing, it will be important to work with an agent who is part of a larger network. Either that or you will need to build a network for yourself.

Some may argue it will be hard to get a great deal from an agent who is an active investor in their own account – especially if the agent also has many other investor clients. This is loser talk and comes from scarcity mentality. The fact is, just the opposite is true.

First of all, there is plenty of real estate in the world, especially since most people don't want to be bothered with investing. Second, most people who are still actively running a brokerage business don't have the wherewithal to buy *every* good deal which comes across their desk. Eventually, they run out of money and will either have to pass the deals on to you (their motivation to do so is to earn a commission – and a generous one at that, if you are wise and want to be first in line) or they might want an equity partner. Either way, you'll probably get a call if you are on excellent terms with your agent(s). Third, and most importantly, an active investment agent will be well connected. He will be able to bring you more and better deals than a novice who is simply dealing in public inventory that is readily available to everyone through the Multiple Listing Service or other "open to the public" databases. Agents who are active investors will know other investors, property managers, and other investment property agents who will have *non-public* information about investment opportunities. Even in a tight market, properties are changing hands as people rearrange their portfolios. You want to make sure you know when properties are available. You do this by being connected to, and well thought of by, the people who have access to the deals. Never forget the important role relationships play in successful real estate investing!

The case is much the same when deciding whom to work with to arrange your investment property financing. Remember, most loan arrangers for residential real estate, whether a broker, banker or retail loan officer, tend to focus their attention on owner-occupants. The ads you see on billboards, receive in your mailbox and hear on the radio are aimed primarily at the single-family homebuyer. Again, there's nothing wrong with this, but if you intend to be an active investor, you will find it much less aggravating when you are working with someone who understands the investor mindset and is well-versed in loan programs designed especially for investment properties.

Look for a loan arranger who understands and practices sound investment financing strategy, and is experienced in the types of properties you want to purchase. Most loan arrangers are expert tacticians when it comes to filling out applications, building a credit file, dealing with loan underwriters, and otherwise moving your loan request towards funding. These are all very important services, but you will find it invaluable to have someone who also thinks strategically, understands and can explain financing strategies from a wealth-building optimization perspective, and knows how different loan programs can fit into your personal investment strategy.

Will the most competent professionals charge more for their services? Yes. Should they? Yes. Should you HAPPILY pay? YES! Who wants the discount brain surgeon? After all, how important is your financial future?

Remember, real estate investing is a TEAM sport. You need to have a team that is competent and loyal. You'll find these through referrals. Then, interview them and establish the terms of the relationship. What do they want and what do you want? Seek a win-win relationship (do you detect a theme?). You can't expect someone to be loyal to you, if you aren't loyal in return. You can't expect someone to help you profit if you are unwilling to help him make money also. When you find people who are capable of helping you, you must make sure they *want* to. The best way to do this is for you to help them advance *their* business agenda at the same time as they are helping you to advance yours. In most cases, this means paying full price – and sometimes a little bit more.

Before you chafe against the idea of not beating up your service providers for every penny of profit for yourself, consider carefully how much potential these people have to enrich you. It isn't about what you pay your players, but rather what you get from their efforts. There's a reason championship sports teams often have the largest payrolls.

Let's take real estate commissions for an example. How much should you pay a broker to represent you? The answer, of course, is "It depends!" But what does it depend on?

By law, real estate commissions are negotiable. This doesn't mean it is in your best interest to pay as little as possible. In fact, just the opposite might be true. While you should always seek to minimize your expenses, you can't lose sight of what you came for. You make your money on *owning* the property. Remember, *not* getting the property can also be expensive.

In most marketplaces, real estate commissions are paid by the seller. Brokers may charge the seller a flat-rate commission, or, more commonly, a percentage of the sales price. The commission percentage depends on the type of property, how much work you are relying on the broker to do, and what the local customs are. The commission the seller agrees to pay is typically allocated to remunerate both the agent who represents the seller's interest (the listing agent) and the agent who represents the buyer (the buyer's agent). While it may be possible for a buyer to pay their agent directly, most often the buyer's agents are compensated by a cooperative arrangement with the seller's agent. Keep in mind that agency laws differ from state to state, so you need to make sure you know the local customs.

We had the opportunity to work closely with a real estate developer on the launch of a large luxury condominium project. The developer decided to publicly launch this project in five different cities concurrently. In the process of approaching the real estate brokerage communities in each of the five cities, the developer discovered that one market's customs were considerably different than the other four. While agents in the other four cities were happy to market the property for a 3% commission, the agents in the fifth city were accustomed to much more. The developer couldn't get that city's brokers to even consider marketing the property until he modified the commission structure to be more competitive based on the local customs.

The fundamental question is: how hard do you want your agent to work for you? When you negotiate a low commission, you often negotiate yourself out of favor with the agent. Personally, we want the agents and brokers we work with to feel great about working with us! We want to be their *favorite* client. If an agent knows he will be well compensated, then he will be much more eager to search out good properties and bring them to your attention – and not someone else's. If the agent knows you intend to nickel and dime them every chance you get, or that you might take the transaction to another agent thereby cutting them out completely, they may decide to take the best deals elsewhere – to clients like us, who appreciate them more and compensate them better. Wouldn't you? Do you want first choice at the property or do you want to settle for leftovers after the preferred investors have picked over the deals? Remember, your profit comes from the *property*, not from the real estate agent's and loan broker's commissions. If you need their commissions to make the deal profitable, it probably isn't a deal.

Is it necessary to have an agent represent you in every transaction? Perhaps not, but it will depend on your level of comfort, experience and knowledge. If in doubt, hire a professional. The advantages far outweigh the expense. A professional will bring relationships, technical knowledge, and a more experienced perspective. Also, having a third party through whom to negotiate can be very advantageous. And of course, it is always safer to be represented by a professional who is covered by "errors and omissions" (E & O) insurance. Any one of these by itself is probably worth it, but all of them together make working with a professional a very compelling value proposition.

A Fool for a Client
While we are on the subject of agents, let's talk about one more thing. We are often asked if it makes sense for investors to get a real estate license. Can you guess what our answer is? That's right! It depends.

If you want to earn sales commissions by representing *other* people in the sale and purchase of real property, then in most jurisdictions, you will need to get a license. Servicing other people to help them acquire property is a great way to earn an income while developing knowledge and relationships that will help you in your own personal investing. If you elect to pursue entering the profession, please invest heavily of your time and money in professional education. Even more important, be sure to align yourself with a company that provides extensive training and mentorship. Don't join some rinky-dink outfit because you can get 100% split on the commission.[50] If you

---

[50] In most jurisdictions, real estate commissions may only be legally paid to licensed brokers. A real estate salesperson who does not hold a broker's license must work for a licensed broker and all commissions are paid to the broker who then splits the commission with the salesperson. The percentage of the commission the salesperson receives is referred to as their "split". Some brokers offer higher splits than others, but obviously the less commission the broker retains, the less support he is able to afford to provide the salesperson. When a salesperson receives 100% commission, the broker usually will require a fixed monthly or transactional fee for processing the business.

don't know what you are doing and therefore don't close any transactions, then 100% of nothing is still nothing. Worse, you'll be experimenting on people (probably your friends and family) who trust you, while your inexperience is actually a threat to their financial well-being. Don't be selfish! If you plan to be a real estate agent or loan broker, take a lesser commission split and allow an experienced mentor to earn an override commission on your business. Give the mentor incentives to help you and your clients.

However, if your only motivation for getting your license is to "save the commission" and "find the best deals," then you might want to reconsider. Having a real estate license will hold you to a higher level of responsibility and disclosure in any transactions you are involved in, including your personal ones. In many states, you will be required to disclose to all parties that you are a professional, so they can be "on guard". Any transactions you handle for your own account may be open to greater scrutiny. Certainly, if you get involved in a lawsuit, the benefit of the doubt will typically accrue to the unlicensed person. In a dispute, the licensed person is often deemed to have a professional advantage over an unlicensed person. This is true whether or not the licensee is actually knowledgeable, experienced and competent.

If you want quality professional transactions, then either become a true professional by investing time and money in education and mentoring, or hire a professional and let them make their money. You're going to pay either way, and either one is fine, but there's nothing more irritating to the real estate community than a licensed amateur whose only reason for holding a license is to avoid paying for services they still want or need.

Even though Robert is a licensed real estate agent, he utilizes and pays for licensed agents familiar with the particular property types and markets he is interested in. Why? First, because real estate market knowledge is not neatly packaged up in some analyst's report available online. The way you learn about a market is by living and working in it, talking to the local people, watching what's going on, and staying in close contact with others who are active in that particular market. When you are investing in multiple marketplaces, it is impossible to keep up with each market on your own. Your agents become your eyes and ears on the street. The smart thing to do is work with local professionals who are active in the areas and types of properties you are interested in.

Another great reason to involve professionals is objectivity. Yes, we realize most professionals are commission paid, so their advice has a potential agenda, but when you are aware of the agenda, it is less of a concern. The fact that the advisor gets paid when a transaction consummates simply means that he will have a propensity for action and a commitment to completion, which we think is a good thing. More people end up regretting *not* buying far more often than they regret buying. Real estate is very forgiving over time. Even a bad buy looks pretty good after ten years of appreciation. Besides, if you have built a strong personal relationship with your agents, they care about you as a person. And when you are generously rewarding them with commissions and referrals, then it is in their own best interest to see you be successful in the long-term, even if it means they encourage you to pass on a bad deal and they don't get paid until the right deal comes along.

The "objectivity" we are seeking from our agents is the ability to look at a challenge or an opportunity from a perspective that only comes when it is not your own money at risk. This is why hospitals do not allow surgeons to operate on their own loved ones. Sometimes you can care too much and it compromises your judgment.

Don't be afraid of other people's perspectives, even if they may have an agenda. As long as you are aware of the agenda (you should always know how your service providers are getting paid), you can put any advice they give you in context. Ultimately, every investing decision is yours and you should never do anything you don't understand and agree with. Other people's ideas aren't a threat, but rather a tremendous asset which can help you better understand your options, see a bigger picture, and make wiser investment decisions.

In regard to getting licensed as a way to find the best deals, we think empowering a seasoned agent to find deals on your behalf is generally much more efficient than spending your time scouring the Multiple Listing Service or internet for hot properties. This isn't to say you can't find a deal there, but as you might imagine it is the place most people go to look, so there is more competition. Furthermore, while we think the MLS is one of the best marketing tools ever created, many of the best investment properties never make it onto the MLS.

Consider the do-it-yourself investors who limit the properties they consider to only those they find in the newspaper. Which properties do you think local agents advertise in the paper – the hottest deals or the properties that aren't selling any other way? By the time an investment property makes it to the classifieds, most of the serious investors have already passed on it.

"But," you say, "I've seen really good deals in the paper!" Of course you have. Good deals, just like low mortgage rates, and "crazy" low prices on the hottest new car ("only one at this price"), are often not really for sale. They just make the phone ring. Think about it for a minute. If you are an active real estate agent, you have a big database of clients. Some of your clients have the potential to do lots of future business and/or refer lots of new clients. This is especially true with your investor clients because they do many more transactions than a typical homeowner. When a hot deal comes along, do you advertise it in the paper so some stranger can buy it? No! You give the hot deal to your best client, and then run the ad to make the phone ring so you can meet new people.

● ● ●

Nat and three partners put together a group to invest in real estate. They learned a technique whereby they sent letters directly to homeowners looking for someone who would sell them a property directly, without the cost of a real estate agent. By the time Nat joined our mentoring club, he and his partners had already acquired their first property from a response they got to their letter campaign.

The partners spent the next few months fixing up the property. They were open enough to share their project with the mentoring club. They brought in "before" and "after" pictures, along with a list of what they had invested in the rehab. Since Nat's partners all had full-time jobs and Nat did not, he was the one who ended up doing most of the hands-on work. In fact, he lived in the house (actually, its garage) for more than six weeks while conducting the renovation.

When we looked over Nat's projections, just before he was ready to market the rehabbed property, we noticed he had only budgeted 2% for sales expense. However, the property was in a market where the traditional sales commission rate was closer to 6%. When questioned about the thinking behind this tactic, Nat explained that because they bought the property without an agent, they were going to try to sell it without an agent and therefore "save" the commission.

Week after week of open houses went by without a sale. Finally, they asked us for a referral to a local agent who could help them sell the house. Ten days later the house was sold! So, why didn't Nat sell the house on his own?

In this case, Nat had two things working against him. First, because he did not list the property with a real estate agent, he did not have the benefit of exposing the property to the largest amount of available buyers through the Multiple Listing Service. He did not have a real estate agent actively promoting the property at any of the many networking meetings real estate professionals regularly attend. There were no real estate agents touring the property to become familiar with it so they could better identify a suitable buyer.

Beyond the problem of less exposure through the real estate agent network and the MLS, Nat also handicapped himself by diminishing the financial incentive for the local real estate professionals to put much priority on selling his property. By offering to pay only 2% to any real estate agent who brought in a buyer, Nat was offering 33% less pay compared to the customary 3% (the half of the area's customary 6% listing agent's commission) that competing sellers were offering. Nat had essentially alienated the entire local professional real estate community from marketing his property.

If you happen to have a property so unique and in demand that there are no competing properties, then agents might be willing to sell your property for 33% less pay. In Nat's case, it was a relatively ordinary property, so there were a fair amount of competing properties available on the market. If you were a real estate agent with a ready, willing and able buyer, and you managed to stumble over an unrepresented amateur seller who was offering 33% less pay, would you show your prospective buyers this property first or last? Or perhaps not at all?

You see, the real estate community could see this transaction was going to require *more* work for 33% less pay. With no listing agent, the buyer's agent would end up doing the work of *both* agents. Understandably, no local agents promoted the property and it sat unsold. Nat had been penny wise, but pound foolish. Meanwhile, carrying expenses continued on the property and Nat's working capital sat idle, thereby significantly eroding his already thin profit margin.

After the property finally sold, Nat shared the results and lessons of the project with the mentoring club. While Nat and his partners did end up making a very slight profit, the rate of return was diluted by the fact the house took so long to sell. If they had only marketed it with a professional earlier, the annualized return on investment would have been much better.

Did the experience sour them on doing fixers? Not at all! Nat believed going through the entire process was one of the best educational experiences he ever had. Fortunately, because he was willing to share the lesson, we were all able to learn from it without having to pay the price Nat did.

• • •

Selling a property is hard enough for someone who does it for a living. Attempting to sell a property *without* the help of a professional can be a daunting undertaking. Robert's father Bob always tells people who want to sell their own properties, "If you can really do my job, then you deserve my commission." Of course, most people are not trained or experienced in what it takes to successfully sell a property for the optimal price. We've heard that over 70% of real estate disclosure lawsuits involve transactions where one or more of the principals were *not* represented by an agent. After seventeen years of practice, Robert can see why. There are a significant amount of forms, protocols, and laws which need to be carefully observed in order to complete a successful transaction. It is naïve to think an amateur with next-to-no experience is going to do a competent job.

During an interview on the radio show, best-selling author, businessman and investor, Robert Kiyosaki made a great point, "Why is it that some people routinely pay 15-20% gratuity for average service at a restaurant, but complain about paying 6-7% to real estate professionals who can actually help with a transaction which can earn tens of thousands of dollars?" This is something that baffles us also.

There have been many studies conducted regarding the value of hiring a real estate agent and paying a commission. Some time ago, Robert came across a study by a state department of real estate. The survey found that sellers represented by an agent received nearly 9% more for their properties on average than those sellers who represented themselves. If the average commission is only 6%, but by paying it you receive a 9% higher price, then do you really save money when you don't pay commission? Do the math, but focus on what you get, not what you pay. Is it so bad that a service provider makes money if they are helping you make money? We don't think so.

If you have always been a consumer and an employee, one of the very first things to do is get crystal clarity on the important differences between "spending" and "investing". "Spending" is when money goes out and there is no expectation, hope or plan for it ever to return, much less with profit. Spent money is gone forever. However, investing is completely different. Money that is invested goes out with the expectation, or better, the demand, that it will return with an increase or benefit. Investing is *not* spending.

If one of the most valuable assets of a business is good will, then money spent on developing good will should be considered a wise investment. When you pay a top professional generously for providing products, services, advice or influence that has the potential to earn you a sizable profit, our advice to you is to pay early, often and gladly. Take care of the people you want to take care of you!

The moral of the story is this: don't major in the minors and step over dollars to save pennies. More often than not, the old adages are true. You get what you pay for and you reap what you sow. If you sow bad will, you will reap bad will. If you sow good will, you will reap good will. In a business like real estate investing, where personal relationships, trust, reputation and inside knowledge are all major components of success, can you really afford to be a miser?

Pass It Forward

One of the greatest ways to build good will and a positive self-image is to share. As you acquire knowledge, build relationships, have financial success and gain experience, make it your habit to share your joy, optimism and success with others. Every time you "pass it forward" you add something positive to the world. It may sound like metaphysical hogwash to engineers and atheists, but all we know is that it works.

Here are some practical ideas for "Passing It Forward:"

- **Volunteer** – especially with children. For several years, Russ volunteered as a speaker in high schools, church youth groups, and junior high schools. He spoke to young people about healthy lifestyle choices and decision-making skills. Each year, we do a free seminar called *Real Estate FUNdamentals for Young People* for junior high through college age students. You'll be amazed at the great things that will come your way when you give back.

- **Teach** – Share the things you are learning with your family, friends and co-workers. Don't worry if not everyone understands or even wants the information. Some people will be suspicious of your motives. Cynicism isn't a reflection of you; it's simply the other person expressing their fear. Just share. If people express an interest, then teach. You'll actually be surprised how much you know! You'll be even more surprised at how, when you teach, you will reinforce what you know and develop many original thoughts. Teaching will make you a better investor.

- **Refer** – When you find a great seminar, workshop, book or service provider, be sure to tell other people about it. It will start conversations, build goodwill, and get you into relationships with people who are like-minded. Remember, you are just one relationship away from an explosion in your business.

- **Give** – There are so many worthwhile organizations out there which are struggling to do noble work with far too few resources. Robert lost his mother to breast cancer and now supports the fight to find a cure. Find a group or cause you support and make generous donations of your time, expertise and money.

- **Smile!** It sounds simple, right? If you are joyfully pursuing your goals, are hopeful and optimistic, then share your joy with others! Too many people are living discouraged, defeated lives. Add value to the world simply by being happy and showing it! Enthusiasm is contagious. It doesn't cost you anything and it can make a big difference in someone's day.

When you do these types of things, you feel better about *you*. Serving others helps you feel more deserving of the success you are working towards. A big part of your success will be managing your personal development in all areas of your life. There is no value in building a multi-million dollar portfolio only to lose it all because others areas of your life are in disarray. You don't want to end up engaging in self-destructive behavior because you don't feel worthy of your financial success. We're not psychologists, but we see it happen all the time in business, athletics, and entertainment. People work hard and start having some success, then they do something shockingly stupid and destroy it all. The purpose of this book is to share with you what we think it takes to be successful in real estate. Managing your self-image is a very important part of successful real estate investing.

CHAPTER 13
May There Never Be One!

This book has no Chapter 13 for two reasons:

1. We hope there will be no Chapter 13 (bankruptcy) in your real estate investment future. Far be it from us to create one for you!

2. Many of the taller buildings we look at throughout the country do not have a 13th floor. Out of respect for this superstitious behavior, we have no 13th chapter.

CHAPTER 14
Twenty Years from Now

The Main Thing is to Keep the Main Thing the Main Thing
Many of the people who come to our *Equity Happens Real Estate Investing Seminar* are just beginning the process of looking into real estate as an investment vehicle. They may have seen, or even purchased, one or more of the real estate programs they've seen on late-night television. Some are taking classes at the local community college. Several have begun or completed the process of getting their state real estate license. The common denominator with almost every person in the audience is that they came to make changes in the direction of their lives. They are looking for more information to help them do this.

At the beginning of the event, Robert will ask everyone, "How many of you came here today to learn more about real estate?" Invariably, nearly every hand goes up. Then Robert asks a follow-up question, "How many of you are here because you want to *own* more real estate?" Once again, virtually all hands go up.

Then Robert proceeds to explain the profound difference between simply learning and actually doing. As we have throughout this book, Robert then challenges the audience, as we have challenged you throughout the book, with, "How much money can you make on real estate you *don't* own?" You may not need to own real estate for very long to make a profit. In fact, you may never need to actually take title to a property to make money. But you absolutely need to gain control of it. The only way you gain control of property is to take action. You have to get up out of your chair, get out of the house, and go out into the real world, because that's where the action is.

We formed, and continue to expand, Advisor Financial Alliance (AFA) for the purpose of bringing together experienced professionals from the financial services and real estate businesses. Members and affiliates of AFA must be willing to lead with education. We believe ignorance is expensive, but information is powerful. However, we are keenly aware that information is only powerful when acted upon. So we developed a slogan for AFA, *Education for Effective Action*™.

When we created our educational events, and as we contemplated writing this book, we didn't just want to be another voice in an already crowded field. We wanted to bring something unique and needed.

In our experience, the missing component, the one thing that causes most people to miss out on the opportunities all around them, is focus. So many people just can't seem to stay focused for extended periods of time.

When people enter our *Real Estate Investor Development Program*™ and we visit with them during their strategy consultation, we always invest time talking to them about their focus. Investors come to us for technical training, but they become attached to us because we help them get and stay focused. It's like *Weight Watchers* (or so we've heard!). Most people already know how to lose weight, they just need some accountability and encouragement to help them stay focused.

We provide the monthly mentoring clubs, weekly radio show, a growing collection of audio and video programs, and a continuous menu of affordable seminars taught by us or our authorized teachers, to help investors stay focused and deal with the real issues holding them back from taking effective action towards building the life and lifestyle they desire.

Robert tells stories from his vast reservoir of experiences. His entertaining style captivates the audience, but all the while he is pushing great information and attitudes into their minds. Russ puts numbers and logic to the concepts to help people see the reality of the returns that are possible if they are willing to step out and take the risk. He gives them a rational reason to believe.

So why don't more people invest in real estate? After all, it's easy to do! Jim Rohn says the reason people fail to achieve their fullest potential is quite simple, "While doing the things that are essential to success are easy to do, they are also easy *not* to do." How true! In fact, many times it's easier not to do the important things. Too many people gravitate toward only doing the easiest thing.

Are you capable of reading some books on real estate, attending some classes, brainstorming with other investors, and talking to professionals in the field? Of course you are! Unless you live in some tyrannical or oppressed country, you have the freedom to do all these things. But the same freedom which allows you to do these things, also allows you to choose freely not to do them. You can stay home and watch television. You can spend every weekend asleep in the hammock or out at the movies. Remember: where you are right now is the result of the decisions you've made up until now. Where you end up twenty years from now will be the result of the decisions you make from now until then.

Here's some sobering news for you: twenty years from now it will be twenty years from now — whether you grow personally and financially or not. You are now equipped with some new ideas, some fresh perspectives, and, we hope, a renewed sense of what is possible for you. Three words forever changed the way Russ looks at life: "Why not me?"

Parents and teachers mean well. In an effort to protect children from risk, pain and disappointment, well-meaning parents warn children, when they are young and highly impressionable, that there are people smarter, better, more experienced, and more capable. Someone else is always #1 in whatever the child is dreaming about doing or achieving.

This paradigm isn't *intended* to limit the young person's belief in his potential. In fact, parents can be very encouraging when telling the child he can be anything he wants to, but when it comes time to go for it, deep down inside, the child still believes there is always someone else who is the best, who probably already thought of it, who is better positioned or equipped to do it bigger and better. In other words, the obstacles are larger than the opportunities. This is a very subtle, but powerfully limiting mindset. It is so easy for loving, well-meaning parents, teachers and coaches to burden a child with limiting beliefs in a misguided effort to protect the child (and perhaps the adults) from the disappointment of failure.

The truth is that obstacles cannot be avoided. They are the part of a venture that makes success possible. Without an opponent to overcome, there can be no victory. When you begin to change your thinking and say, "Why not *me*? Why can't I start a business? Why can't I be a millionaire? Why can't I be the best there is at something? Someone out there is going to do it. Why not me?" Those three words and the attitude behind them can free you to go for it! The perception of your opportunities must become more powerful than the fear of the obstacles on the road to success.

Today, we operate from both the belief and the expectation we can be the best – as individuals and as an organization. We have big dreams and have been amazed at the results we've experienced in just a short period of time. Best of all, we feel like we haven't even gotten started. The best is yet to come! Until you are experiencing this wonderful feeling on a regular basis, we contend that you aren't fully living! We know we weren't.

The roots of greatness lie in making a decision. That's really the hardest part. Making a decision to be successful is something most people never do. Beyond decision, you must commit. Commitment isn't hoping. It isn't wishing. It isn't dreaming. Commitment isn't sticking your toe in the water. Commitment isn't trying. As Jedi Master Yoda counseled young Luke Skywalker in the *The Empire Strikes Back*, "Do! Or do not. There is no try." One of Russ's heroes in business, Art Williams, used to say, "The first step to greatness begins with TOTAL commitment!" It's true! We don't want to belabor this point, but it is the single most important "secret" to success we can share with you. You must commit to win.

What about you? Are you willing to commit to create wealth with real estate, and then stand by that decision? Rest assured, you won't be alone – not often and not for long. As soon as you make the decision, people and resources will open up for you in ways you haven't even imagined. In the next twenty years many people will make a fortune by investing in real estate – this much is certain. The only question you need to ask yourself is: "Why not me?"

Robert always says, "Remember to live this life as though it were your last!" Great advice.

We wish you tremendous personal growth and financial success. May you achieve your fullest potential and be a blessing to all whose lives you touch. We hope to see you along the way!

The Guys' Reading List

Filling your mind with great ideas is one of the most important disciplines you can and should develop. If we lived a thousand lifetimes, we couldn't read all the books we would like to. In fact, with all the great books out there, we are honored you would take the time to read ours. There have certainly been many great thinkers who have taken the time to put their deepest thoughts into writing to share with others. For that, we are eternally thankful. Here is a list of just some of our very favorites which are related to the subject of developing yourself as a real estate investor. Keep in mind that we don't necessarily agree unequivocally with everything each author has to say, but their work has stimulated our thinking and played an important role in our personal development.

We hope you take the time to read some or all of these, and that you enjoy them as much as we have! Please visit www.equityhappens.com from time to time. We will be regularly updating our recommended reading list – and we'd love to get your feedback on *Equity Happens*.

All You Can Do is All You Can Do by Art Williams

Before You Quit Your Job by Robert T. Kiyosaki and Sharon Lechter

How to Master the Art of Selling by Tom Hopkins

The Five Rituals of Wealth by Tod Barnhart

How to Win Friends and Influence People by Dale Carnegie

IRA Wealth by Patrick Rice

Proverbs – The Bible

Rich Dad, Poor Dad by Robert T. Kiyosaki and Sharon Lechter

The Richest Man in Babylon by George S. Clason

The Seven Habits of Highly Effective People by Steven R. Covey

The 106 Mortgage Secrets All Homebuyers Must Learn, But Lenders Don't Tell by Gary W. Eldred

The 106 Mistakes Home Buyers Make (and How to Avoid Them) by Gary W. Eldred

The E-Myth Revisited by Michael Gerber

The Five Major Pieces to the Life Puzzle by Jim Rohn

Think and Grow Rich by Napoleon Hill

Glossary

Far from comprehensive, this glossary defines some of the many words and phrases that make up the "lingo" of real estate investing. In some cases, they are words or phrases we have coined. In all cases, the definitions are ours and reflect the meaning of the words and phrases as we use them in our daily lives, our educational program and throughout this book. If you want the strict legal definitions, you should refer to *Black's Law Dictionary* and any generally accepted English dictionary.

1031 Tax-Deferred Exchange – A provision in the tax code which allows an investor to defer capital gains tax due upon the sale of an appreciated investment property by using the equity in the property to purchase another income property (or group of properties). There are a significant number of rules to be followed when executing a proper exchange. You should work carefully with your tax advisor and an experienced 1031 tax-deferred exchange intermediary when planning and executing a 1031 tax-deferred exchange.

Absolute Dollars – We use this term when referring to the amount of profit dollars in a transaction irrespective of rate of return.

Absolute Return – We use this term when referring to the amount of profit as a percentage of investment irrespective of rate of return. For example, $10,000 of absolute profit dollars on $100,000 investment would be an absolute return of 10%. The actual rate of return (annualized return) would depend upon how long it took to earn the profit.

Accelerated Depreciation – The tax code provides the opportunity to accelerate depreciation on certain items related to your property. For example, while a two-unit residential income property structure (the building) may be depreciated over 27.5 years, there may be personal property and other items that can be depreciated much faster – only five years in some cases. When the depreciation schedule is shorter, each year's depreciation and the resulting deduction are much larger. This will improve your cash-flow. You should review this concept with a qualified and experienced tax advisor. Accelerated depreciation can help you more comfortably handle the cash-flow on an income property in the early years of ownership, when cash-flow can be the most challenging.

Adjusted Gross Income – AGI is the amount of income you have which is taxable. It is determined by taking your gross income less all of your allowable deductions. AGI is important to real estate investors because Passive Activity Loss eligibility is based upon AGI.

After-Tax Cash-Flow (ATCF) – This is the amount of net cash-flow remaining after paying all required and currently due income taxes. Work closely with your tax advisor on this because depreciation schedules and passive activity loss rules change from time to time.

Amortization – The gradual pay down of a loan balance. Each monthly payment contains both pay down of a portion of the principal (the original borrowed amount) and interest. The portion of the payment that reduces the principal is what we call "amortized equity". Amortization is not tax-deductible.

APOD – Annual Property Operating Data. This is a detailed cash-flow analysis of an income property. It takes into account income, expenses and debt service. It is the profit and loss statement of a rental property.

Appreciation – One of our absolute favorite things! Appreciation simply means the value of the property is going up. This, of course, is something we appreciate.

Arithmephobia – An acute and paralyzing fear of arithmetic. Russ suffered from this when he was a child in school, but became cured when the accounting text books placed dollar signs in front of the numbers (yes, we made up this term).

Balance Sheet – A balance sheet is the financial statement that tells you what your net worth is. Assets (what you own) less liabilities (what you owe) equals net worth. Since one of the primary objectives of investors is to grow net worth, the balance sheet is an important tool in tracking progress.

Basic Income Formula – This is the calculation used to determine the net operating income on an income property. The formula is "gross scheduled rents" less "vacancy allowance" and less "operating expenses" equals "net operating income".

Before-Tax Cash-Flow (BTCF) – This is the amount of cash-flow an income property generates taking into account income, expenses, and debt service, but does not consider income tax.

Bond – For purposes of our discussion as real estate investors, a bond is essentially a securitized I.O.U. issued by an entity such as a corporation, municipality or government. As opposed to stock certificates, which evidence ownership in a corporation, a bond is debt owed to the bondholder by the issuing (borrowing) entity.

Capital Gain – The positive difference, or profit, between the total acquisition cost and net sales price of a property. For example, a $95,000 property with $5,000 in purchase costs would have a $100,000 total acquisition cost. If later, that property sold to $265,000 with $15,000 if sales expense, the net sales price would be $250,000, making the realized capital gain $150,000. In the real world, the cost basis would be adjusted for any subsequent capital investments (i.e., adding a new room) and depreciation. Keep good records (sometimes for decades) and work closely with your tax advisor.

Cap Rate – Short for "capitalization rate", cap rate is a percentage that shows how much net operating income a rental property produces relative to its purchase price or fair market value. It takes into account operating expenses, but not debt service. Cap rate only accounts for return from operating income and not from appreciation, depreciation or amortization.

Cash-Flow Statement – An investor's cash-flow statement is a simple, but very important tool. It shows income and expenses from all sources. If expenses exceed income, the shortfall must be met from one's balance sheet – either through liquidation of assets or increase of liabilities (debt).

Comparable Market Analysis – A CMA is an estimate of fair market value determined by comparing the subject property with other comparable properties ("comps") in the area. Unlike an appraisal, which is a more formal analysis based only on past sales, a CMA also takes into consideration current listings and pending sales. CMAs are typically generated by real estate agents as a free service to prospective clients as part of the agent's marketing program.

Critical Mass – This is a term we've heard used and have adopted to describe the amount of investable net worth necessary to generate enough income to maintain a target lifestyle. For example, if you wanted $120,000 per year income for the rest of your life and you knew you could get a 10% cash-on-cash return on your invested capital, you would need $1,200,000 of capital. Therefore, $1,200,000 would be your Critical Mass.

Debt Service – The amount of monthly payments required to pay for a loan or loans.

Debt-to-Income Ratio – This is a cash-flow analysis a lender does on a prospective borrower to determine the borrower's financial capability to service debt. For example, if a borrower has $10,000 per month in gross income and required debt payments of $4,000 per month, the borrower's debt-to-income ratio is 40% ($4,000 / $10,000 = .40 or 40%).

Deed of Trust – See *Trust Deed*

Deflation – Deflation occurs when the amount of money in circulation decreases relative to the supply of goods and services. Even when there is demand to buy things, if there is inadequate purchasing power in the economy, then prices decline. This sets off a chain reaction of losses of profits and jobs. If allowed to continue unchecked, deflation results in recession, and in severe cases, economic depression.

Depreciable Basis – This is the amount of the cost of a depreciable asset, such as a rental property, to which the depreciation schedule is applied. Your depreciable basis can be adjusted during the term of your ownership as you invest into the property. Work closely with your tax advisor and keep good records.

Depreciation – Depreciation is an accounting term and accounts for the gradual deterioration of a capital asset held for the production of income. In the case of real estate, it is the improvements (the structure) to the land which deteriorate over time. The tax code makes provision for a property owner to deduct this "loss", which does not necessarily require any actual out-of-pocket expense by the owner. Real estate investors enjoy depreciation because it provides non-cash losses, which can be deducted against real world income. As a side note, both the income and losses generated by income property are "passive". For information about depreciation and passive activity loss rules, refer to IRS publication 925, available at www.irs.gov.

Due Diligence – This is a term that describes the research a prudent investor performs when evaluating markets, properties and service providers. In terms of investment real estate, most contracts should contain a clause which permits a period of time, called "the inspection period," for this research to take place.

Earnest Money – When submitting a real estate offer, it is common practice for a potential buyer to include a check as a show of good faith to the seller.

Equity – One of our favorite words, equity is the net value of a property. It is the difference between the fair market value of a property and any debt owed against it.

Equity Growth Rate – We use this term to describe how fast new equity is being added to current equity. For example, if you own a property with $100,000 in current equity and it is appreciating (adding new equity) $50,000 per year, then your equity growth rate is 50%.

Equity Partner – A co-investor who shares the risk and reward of the ownership, as opposed to a lender, whose risk and rewards are limited. Typically an equity partner brings cash into the deal, but sometimes other contributions such as property, credit, effort, materials, etc., can be counted as purchase equity.

Flip-and-Hold – This term describes the technique of buying a property, then quickly refinancing it to get all invested capital back out, but without relinquishing the property. In other words, you flip the cash, but hold the property for long-term total return.

Forced Equity – We use this term to describe the equity an investor receives from proactively adding value to a property through new development, rehab or conversion – as opposed to simply waiting for the property to appreciate due to limited supply, increasing demand and increasing capacity-to-pay.

Found Equity – This is a term we use to describe the equity an investor immediately receives simply for buying the property, as opposed to the passive equity that occurs gradually over time, or forced equity for which the investor must proactively add value to the property itself. Not all properties have found equity, though we certainly wish they did!

Good Will – The positive feeling people in the marketplace have towards you and your business. It is the thing that gives a business value over and above the actual financial value of the business's assets.

Gross Effective Income – Gross scheduled income less an allowance for vacancy and bad debt (not consumer debt, but rather lost rents from flaky tenants).

Gross Rent Multiplier – GRM is a ratio between the gross scheduled income (GSI) and the purchase price or fair market value (FMV) of a particular income property. GRM is determined by dividing the FMV of the property by the annualized GSI.

Gross Scheduled Income – GSI is the amount of income a rental property is capable of bringing in when it is fully rented and without vacancy or delinquency. It does not take into account any expenses or debt service, but simply shows the maximum potential gross income based on current leases. See also *Pro-Forma*.

Hard Money – refers to funds obtained from private (non-institutional) lenders who specialize in making real estate backed loans. Typically the loans are expensive in terms of fees and interest rates, and are made through loan brokers who specialize in working with distressed borrowers (people who have poor credit, little income, or some other condition which makes conventional lenders refuse to lend to them). Investors like to use hard-money lenders because the lending criteria are much more liberal and loans can get funded much faster. If there is enough profit in a deal, the interest rate and fees on a hard-money loan are justifiable.

HUD – A United States government agency. HUD stands for Housing and Urban Development. HUD is a great source for real estate statistics. For more info, visit www.hud.gov.

Idle Equity – This is a term we coined to describe equity in a property that is sitting on one's balance sheet, but making very little contribution to cash-flow or equity growth. Too much idle equity is one of the biggest mistakes investors make.

Improvements Ratio – The percentage of the acquisition cost of a rental property that represents the value of the improvements. For example, if a property were purchased for $100,000, and it was determined that $80,000 of the value of the property was the building (the improvements to the land), then the improvements ratio would be 80%.

Limited Liability Company (LLC) – This is a statutory entity, like a corporation, which exists to shield the owners from the liability of the venture. Conversely, an LLC can be used to protect an asset held by the entity. Like a partnership, an LLC provides for two primary classes of shareholder (known as "members"): A *managing member* and a *limited member*, though a manager can be a non-owner. The managing member is actively engaged in the operation of the business or management of the asset. The limited member puts up only money and has no active role. In exchange for this passive role, the entity limits the potential liability of the limited member to only the loss of any money invested by the limited member.

Listing – When a seller signs a contract with a real estate broker to market the seller's property, it is known as "listing" the property. The marketing contract is called a "listing agreement" or an "exclusive right to sell agreement".

Loan-to-Value (LTV) – LTV is simply percentage of debt relative to the purchase price of a property. For example, if an investor places $10,000 cash down on a $100,000 property, he would need a loan of $90,000 to complete the acquisition. A $90,000 loan against a $100,000 value would be 90% LTV.

Mortgage – This is a two-party debt instrument secured by real property. The two parties are the borrower and the lender. In the event of a default on the loan by the borrower, the lender may foreclose through a judicial procedure. Aside from the legal technical differences, there is very little real-world difference between a mortgage and a promissory note secured by a deed of trust. In most discussions of real estate financing, the term "mortgage" is commonly used.

Multiple Listing Service – The MLS is the database of properties listed for sale by Realtors® (members of the National Association of Realtors®). It is a co-operative effort of regional agents through a local board of Realtors® to share this information so that any given property is given as much exposure to potential buyers as possible. Prior to the internet, this was a powerful and exclusive tool. Even today, properties which are listed in the MLS tend to sell faster and for more money than those properties which are not listed.

Negative Amortization – When a loan payment is insufficient to pay the entire amount of accrued interest, the unpaid interest is added to loan balance. For example, if a property had a $100,000 loan on it at 6% interest, then the annual interest expense would be $6,000 and the monthly interest expense would be $500. If the borrower only paid $300 on a particular month, then the $200 of unpaid interest for that month would be added to unpaid loan balance of $100,000 and the new outstanding loan balance would be $100,200.

Net Worth – See *Balance Sheet*

Notice of Default – In certain jurisdictions, this is a legal notice filed by the lender when a borrower has defaulted on the payment terms of their loan. It is a public notice that alerts the world that a foreclosure procedure is beginning. It also warns the owner to cure the default or face foreclosure.

Optimization – This is a term we use to describe the balancing of maximum financial result against other important considerations. For example, if an investor were to optimize his portfolio for equity growth, he would use the maximum amount of leverage possible without taking more cash-flow risk than he is willing to. Because each investor's circumstances vary, the maximum amount of leverage available to a borrower may not be what is optimal. What is optimal is very personal and will emerge as an investor develops clarity in their goals and personal investment philosophy.

Option – A contractual obligation by a seller or lender which provides the option holder the right, but not the obligation to do or receive something. For example, an interest-only payment option issued by a lender would provide the borrower the right, but not the obligation, to make a monthly payment which was only enough to over the interest, but not enough to reduce the loan balance. Likewise, a purchase option provides the option holder the right, but not the obligation, to purchase the subject property according to the terms of the purchase option contract.

Owner Carry-Back – This term describes a situation when the seller of a property accepts a promissory note secured by the subject property via mortgage or trust deed from the buyer in lieu of cash. Though sometimes difficult to find and negotiate, seller financing can be a very effective way for a buyer to preserve cash on the front end of a transaction, and for a seller to attract a buyer in a slow market. Owner/seller financing is sometimes advertised as "OWC" for "Owner Will Carry".

Passive Activity Loss – This is a tax term that describes the operating loss on a property. PAL is calculated on federal tax form 1040 Schedule E and, based on the taxpayer's eligibility, may be used to offset earned or passive income. For more information on this important topic, visit www.irs.gov and read Publication 925.

Passive Equity – This is a term we use to describe the increase in fair market value of a property held over time. It is equity for which the investor does not need to do anything other than own or control the property as it appreciates.

Phased Equity – This is a term we use to describe the passive equity which accrues to an investor in a new development project that is being released to the market in phases, and when, at each phase, the developer raises the price. When an investor buys into this type of development in the early phases, the programmed price increases of later phases actually raises the value of the investor's early phase purchase.

Points – Points are interest and commission paid at the origination of a loan. A "point" is 1% of the loan amount.

Profit and Loss Statement – A P&L is simply an accounting of income and expenses. However, depending on the method of accounting, a P&L may be different than a cash-flow statement. When expenses and income are being accrued (counted when earned or owed rather than when received or paid), a P&L might not precisely match a cash-flow statement.

Pro-Forma – This is a fancy word to describe financial projections that are based on "reasonable estimates". In the real world, "pro-forma" can sometimes be synonymous with "made up". Be careful when looking at a pro-forma. Make sure the numbers are based on something close to reality by verifying the assumptions used whenever practical.

Promissory Note – This is simply a document signed by a borrower in favor of a lender and is a contractual promise to pay back money borrowed. In real estate, a promissory note is typically secured by pledging the subject property as collateral for the loan.

Qualifying Income – The amount of income a lender will allow a borrower to use to qualify for a loan. Qualifying income is different than actual income because lenders will use discounts and averages to effectively disallow a portion of certain types of income such as rental income, commissions and bonus income.

ROI – Return On Investment. In the strictest sense, ROI is only calculated on the amount of actual cash returned on a particular investment. "Return" implies a return of cash. When cash isn't being returned, we use *equity growth rate* and *total return* to describe how fast one's wealth is growing.

Seasoned – In some cases, this simply means experience, but in all cases it refers to the passage of time. In the case of conventional real estate loans, they are considered seasoned when the loan has been in place for six months to one year, depending upon the new lender's guidelines.

Stock – Short for "stock certificate" or "shares", stock is simply a piece of paper evidencing ownership in a corporation. Stocks are sometimes referred to as "equities", because you own a piece of the corporation. Stocks can be publicly traded or privately held, but most investors deal in public companies whose stock is traded through the various stock exchanges (New York, NASDAQ, etc.).

Syndicate – An association of individuals formed for the purpose of conducting and carrying out some particular business transaction, ordinarily of a financial character, in which the members are mutually interested. Syndicates may exist as corporations or partnerships (either general or limited). Source: *Black's Law Dictionary*.

Top-Line Real Estate– We generally use this term to describe the gross value of an investor's real estate holding irrespective of equity or debt. In other words, the aggregate market value of all the real estate owned or controlled.

Total Return – This is our term to describe the total amount of growth experienced on a real estate investment, particularly an income property, when taking into account income, amortization, passive activity loss, and appreciation. Some people like to use *internal rate of return* (IRR), but we find it a confusing term. We just want to know what a given investment's total amount of contribution to one's overall finances is when all aspects of contribution (cash-flow, amortization, appreciation, depreciation, etc.) are taken into consideration.

Trust Deed – A trust deed (TD) is a document signed by a borrower, which secures a promissory note on real property and authorizes a third party, typically selected by the lender, called a trustee, to auction off the subject property in the event the borrower fails to make payments according to the term of the note. Although not technically correct, many people simply refer to trust deeds as mortgages. In the real world, the terms are virtually interchangeable. We just say "mortgage".

Vacancy Allowance – An estimate of vacancy expenses that is represented as a percentage of the Gross Scheduled Income. For example, a property that is expected to be vacant five weeks per year would have a vacancy allowance of 10% because 5 weeks is approximately 1/10 of 52 weeks in a year. In the real world, all five weeks may occur concurrently, so for the particular month in which the vacancy occurred, the rate would be as high as 100%. Conversely, the vacancy may not occur in a given year at all. For a cash-flow analysis, the vacancy allowance simply spreads out the anticipated vacancy expense evenly over the entire year, which of course is not the way it really happens.

Whatever – This is a term we use when responding to people who would rather look for excuses than answers, would rather complain than work, want to blame others rather than accept responsibility for their own behavior and investments, or want to otherwise criticize or malign people who are working hard with sincere motives.

Yeah Butter – A person who sees the obstacles as bigger than the opportunities because he is looking for an excuse not to invest and so responds to every offering with "Yeah, but…" Whatever.

Acknowledgments

Behind any endeavor there are champions. Behind every champion there are an army of unsung heroes. At the risk of unintentionally overlooking someone, we would like to acknowledge the contributions of some of the many people who have helped make this book possible, and/or have played an important role in our personal development, including our knowledge and philosophies, as well as our businesses and investments.

First, we would like to thank the multitudes of people who have come through our educational programs, especially those who have taken the education and used it to increase your wealth with real estate. Your success validates our teaching and encourages our hearts.

To Judy Lawrence, Ron Fouts, Julie Saba and Staci Gray for their help in taking this book from manuscript to finished product.

To Louise Olson, Katherine Gibney, Stephanie Gray and Bob Helms for their help in proofreading the original manuscript, and in some cases more than once.

To CPA Dan Kennedy, for his help with the tax concepts discussed and for his contributions as a charter member of the Advisor Financial Alliance Speaker's Bureau.

To 1031 exchange expert Michael Yesk for his help with the section on 1031 tax-deferred exchanges and for his contributions as a charter member of the Advisor Financial Alliance Speaker's Bureau.

To attorneys Jeff and Michelle Lerman for their contributions to our radio show, educational programs, and as charter members of the Advisor Financial Alliance Speaker's Bureau.

To graphic artist John Guzman for the original cover concept and design – and at *least* a dozen revisions.

To graphic designer Morris Jackson for divine patience in typsetting.

To Jack and Jaio Osborne for coming along side us when we really needed you.

To the amazing people at Global Property Network, Advisor Financial Alliance, WOW Events and Catalyst Funding – Thank you for believing in our vision, putting up with our passion, and helping us to pursue our mission.

Russ would like to thank the following people:

To my wife, Cheri – Proverbs 31 says "the heart of her husband trusts safely in her, therefore he shall have no lack of gain." You are truly a Proverbs 31 woman and the wind beneath my wings.

To my children, Stephanie, Staci, Ryan, Kristina and Sean – for allowing me the freedom to invest the time to not only write this book, but to develop the businesses and make the investments from which many of the concepts in this book were gleaned. Thanks for your love, patience and prayers.

A special thanks to my daughter Stephanie, for bravely following your starry-eyed father into the real estate business and contributing so much, not the least of which is your example of faith, hard work, integrity, and loyalty. I am honored to be your father.

Another special thanks to my daughter Staci, for coming along side me and doing so much, with so little, for so long, for far too little compensation or appreciation. You are an amazing person and you inspire me beyond words.

And yet another special thanks to my son, Ryan, for challenging me to walk by faith and commit 100% to this venture. I've never looked back.

To my Mom – You always did your very best for me and asked very little in return. There is nothing like a mother's love.

To my Dad – Thank you for your entrepreneurial example and invaluable assistance in writing the business plan which eventually became the Real Estate Investor Mentoring Club.

To my Uncle Gary, my first business mentor – We didn't get it all right and it didn't work out like we hoped, but I thank you for believing in me when I really needed it, teaching me "big city" sales, and forgiving some of the dumbest things I've ever done in my life.

To Pastor Mike Kiley for boldly proclaiming the gospel that set me free.

To George Backhus for modeling master salesmanship and first introducing me to the concept of personal development.

To Art Williams – You don't really know me, but you and the amazing organization you built taught me so much about what it takes to win and the peace that comes from knowing All You Can Do Is All You Can Do, But All You Can Do Is Enough.

To Jim Douglas, who believed early and helped me get started in the mortgage business – I've always been encouraged knowing you and Cindy were praying for me.

To my brother-in-law Johnnie Johnson – For the pivotal role you played in helping Robert achieve the clarity of vision that empowered our business relationship.

To Bob Helms, who has taught me so much about real estate and what it is to be a truly nice guy – Thank you for believing in me and putting your money, time and heart into helping us make it all happen.

To Mark Sullivan and Len Turner, my two prayer pals – Thank you for your faithfulness!

To my friend, my real estate mentor, my business partner, and co-author Robert Helms – There are no words to express my gratitude for all you mean to my family and me.

Robert would like to thank the following people:

It is with great humility that I thank many of the people who have been such a tremendous influence in my business and life.

To my wonderful extended family, many of whom are actually related to me. You know who you are, and more importantly, so do I.

To my baby sister Deb and our baby sister Jill, momma Doris and brother Joe, and to the Krajewski clan for making me feel like part of the family.

To Walter Sanford who first introduced me to the idea of a Personal Investment Philosophy; Kyle Wilson for his insight, friendship and guidance; Jim Rohn for showing me a new perspective; Brian Tracy for teaching me the power of goals; Tom Hopkins who encouraged me to be my own best client; Robert and Kim Kiyosaki for educating us all; Sharon Lechter for heartfelt encouragement and leading by example.

To Jerry Hicks (my first broker) who taught me that the buyers and sellers were not found in the office; Jeff Culbertson who showed me what real leadership is all about; Charlie Krackeler for an amazing sense of humor; Johnnie Johnson who helped me find clarity; Matthew Pearce for taking the radio show to the next level; David Kang whose thirst for knowledge is matched only by his incredible work ethic; and Jim Thylin for always doing more than I ever have the right to ask.

To Troy Paski and the gang at Hoppy Brewing Company in Sacramento (stop by sometime!); Shayna and Mike Goldstein for betting it all on the Power of the Group; Vicky and Pierre LePres for doing the impossible...again and again; Mick and Eileen Penka for going the extra mile; Bonnie Jean for never giving up; KB and Bobbi for the donuts, Yogurt Bob and the KSJS Brew Crew; and to "one man"...Jorge Buccio (and Candy)!

To Pol vanRhee, my brother, who was there from the beginning of this journey and who continues to contribute on so many levels, and to Helena who has been a part of this crazy dream since she was born!

To the Gray family, who consistently remind me what friendship is all about and who understand faith and commitment at a level I have never seen. The best is yet to come!

To the greatest broker I have ever known, my mentor and father Bob Helms, who taught me by example that if you always do the right thing for the client, the rest will take care of itself.

Abraham Lincoln said, "All that I am or ever hope to be, I owe to my mother." Thanks, Mom. I miss you every day.

To my pride and joy, Ethan "Peanut" Helms; and to Jessica Tami wherever you are.

And finally, to the love of my life and the keeper of my heart, my beautiful wife Kara. God has truly blessed us!

Our Apologies...

There is no doubt in our minds we have missed many very important people who have contributed to who we are and this book in particular. You are all incredible and we have been blessed by you. We only wish there were enough time and paper to list all of you and your invaluable contributions. Thank you!

About the Authors

Russell Gray and Robert Helms

Robert Helms is the host of the nationally syndicated radio talk show *The Real Estate Guys*™. For seventeen years, he was a top-producing real estate agent in partnership with his father and mentor Bob Helms. Robert has real-world expertise in real estate brokerage, property management, and real estate development. Today, Robert is a professional investor and dedicated educator. He has co-founded several real estate related companies with projects, properties and sales in the hundreds of millions of dollars. Robert teaches at the college level and is the featured mentor at the Real Estate Investor Mentoring Club he founded with co-author Russell Gray.

Robert and his wife Kara live in San Jose, California with their young son, Ethan. Robert enjoys reading, concerts and travel.

Russell Gray is a financial and business strategist. He has consulted with several hundred investors on developing their personal investment strategy and optimizing their resources. He is a real estate investor and co-founded a mortgage company which specializes in financing investment properties. As a former faculty member for the California Association of Realtors®, Russ has taught real estate finance to real estate agents pursuing the prestigious GRI designation. Russ began consulting with Robert Helms in 2001 and together they co-founded the Real Estate Investor Development Program™, Advisor Financial Alliance and the Real Estate Investor Mentoring Club. Russ is a regular on *The Real Estate Guys*™ radio show.

Russ and his wife Cheri live in San Jose, California. They have five children. Russ enjoys football, motorcycles and writing.

Please visit our website
www.EquityHappens.com

✓ Updated Case Studies
✓ Additions to Robert and Russell's Recommended
  Reading List
✓ Answers to Frequently Asked Questions
✓ Reports, Articles, Commentary and Offers
✓ Special Information for Real Estate and Financial Services
  Industry Professionals
✓ Dates and Locations of Events, Seminars and Personal
  Appearances by Robert Helms and Russell Gray